Inclusion and Behaviour Management in Schools: Issues and Challenges

D0493431

The companion volumes in this series are:

Understanding Pupil Behaviour in Schools: A Diversity of Approaches, edited by Janice Wearmouth, Robin C. Richmond, Ted Glynn and Mere Berryman

Addressing Pupils' Behaviour: Responses at District, School and Individual Levels, edited by Janice Wearmouth, Robin C. Richmond and Ted Glynn

These three volumes constitute part of a course jointly developed by the Open University in the UK and the University of Waikato in New Zealand. The Open University course is E804 *Managing Behaviour in Schools.* The University of Waikato course comprises three modules: HDCO534 - Theorising Behaviour in Schools; HDCO535 - Behaviour Assessment and Intervention in Schools; HDCO536 - School Behaviour Policies

The Open University Course E804 - *Managing Behaviour in Schools*

The course is offered within the Open University Master's Programme in Education. The Master's Programme provides great flexibility. Students study at their own pace and in their own time anywhere in the European Union. They receive specially prepared study materials, supported by face-to-face tutorials where they can work with other students.

The MA is modular. Students may select modules from the programme which fit their personal and professional interests and goals. Specialist lines of study are also available and include special and inclusive education, management, applied linguistics and lifelong learning. The attainment of an MA entitles students to apply for entry to the Open University Doctorate in Education Programme.

How to apply

If you would like to find out more information about available courses, please write, requesting the *Professional Development in Education* prospectus, to the Call Centre, PO Box 200, The Open University, Walton Hall, Milton Keynes, MK7 6ZW, UK (tel: 0 (0 44) 1908 653231). Details can also be viewed on our web page http://www.open.ac.uk

The University of Waikato *Postgraduate Diploma in Managing Behaviour in Schools PGDip (MBS)*

This postgraduate diploma is offered within the University of Waikato Master of Education programme, and utilises the same specially prepared study materials, supported by face-to-face classes and tutorials offered flexibly through summer school sessions and intermittent Saturday sessions. Each module is offered as a Master's level course, and can be credited towards a Master's degree in Education. The PGDipMBS requires one additional course in research methodology (on-line options available). Holders of the Postgraduate Diploma are able to complete a one-year Master's Degree in Education by thesis or course work, across a wide range of areas, such as inclusive education, Maori and bilingual education, educational policy and educational leadership.

How to apply

If you would like to find out more about the PGDipMBS and other available courses, please contact the Administrator, Graduate Studies in Education, School of Education, University of Waikato, Private Bag 3105, Hamilton, New Zealand (tel: 64-7-838-4500 or fax 64-7-838-4555). Details can also be accessed via e-mail: educ_grad@waikato.ac.nz or viewed on our website: http://www.waikato.ac.nz/education/grad

Inclusion and Behaviour Management in Schools: Issues and Challenges

Edited by

Janice Wearmouth, Ted Glynn,
Robin C. Richmond and Mere Berryman

David Fulton Publishers
London

in association with
The Open University and
the University of Waikato

The
University
of Waikato
Te Whare Wānanga
o Waikato

The Open
University

David Fulton Publishers Ltd
The Chiswick Centre, 414 Chiswick High Road, London W4 5TF

www.fultonpublishers.co.uk

First published in Great Britain in 2004 by David Fulton Publishers

David Fulton Publishers is a division of Granada Learning, part of ITV plc.

10 9 8 7 6 5 4 3 2 1

Note: The right of the authors to be identified as the authors of this work has been asserted by them in accordance with the Copyright, Designs and Patents Act 1988.

Copyright © 2004, compilation, original material and editorial material, The Open University. See Acknowledgements for copyright holders for other sections.

British Library Cataloguing in Publication Data
A catalogue record for this book is available from the British Library.

ISBN 1 84312 229 4

All rights reserved. No part of this publication may be reproduced, stored in a retrieval system or transmitted, in any form or by any means, electronic, mechanical, photocopying, or otherwise, without the prior permission of the publishers.

Typeset by RefineCatch Ltd, Bungay, Suffolk
Printed and bound in Great Britain

Contents

Part 2: Practitioner research issues   101

Part 3: Cultural issues   167

Part 4: Inclusive practices   263

Acknowledgements

We would like to thank all those who have contributed chapters to this reader or have approved their reprinting from other publications. Grateful acknowledgement is made to the following sources for permission to reproduce material in this book. Chapters not listed have been newly written. All chapters are edited.

Chapter 3: Thomas, G. and Loxley, A. (2001) 'The great problem of "need": a case study in children who don't behave', *Deconstructing Special Education*, Buckingham, Open University Press. Reproduced by permission of Open University Press.

Chapter 4: Didaskalou, E.S. and Millward, A.J. (2002) 'Breaking the policy log-jam: comparative perspectives on policy formulation and development for pupils with emotional and behavioural difficulties', *Oxford Review of Education* 28(1), 109-21.

Chapter 5: Munn, P., Cullen, M.A., Johnstone, M. and Lloyd, G. (2001) 'Exclusion from school; a view from Scotland of policy and practice', *Research Papers in Education* 16(1), 23-42.

Chapter 7: Sapsford, R. and Abbott, P. (1996) 'Ethics, politics and research' in *Data Collection and Analysis*, ed. Sapsford, R. and Jupp, V. London: Sage Publications.

Chapter 8: Zeichner, K. (2001) 'Educational action research', in *Handbook of Action Research*, eds Reason, P. and Bradbury, H. London: Sage Publications. Reproduced by permission of Sage Publications.

Chapter 9: Bishop, R. and Glynn, T. (1999) 'Addressing power and control issues in educational research', *Culture Counts*, Palmerston North, New Zealand: Dunmore Press.

Chapter 10: Bruner, J. (1996) 'Culture, mind and education', *The Culture of Education*, Cambridge, Mass.: Harvard University Press. Reproduced by permission of Harvard University Press.

Chapter 11: Gillborn, D. (2001) 'Racism, policy and the (mis)education of Black children', in *Educating Our Black Children*, ed. Majors, R. London: RoutledgeFalmer.

Chapter 12: Wright, C., Weekes, D. and McGlaughlin, A. (2000) 'Future prospects – towards inclusive education for all', in *'Race', Class and Gender in Exclusion from School*, eds Wright, C., Weekes, D. and McGlaughlin, A. London: Falmer Press.

Chapter 13: Schweigert, F.J. (1999) 'Moral education in victim offender conferencing', *Criminal Justice Ethics*, 18(2), 29-40. Reproduced by permission of The Institute for Criminal Justice Ethics, 555 West 57th Street, New York, NY 10019-1029.

Chapter 15: Lindsay, G. (2003) 'Inclusive education: a critical perspective', *British Journal of Special Education* 30(1), 3-12.

Chapter 16: Greenhalgh, P. (1996) 'Working with the group dimension', *Emotional Growth and Learning*, London: Routledge.

Chapter 19: Gerber, M. (1996) 'Reforming special education: beyond inclusion', *Disability and the Dilemmas of Education and Justice*, eds Chrisensen, C. and Rizvi, F. Buckingham: Open University Press.

Preface

Inclusion and behaviour management in schools: issues and challenges

Janice Wearmouth

In many countries of the world where education for all young people is compulsory, since the latter part of the twentieth century there has been a growing concern for equality of opportunity in the education system and social cohesion in society at large. Internationally there is a move towards inclusive education: provision for a wider range of learners in local mainstream schools. This has sharpened the need to take seriously the issue of behaviour management in schools and how to make educational provision for all students, including those whose presence is perceived to be detrimental to the education of their peers.

This book is designed to offer an international audience interested in education an overview of many of the issues crucial to an understanding of inclusion and behaviour management in schools. It covers these issues in relation to four areas: policy, practitioner research issues, cultural issues and inclusive practices.

The book opens with an introductory chapter by Wearmouth and Glynn which sets the scene by arguing that current moves towards inclusive education require a conceptualisation of the student as having active agency in his/her own learning, of both learning and behaviour as situated, dynamic and interactive between learner and environment, and of the practice of teaching as needing to be reflective.

Part 1, *Policy issues*, includes discussion and analysis of policy in relation to student behaviour in schools at national and local level. In Chapter 2, Cole discusses both the history of provision for young people assumed to 'have emotional and behavioural difficulties' against which current provision can be understood, and possible future developments. Chapter 3 by Thomas and

Loxley outlines a view that constructing 'emotional and behavioural difficulties' as an attribute of individual students militates against schools taking action to make the learning environment more humane and inclusive. In the following chapter, Didaskalou and Millward suggest that, in England, the emphasis on managing the behaviour of students seen as the most disruptive in schools has deflected attention away from the need to address the extreme emotional needs of some students. Chapter 5 by Munn, Cullen, Johnstone and Lloyd reports research on exclusion from Scottish schools in the years 1994–6 and discusses the findings in the context of policy concerns about social exclusion. The final chapter in Part 1 by Sproson discusses policy and practice in relation to a local education authority behaviour support service to schools in one local education authority in England.

Part 2, *Practitioner research issues*, addresses areas of concern which are particularly pertinent to those researching in the context of schools. It begins with Sapsford and Jupp's chapter, which discusses largely ethical and policy issues related to research and continues with Chapter 8 by Zeichner and an outline of traditions and practices in action research in the context of education. This section concludes with Bishop and Glynn's chapter, which addresses issues of power and control relations in educational research. This material relates specifically to the New Zealand Māori context, but also has wider implications.

Part 3, *Cultural issues*, focuses on race, ethnicity, school discipline and exclusion. Chapter 10, by Bruner, examines a psycho-cultural approach to education, working from a view that educational theory lies at the intersect 'between questions about the nature of mind and questions about the nature of culture'. This view is particularly important in the area of student behaviour management. It assumes that failure to support students to acquire skills for understanding and acting in social situations risks not only social incompetence but also alienation, marginalisation and acts of defiance. Gillborn's chapter then examines national policy approaches to race equality most particularly in the UK and adopts a view that the discourse of 'tolerance' and 'understanding' which has featured in policy documents for a long time has been unsupported by clear, targeted action. Chapter 12 by Wright, Weekes and McGlaughlin looks at ways in which the negative social consequences of school exclusion, especially as it relates to minority ethnic students, can be avoided. Schweigert's chapter then goes on to argue that one way to address the issue of the re-offending of those who flout the law is to re-educate the offender in local cultural values and re-connect him/her to the local community through victim–offender conferencing. Chapter 14 is written in the context of New Zealand and discusses the significance of taking a bi-cultural approach to home and school behaviour management.

Part 4, *Inclusive practices*, comprises discussion of approaches to the education of all students in the mainstream. Lindsay's chapter begins by offering a critique of current notions of inclusion and of current approaches to research. Chapter 16 by Greenhalgh then examines the issue of the dynamics of group relations in classrooms. This is crucial in understanding and addressing the area of challenging behaviour which can often be expressed in relationships within groups. In Chapter 17 Sproson discusses the attributes of teachers who are effective in dealing with student behaviour that is viewed as difficult to manage in schools. The following chapter by Davies addresses the critical part played by schools in shaping a student's sense of 'self', that is his/her confidence in his/her ability to initiate and complete actions. It discusses the basic human need for a sense of acceptance in a social group which shows care and respect for its members and highlights how the sense of belonging to, or marginalisation from, a school community affects every aspect of participation and learning within it. The book concludes with a chapter by Gerber. Writing in the context of education in the USA he describes how, in his view, the over-zealousness of some educators and researchers to promote inclusion in the mainstream for all students has priviledged location over genuine educational content and opportunity.

Chapter 1

Issues in inclusion and the management of student behaviour in schools

Janice Wearmouth and Ted Glynn

Introduction

Historically the response to students whose behaviour is perceived as
threatening to the social order in schools has been to assume a deficit model
of the individual and use medical and/or psychological approaches to
assessment to justify the provision of some sort of 'treatment' out of the
mainstream educational context. The law continues to support a notion of
the learner as passive and of behaviour that is difficult to manage as simply
an attribute of the individual student. In this chapter we argue that current
moves towards inclusive approaches for all students of statutory school
age requires a re-conceptualisation of the learner as active agent in his/her
own learning, and of both learning and behaviour as situated, dynamic and
interactive between students and the learning environment. It also requires
a conceptualisation of the learning environment as needing to adapt to the
needs of students if they are to become active participants in schools'
communities of learners (Lave and Wenger, 1991; 1999). If this is to occur,
teachers need to be able to reflect critically on notions of 'behaviour
difficulties', inclusion and the values associated with them. Consequently,
emphasis in teacher professional development should be given to reflective
practice (Schön, 1983; 1987) no less than to training in competencies and the
'tools' of the trade.

A historical overview

There are many ways in which a national education system might be structured to provide for the whole diversity of its student population. In recent years many countries have witnessed a move towards a policy of inclusion in mainstream schools for all students, including those whose behaviour is perceived as difficult to manage, or otherwise troubling to the staff within them. This development is a product of its own history as well as of the structure of today's society. It is important therefore to set within a historical context any understanding of provision for students who may behave in ways that are threatening or challenging to the social order in schools.

Challenging behaviour has a history 'as long as mass education itself' (Furlong, 1985). The problem of disruptive, challenging behaviour by students in schools is long-standing. In the seventeenth century in the U.K., for example, students were often armed and occasionally took part in violent mutiny (ibid). There appear to be recorded instances of students destroying all of the most famous public schools at least once (Ogilvie, 1957). There is a record from the late nineteenth century of the schoolteacher in Newchurch Primary School on the Isle of Wight requesting money from the school managers for shin pads for himself because his students hated school so much that every time they came into the classroom they kicked him (Wearmouth, personal communication). They would rather have been earning money working on the land.

Ford *et al*. (1982) note that, once education became compulsory for all children, the issue of the social control of potentially difficult students, expected to come mostly from the lower classes in society, assumed paramount importance. In England, for example, after the Elementary Education Act of 1870 and the beginning of compulsory state education, policy makers were faced with the fundamental dilemma of how to make educational provision for all students, including those whose presence in the classroom was felt to be holding others back. One solution was the kind of categorisation and segregation of students that resulted from a largely medical and, subsequently, psychological response to the problem. In the late nineteenth and early twentieth centuries, students might be assessed as 'idiots', 'feeble-minded' and 'imbeciles' through the expertise of doctors and/or the growing profession of psychologists, and separated off from the rest for the good of the majority. Admission to asylums was considered suitable for those categorised as 'imbeciles', the 'feeble-minded' were educated in special schools or classes whilst the group labelled 'idiots' was not thought to be educable (Department of Education and Science, 1978).

A glance at the history of the rise and demise of the term 'maladjusted' within special education illustrates how far categorical notions of student attributes become pervasive and fixed to suit the existing national context. Until 1945 there was no formal category of 'maladjustment' enshrined in central government regulations. It had its origins both in early labels of mental deficiency:

> The 1913 Mental Deficiency Act created a category of moral imbeciles or defectives, and children who displayed emotionally disturbed or disruptive behaviour came to be associated with both mental defect and moral defect.
>
> (Galloway *et al.*, 1994, p. 110)

in the unstable, nervous child identified in Board of Education Reports in the 1920s, and also in the

> 'difficult and maladjusted' child recommended in the 1929 Board of Education report as in need of child guidance.
>
> (op cit, p. 112)

After 1945 all local education authorities had a responsibility to establish special educational treatment in special or ordinary schools for students defined in this way. The concept was still relatively new when the Underwood Committee was set up in 1950 to enquire into 'maladjusted' children's medical, educational and social problems. The nearest this Committee's (1955) report could come to a definition read as follows:

> In our view, a child may be regarded as maladjusted who is developing in ways that have a bad effect on himself or his fellows and cannot, without help, be remedied by his parents, teachers and other adults in ordinary contact with him.
>
> (Ministry of Education, 1955, p. 22)

'Maladjustment' is a vague term. Nevertheless, there is a major problem in that once a category has been 'invented' it creates its own discourse:

> Discourses are about what can be said and thought, but also about who can speak, when, and with what authority. Discourses embody meaning and social relationships, they constitute both subjectivity and power relations. Discourses are 'practices that systematically form the objects of which they speak ... Discourses are not about objects; they do not identify objects, they constitute them and in the practice of doing so conceal their own invention' (Foucault 1974: 49).
>
> (Ball, 1990, p. 2)

In his epidemiological study, which attempted to assess the prevalence of specific categories of difficulties in the school student population, Rutter (1970) considers that use of the term may be seen as the justification for special educational provision:

> Maladjustment has been defined in a variety of ways but most definitions have included the concept of need for treatment (sometimes specifically educational

treatment), and its chief purpose (in the country) has been to provide a label under which special education may be provided according to the Handicapped Students and School Health Service Regulations (Ministry of Education, 1945 and 1959).

(Rutter, 1970, p. 147)

Invent the category, create the student. The category floats around waiting to 'gobble up' victims (Mehan, 1996):

> … the possibilities for meaning and for definition are preempted through the social and institutional position held by those who use them. Meanings thus arise not from language but from institutional practices, from power relations. Words and concepts change their meanings and their effects as they are deployed within different discourses. Discourses constrain the possibility of thought. They order and combine words in particular ways and exclude or displace other combinations.

(Ball, 1990, p. 2)

Between 1945 and 1960, the numbers of students classified as maladjusted rose from 0 to 1742. By 1975, there were 13,000 'maladjusted' students (Furlong, 1985).

Although many labels once attached to students became unacceptable as a result of the changing social and historical context of provision during the twentieth century, the practice of constructing categories of, and thus reifying, difficulties in learning and behaviour for the purpose of organising and maintaining the education system has been maintained. In England and Wales, of the total number of students, approximately 2% are seen by policy makers and resource-providers as likely to have difficulties which require additional or extra resources to be provided for them (DfE, 1994a, para. 2:2). This figure of 2% is an arbitrary one, drawn from a count of students in special schools in 1944.

In the latter half of the twentieth century, there was a growing concern for equality of opportunity in the education system and social cohesion in society at large. The 1981 Education Act attempted to translate into legislation the (1978) Warnock Report which reaffirmed the principle of integration and introduced the concept of 'special educational needs' in place of categorisation of handicap. However, the law in England, as in the whole of the UK, is still based on individually-defined need which must be assessed and quantified for the purpose of resource-allocation. Those thought to have 'emotional and behavioural difficulties', a term first introduced by Warnock to apply to students whose behaviour is seen as difficult to manage, have been identified as one group whose problems prevent them from learning in the same way as other students, and who therefore might need special provision. There is considerable confusion surrounding this term, which Gains and Garner (1996) feel is hardly surprising:

> given that the terms 'emotion' and 'behaviour' are amongst the most difficult concepts in the educational lexicon. Moreover, further difficulties arise because definitions of

what comprise EBD are closely bound up with the personality and professional experiences of the person who is assessing the student.

(Gains and Garner, 1996, p. 141)

The notion of 'emotional and behavioural difficulties' employed by the 1993, now the 1996, Education Act clearly adopts a within-person, deficit model. Circular 9/94, *The Education of Children with Emotional and Behavioural Difficulties*, which is associated with the 1996 Education Act, asserts that:

> Prevalence (of EBD) varies according to:
> - sex – boys rather than girls;
> - age – adolescents, rather than younger children;
> - health and learning difficulties – rates are higher among children with other difficulties;
> - background – rates are higher in inner city areas and socially deprived families.

(DfE, 1994b, para. 5)

Circular 8/94 continues with the theme of the deficit model of difficulty, implying that 'having EBD' is a fixed state, that the causes may be family background or sensory impairments and that schools may alleviate or worsen the student's 'condition' by their mode of operation and organisation and by individual teachers' behaviour:

> Causes:
> There may be one or many causes:
> - Associated factors may be family environments or sensory impairments.
> - EBD children always have special educational needs because they are facing barriers which cause them to have significantly greater difficulty in learning than most of their peers.
> - EBD is often worsened by the environment, including schools'/teachers' responses.
> - Schools vary widely in the extent to which they help children overcome their difficulties.

(DfE, 1994a, paras 1–9)

The current approach therefore continues to predispose to a reification of the concept 'special educational needs' and, therefore, to a reification of categories of need on which funding ultimately depends. Without an objectified category of need, quantifying how a student is special enough to warrant additional or alternative provision is highly problematic.

Current emphasis on inclusion

The law supports a deficit notion of students with behaviour problems. Young people 'with special educational needs' that result from difficult behaviour are entitled, in law, to have those needs identified, assessed and then met with appropriate provision guaranteed by their LEA. At the same time, however, for many years, and in some ways in contrast to the letter of the law, in the field there has been a recognition that the source of students' difficulties in behaviour and learning is not always intrinsic to the learner. These difficulties may also arise as a result of aspects of the learning environment. Hargreaves (1975), exploring the relationship between the student and the learning environment, noted that any disruption or disturbance is representative of a discordance within the system to which the student belongs. This discordance is indicated by a failure to match between the student and the system where the student/system interaction causes disruption (Bronfenbrenner, 1979). If a student belongs to a specific social system, both the responses of that student to the surroundings and the responses of significant adults and peers to that student have to be taken into account when assessing the significance of individual acts. Fulcher (1989) has noted that disaffection in the form of disruptive behaviour can be provoked by the demand for compliance from unwilling students by those in authority seeking to establish control in the classroom:

> Classroom order requires docile bodies ... Herein lies some of the resistance to integrating those with less docile bodies: ... larking about ... absence, verbal abuse, etc., all instance the failure to subordinate bodies to the requirements of classroom docility. The control responses to these forms of disruption include ... suspension and other sanctioning practices ... It may therefore be argued that it is the educational apparatus's failure to provide an inclusive curriculum ... rather than the problems specific disabilities pose, which constructs the 'problems' and politics of integration.
>
> (Fulcher, 1989, pp. 53–4)

At the level of the student in the classroom, the effects of classroom peer groups, and individual teachers (Hargreaves, 1982), teacher expectation (Rosenthal and Jacobsen, 1968) and lack of self-esteem of the individual student (Coopersmith, 1968) have been seen to influence students' attitudes and behaviour.

More recently, the source of difficulties has been described as stemming from the interaction between the characteristics of the learner and those of the context (Wedell, 2000; Mittler, 2000). There is, however, no adequate definition or theorising of the nature of this 'interaction' or its implication for a model of learning and the difficulties that are experienced. The learner tends not to be seen as having active agency in his/her learning and there remains a sense that her/his characteristics are static and fixed. In many countries there has also been a move towards 'inclusion' of all students in mainstream schools. This is problematic in some respects. For example, it has lacked clear definition of the term, or consensus about what 'inclusion' entails. Booth et al (2000, p. 12) describe 'inclusion' as a process of 'increasing the participation of students' in local schools without adequately defining what is meant by 'participation'. Mittler (2000, p. 10) describes 'inclusion' as 'based on a value system that welcomes and celebrates diversity arising from gender, nationality, race, language of origin, social background, level of achievement or disability' from a human rights view. In addition, since 1981 there has been an uneven degree of integration of students perceived as experiencing difficulties of different kinds. Education in mainstream schools is still generally organised on the basis of group instruction and not to meet the diversity of students' learning needs. Many of the market-oriented education policies implemented by national government since the 1988 Education Act, for example the publication of 'league tables' of examination results, have resulted in schools being less willing to accept some students. In England, those who might lower mean exam or standard assessment task (SAT) scores through their effects on others (Rouse and Florian, 1997) and those who are perceived as 'difficult to manage' may be particularly unpopular. The significant increase in exclusions in England during the 1990s (see OFSTED, 1996) testifies to this fact.

Creating an inclusive environment is not compatible with the competitive climate encouraged currently by a central government intent on target setting and narrowly-conceived achievement. An inclusive approach shifts the focus onto the school rather than the student. The new 'inclusive' notion that all students have the right of membership in the mainstream implies that mainstream class teachers must themselves be committed to this ideology and believe that all students will thrive there. Disadvantaged students should not be excluded from mainstream education. The notion of inclusion therefore appears to be concerned, above all, with human rights issues. Inclusion is a question of rights and concerns a philosophy of acceptance and a framework within which individuals can be valued, respected and enabled to learn. It is also consonant with inclusivity in society as a whole (Centre for the Studies of Inclusive Education (CSIE), 1997).

There is a conflict, therefore, between central government's focus on standards achieved through competition between schools, and the notions of an inclusive environment. This conflict has been made sharper in the UK since the advent of the Labour Government in 1997 and official recognition of the need to take seriously the issue of social inclusion of those groups seen to be marginalised in society. In England and Wales the government's 'social inclusion' agenda has led to the issuing of further guidance to schools about ways to reduce student disaffection and, consequently, challenging behaviour, in order to keep students in school and in touch with mainstream education. The real dilemma for schools is how to *act* in a situation which is beset by often irreconcilable tensions.

What is required is a view of learning and behaviour, both of students and those who teach them, as situated, dynamic and interactive between learner and context and, therefore, of difficulties in learning and behaviour as situated also. Where difficulties are situated and dynamic, conceptualisation of an inclusive environment in schools is often complex, rather than fixed and clear. The model of the teacher as reflective practitioner is consistent with this view of school provision. Consistent, also, with this view is a notion of teacher-practitioner research into problematic or puzzling areas of provision as a legitimate form of enquiry. Both a dynamic interactive view of learning and a view of teachers as needing to be reflective in their practice and proactive in research in schools have a clear significance for the future direction of research and practice in the area of behaviour management and inclusion.

The situative perspective shifts the focus from 'individual behaviour and cognition to larger systems that include behaving cognitive agents interacting with each other and with other subsystems in the environment' (Greeno, 1998, p. 5). Consonant with this perspective is a view of both research and practice as incorporating the notion of interactivity and as having the potential to address issues of theory and practice within the area of 'inclusion' more clearly than before.

It is important to recognise that, in a situative perspective, issues of affiliation to communities of practice are highly significant in contributing to a positive orientation towards activities of learning and construction of knowledge' (Belencky *et al.*, 1997).

> Individuals' beliefs and patterns of participation in activities of learning are shaped by their interactions in families as well as in schools and other organisational settings, where they and others develop expectations of participating authoritatively or in subservient relations to others on matters of knowledge and intellect.
>
> (Greeno, 1998, p. 10)

From a situative view, 'inclusion' can be defined as 'learning to become more effective in one's participation' in, and 'more central to', the practices in which individuals take part (Lave and Wenger, 1991). Practice within a situated view of difficulties in learning can be conceptualised to incorporate 'principles of curriculum design and the organisation of learning environments' (ibid). In valuing students' learning to participate in sense-making in communities of practice it is consistent both with a sense of 'inclusion' as a human rights issue (Mittler, 2000) and as a notion of greater participation in the mainstream (Booth *et al.*, 2000). The importance of arranging learning environments as the context in which students construct knowledge has already been highlighted by Dewey (1933). A situated view does not indicate which practice should be adopted. However, 'it does say that the activities of different learning practices are important … because participation in these practices is fundamental in what students learn (Greeno, 1998, p. 14). Student groupings, for example, can be arranged to support both the learning of subject content and the skills required to complete the tasks set and also their learning to participate in, and develop affiliation with, the local community of practice, and to develop their understanding of themselves as active, engaged learners.

Linked to a notion of learning, and difficulties in behaviour and learning, as situated is a conceptualisation of the teacher as needing to be reflective and analytical in order to address the complexities of the situation. Where knowledge creation both for teachers and students who experience difficulties is seen as situated, there is a clear rationale for focusing very clearly on the issue of reflective practice and the usefulness of concepts of the reflective conversation, reframing and reflection-on-action within the area of teacher professional development in the area of special educational needs.

Schön takes the view that there is an epistemology of practice where professional actions are based on implicit 'theories in use' which need to be made explicit and open to criticism if professional development is to occur (Schön, 1983; 1987). One aspect of knowledge is to be identified with 'reflection-in-action' within the 'action present'. The term 'reflection-in-action' has been a matter of some debate both as to its authenticity as a unitary concept applied consistently and as a concept within the domain of what constitutes 'knowledge' rather than a 'metacognitive skill' (Eraut, 1994). Nevertheless there is general agreement about the usefulness to notions of professional practice of particular aspects of Schön's work, for example the deliberation implied in the notion of reflection-in-action over a longer period within the action present and his identification with the concept of 'reflective conversation', the concept of 're-framing' at the point of problem-setting to achieve solutions in difficult situations, and the potential for reflection-on-action after the event to result in the creation of new understandings among practitioners (ibid).

Conclusion

The area of special educational provision, especially for those students whose behaviour is perceived as difficult to manage, is historically 'grounded as a form of control, structuring and setting horizons for practice, defining and legitimising knowledge' (Muffoletto, 2001, p. 292) and constructing challenging behaviour as an attribute of the individual who 'has emotional and behavioural difficulties' (DfE, 1994). The area of special educational needs is 'driven by the need to identify solutions for reaching identified outcomes in efficient, effective and accountable ways' (Muffoletto, 2001, pp. 292–3) the outcome of which needs to be observable, measurable and manageable.

The specific term that is applied to individual students' behaviour on any one occasion is not neutral. It is influenced by the fact that at particular points in time certain categories of difficulties are defined as constituting needs which must be met either by the allocation of additional resources, re-deploying existing resources or by the removal of a student into an alternative location.

Where students have been identified and labelled as having behaviour problems, the tendency has been for the education system to respond by providing alternative forms of provision. This has often been in the form of special schools, 'off-site' units, or provision nominally in mainstream but which provides different curricular initiatives and social relationships between teachers and students than those perceived to exist within ordinary classes. Government rhetoric asserts that special or alternative provision is intended to be in the interests of the individual learner. Under the terms of the 1996 Education Act, students are entitled to have their special educational needs assessed and met. This includes those needs resulting from lack of progress in learning resulting from behaviour seen as challenging. However, there is an inherent contradiction between this entitlement and the fact that, as Mehan (1996) notes, once a category has been created it can float around ready to 'gobble up' victims. Professionals' use of terminology which allows them to do things for or to students, whose behaviour carries with it connotations of challenge to the self as a part of the institutional organisation from which the student is disaffected, is not therefore neutral. Reification of 'behaviour difficulties' 'delivers the educational "texts" that students and teachers use to construct and structure the world in which they live and make understandable' (Muffoletto, 2001, p. 293). The corollary of this is an assumption that conceptualising special educational provision in schools is clear and fixed, that the goal of such provision is consensual and that effective practice therefore requires the establishment of the most cost-effective and efficient way to reach that goal. This approach is, however, inappropriate to manage special educational provision in schools where, as discussed above, the real world of schools is characterised by complexity, confusion, instability and conflicting values and often the problem space is emergent. The need for a reflective position with regard to the whole issue of student behaviour in schools, including the dominant approach driving policy in the area, is crucial for practitioners working in the field. Otherwise they can never step outside the thinking that defines 'good practice' through 'Standards' (TTA, 1999), policies it through OFSTED inspections and supports it through competency-based teacher professional development.

> To move beyond a normalised, commonsense understanding of theory and practice in relation to technology and education, a reflective historical process that questions the assumptions of practice and the limits of discourse in the field needs to be recognised and practiced (sic).
>
> (Muffoletto, 2001, p. 286)

In the real world, it is not just the system of special provision that needs to be considered, it is also its effect on the lives of those who experience(d) special provision, both service providers, students and their parents and carers. The purposes and effects of school curricula need to be reflected on and discussed openly if such provision is to serve the interests of those it is supposed to benefit, especially since issues of human rights, entitlements and equity are open to question. If there is no opportunity for reflection, there is the danger that educators, students and parents, immersed in the dominant discourse of the world as it has been rationalised, will be less able to see how the world is constructed and therefore conceptualise alternative ways of working in the messiness of the real world situation.

Current understandings of difficulties in learning and behaviour are moving towards a view that they are situated. Curricular experiences offer students ways of knowing the world. Within an institution, educators and students are defined by that institution's social practices. The understanding of the individual whose behaviour is seen as challenging is part of that social practice. Teachers need to be able critically to reflect on the notion of 'behaviour difficulties' and, allied to that, 'inclusion', and the beliefs and values that are associated with them, in order to see them for what they are, as social constructs. As Eraut comments:

> New knowledge is created … in each professional community … The particularistic nature of knowledge gained by practising professionals presents yet another barrier to knowledge creation: both its exchange with other professionals and its incorporation into theory are limited by its specificity, and often by its implicitness.
>
> (Eraut, 1994, pp. 20–1)

For many students, the only route from disadvantage is through education. It is crucial to maintain a reflective stance towards situations of practice in the area of behaviour management and inclusion. Otherwise it is difficult to see how we are to understand the student behaviour that is difficult to manage in the real world of schools, open up students' opportunities for learning and show genuine concern and respect for the professionals who have to deal with them.

References

Ball, S.J. (1990) *Foucault and education: disciplines and knowledge*, London: Routledge.

Belenky, M.F., Bond, L.A. and Weinstock, J.S. (1997) *A tradition that has no name: nurturing the development of people, families and communities*, New York: Basic Books.

Booth, T. and Ainscow, M. (2000) *Index for Inclusion: developing learning and participation in schools*, Bristol: CSIE.

Bronfenbrenner, U. (1979) *The ecology of human development*, Cambridge, Mass: Harvard.

Coopersmith, S. (1968) 'Studies in self esteem', *Scientific American*, 218, pp. 96–106.

CSIE/Wertheimer (1997) *Inclusive Education: A Framework for Change*, Bristol: CSIE.

Department for Education (DfE) (1994) *Code of Practice for the Identification and Assessment of Special Educational Needs*, London: HMSO.

Department for Education (DfE) (1994a) *Circular 8/94: Pupil behaviour and discipline*, London: DfE.

Department for Education (DfE) (1994b) *Circular 9/94: The education of children with emotional and behavioural difficulties*, London: HMSO.

Department of Education and Science (DES) (1978) *Special educational needs. Report of the Committee of Enquiry into the Education of Handicapped Children and Young People* (Chairman: Mrs H.M. Warnock), London: HMSO.

Dewey, J. (1933) *How we think*, Boston: Health (original work published 1909).

Eraut, M. (1994) *Developing professional knowledge and competence*, London: Falmer.

Ford, J., Mongon, D. and Whelan, M. (1982) *Special education and social control*, London: Routledge.

Foucault, M. (1974) *The archaeology of knowledge*, London: Tavistock.

Foucault, M. (1988) 'The ethic of care for the self as a practice of freedom', in J. Bernauer and D. Rasmussen (eds) *The final Foucault*, Cambridge, Mass: MIT Press.

Fulcher, G. (1989) *Disabling policies: a comparative approach to educational policy and disabilities*, London: Falmer.

Furlong, V.J. (1985) *The deviant pupil: sociological perspectives*, Milton Keynes: OU Press.

Gains, C. and Garner, P. (1996) 'Models of intervention for children with emotional and behavioural difficulties', *Support For Learning*, 11(4), pp. 141–145.

Galloway, D.M., Armstrong, D. and Tomlinson, S. (1994) *The assessment of special educational needs: whose problem?*, Harlow: Longman.

Greeno, J.G. (1998) 'The situativity of knowing, learning and research', *American Psychologist*, 53(1), pp. 5–17.

Hargreaves, D. (1982) 'The two curricula of schooling', in *The challenge for the comprehensive school*, London: Routledge.

Hargreaves, D. et al (1975) *Deviance in classrooms*, London: Routledge.

Lave, J. and Wenger, E. (1991) *Situated learning: legitimate peripheral participation*, Cambridge: Cambridge University Press.

Lave, J. and Wenger, E. (1999) 'Learning and pedagogy in communities of practice', in J. Leach and B. Moon (eds) *Learners and pedagogy*, London: Paul Chapman.

Mehan, H. (1996) 'The politics of representation', in S. Chaiklin and J. Lave (eds) *Understanding practice: perspectives on activity and context*, Cambridge: Cambridge University Press.

Ministry of Education (1955) *Report of the Committee on Maladjusted Children* (Chairman, J.E.A. Underwood), London: HMSO.

Mittler, P. (2000) *Working towards inclusive education: social contexts*, London: David Fulton Publishers.

Muffoletto, R. (2001) *Education and technology: critical and reflective practices*, Cresskill, N.J.: Hampton Press.

Office for Standards in Education (1996) *Exclusions from secondary schools, 1995/6*, London: HMSO.

Ogilvie, V. (1957) *The English public school*, London: Batsford.

Rosenthal, R. and Jacobsen, L. (1968) *Pygmalion in the classroom*, New York: Holt, Rinehart and Winston.

Rouse, M. and Florian, L. (1997) 'Inclusive education in the market place', *International Journal of Inclusive Education*, 1(4), pp. 323–336.

Rutter, M. et al (1970) *Education, health and behaviour*, London: Longman.

Schön, D. (1983) *The reflective practitioner*, New York: Basic.

Schön, D. (1987) *Educating the reflective practitioner*, London: Jossey-Bass.

Social Exclusion Unit (1998a) *Truancy and school exclusion*, London: The Stationery Office.

Social Exclusion Unit (1998b) *Bringing Britain together: a national strategy for urban renewal*, London: SEU.

Teacher Training Agency (TTA) (1999) *National special educational needs specialist standards*, London: TTA.

Wedell, K. (2000) Audio interview in E831 *Professional development for special educational needs co-ordinators*, Milton Keynes: Open University.

PART 1
Policy issues

Chapter 2

The development of provision for children and young people 'with emotional and behavioural difficulties (EBD)': past, present and future

Ted Cole

After sketching definition difficulties, this chapter examines aspects of the evolution of provision for children and young people 'with emotional and behavioural difficulties' [EBD][1], which help to explain the untidy and varied array of services existing in the present decade. The latter is then summarised before some conclusions are offered on 'EBD', inclusion and needs for future provision.

The chronic difficulties of definition

Children and young people now said to 'have EBD', to be 'disruptive' or to have 'behavioural disorders', have in the past been described by a range of descriptors – particularly the term 'maladjusted'. The range in part reflects the different government and voluntary agencies (justice, welfare, health and education) who, historically, have identified and then provided services for them. Cole, Visser and Upton (1998) cite evidence (e.g. DES, 1974a) for the following view:

> While the maladjusted were conceptualised as a separate group, in fact, many children thus labelled could equally have been described as socially deprived, disruptive, disaffected, delinquent, mentally ill or mentally deficient. (p.5)

Other descriptors have included 'children of the perishing and dangerous classes' (Mary Carpenter, 1851), 'Street Arabs' (later Victorian era), 'moral imbeciles' (early 1900s) and 'maladjusted children' (from c.1930 to the 1980s) (Cole, 1989). In their national study, Wilson and Evans (1980) opted to talk of 'disturbed children' while Galloway and Goodwin (1987) argued that the descriptor 'disturbing children' was more accurate, given the often social construction of maladjustment and deviance. The present term 'EBD' appeared briefly in the Underwood Report (Min. of Ed., 1955) but did not enter common parlance until the late 1980s, and then only in educational circles. Social services have sometimes opted for 'troubled and troublesome' (e.g. Dimmock, 1993) while health service commentators now subsume many aspects of EBD under 'mental health disorders' (Gowers, Bailey-Rogers, Shore and Levine, 2000; Cole, Sellman, Daniels and Visser, 2002). In America, various clinically identifiable categories have emerged over recent decades. These include 'conduct disorders', 'oppositional defiance disorders' (ODD) and 'attention deficit/hyperactivity disorders' (ADHD) (Kauffman, 2001).

The contrasting nature of these labels points to the historical and continuing problems in defining what 'EBD' is and who can fairly be said to have such difficulties. Indeed Thomas and Glenny (2000) talked of 'bogus needs in a false category'. In recent decades a number of English writers have attempted to give a typology, amongst them the Warnock Committee (DES, 1978), Smith and Thomas (1993), DFE (1994) and Cooper (1996). Cole et al. (1998) attempted a definition by examining the characteristics of pupils attending the nation's EBD special schools. The first and second government Codes of Practice for Identifying and Assessing Special Educational Needs (DFE, 1994b; DfEE, 2001) gave incomplete and contradictory descriptions. All the above points to the fact that defining the characteristics of this disparate group of students remains difficult and possibly impossible. Laslett (1983, p.6) described the precursor category of maladjustment as 'a kind of catch-all for children showing a wide range of behaviour and learning difficulties'. It is probably wise to accept that the same applies to EBD and not to waste further effort on seeking a precise definition. That offered in the still current government guidance on EBD, Circular 9/94 (DFE, 1994a), is probably as complete as can be achieved.

Historical patterns of provision

The 1944 Education Act first created a legal category in England of maladjusted children and required all LEAs to make suitable provision for these young people. This led to a large expansion in the numbers of special schools for the maladjusted (usually in disused country mansions). But, as indicated above, children whose behaviour was experienced as worrying had been identified long before the end of the Second World War. Both before and after the 1944 Act, they might have received education and/or care through a range of services other than the special school run by a local education authority.

Types of provision included juvenile prisons (post-1840), large poor law residential schools (1860–1970s), day and residential industrial schools (from 1857, transmuting into approved schools in 1933, and community homes with education [CHEs] after the 1969 Children and Young Persons Act), fostering and attending local day schools (mid to late 1800s), National Children's Home or Barnardo's 'cottage' and 'village' homes (after about 1880), residential schools for the maladjusted/EBD (from c.1920), special day schools (rare before the 1970s), mental or psychiatric hostels, residential hostels from which the maladjusted would attend mainstream schools (post-1945), special classes attached to mainstream schools (mainly post-1970), off-site special units (seen in London in 1950s but mainly post-1970), educational units attached to Child Guidance Clinics, sometimes based in hospitals (mainly post-1945), classrooms in children's homes/observation and assessment centres (mainly post-1969 Children and Young People Act). In fact some forms of provision, seen in the 1980s and 1990s as progressive alternatives to 'segregated', often residential special schools, which furthered the movement towards greater school and community inclusion, already had a long history.

Within the English/Welsh system, particular types of intervention were developed, sometimes enjoying an ephemeral predominance, sometimes remaining popular over generations. There were short-term industrial schools where persistent truants were initially locked in solitary confinement, 'feeding schools' providing meals and baths for 'at risk' working class poor (pre-1900), and nautical schools to train the crew for the empire's navy (pre-1900 to post-1945). In deliberate contrast to the often harsh, militaristic regimes of many reformatory and industrial schools, some of the pioneer schools for the 'maladjusted' opted for democratic and permissive regimes (Bridgeland, 1971) from Homer Lane's 'Little Commonwealth' (1914–1918), through A.S. Neill's early Summerhill to therapeutic regimes after 1945 (Cole, 1989). Here the views of children were sought, for example through daily school meetings and pupils sometimes allowed to dictate schools' policy in a way that could frighten orthodox school inspectors (Bridgeland, 1971; DES, 1974a; Cole, 1989).

Where a choice existed, a child's placement could relate to local and personal belief of particular professionals. Those responsible for allocating approved school or later CHE places might believe in a disciplinarian, punitive approach or a clearly rehabilitative one. A local psychologist or education officer might be sympathetic to a particular therapeutic community. The local LEA might have particular historical experience of placing children in specific residential or day special settings. More widely, the behaviour of the young person might be seen as a personality disturbance that could be 'treated' (the medical model) or as a rational reaction to an adverse environment that might be changing the environment through choice of a different home or school (Min. of Ed., 1955; Laslett, 1983).

Theories, guidance and the elements of good practice

After the Second World War, a few settings were influenced by advances in science and accounts of Freudian-influenced practice in the USA. This could take the form of psychotherapy in a few schools, such as Otto Shaw's Red Hill, or in the growing number of Child Guidance Clinics where psychiatrists, psychologists and psychiatric social workers were employed. By the 1970s, the legacy of Skinner and Watson appeared tentatively on the British scene (Wilson and Evans, 1980) and fairly sophisticated behaviour modification was practised at a few schools (Cole, 1986). The Underwood Report (Min of Ed., 1955) and the Schools Council national study (Wilson and Evans, 1980) recorded contrasting views on the effectiveness of differing educational and care approaches. Perhaps under-reported was the influence of staff moving from the approved school (or CHE sector) to the expanding schools for maladjusted children. These staff were known to bring with them points and reward systems and sometimes a concern for imposed discipline that would set them at odds with staff favouring a more liberal and psychodynamic approach (Cole et al., 1998). By the mid to late 1990s, simple forms of behaviourism (baselining, target-setting, points and token reward systems) were found to exist in most English EBD schools although mixed with a concern for listening and talking to children and building self-esteem (a humanistic or cognitive-behavioural approach) (Cole et al., 1998).

Institution's or service's policies and pupils' programmes also had to respond to government laws and guidance. An uneasy and shifting rapprochement had sometimes to be achieved between 'front-line' staff's beliefs rooted in their working practice and demands of government sometimes perceived as misguided. Tensions were apparent between special schools (industrial schools) and government inspectors in Victorian times, special schools/units and HMI after 1945 (Cole, 1989) and social service inspectors interpreting the 1969 Children and Young Persons Act or more recent 1989 Children Act in relation to more recent special schools (Cole et al., 1998). Recurrent interwoven dilemmas affecting the development of policy and practice included:

- The extent to which the institution or service was one of social control, therapy, welfare or education.

- The extent to which the education offered should replicate the mainstream education that a child-rights perspective might indicate should be provided.
- The optimum balance between delivering programmes that lessen the child's present difficulties and those that develop his/her capacity for an independent and fulfilled adult life style.
- How far the views and preferences of the individual child in a complex school community could be reconciled with the needs of the larger group.
- In relation to personal, social and educational development, the extent to which adults could or should impose their will on sometimes resistant youth.

Cole and Visser (1998) noted that different officials and individuals within institutions offer contrasting answers to these questions. In history, balancing conflicting opinion on these key issues has led to shifting compromises that on occasion have advanced practice in one direction while forcing retreat in others.

Of the greatest importance to determining 'quality' in individual sites or local systems were the values, motivation and resources of the teaching, care and support staff who were in extended often daily contact with the young people. The quality of adult–child relationships has long been seen to reside at the heart of improving troubled young people's social functioning and general mental health. Such relationships were established more through skilled use of the *affective* or in Bernstein's (1977) terms, *expressive* aspects of the teacher or carers' personality and behaviour than through their cognitive skills or because of their training. This was apparent to Victorian pioneers (Cole, 1989) and was emphasised in more recent research (e.g. Wilson and Evans, 1980; Cooper, 1993; Cole et al., 1998). In line with modern cognitive-behaviour (and eco-systemic) theory, staff were needed who had the capacity and experience to win the respect, trust and often the liking of young people who had often become deeply adult-suspicious and -aversive, particularly in relation to teachers and social workers. Staff had to help the young person to take a more optimistic view of self and of his or her potential for positive development. These staff had to hold power in their institution and counteract the effects of colleagues who perhaps did not share their values, skills or commitment. Research by Millham, Bullock and Cherrett (1975) into the operation of Home Office approved schools in the late 1960s noted the tendency of sites to allow *organisational* goals that made life more comfortable for staff to predominate over pupil-oriented *expressive* or *instrumental* goals. In EBD and approved schools, there could be an ongoing struggle to check this tendency.

Cooper (1993), reporting his research in the late-1980s, stressed the need for staff to use democratic, collaborative approaches, listening and responding to the views of the individual pupils. This is now a common message but *how far* sites of practice should proceed down this road has been a topic of sometimes intense debate and subject to the current values and beliefs of government departments and individuals. The history of provision for troubled youth indicates the apparently effective work of many of a highly paternalist attitude. In some schools staff were open about claiming to know what was best for the immature and uncertain children in their care (see, for example, Bridgeland, 1971 for pioneer maladjusted schools; Millham et al., 1975 in relation to 'approved schools'). Where the adults were respected, the young people could be content to accept the safety and escape from the personal responsibility of decision making, offered by these paternalist 'significant others'. The flattened hierarchies and 'permissive' nature of therapeutic communities rarely won HMI approval (Cole, 1989) but could appeal more to some psychiatrists and social workers from health-service child guidance clinics. HMI in the past, as now, tended to favour an educational approach with expectations of 'normal' behaviour within clear boundaries set by staff.

An important element of 'good practice' is the physical environment. Here values (and consequently prioritisation of resource allocation) come into play and have affected the design and quality of the built environment. The provision of privacy, comfort and wide-ranging facilities is recognised as relevant to the achievement of effective intervention (DHSS, 1970; Cole et al., 1998). Yet government inspectors have too often found it necessary to condemn the ill-kept mansions or temporary 'huts' in which troubled youth have so often been cared for and educated (e.g. DES, 1989b). Improving physical facilities obviously related to the availability of – or at least *choosing* to make available – financial resources.

Indeed financial issues have always impacted upon the achievement of effectiveness. Providing any service for pupils with EBD (special classes, day and boarding schools, child guidance clinics, 'tutorial centres'), that of necessity, given the challenges presented by troubled youth, have to be labour intensive, has always been expensive. Cost has posed recurrent worries for local government and practitioners over the last two centuries and increasingly since the 1944 Education Act and compulsory secondary education. If national or pressure group expectations led to new government laws or guidance requiring more generous staffing levels or better training, then the pressures increased and contributed to the demise of many institutions (see Hyland, 1993 in relation to CHEs). Relating this to values: how much money is it worth spending on a tiny minority of children when the prognosis for investment may be poor? Or, does money spent on early intervention save society greater expense in the future? The answers given in the past have related to personal beliefs and local tradition or experience. In comparison to providing other holistic services, such as children's home placement or foster care allied to day education, residential education may provide value for money (Berridge et al.,

2002) although this view has been at odds with the perspective of budget holders looking solely through LEA eyes (Topping, 1983; Galloway, Armstrong and Tomlinson, 1994; Cole et al., 1999).

The paragraphs above indicate continuing debates about the control, therapy, welfare and education functions of provision/programmes for children with EBD. Whatever the ongoing tensions, a consensus has emerged on key aspects of effective practice. Cole et al. (1998), echoing Wilson and Evans, (1980) found many senior staff believing that central to successful approaches were

- the importance of working through positive relationships;
- building self-esteem through successful basic skills, wider educational and social achievement;
- high educational expectations, linked to a 'normal' curriculum;
- the creation of caring communities, where the voice of the child was heard;
- clearly understood routines and behavioural boundaries.

Government guidance contained in Circular 9/94 (DFE, 1994a) supported the above. Cooper (1993) and Cooper, Smith and Upton (1994) offered a similar message, distilling the essence of provision of good practice into the '3Rs' of *relationships, respite* from adverse experience and *re-signification* of self whether in special school or mainstream settings.

Patterns of provision in the late 1990s/early 2000s

In the 1990s, new developments influenced provision for pupils said to have EBD. Local government reorganisation led to the creation of over forty new unitary local education authorities (LEAs) and the displacement of some existing services. The Office for Standards in Education (OFSTED) stressed its worries about perceived low standards in an expanding system of off-site special units called 'Pupil Referral Units' (PRUs) (OFSTED, 1995) and the quality of many EBD schools (e.g. OFSTED, 1997). A new government published a Programme of Action (DfEE, 1998a) for special educational needs following a Green Paper (DfEE, 1997) with an inclusionist message (except for pupils with EBD). Between 1990/1 and 1997/8 the number of pupils recorded as 'permanently excluded' from schools rose from 2900 in 1990/1 to 12,298 in 1997/8 (Harris, Eden with Blair, 2000). This high number of exclusions under a Labour government committed to inclusion was seen by some (e.g. Parsons, 1999) as a consequence of the continued operation of elements of the neo-liberal market in education established under the previous administration (Booth, Ainscow and Dyson, 1998). Meanwhile government pressure for 'joined up' solutions as a response to the problems of social exclusion was witnessed in Circular 1/98 (DfEE, 1998b). This called for LEAs to create comprehensive and coherent arrangements for pupils with behavioural difficulties to be called *behaviour support plans* (BSPs) by the end of the year and to revise these plans in 2001.

It is not easy to evaluate the effect these developments had on patterns of provision, given the difficulties of definition and lack of clear, published government statistics. However, Cole, Daniels and Visser (2003a), using figures supplied by the English government for 1998 and other sources, notably over 140 of the first BSPs, have made a careful attempt to do so.

Table 2.1 (from Cole et al., 2003b) gives an historical overview of numbers in state and 'approved'[2] independent EBD special schools before presenting figures for 1998. In 1998, Cole et al. (2003a) estimated that there were about 350 maintained, non-maintained and independent special EBD schools. Cole (2002) also reported that the numbers of pupils sole-registered in PRUs increased from 5043 in 1995 to nearly 10,000 in 2002, which more than offset reduction in places provided in EBD schools. OFSTED reports also make clear that many PRUs, contrary to their official purpose of being 'revolving door', short- to medium stay placements for pupils without statements for EBD, were accommodating for, long periods, sometimes years, significant numbers of pupils who clearly had severe EBD (Cole, 2002). PRUs have some success but also great difficulties in achieving the re-inclusion into mainstream schools of their pupils (Howlett and Parsons, 2001; Daniels et al., 2003).

Table 2.1 Numbers of full-time pupils in special schools for the 'maladjusted' or children with EBD and of pupils educated otherwise (EBD schools excluding schools for pupils with EBD and learning difficulties)

1st Jan	1963	1973	1983	1994	1998
A. Maintained and non-maintained schools	2440	7605	11,771	9500/10,000	c.9900
(includes boarders: as % of total full-time pupils)	(1829: 75%)	(4101: 54%)	(5367: 46%)	(c.3700:) c.38%)	(c.3000: c.30%
B. 'attending independent schools' (mainly boarders)	1764	3515	4376	c.1500/2000	c.1500
Total of A + B	4204	11,120	16,147	11 to 12,000	c.11,400
C. 'Pupils otherwise than at school'/PRUs	450	1604	2645	c.7000 (Parsons, 1995)	7740 in PRUs
Total : A + B + C	4654	12,724	18,792	c.20,000	c.19,000

Sources: DES (Table 25; 1964); DES (Table 25, 1974b); DES (Table A22/83; 1984): Visser and Cole (1996)

Cole et al. (2003b) suggested that if the children who might be defined as EBD and who were placed in Social Services or other voluntary establishments were included and pupils on 'home tuition' not on the rolls of PRUs, in excess of 20,000 pupils who might be said to have EBD received most of or all their education outside mainstream schools in early 1998. There were 6, 517, 300 children of compulsory school age in 1998 (DfEE, 1999b). The population of pupils with EBD outside mainstream schools therefore equated to about 0.3% of the total compulsory school-aged population at that time. This figure rises to about 0.4% if children with EBD placed in schools for pupils with both EBD and learning difficulties are included, virtually the same proportion as that reported by the Elton Report (DES, 1989a – see below).

EBD schools that provide boarding are expensive, difficult to staff and challenging to run effectively (OFSTED, 1997; Cole et al., 1998; OFSTED, 1999a; Cole et al., 2003b). They have been portrayed (probably unfairly) as the most marginalising and segregated form of provision (Topping, 1983) and, following the inclusionist 1981 Education Act, the 'dinosaurs of the education system' (headteacher to Cole, 1986). A trend away from boarding (see Visser and Cole, 1996) was therefore to be expected. From a peak in the mid-1980s there has been a sharp decline in the number of boarders, accompanied by a move away from seven nightly boarding to young people typically spending only four or five nights a week in the boarding schools or returning home every second weekend (Cole et al., 2003b). Nevertheless, the DfEE data show that for 1998, of the maintained and non-maintained EBD schools 49% still contained boarders (although some had very few boarders) and 77% of the available boarding places were occupied. Independent schools are mainly boarding schools and some remain much in demand (Cole et al., 2003b; OFSTED, 2002). A limited amount of recent research (Cooper, 1993; Grimshaw with Berridge, 1994; Cole et al., 1998) highlights the positive benefits of the residential approach as evidenced by the boarders themselves. The continuing use of boarding is also explained by placements in residential EBD schools being socially rather than educationally driven (Grimshaw with Berridge, 1994; Cole et al., 1998; Cole, 2001). The need for this function has perhaps increased as social service departments have severely limited the placement options available to them by closing many children's homes and CHEs.

Given a lack of data, gauging the numbers of pupils with EBD or those deemed seriously disruptive in mainstream settings is even more difficult (Daniels, Visser, Cole and de Reybekill, 1998). Cole et al. (1999, 2003a) found that in thirty LEAs the percentage of their compulsory school-age population for whom statements of special educational needs for EBD were maintained ranged from 0.2% to 1.07%. Helping to explain the variations (and highlighting again the difficulties of definition) the following comment was found in one BSP: 'The lively youngster in one setting can be deemed a major problem in another'. However, in the light of some data available to Cole et al. (1999) and other research studies, the tentative view can be offered that nationally the percentage of pupils presenting significant disruption or EBD is likely to be close to Fortin and Bigras' (1997) suggestion that in America and Canada about 4% of pupils usually have behaviour problems. This reflects Kauffman's (2001) conclusion, from an extensive review of evidence in the USA, that the proportion of students lies within the range of 3% to 6%.

Suggestions that there are perhaps three or more times that number of children with serious and enduring behaviour difficulties (e.g. BBC, 1999) seem unduly alarmist. The Audit Commission (1999) reported that estimates of children with childhood mental health problems (definitions of which overlap considerably with the DFE Circular 9/94 definitions of EBD) ranged from 10–33% with 'a fairly close consensus on a prevalence rate of 20%' at any one time. Such figures depend on very broad definitions favoured by health professionals (Cole et al., 2002).

In their first BSPs, some LEAs were clearly worried about the lack of special provision for girls. This was unsurprising given that the gender ratio for children categorised as maladjusted in maintained and non-maintained maladjusted schools was about four boys to one girl from 1950 to 1982 but changed dramatically to 12.5 : 1 in EBD schools in 1998 (Cole et al., 2003a). Explanations for the gender ratios can only be speculative given a lack of research in this area. Teachers sometimes say that boys tend to 'act out' more than girls. It is known that externalised disruptive behaviour in mainstream schools tends to elicit transfer to EBD special schools (Cole et al., 1998).

By 1998, in keeping with the advice of the Green Paper (DfEE, 1997), a few EBD schools had or were about to relocate most or all provision for pupils aged 14–16 to units based in their local further education (FE) colleges. Some mainstream secondary schools and/or their LEAs were actively developing links with FE colleges for pupils who were at risk of being, or had been, excluded, including pupils deemed as 'having EBD'. It is clear that there has been a substantial growth across England in programmes in FE colleges designed for disaffected pupils, aged 14 to 16, including students 'with EBD' (see also Daniels et al., 2003).

It was a common theme in first BSPs that behaviour support services (BSS), constituted of specialist advisory and support teachers working alongside specialist educational psychologists, following the lead of DES (1989), would like to devote their energies to preventive work in mainstream schools. However, often they could not escape a 'fire-fighting' and maintenance role with long-term excluded or pupils on the cusp of exclusion. 'As and when the number of permanently excluded falls, more of the service resources can be used for in-school support' the writer of one BSP said. In a few LEAs, BSS emanated from the local EBD school (i.e. pioneering approaches favoured by the DfES report on the future of special schools: DfES, 2003).

To conclude this section: in January 1998 (prior to the creation of the final tranche of new 'unitary' LEAs):

- 101 out of the 131 LEAs then existing (77%) maintained one or more EBD schools;
- 110 out of 131 LEAs (84%) had one or more PRUs;
- many LEAs possessed and hoped to expand their behaviour support services to reduce difficulties in mainstream schools and dependence on segregated provision.

The BSPs made clear that the LEAs lacking their own special facilities had access to either other LEAs or non-maintained or independent schools. Sometimes this had been necessitated by the progressive fragmentation of support services by local government re-organisations. Many BSPs referred to the need to expand staffing and the range of facilities outside mainstream schools (Cole et al., 2003a).

Conclusion: pupils with EBD and inclusion

We might question what this last section says about LEAs' attitudes and practice towards school inclusion for children and young people with EBD and the extent to which some LEAs see separate schools for pupils with EBD as an anachronism and the denial of fundamental human rights as is claimed for example by the Centre for Studies in Inclusive Education (CSIE, 1999). A few LEAs prefaced their first BSPs with strong statements about the rights of children to inclusion, with two citing the UN Convention on the Rights of the Child. However, another BSP was more typical in diluting this for children 'with EBD' saying that such pupils should be included in the mainstream whenever this was 'desirable and practicable'. The BSPs showed LEAs seeking to move towards more inter-agency working, early identification and preventive interventions that, arguably, might lessen the need for alternative provision (shortly afterwards to be encouraged by Circular 10/99 – DfEE, 1999b) without giving a convincing picture of how this reduction of need would be achieved. Although a few LEAs claimed to be progressing towards locational inclusion (educating children with EBD on the same physical sites as mainstream schools – see, for example, Barrow, 1998), the vast majority, as we have seen, found it necessary to maintain or to access a spectrum of off-mainstream-site provision from residential schools and PRUs to 'alternative' and 'vocational' FE courses. Some data pointed to LEAs' ideals being compromised by the practical day-to-day challenges presented by pupils 'with

EBD', thereby backing the research of Clark, Dyson, Millward and Robson (1999) which stressed the challenge to inclusion presented even in the most inclusive schools by intractable and perhaps increasing behaviour difficulties. One LEA, which had one of the lowest rates of children placed outside the mainstream, now recognised that a greater range of alternative provision was required. Another, which closed its EBD schools in the early 1980s, aimed to extend its 'alternative' day provision at the end of the decade.

In short, behind the rhetoric of inclusion employed by LEAs in their BSPs, and government in various documents, there commonly seemed a recognition of the need to continue practices which ran in a contrary direction. A few BSPs openly stated that an important concern was that the minority of pupils with EBD must not disrupt the majority. One contained the following: 'Every child is entitled to an education which promotes his or her development in a safe and secure environment, free from distraction'.

Such teacher and administrator concerns were clearly recognised by the DfEE (1998a). This Programme of Action stressed that the Labour government's approach would 'be practical, not dogmatic' and claimed to put the needs of individual children first (para. 3.2, p.13). Special schools would 'continue to play a vital role' (para. 3.5). OFSTED (1999a) and later DfES (2003) took a similar stance: there needed to be a range of appropriate provision, including PRUs and high quality special schools as well as imaginative approaches to curricula and FE links. In practice, beneath the inclusionist veneer, the government message remained similar to that of the Elton Committee, which had stressed in 1989

> that ordinary schools should do all in their power to retain and educate all the pupils on their roll on-site. However, we recognise that in the case of a small number of pupils this may be difficult, and in some cases impossible (DES, 1989a, para. 6.39, p.152).

My various research projects suggest the wisdom of this approach. The realistic goal is to seek to bring about reform in attitudes, ethos and curriculum and to develop staff skills so that mainstream schools can successfully accommodate and address the needs of progressively more pupils currently deemed disaffected, disruptive or EBD. 'Learning support units', as advocated in Circular 10/99 (DfEE, 1999b) might avoid the 'sin-bin' function of their predecessors, and become vehicles for attitudinal change as well as keeping more pupils in the mainstream (see OFSTED, 2002). Hallam and Castle's (1999, 2001) study holds out some hope although Sutton (2002) presented a less optimistic view. It seems that many special schools and alternative forms of provision will continue to be required, as DFES (2003) clearly recognises. Professional pragmatism will continue to take precedence over politically preferred ideology.

Is this necessarily a denial of children's rights or perpetuation of damaging social exclusion? Campaigners for total school inclusion might usefully reflect on DfEE's (1998a) belief that special schools for pupils with EBD were sometimes 'valued by parents and pupils' (para. 3.11, p.13). This is not an unexpected statement given similar evidence offered by Wilson and Evans (1980), Cooper (1993), Sanders and Hendry (1997), Cole et al. (1998) and OFSTED (1999a). Berridge et al.(2001) and Daniels et al. (2003) and some inspection reports (e.g. OFSTED, 1999b; Cole, 2002) also indicate that similar parental and pupil appreciation can be found for some PRUs. Special, unit or other 'alternative' provision, though in the past often flawed, can sometimes be more supportive and educationally appropriate than mainstream settings for pupils with behavioural difficulties, although these children and young people constitute a tiny minority, probably numbering no more than 0.5% of the compulsory school-age population.

Notes

1. For simplicity the initials 'EBD' are employed although government now tends to attach 'S' for social (either ESBD or BESD). I, and the Association I work for, prefer the Scottish ordering 'SEBD' as it is clearly the social and the emotional that need to be understood and addressed before the behaviour is likely to be ameliorated.
2. LEAs are allowed to place a child at 'approved' independent schools without seeking permission from DfES. The 'approved' schools tend to be long-established schools which have 'passed' OfSTED and earlier HMI inspections. At 'registered' schools, specific permission has to be sought first by the LEA from DfEE to place a child. 'Registered' schools tend to be new schools or a few institutions that pursue an educational and/or care curriculum which is in contrast to the usual maintained or 'approved' school offer, e.g. a 'therapeutic community' giving less prominence to the National Curriculum.
3. In many LEAs, before 2002, there were pupils receiving small amounts of 'home' or 'community based' tuition (for example, in local libraries) who were not on the rolls of PRUs. These included those excluded from PRUs and those refusing to attend PRUs or any form of education or training.

References

Audit Commission (1999) *Children in Mind: Child and Adolescent Mental Health Services*. London: Audit Commission.

Barrow, P. (1998) *Disaffection and Inclusion: Merton's Mainstream Approach to Difficult Behaviour*. Bristol: CSIE.

Bernstein, B. (1977) *Class, Codes and Control*, rev. edn. London: Routledge.

Berridge, D., Brodie, I., Pitts, J., Porteous, D. and Tarling, R. (2001) *The Independent Effects of Permanent Exclusion from School on the Offending Careers of Young People*. London: Home Office.

Berridge, D., Beecham, J., Brodie, I., Cole, T., Daniels, H., Knapp, M. and MacNeill, V. (2002) *Costs and Consequences of Services for Troubled Adolescents: An Exploratory Analytic Study*. Sponsored by Dept of Health, Luton: University of Luton.

Booth, T., Ainscow, M. and Dyson, A. (1998) 'England: inclusion and exclusion in a competitive system'. In Booth, T. and Ainscow, M. (1998) (eds) *From Them to Us*, pp.193–225. London: Routledge.

Bridgeland, M. (1971) *Pioneer Work with Maladjusted Children*. London: Staples.

British Broadcasting Corporation (1999) *Eyes of a Child*. 6th September, 1999.

Carpenter, M. (1851) *Reformatory Schools for the Children of the Perishing and Dangerous Classes, and for Juvenile Offenders*. London: Gilpin.

Centre for Studies in Inclusive Education (1999) *More Disabled Children in Special Schools*, press release, 17th Sept, 1999. Bristol: CSIE.

Clark. C., Dyson, A., Millward, A. and Robson, S. (1999) 'Theories of inclusion, theories of schools: deconstructing and reconstructing the inclusive school'. *British Educational Research Journal*, **25**(2), 157–177.

Cole, T. (1986) *Residential Special Education: Living and Learning in a Special School*. Milton Keynes: Open University Press.

Cole, T. (1989) *Apart or A Part? Integration and the Growth of British Special Education*. Milton Keynes: Open University Press.

Cole, T. (2002) 'Pupil Referral Unit Review', *National Newsletter of AWCEBD*, (Autumn), 7–9.

Cole, T., Daniels, H., Berridge, D., Brodie, I., Beecham, J., Knapp, M. and MacNeill, V. (2003b) *Residential Schools for Pupils with Emotional and Behavioural Difficulties: Client and Organisational Characteristics*. Birmingham: School of Education.

Cole, T., Daniels, H. and Visser, J. (1999) *Patterns of Educational Provision Maintained by Local Education Authorities for Pupils with Behaviour Problems*. A report sponsored by the Nuffield Foundation. Birmingham: University of Birmingham.

Cole, T., Daniels, H. and Visser, J. (2003a) 'Patterns of provision for pupils with behavioural difficulties in England.' *Oxford Review of Education*, **29**(2), 187–205.

Cole, T., Sellman, E., Daniels, H. and Visser, J. (2002) *The Mental Health Needs of Children with Emotional and Behavioural Difficulties in Special Schools and Pupil Referral Units*. Mental Health Foundation. www.mentalhealth.org

Cole, T., Visser, J. and Upton, G. (1998) *Effective Schooling for Pupils with Emotional and Behavioural Difficulties*. London: David Fulton Publishers.

Cole, T. and Visser, J. (1998) 'How should the effectiveness of schools for pupils with EBD be assessed?' *Emotional and Behavioural Difficulties*, **3**(1), 37–43.

Cooper, P. (1993) *Effective Schooling for Disaffected Pupils*. London: Routledge.

Cooper, P. (1996) 'Giving it a name: the value of descriptive categories in educational approaches to emotional and behavioural difficulties'. *Support for Learning*, **1**(4), 146–150.

Cooper, P., Smith, C. and Upton, G. (1994) *Emotional and Behavioural Difficulties*. London: Routledge.

Daniels, H., Visser, J., Cole, T. and de Reybekill, N. (1998) *Emotional and Behavioural Difficulties in the Mainstream*. Research Report RR90. London: DfEE.

Daniels, H., Cole, T., Sellman, E., Sutton, J., Visser, J. with Bedward, J. (2003) *Study of Young People Permanently Excluded from School*. London: DfES.

Department for Education (1994a) *Emotional and Behavioural Difficulties*. Circular 9/94. London: DFE.

Department for Education (1994b) *Code of Practice on the Identification and Assessment of Special Educational Needs*. London: DFE.

Department for Education and Employment (1997) *Excellence for All Children: Meeting Special Educational Needs*. Cm 3785 (Green Paper). London: The Stationery Office.

Department for Education and Employment (1998a) *Meeting Special Educational Needs: a Programme of Action*. London: DfEE.

Department for Education and Employment (1998b) *LEA Behaviour Support Plans*. Circular 1/98. London: DfEE.

Department for Education and Employment (1999a) *School Absence Tables*. London: DfEE.

Department for Education and Employment (1999b) *School Inclusion: Pupils Support*. Circular 10/99. London: DfEE.

Department for Education and Employment (2001) *Revised Code of Practice on the Identification and Assessment of Special Educational Needs*. London: DFEE.

Department for Education and Skills (2003) *The Report of the Special Schools Working Group*. London: DfES.

Department of Education and Science (1964) *Statistics of Education, Vol. 1: Schools*. London: HMSO.

Department of Education and Science (1974a) *The Health of the School Child, 1971–2*. London: HMSO.

Department of Education and Science (1974b) *Statistics of Education, Vol. 1: Schools*. London: HMSO.

Department of Education and Science (1978) *Report of the Committee of Enquiry into the Education of Handicapped Children and Young People (the Warnock Report)*. London: HMSO.

Department of Education and Science (1984) *Statistics of Education, Vol. 1: Schools*. London: HMSO.

Department of Education and Science (1989a) *Discipline in Schools: Report of the Committee of Enquiry chaired by Lord Elton*. London: HMSO.

Department of Education and Science (1989b) *A Survey of Provision for Pupils with Emotional/Behavioural Difficulties in Maintained Special Schools and Units*. Report by HMI. London: DES.

Department of Health and Social Security (1970) *Care and Treatment in a Planned Environment*. Advisory Council on Child Care. London: HMSO.

Dimmock, B. (1993) *Working with Troubled and Troublesome Young People in Residential Settings: a directory of training materials*. London: Department of Health/Open University.

Fortin, L. and Bigras, M. (1997) 'Risk factors exposing young children to behaviour problems'. *Emotional and Behavioural Difficulties*, 2(1), 3–14.

Galloway, D., Armstrong, S. and Tomlinson, S. (1994) *The Assessment of Special Educational Needs: Whose Problem?* London: Longman.

Galloway, D. and Goodwin, C. (1987) *The Education of Disturbing Children*. London: Longman.

Gowers, S., Bailey-Rogers, S., Shore, A. and Levine, W. (2000) 'The Health of the Nation Outcome Scales for Child and Adolescent Mental Health (HONOSCA)'. *Child Psychology and Psychiatry Review*, 5(2), 50–56.

Grimshaw, R. with Berridge, D. (1994) *Educating Disruptive Children*. London: National Children's Bureau.

Hallam, S. and Castle, F. (1999) *Evaluation of the Behaviour and Discipline Pilot Projects (1996–99) Supported under the Standards Fund Programme*. Research Report, RR163, London: DfEE.

Harris, N., Eden, K. with Blair, A. (2000) *Challenges to School Exclusion*. London: Routledge.

Hyland, J. (1993) *Yesterday's Answers: Development and Decline of Schools for Young Offenders*. London: Whiting and Birch/Social Care Association.

Kauffman, J. (2001) *Characteristics of Emotional and Behavioral Disorders of Children and Youth*, 7th edn. New Jersey: Merrill Prentice Hall.

Laslett, R. (1983) *Changing Perceptions of Maladjusted Children, 1945–1981*. London: AWMC.

Millham, S., Bullock, R. and Cherrett, P. (1975) *After Grace – Teeth*. London: Chaucer.

Ministry of Education (1955) *Report on the Committee on Maladjusted Children (The Underwood Report)*. London: HMSO.

OFSTED (1995) *Pupil Referral Units: the First Twelve Inspections*. London: OFSTED.

OFSTED (1997) *Standards and quality in Education, 1995/6, The Annual Report of Her Majesty's Chief Inspectorate of Schools*. London: HMSO.

OFSTED (1999a) *Principles into Practice: Effective Education with Pupils with EBD*. HMI report. London: OFSTED.

OFSTED (1999b) *Inspection Report: West Cumbria Learning Centre Pupil Referral Unit*, Contract No 704725. London: OFSTED.

OFSTED (2002) *Independent Schools for pupils with SENs: a review of inspections, 1999–2002*. London: OFSTED.

Parsons, C. (1999) *Education, Exclusion and Citizenship*. London: Routledge.

Parsons, C. and Howlett, K. (2000) *Investigating the Re-integration of Permanently Excluded Pupils in England*. Cambridge: Include.

Sanders, D. and Hendry, L. (1997) *New Perspectives on Disaffection*. London: Cassell.

Smith, A. and Thomas, J. (1993) 'What's in a name: some problems of description and intervention in work with emotionally disordered children.' *Pastoral Care*, **295**, 3–7.

Sutton, J. (2002) 'Learning Support Units: Promoting inclusion or Internal Exclusion'. *National Newsletter of AWCEBD*, (Autumn), 11–12.

Thomas, G. and Glenny, A. (2000) 'Emotional and Behavioural Difficulties: bogus needs in a false category.' *Discourse: Studies in the Cultural Politics of Education*, **21**(2), 283–298.

Topping, K. (1983) *Educational Systems for Disruptive Adolescents*. Beckenham: Croom Helm.

Visser, J. and Cole, T. (1996) 'An overview of English special school provision for children with EBDs'. *Emotional and Behavioural Difficulties*, **1**(3), 11–16.

Wilson, M. and Evans, M. (1980) *Education of Disturbed Pupils*. London: Methuen.

Chapter 3

The great problem of 'need': a case study in children who don't behave

Gary Thomas and Andrew Loxley

Introduction

This chapter focuses on children who don't behave at school. It makes the point that the metaphors and constructs which are used to generate understanding about such difficult behaviour are often misleading, evoking as they do all kinds of quasi-scientific explanation. For the mélange of disparate metaphor and theory around which understanding of people's behaviour is popularly constructed – in both lay and professional circles – rests in the reification of what is little more than tentative psychological conjecture.

Whatever the register in which one chooses to discuss it, there have, we argue in this chapter, been some unfortunate consequences of this kind of discourse for schoolchildren. Further, in the more recent school-orientated approaches to helping avoid troublesome behaviour at school – approaches which put the emphasis on change by the school rather than change in the child – is found merely a replication of the exclusionary phenomena of the past. Those phenomena are created by certain kinds of mindsets and professional systems which accentuate rather than attenuate difference.

We contend that a relatively recent concept, that of 'need', has come to reinforce these concepts of deficit and disadvantage. Intended to be helpful, to place emphasis on a child's difficulties rather than simply naming a supposed category of problems, the notion of need has instead come to point as emphatically as before at the child. It has allowed to remain in place many of the exclusionary practices associated with special education.

The notion of emotional and behavioural difficulties: the root of the problem

A search through the last ten years' issues of five leading national and international journals finds not a single paper which discusses in any detail the provenance, status, robustness, legitimacy or meaning of the term 'emotional and behavioural difficulties' (EBD). This is surely a cause for concern. The term is widely and unquestioningly used in the UK (and other countries have their own equivalents) as an administrative and quasi-clinical category. Uniquely, it proffers a category which is specific to children, and which combines legal, medical and educational connotations and meanings.

Although EBD is not an official category in Britain, it exists as one in everything but name. Categories officially ceased to exist following the report of the Warnock Committee (DES, 1978) and the 1981 Education Act. Yet for all practical purposes EBD is indeed a category and it forms in the minds of practitioners, professionals and administrators one of the principal groups of special needs. It has been used as a category in the local statementing procedures which have followed from section 5 of the 1981 Education Act and the Education Acts which have succeeded it. It appears unquestioningly in papers in reputable academic journals (for example Smith and Thomas, 1992), and it appears as a descriptor in official documents and papers (for example DES, 1989a, 1989b; DfEE, 1995; Mortimore, 1997).

The term 'EBD', then, reveals no frailty. The resilience it shows is demonstrated in its ability to survive and prosper over the past few years, when attention has moved from the child to the institution, with for example, the Elton Committee's (DES, 1989c) emphasis on whole-school approaches to discipline. Respected academics could, for example, as recently as 1994 frame their book (Chazan *et al.,* 1994: 27) around section headings such as 'Identification of EBDs' and 'Factors associated with EBDs in middle childhood' (1994: 36). The agenda is of deficit, deviance and disadvantage in the child, and while school systems are usually mentioned in discourse such as this, they seem to appear almost as an afterthought. It is clear that the real problem is considered to be dispositional: that of the child – and the emphasis is thus on individual treatment. The term 'EBD' induces a clinical mindset from which it is difficult to escape.

This mindset operates within more all-encompassing ideas about need. The notion of need is seldom questioned. It is seemingly so benign, so beneficial to the child that it has become a shibboleth of special education thinking and policy. But we contend in this chapter that 'need' is less than helpful, and that it is a chimera when difficult behaviour is being considered. The notion of need here is based on a belief that a *child's* problems are being identified and addressed. 'Need' in this context, however, is more usefully seen as the school's need – a need for calm and order. The language of the clinic, though, invariably steers the response of professionals toward a child-based action plan.

This focus on emotional need substitutes a set of supposedly therapeutic practices and procedures for more down-to-earth and simple-to-understand sanctions. It also diverts attention from the nature of the environment which we expect children to inhabit. The ambit of the 'helping', therapeutic response invoked by the idea of EBD is unjustifiably wide, being called on neither at the request of the young person involved (or at least very rarely so), nor because of some long-standing pattern of behaviour which has demonstrated that the young person has a clinically identifiable problem, but rather because the behaviour is unacceptable for a particular institution. But because these therapeutic practices and procedures notionally constitute 'help', they are peculiarly difficult to refuse.

Likewise, it is difficult to refute the kindly, child-centred, humanitarian tenets on which they supposedly rest. The tenets on which therapeutic practice rest may be all these good things (kind, humanitarian, child-centred) but they have developed during an era when the intellectual climate eschewed – or, rather, failed even to consider as meaningful concepts – ideas about the rationality and rights of the child. In such a climate it was considered appropriate and necessary for decisions to be made about and for children by concerned professionals. Whereas systems for rule-breaking adults have come to incorporate strict procedures to protect rights, systems could develop in schools to deal with rule infraction which would incorporate no such protections – since the protection was considered to be automatically inherent in the beneficial action of the professionals acting on the child's behalf.

But those actors and advocates would often be the very same people who were offended by the child's behaviour. In the adult world, political and legal systems are particularly sensitive to the boundary between wrongdoing and mental illness, and it is a commonplace that in certain circumstances in certain political regimes it is only too convenient to brand wrongdoers and rebels 'mad'. In more favourable political circumstances, by contrast, fastidious care is taken to differentiate between law breaking, rebellion and mental illness.

But for children and young people at school, because of assumptions about their vulnerability and their irrationality, and presuppositions about the beneficial actions of professionals acting on their behalf, those protections do not exist. Their absence has enabled in education a label like 'EBD' to be compiled out of a range of disparate ideas about order and disturbance. Those ideas are elided yet their elision is rarely acknowledged or addressed.

The elision of ideas represented in the notion of EBD has done little, we contend, for the individual child. Yet it also exercises an influence even on supposedly whole-school approaches to behaviour management at school. The notion of EBD distorts the way that management or organizational issues at school are defined and handled. A whole-school approach to behaviour difficulties existing in the same universe as a thriving notion of EBD means that behaviour difficulties are invariably seen through a child-centred, clinical lens. For this clinical lens is more convenient for everyone: it offers immediate response (often the removal of the child) rather than the promise of an improvement in a term or a year; it offers ready-made routes into existing professional systems which distract attention from possible shortcomings of the school, and it avoids the large-scale upheaval and expense of whole-school reform.

A different view about how to respond to difficult behaviour at school can emerge out of current thinking on inclusion. The inclusive school should best be seen as a humane environment rather than a set of pre-existing structures and systems for dealing with misbehaviour. These traditional structures and systems inevitably invoke already-existing professional responses. But our contention is that schools contain such an odd collection of rules and practices that unless these are themselves addressed and altered, misbehaviour from children is an almost inevitable consequence.

Whose needs?

The blanket ascription of 'need' when behaviour is found difficult at school needs some examining. Whose needs are being identified and unravelled here? The route taken is nearly always to assume that the child needs something, and the assumptions about need proceed to imputations of intent, weakness and problem in the wrongdoer.

Foucault (1991) analysed this process as it has taken place in juridical practice over two centuries. According to his analysis, modern times have seen a transformation in society's response to wrongdoing. Because historically responses to wrongdoing were often so shockingly cruel, new 'kinder' techniques of control have supplanted them. Foucault's *Discipline and Punish* (1991) begins with an example. It begins with a picture of a savage punishment in pre-revolution France, where a prisoner, Damiens, has his limbs carved from his body. But it is not principally condemnation of this cruelty which follows from Foucault. Rather, he has drawn the picture to contrast it with the kinds of punishment which have come to succeed it. Because of the conspicuous savagery of punishment regimes in Europe until the mid-nineteenth century, Foucault says, a backlash forced attempts to be more gentle, to have 'more respect, more "humanity" ' (1991: 16). It is these successors to the punishment of Damiens for which Foucault reserves his sharpest critique. For these systems – this 'gentle way in punishment' (1991: 104) – are quieter, more insidious.

These new techniques, relying on the constructs and knowledge of the new social sciences, constructed various forms of understanding of the wrongdoer which made imputations of intent and assumptions about motive. This would not be so bad were it not for the fact that the understandings provided by the new sciences depended on tentative, fallible theories which were treated as though they were scientific fact. In fact, they were merely making new kinds of judgement about misbehaviour, but judgements which were given added credence and respectability by their association with supposedly scientific thinking and understanding – understanding which had been so successful in the natural sciences. In short, what has occurred, the analysis of Foucault suggests, has been a movement from simple judgement and punishment of someone's disapproved-of act to complex and unjustified judgements about his or her 'soul'.

EBD provides an excellent case study of this elision from punishment to judgement. It provides a clear example of a category created from an intermingling, on one side, of certain systems of knowledge (like psychology and medicine) and, on the other, of a need for institutional order.

Our specific focus here, is on the almost explicit conflation of administrative need with quasi-medical category; of the transition from naughty-therefore-impose-sanctions, to disturbed-therefore-meet-needs. It is the nature of the transition which we wish especially to examine: the gradient from punishment to 'help' down which the child tends to descend once 'need' has been established.

There are taken-for-granted assumptions of 'help' in the 'meeting need' mantra of contemporary special education protocols, and these 'needs' have been silently transmuted with the assistance of the constructs of academic and professional psychology from the *school's* needs for order, calm, routine and predictability to the *child's* needs – supposedly for stability, nurture, security, one-to-one help, or whatever.

In the unspoken assumptions behind special education procedures there is no acknowledgement of the manoeuvre which has occurred here – no recognition of the frailty of the idea of an 'emotional need' – and no willingness to entertain the possibility that emotional needs may be a fiction constructed to escape the school's insecurities about failing to keep order.

But unacceptable behaviour is rarely a problem of the child. While this behaviour is a problem for the school, it rarely constitutes a clinical problem. Neither does it point to some abnormality or deficit.

An elevation in the status of psychological knowledge has meant that simple understandings about what is right or wrong have in themselves become insufficient to explain difficult behaviour. A new epistemology has emerged wherein a lexicon of dispositionally orientated words and phrases govern and mould the way unacceptable behaviour is considered. Thus, if children misbehave at school, education professionals are encouraged to examine the background, motivations and supposed traumas of the students rather than the simple humanity of the school's operation – its simple day-to-day processes and routines.

Foucault (1991) warns against the assumption that the knowledge of disciplines like psychology and sociology can inform the working practices of staff in schools and hospitals. It is not disinterested knowledge; it is the same perhaps as what Bourdieu calls 'doxa': a kind of taken-for-granted knowledge, naturalized knowledge, 'things people accept without knowing' (Bourdieu and Eagleton, 1994). In other words, the knowledge of psychology and psychiatry have infiltrated our everyday understanding of disorder and deviance so that they are now almost as one: disorder has somehow become melded with disturbance in such a way that thought about behaviour which is out of order at school can hardly be entertained without the collateral assumption of emotional disturbance and special need.

Meeting need

In education, this last reconceptualization occurs under the cloak of *meeting individual need*. The 'meeting need' notion satisfies two conditions for the educationist. First, it enables the labelling of madness (a Bad Thing) to be transformed into the identification of a need in the child (a Good Thing). Thus, the educator, with a stroke of a wand, is changed from labeller (this child is maladjusted) to benefactor and helper (this child has special needs and I will meet them). Second, an institutional need for order is transformed to a child's emotional need. The child who misbehaves has special needs which are rooted in emotional disturbance, the vocabulary at once invoking psychological, psychoanalytic and psychiatric knowledge. Once need is established, the psychological genie has been released.

It is strange that psychologists and educationists should have managed to pull off such a feat of alchemy, since a moment's thought discloses the fact that the things which children habitually do wrong at school rarely have any manifest (or indeed covert) association with their emotional makeup. They concern the school's need to regulate time (punishing tardiness and truancy), activity (punishing lack of effort or overactivity), speech (punishing chatter or insolence), and the body (punishing hairstyles, clothes, the use of make-up or the degree of tidiness of the individual). As Cicourel and Kitsuse (1968: 130) put it, 'the adolescent's posture, walk, cut of hair, clothes, use of slang, manner of speech … may be the basis for the typing of the student as a "conduct problem" '. And the term 'conduct problem', or more likely 'conduct disorder', is still alive and well in special education.

But being unpunctual, lazy, rude or untidy were never, even by early twentieth-century standards, qualifications for madness, or even emotional difficulty. They concern, as Hargreaves *et al.* (1975) point out, rule-infractions. They have little or nothing to do with an individual's emotional need, but everything to do with the school's need to keep order. Maintaining order through the upholding of these codes is necessary, school managers would argue, for the efficient running and indeed for the survival of the school.

Institutions which require the collecting together of groups of 20 or 30 in classes, and hundreds in assemblies, need ways of keeping order. To maintain order, there is a need for disciplinary methods through the regulation of the use of space and the control of activity. Mostly these work.

It is when they don't work, when children fail to conform and fail to respond to the 'gentle punishments', that the manoeuvre occurs in which need is passed from school to child. Unable to understand the stubbornness of the individuals concerned and fearful of the consequences for order, those responsible for order in the school then, following the precepts learned in teacher education and reinforced by the service system provided by the local education authority, reconceptualize the students as having emotional and behavioural difficulties.

Although recent changes in discussion about policy (DfEE, 1997) have stressed the importance of an inclusive ethos in schools (that is, one in which the comprehensive ethos of the school is clearly articulated, and the systems of the school are established to ensure inclusion), there remains a firm resistance to such an ethos. Croll and Moses (2000: 61), for example, found that more than half of the 48 headteachers they interviewed felt that 'More children should attend special schools', and in the case of 'children with emotional and behavioural difficulties' this figure rose to two-thirds (see also Mousley *et al.*, 1993). In the language of attribution theorists, the problem is that of 'fundamental attribution error' (Ross *et al.*, 1977) – the easy over-attribution of events to the disposition of individuals rather than to the failings of institutions. (It is worth noting that of Croll and Moses's sample under 1 per cent of headteachers and only 2 per cent of teachers attributed 'emotional and behavioural difficulties' to 'school and teachers'.)

Once established as having emotional difficulties, children are diverted along a new path which separates them, and which ends in their being 'helped'.

The arcane paraphernalia of assessment procedures confirm the diagnosis of emotional difficulties. Once so labelled, your every word becomes untrustworthy. Your complaints can be ignored, as the response to increasing irrationality is to pile on more and more 'help'.

The result is incarceration by smothering: the entrapment of the child in a cocoon of professional help. One is launched on what Goffman (1987: 79) calls a 'moral career' in which both the individual's image of self and his or her 'official position, jural relations, and style of life' change in sequence as the child graduates through his or her career as sufferer and victim. Escape comes only by 'acknowledgement' and 'acceptance' of one's problems. It helps if one can learn the vocabulary and the semiology of the therapeutic system and parrot it back to the therapeutic agent.

From simple wrongdoing to disturbance and treatment

How does all this happen? The impedimenta, vocabulary and constructs of the new professionals have come to invade the simple systems of judgement which preceded them. The act itself ceases to be condemned in simple terms; instead, it is an estimation of the *student* which is made.

The delineation of emotional disturbance interrupts the procedure of simply judging whether an act is right or wrong, good or bad. Simple moral judgement is suspended. It is displaced by a morass of half-understood ideas about disturbance, a jumble of bits and pieces from psychoanalysis, psychology and psychiatry, a bricolage of penis envy and cognitive dissonance, of Freudian slip and standard deviation, of motivation and maternal deprivation, regression and repression, attention seeking and assimilation, reinforcement and self-esteem – ideas corrupted by textbook writers and mangled by journalists and the writers of popular culture. But these ideas are not only half-understood. Even if those who use the ideas in defining 'need' understood them as well as it is possible to understand them, they would be on shaky ground epistemologically and empirically (Nagel, 1959; Cioffi, 1975; Macmillan, 1997), for the models which stand behind notions of emotional disturbance are, as Crews (1997: 297) points out, characterized by faulty logic, the manufacturing of evidence and facile explanation.

Explanatory and therapeutic currency is widely lauded by the psychological community in a small rainforest of 'scientific' journals, yet there is little sign of a diminution in unhappiness resulting from these supposed advances in understanding. Indeed, Smail (1993: 13) asserts that 'There is certainly no evidence that the wider availability of psychological theories and techniques is leading to a decrease in psychological distress.' He suggests that in the burgeoning of psychological techniques to alleviate distress, there is far less a breakthrough in enlightened understanding, and more 'the success of an enterprise' (1993: 13). The mass of techniques make a bazaar in which plausible homily, mixed with large portions of psychoanalytic and psychological vocabulary, take the place of a rational consideration of children's behaviour at school. Nor is there much evidence in education of the successful impact of this burgeoning enterprise: numbers of children excluded from school continue to rise.

It is strange that the therapeutic mindset behind notions of maladjustment and EBD should have been so resistant to suffocation in the absence of supporting evidence. Smail suggests that an ostensibly therapeutic approach survives first because people want it to, and second because it is impossible to demonstrate that it *isn't* effective. The result of this mock-scientific approach to behaviour is the sanctification of the agent of therapy (and even the agent of assessment), so that the whole assessment-therapy process surrounds itself with what Smail calls 'an aura of almost moral piety' in which to question putative benefits 'comes close to committing a kind of solecism' (1993: 16).

It is not only 'abnormal' psychology (as a sub-area of psychology) which is playing a significant part in the 'clinicizing' of unacceptable behaviour. For educationists the notion of need *in the child* is reinforced by key psychological theories such as those of Piaget. Important for reports such as that of the influential Plowden (DES, 1967), these theories have stressed the genetic determinacy of development, leaving explanation for behaviour problems or learning difficulties to be made in terms of developmental defect or emotional deprivation, the vocabulary again invoking psychological or social explanation for behaviour at school.

Many have pointed to not only the tenuousness of the theories on which such educational and social policy is based (e.g. Elkind, 1967; Gelman, 1982; Bryant, 1984; James and Prout, 1990; Rutter, 1995), but also to the way in which attention is distracted from the nature and significance of the school environment in itself constructing the difficulties (e.g. Walkerdine, 1983; Alexander 1984). But frail as these theories are, they are perennially attractive (as the persistence of Piaget's theories in teacher education syllabuses demonstrates) and it is the ideas which stem from them that influence the professional as he or she works with the reconceptualized child: the child with needs.

Categories for children, not adults

Ideas about psyche, motivation and background form the substrate out of which new descriptors emerge. They also contribute to and exaggerate the unequal power balance between adult and child, for in no *adult* system is the official process of packaging and labelling aberrant behaviour as well-formed, sophisticated and widely accepted as it is in EBD for these minors. Concomitantly, the rules, punishment regimes and labelling tolerated within schools would not be tolerated within any adult organization (other than the prison). It is perhaps significant that although twenty-five years ago a ferment of discussion under the leadership of Laing (1965) and Szasz (1972) surrounded the issue of whether difficult behaviour constituted mental illness, little of the significance of that discussion was assimilated into debate about what was then called 'maladjustment' – perhaps because a central pillar of the superstructure of children's services and special education has been the taken-for-granted assumption of doing good, of acting in *loco parentis*, of guardianship. These ideas have flourished partly because of a tradition of seeing the child as not only vulnerable and helpless but also as irrational.

The process of understanding children to be not only irrational but *also* emotionally disturbed effectively condemns them to voicelessness. Being seen as irrational (rather than simply stupid) is particularly damning, for it means that you are deemed unworthy even of consultation about what is in your best interests.

The system of soft categories (like EBD), spongy quasi-legal procedures – such as in the Code of Practice (DfE, 1994a), quasi-medical diagnoses (like Attention Deficit Hyperactivity Disorder – ADHD) and mock-scientific assessments, though it doesn't stand up to rigorous scrutiny, has its effects insidiously. Partly because children are taken to be not only irrational, but also in need of protection, it has been possible for a network of special procedures – supposedly protective and therapeutic – to grow around them, in a way that they have not grown around adults.

For adults, unacceptable behaviour is punished – but a comprehensible (if less than perfect) system of procedures and protocols protects them. Even if the protection is written in legal jargon, it is at least in the language of straightforward relations: you have done wrong, we will punish you with x, but you are entitled to y. For children, by contrast, repeatedly unacceptable behaviour leads them into a set of arcane official and semi-official procedures (detention, exclusion, referral to the psychologist, statementing, placement in special education) in which their rights are unclear not only to them and their parents but also to the administrators and professionals who work with them (and hence the need for the setting up of the Special Needs Tribunal). Ad hoc collections of people, such as governors in exclusions panels, decide about their rights to attend school, and decisions (unrestricted by anything so mundane as a time limitation) are made by teachers, psychologists and administrators about their lives. For children, protection takes on a wholly different meaning from the protection which the law gives to the adult suspected of law breaking. The protection given to the child is a paternalistic protection, for example in the 'protection' of a statement, where supposed 'needs' are constructed and then met. It is far harder to argue against someone who is meeting your needs than someone who is accusing you of breaking the rules.

Making schools more humane as environments: common talk in humane schools

Lest it appears that we are endorsing misbehaviour, violence or abuse, let us stress that we are not. We do not seek in any way to condone violence or to romanticize difficult behaviour. Nor do we seek to play down or underestimate the school staff's need for disciplinary techniques to keep order. Instead we are seeking to point out that misbehaviour seems to be an endemic part of institutions that organize themselves in particular ways and that if we seek to reduce such behaviour we have to recognize its provenance. We must recognize the possibility that the origins of misbehaviour lie less in children's emotions or even in their 'disadvantage' and lie more in the character of the organization which we ask them to inhabit for a large part of their lives. It is an organization staffed by professionals whose response when faced with trouble is necessarily a professional one. Here, Skrtic (1991) suggests, is its main problem since it operates as a 'professional bureaucracy' (and Weatherley and Lipsky, 1977, and Wolfensberger, 1990, point to similar processes). Professional bureaucracies are organizations which, far from being designed to think creatively about how to change for the better, think rather about how to direct their 'clients' toward some existing professional specialism. Or they may consider how the problem can be absorbed in the professional procedures defined in a local policy document. The mindset induced by the notion of disturbance fits happily into such a system, encouraging the view that specialized sets of professional knowledge exist to deal with misbehaviour.

It is odd that Skrtic's analysis occurs at a time when there has been optimism about the potential of school to influence 'outcomes' for children. For over the last decade or so, academics and policy makers have proposed that in tackling the question of difficult behaviour at school, attention should be paid not only to analysis and treatment of the child's behaviour but also to the operations and systems in the school which may cause or aggravate such behaviour. The positive arguments for such a shift in emphasis from child to institution rest in evidence and analysis from diverse sources. They rest in evidence about the significance of the school's role in influencing behaviour and achievement (e.g. Edmonds, 1979; Rutter *et al.*, 1979; Hallinger and Murphy, 1986; Neisser, 1986; Mortimore *et al.*, 1988; Jesson and Gray, 1991; Sammons *et al.*, 1993; Levine and Lezotte, 1995). They rest in recognition of the potentially damaging effects of labelling (in the work of theorists such as Cicourel and Kitsuse, 1968). And they rest in arguments about the invalidity of interpreting aberrant behaviour as disturbed (in the ideas of Szasz, Laing and others). Resulting models for intervention and help which thus attach significance to the impact of the wider environment, and particularly that of the school, have been given added impetus by the development of thinking in areas such as ecological psychology (following pioneers such as Kounin, 1967; Barker, 1968; Doyle, 1977; Bronfenbrenner, 1979) and systems theory (e.g. Checkland, 1981).

In fact, though, only a small amount of the school effectiveness research has related specifically to behaviour (e.g. Galloway, 1983; Galloway *et al.*, 1985; McManus, 1987). The *Fifteen Thousand Hours* work (Rutter *et al.*, 1979) looked at attendance and 'delinquency' but conceded that the process (independent) variables – that is, the school factors supposedly responsible for influencing outcomes – can contribute only in small measure to predictions concerning those outcomes. The authors say that other (unidentified) variables must be playing an important part in differences between schools in attendance and behaviour.

The tenuousness of the research evidence here has not prevented a widespread acceptance of the idea that schools make a difference when it comes to behaviour. Despite the clear caveat provided by Rutter and his colleagues about the generalizability of effectiveness findings when it comes to behaviour, there has been a near unanimous acceptance of the message which, it appears, policy makers want to hear.

Optimism in the face of lack of evidence is interesting and perhaps related to the laudable desire to do whatever can be done to make schools more congenial places for all who inhabit them. But the general body of school effectiveness literature and research has pushed whole-school responses in the wrong direction. Consistent with the conclusions which would follow from Skrtic's (1991: 165) analysis, the particular professional vocabularies – psychological and psychiatric – induced by the label 'EBD' discourage a move to the necessary creativity. They induce merely what Skrtic calls 'an assortment of symbols and ceremonies' which look and sound like sensible action – things of the sort which appear in the *Elton Report* (DES, 1989c), like writing a bullying policy, or improving liaison procedures – but in fact shift attention from characteristics of the environment to what Skrtic calls aspects of the 'machine bureaucracy': things that have the appearance (but only the appearance) of rational reaction to a problem (see also Weatherley and Lipsky, 1977 in this context).

The system 'bureaucratizes deviance' (Rubington and Weinberg, 1968: 111), with a hierarchy of defining agents – and one may note how this hierarchy has been formalized over the years in the UK system, from Circular 2/75 to the 1981 Education Act to the Code of Practice (DfE, 1994a).

The professional systems operating in schools to manage deviance in fact bureaucratize deviance as reliably today as they did when Rubington and Weinberg wrote about them thirty years ago. They now do so perhaps more sensitively and with more emphasis on the whole-school options suggested by Elton. However, the professional systems encourage and reinforce professional responses, thus diverting attention from ostensibly more mundane but potentially more significant aspects of the world which children have to inhabit. They ensure that the discourse is that of professionals, communicating in their habitual constructs. Discussion and debate about, for example, 'professional liaison' has more cachet than discussion about fair queuing systems at lunchtime, but the bullying policy thus engendered may be little more than an ineffectual sop, doing little to address the actual problems faced by pupils in the school. And liaison with the educational psychologist may do little to address the routine unfairnesses committed every day at school. As the great educator Rousseau (1993) noted more than two centuries ago, some observations are considered too trivial to be true. They have to have a theoretical or professional spin to make them seem significant.

A nice example of simple, non-theoretical, aprofessional thinking is given by Clarke (1997) as headteacher of a large urban comprehensive school. He notes:

> Some years ago, having taken issue with a teacher (male) for shouting at a student (female), I was invited at a staff meeting (under any other business!) to outline my 'policy on shouting'. Three points occurred to me:
> (i) if mature adults disagree, they generally don't shout at each other;
> (ii) it is hard to ask students to keep their voices down if the teachers shout;
> (iii) it is impossible to say, hand on heart, that we do not have bullying if big, powerful men verbally assault small, powerless young women.
>
> (Clarke, 1997: 154)

This kind of intervention emerges from Clarke's values and beliefs as a teacher and as a person. It has nothing to do with any professional knowledge, theoretical archive, or government code of practice. It is only this brave kind of thinking and action which emancipates one from the machine bureaucracy of which Skrtic writes.

An analogy can perhaps be drawn with successful action currently being taken on housing estates to manage the behaviour of unruly youngsters. This involves a deliberate move away from the pattern of response which would usually have taken place five or ten years ago – a response which involved 'understanding' the 'problems' of the young people involved, an understanding predicated on the theoretical assumptions of certain professional groups, which imputed 'need' to certain kinds of behaviour. The move is toward more community action, which involves – on one side – increasing the likelihood that the perpetrators of misdemeanours will be caught, disapproved-of and, if necessary, punished, and – on the other – making systematic efforts to provide activity for the young people involved. It is through an engagement with the political (and a corresponding disengagement with the patronizing psychobabble of 'understanding') that the patent truth of Postman's statement can shine out:

There is no question that listlessness, ennui, and even violence in school are related to
the fact that students have no useful role to play in society. The strict application of
nurturing and protective attitudes toward children has created a paradoxical situation
in which protection has come to mean excluding the young from meaningful
involvement in their own communities.

(Postman, 1996: 103)

It is only by thinking in this way – outside the boundaries presented by the
school walls – that genuinely inclusive solutions can emerge to the routine
challenge presented by children's difficult behaviour. The champion of children's
rights, Eric Midwinter, said something similar a quarter of a century ago:

I gaze half-benignly on cuts in public expenditure. If those cuts can mean (it is a large
'if') the properly directed deprofessionalisation and deinstitutionalisation of our
public services and the controlled mobilisation of community resources, then I am
convinced the overall quality of services would be improved.

(Midwinter, 1977: 111)

The reflex response of education cannot in other words be a unilateral one
using its familiar constructs and professional routes. Those constructs and
routes inevitably involve separate action and sometimes segregated provision.

Conclusion

In the use of the term 'EBD' there is an indolent espousal of a term which too
conveniently packages together difficult, troublesome children with emotional
disturbance. In its use is an insidious blurring of motives and knowledges
which imputes problems to children that in reality are rarely theirs. In the
dispositional attributions which are therein made, unnecessarily complex
judgements about putative need take the place of simple judgements about
what is acceptable or unacceptable behaviour for a particular institution. Use of
the term 'EBD' enables the substitution of the former for the latter – of the
complex for the straightforward – and this in turn perpetuates a mindset about
behaviour which distracts attention from what the school can do to make itself
a more humane, inclusive place.

Recent understandings about the rights of the child have made little impact
on the processes which formalize these attributions, fraught as those processes
are with difficulties concerning the extra-judicial judgements being made on
children's aberrant behaviour. Neither have questions which have been posed
about the effectiveness and appropriateness of 'helping' services in adult
clinical psychology and psychiatry been addressed to anywhere near the same
extent in children's services. In fact, the professional services which exist
notionally to support children exist often in reality to support the institution

(a distinction which is sometimes overtly and unselfconsciously made) and may set into train routines and rituals which have the appearance of effective response, but in practice do little other than distract attention from significant aspects of the environment which children are being asked to inhabit.

By retaining and using the label 'EBD', sight is often lost of the fact that schools for many children present an environment with which it is difficult to come to terms. By packaging this difficulty as a problem of the children we divert our own attention from ways in which schools can become more congenial and inclusive places.

Summary

The legacy of the thinking behind special education is a set of ideas which perpetuate exclusion. In this chapter we focus on 'emotional and behavioural difficulties' (EBD), which we suggest represents a confused collation of notions. It rests on an unsteady foundation – a mélange of disparate ideas which nevertheless share one feature: the attribution of behaviour problems to the disposition of the child and his or her personal circumstances. Out of this mix of notions and attributions has emerged EBD – a category which substitutes quasi-clinical assessments about putative need for more straightforward judgements about right and wrong. It enables and legitimizes clinically orientated judgements about the causes of misbehaviour – 'emotional difficulties' – which allow the school to evade serious scrutiny of its own routines and procedures. Moreover, the judgements made about children occur in the absence of the panoply of protections which exist for adults who behave oddly or unacceptably. This difference between the way adults and children are treated is an increasingly untenable anomaly at a time when policy debate correctly pays more attention to children's rights. The predominantly clinical and child-centred mix of notions and attributions behind EBD influences also supposedly whole-school approaches to behaviour difficulties and distracts attention from ways in which schools can be made more humane, more inclusive places.

References

Alexander, R. (1984) *Primary Teaching*. London: Holt.

Barker, R.G. (1968) *Ecological Psychology*. Stanford, CA: Stanford University Press.

Bourdieu, P. and Eagleton, T. (1994) Doxa and common life: an interview, in S. Zizek (ed.) *Mapping Ideology*. London: Verso.

Bronfenbrenner, U. (1979) *The Ecology of Human Development*. Cambridge, MA: Harvard University Press.

Bryant, P.E. (1984) Piaget, teachers and psychologists, *Oxford Review of Education*, 10(3): 251–9.

Chazan, M., Laing, A.F. and Davies, D. (1994) *Emotional and Behavioural Difficulties in Middle Childhood*. London: The Falmer Press.

Checkland, P. (1981) *Systems Thinking, Systems Practice*. Chichester: Wiley.

Cicourel, A.V. and Kitsuse, J.I. (1968) The social organisation of the high school and deviant adolescent careers, in E. Rubington and M.S. Weinberg (eds) *Deviance: the Interactionist Perspective; Text and Readings in the Sociology of Deviance*. London: Macmillan.

Cioffi, F. (1975) Freud and the idea of a pseudo-science, in R. Borger and F. Cioffi, *Explanation in the Behavioural Sciences: Confrontations*. Cambridge: Cambridge University Press.

Clarke, B. (1997) What comprehensive schools do better, in R. Pring and G. Walford, *Affirming the Comprehensive Ideal*. London: Falmer.

Crews, F. (1997) *The Memory Wars: Freud's Legacy in Dispute*. London: Granta.

Croll, P. and Moses, D. (2000) *Special Needs in the Primary School*. London: Cassell.

DES (Department of Education and Science) (1967) *Children and their Primary Schools (Plowden Report)*. London: HMSO.

DES (Department of Education and Science) (1978) *Special Educational Needs*. Report of the Committee of Enquiry into the Education of Handicapped Children and Young People, Cmnd 7212. London: HMSO.

DES (Department of Education and Science) (1989a) *A Survey of Provision for Pupils with Emotional/Behavioural Difficulties in Maintained Special Schools and Units. A Report by HM Inspectors*. London: HMSO.

DES (Department of Education and Science) (1989b) *Special Schools for Pupils with Emotional and Behavioural Difficulties*, Circular 23/89. London: HMSO.

DES (Department of Education and Science) (1989c) *Discipline in Schools (Elton Report)*. London: HMSO.

DfE (Department for Education) (1994a) *The Code of Practice on the Identification and Assessment of Special Educational Needs*. London: HMSO.

DfEE (Department for Education and Employment) (1995) *Special Educational Needs in England, 1995*. London: HMSO.

DfEE (Department for Education and Employment) (1997) *Excellence for All Children: Meeting Special Educational Needs*. London: DfEE.

Doyle, W. (1977) The uses of non-verbal behaviours: toward an ecological view of classrooms, *Merrill-Palmer Quarterly*, 23(3): 179–92.

Edmonds, R. (1979) Effective schools for the urban poor, *Educational Leadership*, 37(1): 15–23.

Elkind, D. (1967) Piaget's conservation problems, *Child Development*, 38: 15–27.

Foucault, M. (1991) *Discipline and Punish* (trans. A. Sheridan). London: Penguin.

Galloway, D. (1983) Disruptive pupils and effective pastoral care, *School Organisation*, 13: 245–54.

Galloway, D., Martin, R. and Wilcox, B. (1985) Persistent absence from school and exclusion from school: the predictive power of school and community variables, *British Educational Research Journal*, 11: 51–61.

Gelman, R. (1982) Accessing one-to-one correspondence: still another paper about conservation, *British Journal of Psychology*, 73: 209–21.

Goffman, E. (1987) The moral career of the mental patient, in E. Rubington and M.S. Weinberg (eds) *Deviance: The Interactionist Perspective*, 5th edn. New York, NY: Macmillan.

Hallinger, P. and Murphy, J. (1986) The social context of effective schools, *American Journal of Education*, 94(3): 328–55.

Hargreaves, D.H., Hestor, S.K. and Mellor, F.J. (1975) *Deviance in Classrooms*. London: Routledge and Kegan Paul.

James, A. and Prout, A. (1990) A new paradigm for the sociology of childhood? Provenance, promise and problems, in A. James and A. Prout (eds) *Constructing and Reconstructing Childhood: Contemporary Issues in the Sociological Study of Childhood*. London: Falmer.

Jesson, D. and Gray, J. (1991) Slants on slopes: using multi-level models to investigate differential school effectiveness and its impact on schools' examination results, *School Effectiveness and School Improvement*, 2(3): 230–71.

Kounin, J.S. (1967) An analysis of teachers' managerial techniques, *Psychology in the Schools*, 4: 221–7.

Laing, R.D. (1965) *The Divided Self*. London: Penguin.

Levine, D.U. and Lezotte, L.W. (1995) Effective schools research, in J.A. Banks and C.A. Banks, *Handbook of Research on Multicultural Education*. Nebraska, NE: Macmillan.

McManus, M. (1987) Suspension and exclusion from high school – the association with catchment and school variables, *School Organisation*, 7(3): 261–71.

Macmillan, M. (1997) *Freud Evaluated: The Completed Arc*. London: MIT Press.

Midwinter, E. (1977) The professional-lay relationship: a Victorian legacy, *Journal of Child Psychology and Psychiatry*, 18: 101–13.

Mortimore, P. (1997) *The Road to Success: Four Case Studies of Schools Which No Longer Require Special Measures*. London: DfEE.

Mortimore, P., Sammons, P., Stoll, L., Lewis, D. and Ecob, R. (1988) *School Matters: The Junior Years*. Exeter: Open Books.

Mousley, J.A., Rice, M. and Tregenza, K. (1993) Integration of students with disabilities into regular schools: policy in use, *Disability, Handicap and Society*, 8(1): 59–70.

Nagel, E. (1959) Methodological issues in psychoanalytic theory, in S. Hook (ed.) *Psychoanalysis, Scientific Method and Philosophy*. New York, NY: New York University Press.

Neisser, U. (ed.) (1986) *The School Achievement of Minority Children*. Hillsdale, NJ: Lawrence Erlbaum.

Postman, N. (1996) *The End of Education*. New York, NY: Alfred A. Knopf.

Ross, L.D., Amabile, T.M. and Steinmetz, J.L. (1977) Social roles, social control and biases in social-perception processes, *Journal of Personality and Social Psychology*, 35: 485–94.

Rousseau, J.-J. ([1762] 1993) *Émile* (trans. B. Foxley). London: J.M. Dent.

Rubington, E. and Weinberg, M.S. (eds) (1968) *Deviance: The Interactionist Perspective; Text and Readings in the Sociology of Deviance*. London: Macmillan.

Rueda, R. and Mehan, H. (1986) Metacognition and passing: strategic interactions in the lives of students with learning disabilities, *Anthropology and Education Quarterly*, 17: 145–65.

Rutter, M. (1995) Clinical implications of attachment concepts: retrospect and prospect, *Journal of Child Psychology and Psychiatry*, 36(4): 549–71.

Rutter, M., Maughan, B., Mortimore, P. and Ouston, J. (1979) *Fifteen Thousand Hours: Secondary Schools and their Effects on Children*. London: Open Books.

Sammons, P., Nuttall, D. and Cuttance, P. (1993) Differential school effectiveness: results from a re-analysis of the Inner London Education Authority's Junior School Project Data, *British Educational Research Journal*, 19(4): 381–405.

Skrtic, T.M. (1991) The special education paradox: equity as the way to excellence, *Harvard Educational Review*, 61(2): 148–206.

Smail, D. (1993) *The Origins of Unhappiness*. London: Harper Collins.

Smith, A.J. and Thomas, J.B. (1992) A survey of therapeutic support for children with emotional and behavioural disturbance (EBD) in special schools in the United Kingdom, *School Psychology International*, 13: 323–37.

Szasz, T.S. (1972) *The Myth of Mental Illness*. London: Paladin.

Walkerdine, V. (1983) It's only natural: rethinking child-centred pedagogy, in A.M. Wolpe and J. Donald (eds) *Is There Anyone Here from Education?* London: Pluto.

Weatherley, R. and Lipsky, M. (1977) Street level bureaucrats and institutional innovation: implementing special educational reform, *Harvard Educational Review*, 47(2): 171–97.

Wolfensberger, W. (1990) Human service policies: the rhetoric versus the reality, in L. Barton (ed.) *Disability and Dependency*. London: Falmer.

Chapter 4

Breaking the policy log-jam: comparative perspectives on policy formulation and development for pupils with emotional and behavioural difficulties

Eleni S. Didaskalou and Alan J. Millward

Introduction

Education systems in a number of countries continue to express concerns about an apparently inexorable increase in the number of pupils displaying difficult behaviour in schools and classrooms. This 'rising tide of disruption' poses a number of complex problems not just for those who have to deal with difficult pupils on a regular basis but also for policy makers and other services. In England, for example, there have been a number of recent oscillations in policy advice for schools over how they should respond to the most difficult pupils in the system. The 'New' Labour government, concerned about adverse publicity from the rising number of pupil exclusions (see, for example, Imich, 1994; Blyth & Milner, 1993; Parsons & Howlett, 1996; Morris, 1996; Castle & Parsons, 1997; Hayden, 1997; Smith, 1998; Parsons, 1999, among others), has found it difficult to provide consistent advice to schools as to whether or not the most problematic pupils should or should not be 'excluded'. Traditionally, of course, the English system has made use of provision for disruptive pupils in 'special' schools, units and latterly through Pupil Referral Units (PRUs). However, the recurring vacillations in policy over the extent to which such provisions should be used in favour of schools seeking to develop more effective 'in-house' and 'inclusive' responses have helped in establishing an inconsistency for those in both mainstream and special sectors. In the face of this lack of consistency we will argue that there is a significant danger that by focusing too narrowly on the needs of those pupils with the most obvious and pressing behavioural difficulties the needs of those with emotional problems will be overlooked. In support of this we will draw from the extensive research literature that already exists and also from a recent large-scale survey undertaken in Greece. This survey of teachers' attitudes provides an important comparative dimension in understanding the dangers that exist for policy makers and practitioners in the face of increasing disruption within schools and classrooms.

An emphasis on behaviour problems: some implications

It is now over four years since two landmark articles (Bowers (1996), 'Putting back the "E" in EBDs' and Maras (1996), 'Whose Are The "Es" in EBDs?') alerted policy makers to the danger of forgetting the emotional needs and problems of pupils. In these two articles a number of important issues concerning current conceptualisations and practices for pupils who experience Emotional and Behavioural Difficulties (EBDs) were addressed by the authors. In particular they identified two points that have considerable significance for this paper. First, they pointed out how official policy overemphasised issues of the control and management of behaviour as reflected in the surfeit of advice and guidance that was forthcoming at the time (see, for example, DfEE, 1994a, b). Second, they highlighted a worrying trend regarding the attitudes of mainstream teachers to pupils' emotional problems suggesting that such problems were regarded as less problematic and warranted less attention than behavioural difficulties.

Significantly, this theme was explored some two years later by one of the major figures in the field. Cooper (1998) felt moved to note that the deluge of policy guidance at the time reflected an emphasis on the control of disruption potentially ignoring the needs of those with emotional difficulties. Such an emphasis was of course in line with the policy prerogative implicit in the Green Paper (DfEE, 1997) that schools should become more inclusive, in particular by demonstrating that they could wherever possible 'consume their own smoke' by retaining their 'special' pupils without recourse to placements outside the mainstream. A focus on the need to retain those with the most pressing behaviour problems was therefore an understandable priority but, as Cooper

(1998) and others (Bowers, 1996; Maras, 1996: Vulliamy & Webb, 2000) warned, there was a danger that the needs of those with emotional problems would be overlooked.

Recent evidence on the rate of exclusions from schools points to some success in the Government's attempts to address what was previously regarded as a major problem within the education system. This evidence also suggests that schools supported by Local Education Authorities have also increased their capacity to deal with those pupils who present the most pressing behavioural problems (DfEE, 2000a). In the light of this success, and after such a considerable time spent on the needs of those with behaviour problems, now may be an opportune moment for policy makers and practitioners to begin a dialogue which addresses the needs of those with emotional problems. Such a dialogue, we suggest, needs to take account of a number of developments which have contributed to the downplaying of the needs of those with emotional problems. Amongst these developments are: the absence of up-to-date research evidence on the extent of emotional problems; a policy context emphasising achievement at the expense of social and emotional development; and a dominant paradigm exerting considerable influence on professional training and practice.

The research agenda: some implications

Significantly, the research agenda in this area has been dominated by the need to gauge the extent of the difficulties teachers are facing by focusing on tangible issues such as the level of exclusions. However, it is interesting to note that even in the landmark national survey conducted into the issue of discipline in schools (Elton Report, 1989) there was a noticeable absence of data collected on the 'emotional' problems of pupils in schools. This well documented report emphasised that in the main teachers and schools were confronted not by major acts of defiance but with a much higher incidence of relatively low level disruptions which had a wearing effect on teachers, testing their patience and preventing them from teaching to the maximum efficiency. As a consequence, the recommendations from this report subsequently reinforced in the 1994 Circulars were that schools and teachers should have, as a minimum, systems of rewards and sanctions aimed at suppressing these low level disruptions through a 'carrot and stick' approach (DfEE 1994a, 1994b, 1994c). Such an approach built substantially on the work of a number of key contributors active at the time (e.g. Wheldall & Merrett, 1988) whose background was in the field of educational psychology. Significantly, previous landmark research (Rutter *et al.*, 1975; Kolvin *et al.*, 1981) which had given a much greater emphasis to the emotional needs of pupils and the capacity of teachers to recognise such needs was surprisingly absent from the Elton Report. From the time of the publication of the Elton Report the dominant discourse became that of educational psychology and it is only relatively recently that other 'voices' (Bowers, 1996; Maras, 1996; Cooper, 1998; Vulliamy & Webb, 2000) have, as we intimated, attempted to redress this emphasis. One consequence of the dominance of educational psychology in the field has been that there is a wealth of evidence about the incidence of behaviour problems, rates of exclusion and also a corresponding volume of advice on appropriate techniques for managing behaviour problems in the classroom. This has culminated in the endorsement in one recent government policy document (DfEE, 1998) of the use of Assertive Discipline (Canter & Canter, 1992). Such advocacy is perhaps not altogether surprising given a policy context which has stressed the role of schools in driving up standards and raising attainment. In this context, the absence of both substantive recent research such as that undertaken by Kolvin *et al.* (1981) and also policy guidance into the emotional needs of pupils is therefore not altogether surprising.

The shift in policy: some dilemmas

Just as the Elton Report (1989) marked a sea change in the dominant discourse in the areas of behaviour difficulties, so the 1988 Education Act changed the emphasis within education in general and special education in particular. The Education Act (1988) and subsequent legislation reflected the desire of the then government to bring state-maintained education within the embrace of its espoused 'free-market' policies. Taken as a whole, the reform shifted public and professional concern on to school performance and the improvement of academic standards. The National Curriculum and OFSTED inspections provided for the first time the means by which children throughout England and Wales might be tested and judgements made about the effectiveness of schools. Schools were required, for the first time, to compete for pupils and to publish the results of national testing and regular inspection reports, enabling parents to decide which schools could most appropriately provide an education for their child.

Pupils with Special Educational Needs (SEN) were not excluded from this agenda and the introduction of the National Curriculum required that all pupils be taught a common curriculum which was broadly balanced and suitably differentiated. However, the strong academic focus of the National Curriculum has increasingly been considered as not always appropriate for addressing the needs of some pupils with SEN and moreover may be viewed as contributing to the increase reported over the period of pupils experiencing behaviour problems (Dyson & Millward, 2000).

It can be argued that this new policy context resulted in a downplaying of the emphasis that previous legislation (see, for example, DES, 1978; Education Act, 1981) had placed on special needs and a reduction in the time (Crowther *et al.*, 2000, 2001) that, for example, SEN Co-ordinators could devote to the needs of the pupils. This is despite the plethora of guidance that has surfaced in this period (DfEE, 1994a, 1994b, 1994c, 1997, 1998, 2000b) and the desire of the New Labour government to create a more 'inclusive' education system. Indeed it is now a commonplace to identify the existence of an apparent contradiction in policy, with schools being encouraged to drive up standards and raise attainment while at the same time delivering greater inclusivity (Dyson & Millward, 2000). These potentially contradictory policy imperatives presented schools and teachers with a dilemma. How were they to retain an inclusive profile while at the same time surviving in a competitive educational environment? Vulliamy and Webb (2000) suggest that the recent rising tide in exclusions is a consequence of this dilemma and can be seen as one response by schools to the pressures and dilemmas arising from conflicting policy imperatives. Given the negative implications that the number of exclusions have for the realisation of the government's agenda and the more widespread concern that this phenomenon generates, it is not altogether surprising that the policy agenda has had to revisit matters of discipline and disruption. Such a focus can be seen plainly in the significant proportion of the 1997 Education Act being devoted to issues of discipline and the management of behaviour problems. Its recommendations mainly draw, unsurpisingly, from the principles of behaviourism with an emphasis on control, rather than suggesting any review of the circumstances which might be contributing to the problem. Cooper (1998), considering the implications that the new Act had for pupils with EBDs, argued that it reflected a coercive and punitive approach which was likely to exacerbate rather than eliminate problems in schools. This emphasis can also be seen to have impacted elsewhere in the system. Most notably, it has had a marked influence in the field of professional development and training.

A hegemonic paradigm and its implications for professional training and practice?

To support its emphasis on standards and achievement the government has sought to exert increased influence over the content and direction of professional training and development. In terms of the focus of this paper, this attempt to influence training and development can be seen in a number of areas. We have, for example, noted how the emphasis given in the Elton Report (1989) has been reinforced (DfEE, 1994a, 1994b, 1994c) and extended with the advocacy of the advantages to schools and teachers of using, for example, the techniques suggested by Canter and Canter in their Assertive Discipline programme (DfEE, 1998). This endorsement of the principles of behaviour theory and behaviourally-based classroom management programmes can be also seen in a proliferation of similar packages (see, for example, Laing & Chazan, 1987; Wheldall & Merrett, 1989; Wheldall, 1991; Canter & Canter, 1992; Galvin & Costa, 1994; Smith & Laslett, 1995 among others). Offering an apparently endless source of techniques and 'practical' advice capable of being applied in schools and classrooms, such approaches and their underlying philosophy have exerted what can be regarded as an hegemonic influence over the professional training and development of teachers.

The degree of this monopolistic hold over the culture of professional training has been accelerated considerably by the rapid decline in the influence of the 'psychomedical' paradigm (Clark *et al.*, 1998). The reduction of the influence of the medical model within special education has been widely welcomed (see for example Cooper *et al.*, 1994; Clark *et al.*, 1998; Laslett, 1998, among others). It is suggested that such a reduction has advantages. On the one hand it places a much greater emphasis on the need for the development of 'educational' theory to inform and guide educational practices. On the other hand it creates a context in which teachers and schools can take a much more direct role in managing and directing the response to pupils rather than being dependent on techniques and explanations which were not part of their professional domain. We will argue that while such a development has had undoubted benefits for the advancement of education as a professional discipline, it has nevertheless contributed to the emphasis on the management of behaviour through behaviourally-based approaches and techniques. We do not wish to underestimate the contribution that these approaches and techniques have offered to schools and teachers. They provide an essential framework which teachers can use to support their management of pupils. Our contention, however, is that the hegemonic influence that this discourse has over current practices can result in what has been referred to as a 'reductionism' (Skidmore, 1996) both within the theoretical conceptualisations and practical interventions relating to the management of behaviour. Many commentators (Conway & Izard, 1995; Hanko, 1995, Lloyd-Smith & Davies, 1995; Slee, 1995, among others) have suggested that behaviourally-based approaches oversimplify the nature of behaviour difficulties and overemphasise external control while ignoring the complex dynamics of the classrooms and the personalities of pupils. It is, for example, argued that a reliance on a mechanistic manipulation of the environment may prevent pupils from developing an intrinsic motivation and control of their actions and that this encourages teachers to underestimate the complexity of the management of behaviour. Moreover, it is suggested that teachers may rigidly apply the skills and practices suggested by these programmes without necessarily engaging with this complexity.

Furthermore, we argue that such a rigidity may inhibit a more effective approach and a desire to search for alternative approaches that take into consideration pupils' emotional needs and the difficulties that some experience in the psychological domain.

In terms of professional training and development the problem becomes one of finding ways in which such approaches can be incorporated alongside the obviously more appealing 'quick-fixes' offered by behaviourally-based programmes. Although alternative approaches such as cognitive, problem-solving methods, ecosystemic interventions and counselling which stress pupils' empowerment in controlling their own behaviour and promote pupils' emotional growth are available, their incorporation in training programmes for teachers are somewhat more problematic. They do not offer the apparently sure-fire and instant solutions of more behaviourally-based approaches and in the light of the prevailing policy context have been squeezed out of both initial and continuing teacher training programmes.

In the light of this it is interesting to establish whether teachers, struggling under the weight of demands to improve standards while having to contend with a population which is apparently more 'disruptive' than ever, are still aware of and sensitive to the needs of pupils with emotional problems. As we have indicated above there are relatively few large-scale studies which have been conducted in England. For this reason we will attempt to highlight these issues by drawing from the findings of a study recently conducted in Greece (see Didaskalou, 2000).

Emotional and behavioural difficulties: a comparative dimension

Questions may understandably be raised about the legitimacy of comparing the situation in Greece with that in England. However, despite a number of obvious contextual differences both countries share some things in common which makes such a comparison legitimate. Both have long-established education systems and have a national curriculum which is academically orientated with the intention of creating a highly educated workforce. Both systems have, over the course of the last decade, sought to reform provision as part of an agenda to raise standards by increasing competition between schools and requiring the publication of information about the relative performance of individual schools. There is a shared requirement that all teachers should be of graduate status and programmes of further professional development are available in both systems.

The study involved a survey of over 600 primary school teachers (see Didaskalou, 2000) and highlighted a number of significant factors relating to teachers' perceptions of the nature, incidence, causes and appropriate responses to behaviour problems. A number of these factors will now be discussed in relation to the argument we have developed in the course of this paper. It is perhaps not altogether surprising to note that teachers in Greece are as concerned as their English counterparts with what they regard as an increase in the number of pupils presenting with behaviour problems. They report that they are having to contend with increased levels of disruption within their classrooms and generally throughout their schools. Pupils, it would appear, are increasingly disrespectful and teachers, who are likely to face an increasing number of challenges to their authority, have to deploy a wider range of strategies to manage increased levels of disruption. We would not wish to suggest that the situation in Greece and England is exactly the same but to point out that in both systems similar patterns and trends are apparent.

What is significant, however, for this chapter is the extent to which Greek teachers report on the incidence of emotional problems and report on their concerns about their ability to respond effectively to pupils who exhibit these characteristics. Over one third of teachers who participated in the survey reported having to deal between two and three times a week with pupils who experience some form of emotional difficulty. Approximately half of the participants considered these difficulties to be 'very serious' and over 40% of teachers found emotional problems 'very difficult' and 'difficult' to deal with. Within classrooms these problems included withdrawn behaviours, unhappiness, timidity, lack of confidence etc. In playgrounds teachers reported the existence of emotional problems such as isolation and lack of close friends. Whether inside the classrooms or in the playground it was emotional problems which presented teachers with most management difficulties.

This evidence presents an interesting contrast with many of the research findings carried out in England and elsewhere, suggesting that there are a number of potential dangers of which policy makers need to be aware. First, there is the concern that in the face of what are 'real' and pressing problems it is only the needs of those that have behaviour difficulties that are addressed in policy. Second, there is the danger, as Skidmore (1996) has pointed out, of this process becoming accelerated as demands for instant action narrows the focus of those responsible for making policy. Finally, as this process continues there is the long-term danger that what may begin as relative minor emotional difficulties become more intractable and potentially damaging conditions. In the light of these dangers we suggest that policy should be developed not only on the basis of responding to the most immediate and apparently pressing behaviour problems but also by taking account of those apparently less severe emotional problems experienced by pupils. In the absence of recent research into this area in countries such as England, there is considerable merit in the process of policy review and development opportunities being informed by evidence from elsewhere. In this way it may be possible to illuminate 'gaps' in existing policy and redress any imbalances.

The brief description of the study undertaken in Greece raises some interesting questions about a policy imbalance in England. We suggest that the existence of the research from Greece offers an opportunity for all those concerned regardless of their national context to reflect and review their current policies and practices. It is for this reason that we will now attempt to draw out what we regard as the key issues in that process.

Analysis and commentary

The apparent sensitivity of teachers in Greece to the needs of pupils with emotional problems begs a number of questions. It raises the issue of whether or not teachers in England are less aware of the needs of these pupils. This may well be the case. However, in line with Maras (1996) we prefer to suggest that an answer to this question has to be considered in the light of a number of societal factors. Although sharing some common features there are, of course, considerable differences between Greece and England, some of which we will highlight here to help understand the apparent discrepancies in the concerns of teachers. We suggest that these differences can be analysed at three levels.

First, there are contextual differences relating to the attitudes and values surrounding education in the two countries. Greece is a country where education is highly valued and where teachers are widely accorded considerable respect. We do not wish to draw a direct comparison with the situation in England but to highlight the implication that this has for the awareness of the emotional needs of pupils. Less pre-occupied about the management of disruptive behaviour, Greek teachers will potentially have more 'space' in which to identify those pupils experiencing emotional difficulties. In England, as we have highlighted above, the incidence of behaviour difficulties is such that there is likely to be much less 'space' to allow any identification to take place. This has implications for both contexts. In England and in other countries experiencing similar pressures there is, as we have seen, a danger that in responding to the demands from the field for advice and guidance on the management of presenting behaviour problems the needs of those with emotional problems are squeezed out of the policy context. For countries sharing a similar context to Greece there is another danger. In their eagerness to replicate the policy and legislative frameworks of more economically developed countries, they may introduce the same market driven reforms and in so doing generate the same problems that currently beset systems in countries such as England. In this context the space that would otherwise be available to those with emotional problems becomes compressed and their needs 'lost'.

Second, and closely associated with the dangers in respect of policy convergence, is the likely impact of changes in society. Greece, in line with many countries at a similar stage of development, retains many of the vestiges of a traditional society. The family still remains central to much of Greek life and forms the basis of relatively stable communities. These are buttressed by religion and an acceptance of traditional authority figures (see, for example, Vassilliou & Vassilliou, 1982; Katakis, 1984; Papastamatis, 1988, among others). However, there is evidence that where these traditions and values are in decline (Harding *et al.*, 1986) countries begin to experience increasing problems (see, for example, Grouspa, 1999; Molosi, 1999; Antoniou, 2000; Persianis, 2000). The impact in schools is likely to be that teachers will face an increasing number of pupils who challenge and undermine their traditional authority. If this situation develops in the ways that it has in countries such as England, the risk is that as teachers have to devote more of their time to managing disruptive behaviour they will have less space in which to identify and respond to the needs of those with emotional problems. In the light of this risk there is a need for policy makers in Greece to ensure that the needs of those pupils who experience emotional problems will not be squeezed out from the policy and guidance context. For England and other countries which share a similar situation, there is a need to reinsert into the policy and guidance context the 'space' to enable emotional needs to be identified. That involves action at the third level, which relates to the professionals' domain.

Third, there is an issue related to the stage of development in the thinking that informs the broad field of special education of which emotional and behavioural difficulties are a part. The history of special education, as we have indicated above, is marked by a decline in the influence of the medical model and its replacement by one which emphasises theories and practices generated from within educational practices. In England this process has seen a growth in importance of educational psychology with its preference for responding to overt rather than latent behaviours. However, in Greece, as with many countries where the development of special education is comparatively recent and remains under the influence of a medical as opposed to an educational model (Stasinos, 1991; Polychronopoulou, 1993; Gavrilidou *et al.*, 1994; Mantarakis, 1994), the influence of educational psychology as it relates to the area of emotional and behavioural difficulties remains limited (Nikolopoulou, 1986; Gavrilidou *et al.*, 1994 among others). One possibly advantageous outcome of this can be seen in the orientation of training in teacher education programmes at both initial and inservice level. There has been no tradition within the initial training or indeed further professional training of teachers of including a component of behaviourally based programmes on classroom management. In the light of this absence and the continuing influence of the medical model it is not altogether surprising that Greek teachers still retain a concern about emotional problems to the extent that they continue to identify them even when, like their colleagues in other countries, they are facing more misbehaving pupils.

However, if the pattern of development of special education in Greece follows that in England we can predict that the role of professionals such as educational psychologists is likely to be enhanced considerably and affect decisively the formulation of educational policies and practices. There is support for this view from within Greece, where Gavrilidou *et al.* (1994) and Nikolopoulou (1986) argue that the process of development is likely to have an adverse impact on behaviour in schools, increasing the influence of educational psychology. Despite the positive impact that the empowerment of educational psychology is likely to have on the development of school-based responses to pupils with EBDs there is, however, a potential risk. The risk is that in responding to the demands that presenting problems place upon schools and teachers there will be an inevitable emphasis on the management of behaviour problems at the expense of pupils' emotional needs and problems.

This process will also have considerable implications for teachers' initial and inservice training. It can be anticipated that pressures for a revision of teachers' training will emerge as teachers find that there is less compliance on the part of pupils and that there is a need for them to become more skilled in the management of behaviour. As a response to these pressures a component of classroom management is likely to be included in the initial training of teachers and a variety of classroom management courses to be offered by psychologists and other professionals to those already in service.

A concern here is that there is every likelihood for the pattern that we have described as having occurred in England being replicated in Greece. Thus the danger for Greece, as for similar countries, is, we suggest, that unless policy makers begin to think about these issues they will also create a situation where in their endeavours to support the demands of their teachers they will 'silence' the needs of those with emotional problems.

Conclusion

We have, in the course of the above, sought to highlight a number of issues regarding pupils with emotional and behaviour difficulties. We have highlighted the existence of a 'gap' in much of the policy and guidance in England regarding pupils with emotional problems. In highlighting this 'gap' we have added our voice to that of others who share a similar concern about the needs of those pupils with emotional problems. In addition to this we have also attempted to extend the explanation of why this situation has occurred, to address its implications for other educational contexts and to suggest ways in which the creation of this gap might be avoided.

In extending the explanation of why this situation has developed we have highlighted the importance for any analysis in this area to take account of the complexities brought about through the interaction of a number of related factors. The interaction of these factors results in a momentum which we suggest produces a convergence in a number of key areas of the educational provision which seeks to meet the needs of these pupils. First, we have described how as education systems develop and become inevitably more complex they generate a level of problems which founding disciplines such as medicine are unable fully to address. Under these conditions the needs of those with emotional problems are in danger of being overlooked as the focus becomes one of addressing increases in behaviour difficulties. Second, along with other contributors, we have suggested that when policy makers focus on the raising of standards they generate pressures in schools and classrooms which bring about an increase in the level of behaviour problems. In these circumstances teachers inevitably demand advice and guidance on the management and control of pupils as a prerequisite to the achievement of other policy imperatives. As the demands of responding to disruption increase they have less and less 'space' to devote to the identification and response to those with emotional needs and problems. Third, we have highlighted the danger of reductionism in policy formulation. As policy makers are presented with the dilemma of reconciling the demands for higher standards and at the same time responding to calls from schools for more guidance to deal with disruption, there is a danger that policy becomes narrowly focused. In these circumstances the needs of the emotional and behavioural disturbed population are compressed in guidance and policy to concentrate on those who present the most management difficulties.

Policy makers both in countries with a well-established history of legislation and guidance in the management of pupils with behavioural problems and in countries seeking to formulate a 'contemporary' response are faced with the same dilemma. We will turn now to a consideration of how such a dilemma might be avoided in both contexts.

We suggest that for those countries such as Greece which have not yet become victims of this apparently inevitable process there are a number of ways forward. First, there is a need to ensure that there is a balance in the research profile in this area. Policy makers need to have a regular flow of high quality information on the needs of pupils with behavioural and emotional problems. In this way the needs of a potentially vulnerable group can be protected. Second, policy makers need to ensure that in training programmes at both pre- and in-service level the needs of both groups of pupils are preserved through an appropriate balance of courses. Third, there is a need to ensure that, despite pressure for educational based solutions to behaviour problems, there is a balance of professional 'voices'.

In countries such as England the situation is somewhat different. As we have explained, the problem is one of seeking a place on the agenda for the needs of a neglected group while there still remains an overriding concern with the problems of managing behaviour. In a context where the research agenda has become somewhat one-dimensional, where the professional training programme has become highly focused and where the professional voice of an important constituency has been progressively silenced, policy makers have a complex task. They have to offset all these factors and look beyond the immediate and the pressing and consider the wider context. As we have argued in the case of emotional difficulties, this might mean reviewing the evidence from other contexts. To take such a step is of course controversial but it is the task of policy makers not just to respond to immediate concerns and pressures but also to take into account the bigger picture. As part of their role they have to remind stakeholders that in the bigger picture there are not only pupils who present real and immediate challenges but also those with equally great needs which are being overlooked.

References

Antoniou, D. (2000) How and why Greek youth break the law (in Greek), *Kathimerini*, 5 March, pp. 13/14.

Blyth, E. and Milner, J. (1993) Exclusion from school: a first step in exclusion from society? *Children and Society*, 7, 3, pp. 255–268.

Bowers, T. (1996) Putting back the 'E' In 'EBD', *Emotional and Behavioural Difficulties Journal*, 1, 1, pp. 8–13.

Canter, L. & Canter, M. (1992) *Assertive Discipline: positive behaviour management for today's classrooms* (Santa Monica, Lee Canter Associates).

Castle, F. & Parsons, C. (1997) Disruptive behaviour and exclusions from schools: redefining and responding to the problem, *Emotional and Behavioural Difficulties Journal*, 2, 3, pp. 4–11.

Clark, C., Dyson, A. & Millward, A. (1998) Theorising special education: time to move on? In: C. Clark, A. Dyson & A. Millward (Eds) *Theorising Special Education* (London, Routledge).

Conway, R. & Izard, J. (Eds) (1995) Student behaviour outcomes: choosing appropriate paths, selected papers from *The National Conference on the Behaviour Management and Behaviour Change of Children and Youth with Emotional and/or Behaviour Problems* (Melbourne, Australian Council for Educational Research).

Cooper, P. (1998) Developments in the understanding of childhood emotional and behavioural problems since 1981. In: R. Laslett, P. Cooper, P. Maras & A. Rimmer (Eds) *Emotional and Behavioural Difficulties Since 1945* (The Association of Workers for Children with Emotional and Behavioural Difficulties).

Cooper, P., Smith, C. & Upton, G. (1994) *Emotional and Behavioural Difficulties* (London, Routledge).

Crowther, D., Dyson, A. & Millward, A. (in press) (2001) Plus ça change, plus c'est la meme chose, *European Journal of Special Needs Education*.

Crowther, D. Dyson, A. & Millward, A. (2000) *The Role of the SENCO in Primary Schools* (Newcastle: University of Newcastle Upon Tyne).

Department for Education and Employment (DFEE) (1994a) *Pupil Behaviour and Discipline*, Circular 8/94 (London, DfEE Publications).

Department for Education and Employment (DFEE) (1994b) *The Education of Children with Emotional and Behavioural Difficulties*, Circular 9/94 (London, DfEE Publications).

Department for Education and Employment (DfEE) (1994c) *Exclusions from Schools*, Circular 10/94 (London, DfEE Publications).

Department for Education and Employment (DfEE) (1997) *Excellence For All Children—Meeting Special Educational Needs* (London, DfEE Publications).

Department for Education and Employment (DfEE) (1998) *Meeting Special Educational Needs: an action programme* (London, DfEE Publications).

Department for Education and Employment (DfEE) (2000a) *Permanent Exclusions From Schools and Exclusion Appeals, England 1998/1999 (provisional)*, 10 May (DfEE, Statistical First Release).

Department for Education and Employment (DfEE) (2000b) *SEN Code of Practice & SEN Thresholds: good practice guidance* (London, DfEE Publications).

Department of Education and Science (DES) (1978) *Special Educational Needs*, Report of The Committee Into The Educational Needs of Handicapped Children and Young People – The Warnock Report (London, HMSO).

Didaskalou, E. (2000) Emerging teacher perspectives in relation to emotional and behavioural problems in Greek primary schools, PhD Thesis, Department of Education, University of Newcastle Upon Tyne.

Dyson, A. & Millward, A. (2000) *Schools and Special Needs – Issues of Innovation and Inclusion* (London, Paul Chapman Publications).

Elton Report (1989) *The Discipline in Schools: Report of the Committee of Enquiry Chaired By Lord Elton*, Department of Education and Science and the Welsh Office (London, HMSO).

Galvin, P. & Costa, P. (1994) Building better behaved schools: effective support at the whole-school level. In: P. Gray, A. Miller & J. Noakes (Eds) *Challenging Behaviour In Schools* (London, Routledge).

Gavrilidou, M., De Mesquita, P. & Mason, E. (1994) Greek teachers' perceptions of school psychologists in solving classroom problems, *School Psychology International*, 32, 3, pp. 293–304.

Grouspa, G. (1999) The increasing rates of single parents in Greece (in Greek), *The News*, 13 May. Online version.

Hanko, G. (Ed.) (1995) *Special Needs in Ordinary Classrooms – From Staff Support to Staff Development*, 3rd edition (London, David Fulton Publishers).

Harding, S., Phillips, D. & Fogarty, M. (1986) *Contrasting Values in Western Europe: Unity, Diversity and Change* (Basingstoke, Macmillan).

Hayden, C. (1997) Exclusions from primary schools: children 'in need', *Emotional and Behavioural Difficulties Journal*, 2, 3, pp. 36–44.

Imich, A.J. (1994) Exclusion from school: current trends and issues, *Educational Research Volume*, 36, 1, pp. 3–11.

Katakis, C. (1984) *The Three Identities of the Greek Family* (in Greek) (Athens, Kedros).

Kolvin, I., Garside, R., Nicol, A., Macmillan, A., Wolstenholme, F. *et al.* (1981) *Help Starts Here* (London, Tavistock).

Laing, A. & Chazan, M. (1987) *Teachers' Strategies in Coping with Behaviour Difficulties in First Year Junior School Children* (Swansea, University College of Swansea).

Laslett, R. (1998) Changing perceptions of maladjusted children, 1945–1981. In: R. Laslett, P. Cooper, P. Maras & A. Rimmer (Eds) *Emotional and Behavioural Difficulties Since 1945* (The Association of Workers for Children with Emotional and Behavioural Difficulties).

Lloyd-Smith, M. & Davies, H. (Eds) (1995) *On The Margins – The Educational Experience of 'Problem' Pupils* (Nottingham, Trentham Books).

Mantarakis, N.Z. (1994) An exploratory policy analysis of issues in special education teacher training in Greece as perceived by elected stakeholders: implications for national and higher-educational policy, Ph.D. Thesis, Leadership and Educational Policy Studies, Northern Illinois University.

Maras, P. (1996) Whose are the 'Es' In EBDs? *Emotional and Behavioural Difficulties Journal*, 1, 1, pp. 14–21.

Molosi, G. (1999) Report (in Greek), *Eleftherotypia*, 31 January, pp. 15–16.

Morris, G. (1996) Excluded pupils – the mismatch between the problem and solutions, *Emotional and Behavioural Difficulties Journal*, 1, 2, pp. 35–38.

Nikolopoulou, A. (1986) School psychology in Greece: an updated view, *Journal of School Psychology*, 25, pp. 147–154.

Papastamatis, A. (1988) Teaching styles of Greek primary school teachers, Ph.D. Thesis, Faculty of Education, University of Manchester.

Parsons, C. (1999) *Education, Exclusion and Citizenship* (London, Routledge).

Parsons, C. & Howlett, K. (1996) Permanent exclusion from school: a case where society is failing its children, *Support for Learning*, 11, 3, pp. 109–112.

Persianis, P. (2000) Education as a panacea: the case of Greece. In: K. Mazurek

& M. Winzer (Eds) *Global Society – A Comparative Perspective* (London, Allyn & Bacon).

Polychronopoulou, S. (1993) *Children with Special Needs* (in Greek) (Athens, University of Athens).

Rutter, M., Cox, A. Tupling, C., Berger, M. & Yule, W. (1975) Attainment and adjustment in two geographical areas iii: the prevalence of psychiatric disorders, *British Journal of Psychiatry*, 126, pp. 493–509.

Skidmore, D. (1996) Towards an integrated theoretical framework for research into Special Educational Needs? *European Journal of Special Needs Education*, 11, 1, pp. 32–46.

Slee, R. (1995) *Changing Theories and Practices of Discipline* (London, Falmer Press).

Smith, R. (1998) *No Lessons Learnt* (London, The Children's Society).

Smith, C. & Laslett, R. (1995) *Effective Classroom Management* (London, Routledge).

Stasinos, D. (1991) *Special Education in Greece* (in Greek) (Athens, Gutenberg).

Vassilliou, G. & Vassilliou, V. (1982) Promoting psychological functioning and preventing malfunctioning, *Paediatrician*, 11, pp. 90–98.

Vulliamy, G. & Webb, R. (2000) Stemming the tide of rising school exclusions: problems and possibilities, *British Journal of Educational Studies*, 48, 2, pp. 119–133.

Wheldall, K. (1991) Managing troublesome behaviour in regular schools: a positive teaching perspective, *International Journal of Disability, Development and Education*, 38, 2, pp. 99–116.

Wheldall, K. & Merrett, F. (1989) *Effective Classroom Behaviour Management: positive teaching in the secondary school* (London, Paul Chapman).

Wheldall, K. & Merrett, F. (1988) What classroom behaviours do primary school teachers say they find most troublesome? *Educational Review*, 40, pp. 13–28.

Chapter 5

Exclusion from school: a view from Scotland of policy and practice

Pamela Munn, Mairi Ann Cullen, Margaret Johnstone and Gwynedd Lloyd

Introduction

Exclusion from school has potentially serious consequences for young people. Their opportunities for academic achievement are curtailed, thereby reducing their chances of gaining educational qualifications and thus progression to further or higher education or into direct employment. Furthermore, exclusion may adversely influence a young person's sense of belonging, self-esteem and general socialization into acceptable behaviour. This chapter reports research on the nature and extent of exclusion from school in Scotland, 1994–6. It places the findings in the context both of research in England and of current policy concerns with social exclusion. It is in four main sections. Section one sets out the legislative framework for exclusion in Scotland, contrasting it to that in England and Wales. Section two reports the nature and extent of exclusions in a sample of Scottish schools, including data from teachers and pupils about the purposes and effects of exclusion. Section three considers the ways in which school ethos affects exclusion and section four briefly considers the findings in terms of broader policy issues.

Legislative background

In Scotland, there are two main grounds for exclusion laid down in the Schools General (Scotland) Regulations 1975 as amended. These are:

- that the education authority are of the opinion that the parent of the pupil refuses to comply or to allow the pupil to comply with the rules, regulations or disciplinary requirements of the school;
- that they consider that in all the circumstances to allow the pupil to continue his/her attendance at the school would be likely to be seriously detrimental to order and discipline in the school or to the educational well-being of pupils there.

The procedures for exclusion are set out in a range of regulations and acts. Key features are:

- the need for oral/written communication between the school/authority and the home on the day of the decision to exclude and subsequently in the event of the exclusion not being resolved, within 7 days;
- the right of appeal against exclusion to an appeal committee and beyond that to the sheriff;
- the recording of information about exclusion in the pupil's progress record;
- the responsibility which the parents have to educate the excluded pupil;
- the registering of exclusion as unauthorised absence as the pupil is deemed to be absent from school without reasonable excuse.

There are a number of important features in the Scottish legislation made explicit in more recent guidance from the Scottish Office (2/98):

- the length of an exclusion is not defined and is a matter for the discretion of the education authority;
- the legislation does not make a distinction between 'temporary exclusion' and 'permanent exclusion'. In legislative terms a pupil is merely excluded.
- under Scottish Office Guidance (2/98, p. 5) the term 'temporary exclusion' should be used when a pupil is excluded but remains on the school register because it is expected that he or she will return to the school. The term 'permanent exclusion' should not be used; instead, when a pupil is excluded (and not expected to return to school) the term 'exclusion/removal from the register' should be used.
- attention is drawn to the special difficulties of excluding a pupil with a Record of Needs (the broad equivalent of a statement), having pronounced specific or complex special educational needs which require continuing review. Scottish Office Guidance (2/98, p. 6) urges education authorities to 'take all reasonable steps urgently to ensure that alternative provision … is made available'.
- there is no national 'tariff' which ties a specific length or type of exclusion to specific behaviours in a rigid or automatic way.

In contrast, in England and Wales, under the 1997 Education Act:

- schools are permitted to exclude pupils up to a maximum of 45 days per year;
- detention outside school hours without parental consent is permitted;
- parents' rights to choose a new school if their child has been excluded from two schools are withdrawn;
- LEAs are required to publish plans for supporting schools with disruptive pupils.

In summary, there are several differences in legislative provision north and south of the border. The key differences are that in England there is a stipulated maximum length of fixed-term exclusions, the curtailed rights of parents to choose a school for their child if the child has been excluded more than once and the widespread use of permanent exclusion. In Scotland many education authorities do not use the term permanent exclusion arguing that their underlying approach is one of inclusion and that the authority retains duties in relation to a child removed from the register of a particular school. It is difficult to determine whether these apparent legislative differences directly influence practice in schools' use of exclusion. As we shall see below, small numbers of pupils were excluded in Scottish schools for six weeks or more in contrast to the rapid rise in pupils permanently excluded in English schools. However, accurate and reliable statistics in this area are difficult to establish (Parsons, 1996). A new standard report form recording exclusions has recently been introduced in Scotland which should, for the first time, provide fairly comprehensive data on exclusions across the country.

While a full consideration of the legislation affecting exclusion from school is outside the scope of this chapter, it is worth highlighting one general point which applies both to Scotland and England. This is the lack of congruence between the Children Act 1989 and the Children (Scotland) Act 1995 on the one hand and education legislation on the other. The welfare principle which underpins the Children's Act in England and Scotland, namely that the child's welfare shall be the court's paramount consideration, has no parallel in the Education Acts.

The research

The research was funded by the Scottish Office and had five main aims: to map Regional Authority policies; to explore headteachers' perception of these policies; to describe the characteristics of a sample of excluded pupils; to investigate perceptions of exclusion and of in-school alternatives; and to provide guidance on best policy and practice. It was carried out in three main phases from 1994 to 1996. Phase 1 on Regional Authority policy involved an analysis of appropriate documents and a telephone interview with a senior education officer with responsibility for exclusion.

Phase 2 consisted of a telephone survey of 176 headteachers, 60 from primary schools and 116 from secondary schools. We also asked headteachers to supply us with details of pupils who had been excluded since August 1995. Some 120 of the 176 did so, providing us with detailed information on 2,710 pupils.

Phase 3 consisted of case studies of eight secondary and four primary schools. Each pair of schools was similar in size and in the socio-economic status of their pupils, but different in their use of exclusion.

The nature and extent of exclusions

Given the important role accorded to education authorities in defining time limits for exclusion it is necessary to report briefly on the diversity of practice in regard to this and other aspects of exclusion. The summary of findings reinforces the point made earlier about the dubious validity and reliability of statistics on exclusion. The research was carried out while the 12 Regional and Island Authorities were still in existence and before the reform of local government created 32 single tier councils. Many of the new councils are in the process of adapting the exclusions policies of their Regional predecessors. The research revealed a wide diversity of policy, a diversity likely to increase with 32 rather than 12 authorities. The main areas of diversity were:

- *informal exclusion* Where pupils were sent home for a 'cooling off' period without any record of such an event being kept. Four authorities permitted this at the time of the research either explicitly or implicitly; three expressly forbade it and five made no mention of it in policy documents.
- *permanent exclusion* Where the pupil could not be readmitted to the original school. This was a feature of policy in three authorities.
- *notification of exclusion to the authority* Five authorities wanted notification of all exclusions while seven required notification only of exclusions of a certain number of days or beyond.
- *stages of exclusion* These included 'at the headteacher's discretion'; two types such as 'under 14 days' and '14 days and over'; 3 stages of varying lengths, e.g. 5/10/15 days, 5/15/30 days.
- *volume and, by implication, status of policy* Some authorities had fairly voluminous documentation and referred to other policies such as those for special educational needs. Others deliberately eschewed a formal policy statement, relying instead on a standard letter to headteachers.
- *policy aims* All authorities stressed that exclusion was a serious step and should be used as a last resort. However, ten authorities emphasized the

overall aim of inclusion, sustaining pupils in mainstream schools; two emphasized the need for accurate record keeping and adherence to the authority's procedures with an eye on legal process.

• *status of an excluded child pending an appeal* In some authorities the pupil remained excluded when an appeal was lodged even if the appeal took place at a time after the pupil could have been readmitted.

The main areas of similarity among most, but not all, authorities were:

• the lack of a systematic collation and analysis of exclusion statistics and hence of a strategic overview in terms of schools, or of pupil characteristics such as age, gender, ethnic origin, special needs or whether the case was referable to the Children's Panel (Scotland's vehicle for youth justice).

• the lack of a strategic overview of the range, quality and cost of alternative, off-site provision, regularly monitored, up-dated and debated.

• the *ad hoc* provision of staff development in the area of pupils with social, emotional and behavioural difficulties.

From the survey of 116 secondary schools and 60 primary schools, information on pupils excluded over a specific eight month period was obtained. Schools generously gave their time to complete a detailed form, 'Pupils Excluded Since August', as well as providing global estimates. The statistics below report *all* exclusions of however short a nature. The sample of secondary and primary schools does not provide a basis for generalization, since the schools were not randomly selected but stratified to maximize the opportunities of collecting data from headteachers who had experience of using exclusions. It is worth adding, however, that the secondary school sample represents over 25 per cent of all secondary schools in Scotland. The figures provide a snapshot of exclusions at a particular period of time. Over this period, August 1994 to March 1995, 202 pupils had been excluded from 39 primary schools and 3,562 pupils had been excluded from 110 secondary schools. A further 969 pupils had been sent home. Thus a total of 4,740 pupils had been excluded over this period. Exclusion most commonly happened only once and for three days or less for most pupils, although a significant proportion had been excluded for longer. About 20 pupils were recorded as a single but long-term exclusion. Table 5.1 shows the number of times pupils had been excluded.

Table 5.2 shows the number of school days lost through exclusion.

Key characteristics of excluded pupils are:

• more boys than girls were excluded (9:1 in primary and 4:1 in secondary);

• the peak stages for exclusion were P5 (9–10 year olds), S3 (14–15 year olds) and S4 (15–16 year olds);

- over half the excluded secondary pupils had a previous history of indiscipline, while almost all excluded primary pupils had such a history;
- the most common reasons for exclusion were fighting/assault, disruptive behaviour, failure to obey rules and abuse/insolence (see Table 3);
- 26 pupils (19 secondary and 7 primary) had been excluded for assault on staff. Almost all were boys.

Most excluded pupils were readmitted to their original schools.

Table 5.1 Number of times each pupil had been excluded, August 1994 to March 1995

Times excluded	Primary school pupils N = 184		Secondary school pupils N = 2,435	
	No. of pupils	%	No. of pupils	%
Once	117	64	1,699	69
Twice	34	18	455	18
3 times	15	8	191	8
4 times	14	8	68	3
5 times	2	1	37	1
Over 5 times	2	1	30	1

Note: Details on some pupils were missing and so totals in the tables may vary.

Table 5.2 Days lost through exclusion per pupil, August 1994 to March 1995

Times excluded	Primary school pupils N = 182		Secondary school pupils N = 2,491	
	No. of pupils	%	No. of pupils	%
1 day	13	7	108	4
2 days	29	16	202	8
3 days	50	27	613	25
4 days	10	5	205	8
5 days/a week	23	13	295	12
6 days to 2 weeks	26	14	526	21
11 days to 3 weeks	12	6	183	7
16 days to 6 weeks	14	8	218	9
More than 6 weeks	5	3	141	6

Figure 5.1 reports the reasons given for exclusion. The reasons stated can reflect no more than the legislative grounds for exclusion and/or the space available on forms. Some of the reasons given are striking for their seeming triviality given the emphasis on exclusion as a last resort to troublesome behaviour reported by the overwhelming majority of headteachers (data not shown). Nevertheless a seemingly minor offence can be the straw that breaks the camel's back in a history of disaffected behaviour and this point was

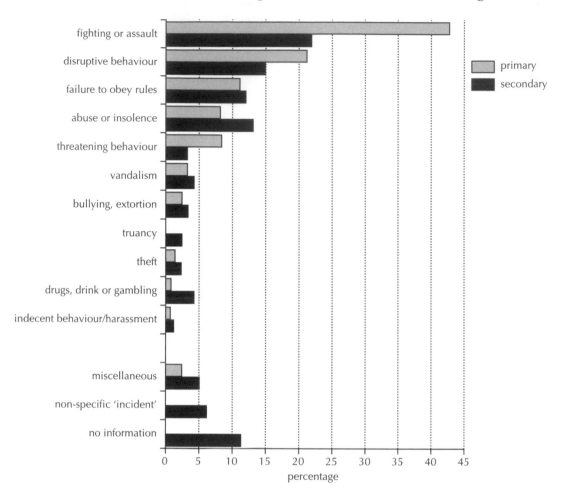

Figure 5.1 Reasons for exclusion

frequently made by teachers in the case study phase of the research. The numbers of pupils excluded for serious offences were small: using or selling drugs (45); assault on staff (26); carrying an offensive weapon (19). Fighting or assault, of course, is a serious issue and we do not seek to minimize it. Most of these incidents seemed to take place in breaks or lunchtimes when pupils may not have been supervised. We have written elsewhere about the need to think constructively about out-of-class activity as a way of minimizing opportunities for fighting (Munn *et al.*, 2000).

Direct comparisons with exclusions in England and Wales are difficult. We know from a number of studies that permanent exclusion from school in England and Wales has risen dramatically over the last six years. Parsons (1996) estimates that over 11,000 pupils were permanently excluded from secondary schools and 1,800 from primary schools in the school year 1995/96. The absolute numbers are worrying in themselves but of greater concern is that numbers are growing with a 45 per cent increase between 93–94 and 95–96 in primary schools and an 18 per cent increase over the same period in secondary schools (Parsons, 1996; Lawrence and Hayden, 1997). Furthermore boys are around four times as likely to be excluded as girls and African-Caribbean pupils are excluded between three and six times more often than their white peers (Commission for Racial Equality [CRE], 1996; Lloyd, 1999).

Turning now to the relationship between the social composition of the school and exclusion, a rather complex picture emerges. There were two proxy indicators of the social composition of the school, the percentage of pupils eligible for free school meals and headteachers' perceptions of the social composition of the school.

All schools with 30 per cent or more pupils eligible for free school meals fell into a high excluding category, excluding 5.1 per cent or more of their roll. It is noteworthy, however, that 13 per cent of schools in the sample had both a high exclusion rate and low percentages of pupils eligible for free school meals. In contrast, headteachers who saw the school as having a majority of pupils with economic and social disadvantages tended to be in schools with higher exclusion rates, although we found three schools reporting no official exclusions with perceived disadvantaged pupils. In brief, schools with perceived majorities of disadvantaged pupils were more likely to be high excluding. As the percentage of pupils eligible for free school meals increased, so exclusion tended to increase but there were exceptions.

It has long been recognized that the social and economic status of individual pupils and of the school population as a whole has a profound effect on many aspects of school life, including attainment, truancy, discipline and staying-on rates. Research on school effectiveness in general (e.g. White and Barber, 1997; Sammons *et al.*, 1997) and on school discipline (e.g. Munn *et al.*, 1992a, 1992b; Slee, 1995; Gray and Noakes, 1993) has demonstrated that schools with similar populations vary in their effectiveness in terms of disciplinary climate. A key factor in explaining such differences is that nebulous concept school ethos, and as part of ethos, the beliefs of senior school staff about the purpose of schooling. This finding emerged very strongly too from the case study phase of the research. In this phase matched pairs of schools in terms of size, socio-economic status of pupils, numbers of pupils with records of needs and geographic location were studied. The schools varied in the use they made of exclusion. The choice of low excluding schools was influenced by headteachers' reports from the larger survey reported above, which had a section on in-school strategies to prevent exclusion. The lower excluding schools studied were selected from schools which claimed to be making an effort to achieve this, rather than schools with no exclusions because they had a history of very few behavioural problems. A small sample of staff, parents, pupils, educational psychologists and others such as social workers was interviewed. A total of 84 interviews took place. All interviews were tape-recorded and transcribed. Our purpose was to explore the perceptions of the use of exclusion by asking respondents to focus on a recent typical case which best illustrated the school's approach to exclusion. We did not set out to explore a specific list of factors affecting the use of exclusion. The factors reported below emerged from a detailed analysis of interviews.

School ethos and exclusion

The dictionary defines ethos as 'the guiding beliefs, standards or ideals that characterise or pervade a group, a community, a people … the spirit that motivates the ideas, customs or practices of a people' (Webster's, 1986). This definition is helpful because it highlights first of all the *pervasive* nature of ethos. In a school, ethos touches all aspects of its operation but its very pervasiveness means that it is hard to pin down. Ethos is so much part and parcel of the taken-for-granted about the way any school goes about its business that it can be hard to describe. Second, the definition illuminates the fact that ethos underpins our *practice*, what we do in schools and how we do it. Thus ethos is not an abstract idea. It helps to explain why we act in particular ways and so why our actions can be different according to the particular school in which we work. Third, the definition focuses on the idea of a group, a *collective understanding* of how things are done. In this section we take four key aspects of school ethos and describe how they influence exclusion. At the end of the section we summarize these aspects in terms of characteristics of schools which tend towards inclusion or exclusion of troubled and troublesome pupils.

The four aspects are:

- beliefs about schools, teaching and pupils;
- the curriculum on offer;
- school relations with the outside world;
- decision-making about exclusion.

Beliefs about schools, teaching and pupils

Understanding exclusion begins with an exploration of staff views about the purposes of the school, the role of the teacher and who counts as an acceptable pupil. This may seem hopelessly abstract and impractical to those engaged in the hurly burly of school life but as our studies of schools with contrasting exclusion rates showed, the more narrowly these questions were answered, the higher the exclusion rate. Schools that saw their main purpose as equipping pupils with good academic qualifications, saw teaching as primarily concerned with subject specific knowledge and acceptable pupils as those who were well behaved, well motivated and from a home that supported the school, tended to have higher rates of exclusion than those which took a broader view of these matters. This is common sense. The more one specifies and delimits the nature of an organization and its members, the greater the scope for excluding those who do not conform.

Leadership, particularly that of the headteacher, has been identified as a key influence on school effectiveness in general and on school discipline in particular. In our study the beliefs of headteachers[1] were associated with their practices regarding exclusion.

In low excluding schools headteachers believed that it was the job of the school to educate all pupils, not just the well motivated and well behaved. The following quotation is typical although it came from a newly appointed headteacher to a high excluding school.

> I think it is a moral thing, that you've got to say that those youngsters should be in education and it's education for all. It's not just education for the few that come in and don't cause us any problems. (Headteacher, Lubnaig Secondary School)

Her beliefs were translated into action by changing the system used to exclude pupils so that all exclusions had to be personally authorized by her. She saw it as a major challenge for the school to adopt inclusive values and she was well aware of the management task ahead in terms of persuading her colleagues of the need for such an approach. Headteachers' beliefs in minimizing exclusion were reflected in practices which sought to value staff and pupil views while at the same time setting the tone about what the school stood for. The same headteacher continued:

> … For many [staff who are nearing retirement] their heyday was in the time when the belt [strap] was about and that was the answer … and many of them haven't moved out of that mind set. So it's hard for them and for me. (Headteacher, Lubnaig Secondary School)

Furthermore, headteachers of inclusive schools saw it as a collective responsibility for the staff to motivate pupils, to make learning fun and to make pupils feel valued, as the following quotation makes clear.

> That's my alternative to exclusions – crazy sports, novelty afternoons, being silly. You're constantly changing things with the kids. It's always keeping them on their toes so they'll enjoy what is happening and want to come to school. They like it. School is fun. It's enjoyable. They know the staff like them and want to be with them and the staff are very good at this. (Headteacher, Menteith Primary School)

In brief, headteachers of inclusive schools saw it as a responsibility to educate all pupils, to nurture social as well as academic achievements, to stimulate pupil motivation and enjoyment in learning and personally to offer practical support and help to teachers under strain from troublesome pupils. Their management style was consultative but they were clear that it was their responsibility to set the tone.

In contrast, headteachers in schools with high exclusion rates tended to specify the school's responsibility in terms of promoting the academic attainment of their pupils, to see pupils causing trouble not being the school's responsibility and to have rather hierarchical line management structures. So, for example, instead of schools having a responsibility to educate all pupils, their responsibility was to educate only those pupils who came willing and ready to learn what the school had to offer.

> I would love not to suspend [i.e. exclude] pupils but, and this is a statement from the school – I do not care if in a month I suspend 100 or I suspend none, as long as, at the end of the month, a quality education has been delivered to pupils who come through the gates wishing to learn. (Acting Headteacher, Tummel Secondary School)

The policy dilemmas for teachers and others in dealing with the needs both of troublesome pupils and with the generality of pupils are considered briefly below. For the moment the point to make is that a headteacher who holds a view like that expressed above is clearly delimiting the school's responsibility. Those excluded are those who do not share the school's highly focused concern with learning and being ready to learn is a *sine qua non* of inclusion in that particular school. The school is not accepting responsibility for young people who are unready to learn nor to change its practices. The school has something to offer and if pupils do not want to take advantages of this, there is no place for them in the school. It is easy to see that a school leader espousing such a set of beliefs will encourage the use of exclusion.

It is important to note that within all schools there were tensions and contradictions in terms of prevailing beliefs about the nature of teaching and the role of pupils. Not all staff showed the same view of where the boundaries ought to lie and resistant cultures were in evidence. Thus in schools where dominant beliefs tended towards inclusion, there were staff who resented this. Some teachers in such schools would sometimes challenge the headteacher's loyalty to themselves as professionals by giving examples of occasions when they had been unsupported or treated unsympathetically in the face of a discipline problem and the headteacher had refused to exclude a pupil. Likewise, in schools which were readier to exclude, some staff believed the approach was wrong and resisted referring pupils with troublesome behaviour to senior management. This was more apparent in large secondary schools where subject departments could provide a natural locus for alternative points of view. It was less in evidence in primaries where open resistance to dominant beliefs would be more conspicuous among a staff of say 10–15. Although senior management, therefore, defined the key assumptions under which the school used exclusions, individual teachers who did not share these assumptions could also influence exclusion. This suggests that headteachers who wish to reduce the use of exclusion need to persuade almost all staff of the rationale for and benefits of such a policy, if it is to be successful.

The curriculum on offer

A key part of a school's ethos concerns curriculum provision and organization. For example, organizing pupils by ability groups or by setting and streaming is seen by many commentators as having harmful unintended consequences (Harlen and Malcolm, 1999; Sukhnandan and Lee, 1998). They point out that when students are divided on the basis of academic criteria, 'they also tend to be segregated by social and academic characteristics' (Gamoran *et al.*, 1995, p. 688). This can send messages about who is valued in the school and about what counts as really useful learning. If young people perceive that they cannot be successful academic learners, anxiety and insecurity can result which in turn leads on to disruptive and avoidance tactics to cover for fear of failure (see Goleman, 1996, pp. 234–7 for an overview).

There was a general consensus in the secondary schools studied that learning difficulties, particularly difficulties in reading and writing, lay at the root of many behaviour problems. Staff saw many of the 14–16 year-olds who were excluded as lacking motivation to learn, as seeing no purpose in school work and schools as 'being not for the likes of us'. Although schools reported similar concerns with the curriculum (namely as being overly academic, the demands of portfolios of work for Standard Grade examinations requiring regular and consistent effort on the part of pupils and the pressures to present all pupils for 7–8 Standard Grades regardless of their ability to cope) they varied markedly in their approach to tackling these concerns.

The lower excluding schools recognized the importance of offering all pupils the opportunity to experience success and acceptance as part of the school community. They did this in many different ways. For example, through the informal curriculum of clubs and societies, developing and valuing participation in drama, music and art through exhibitions, school shows and concerts, pupils were given opportunities to demonstrate creativity, organizational skills and talents in public relations. These schools too also valued personal and social development slots in the curriculum, which were regularly timetabled and had an agreed syllabus. Low excluding schools tended to experiment with the curriculum on offer, being flexible in the number of subjects pupils were expected to study and using learning support as a resource for mainstream staff to consult about differentiating curriculum materials. In contrast, high excluding schools tended to have few out-of-school activities, stressed their core business of teaching the academic curriculum and expected learning support teachers to extract pupils experiencing difficulties from the mainstream classroom.

School relations with the outside world

In this section we look briefly at relations between school and home and between school and 'external professionals' such as educational psychologists and social workers as a way of revealing how school ethos can influence exclusion.

All the primary and secondary schools studied believed that it was crucial for parents to support the school in terms of its behaviour and discipline policy. Parental support was important both in avoiding exclusion in the first place, through working with the school to avoid the escalation of trouble and, if that failed, in making an exclusion effective in changing behaviour. As one senior manager said:

> One of the most crucial things in exclusion … in terms of whether it is a success or not, or whether it is a deterrent or not … is the parental reaction and the extent of parental support. (Deputy headteacher, Ness Secondary School)

This view was not disputed; what did vary between the schools was the degree to which parental support was actively sought, as opposed to being simply expected. Broadly speaking, schools with lower exclusion levels had key staff who worked hard to build a two-way relationship with the parents of children in trouble. These staff were typically designated behaviour support staff and senior managers. Strategies used included inviting parents to meetings where their child's difficulties were the focus of a problem-solving effort by all present. Such meetings were seen as a useful way of breaking down stereotypes on both sides. Although resource intensive in terms of staff and time, such meetings could build up an atmosphere of mutual trust as the following extract from a parent interview makes clear.

> I was totally against them [school] but as time goes on, I realised it's not really their fault and you've got to try and work together and that's what we've done. You're trying to stick up for your children, but we do work well together now. I think that's why (the teacher) puts up with what she does from Matthew, because we've given each other support throughout it all. Otherwise, I think he would have been out of school a long time ago. (Mrs P, Katrin Primary Parent)

All the parents interviewed saw school as worthwhile and even where there were severe behavioural problems had not given up on their children and wanted them to succeed. Thus any perceived failure on the part of school could assume the scale of a major deliberate omission. Feelings of stress and anger were common, particularly from mothers. They 'felt mad', 'felt I could just scream', 'didn't know where to turn' and 'felt at the end of my tether'. These feelings are also reported from other small-scale studies involving parents of excluded children (Parsons, 1996; Cohen *et al.*, 1994).

In these circumstances it is hardly surprising that misunderstandings occur, breakdowns in communication happen and all kinds of motives are impugned to one side by the other. Teachers feel stressed too. Yet low excluding schools were characterized by a commitment to working with parents, being less judgmental about their circumstances and by seeing two-way communication between home and school as really important. High excluding schools tended to expect parents' unquestioning support and to condemn them if this was not immediately apparent.

A similar picture was evident in contrasting approaches to working with external professionals. Where teachers saw themselves as responsible for teaching only the well behaved and ready to learn, external professionals tended to be seen as there to 'cure' disaffected pupils who would then return to mainstream classes or, where this was possible, facilitate out of school placement. Where teachers saw themselves as responsible for teaching all children, these external professionals were viewed as partners in the joint task of helping to solve the problems evinced by the pupils. Rather than offering particular examples of this approach in action we list, on the basis of our data, a number of factors which increased the likelihood of successful joint working. These were that external professionals should be involved:

- early, preferably before the situation reached exclusion stage (indeed, one interviewee felt that the official procedures on exclusion should be slowed down so that appropriate support from, for example, Social Work, had to be tried first);
- appropriately, that is, depending on the nature of the underlying problem and not automatically regardless of the underlying problem;
- as partners with the school and, if possible, with the parents;
- with an agreed purpose and with realistic aims;
- for the shortest effective time relative to the agreed aims.

Of course, it is much easier to set out such factors than to put them into practice in a context of competition for declining resources, increasing workloads on all professionals, and very different professional ideologies. Yet we were given examples of cases of real pupils where successful intervention carrying all these hallmarks took place. Crucially, this resulted from good

Encouraged Exclusion ◄───────────────────────────────► **Discouraged Exclusion**

Beliefs about school, teaching and pupils

narrow definition of teacher's job, focused on subject knowledge, exam results	wide remit, including personal and social development of pupils, as well as exam results
academic goals prominent	social and academic goals
acceptable pupils were those who arrived willing to learn, and came from supportive homes	acceptance of a wide range of pupils, including those with learning and other difficulties

The curriculum

academic curriculum, pressure on pupils, lack of differentiation	curriculum flexible and differentiated
personal and social development curriculum lacks status	personal and social development curriculum highly valued
potential of informal curriculum for motivating less academic pupils not realized	informal curriculum, lively and covering a wide range of activities, such as sport, drama, art, working in the local community

Relations with the outside world

parents expected unquestioningly to support the school	time and effort spent involving parents in decision making about their children
educational psychologists and others seen as there to cure problems	educational psychologists and others seen as partners in working out solutions to problems

Decision making about exclusion

Hierarchical decision-making separating pastoral support staff from those with responsibility for maintaining discipline	Decisions informed by a network of staff with a range of perspectives on the pupil
Tariff systems leading to automatic exclusion	Flexible system, behaviour evaluated in context
Pastoral support staff expected to meet needs of all pupils	Pastoral support staff – an information source on decisions
Learning/behaviour support expected to remove troublesome pupils and solve problems	Learning/behaviour support a source of support and ideas for mainstream staff

Figure 5.2 School ethos and exclusion

personal relations between the key school contact, often a support centre teacher (in secondary) or the headteacher (in primary) and the external professional(s) involved. Such relationships did not happen by chance, but required work over time from all involved. This work was facilitated by open or 'sharing' professional ideologies.

The issues of name calling, though not in a racist context, and of labelling, also featured in Scottish research involving 11 frequently excluded pupils and their families (Cullen *et al.*, 1996, p. 48). 'They [other pupils] call you names and nag at you and you end up just striking back because you get sick of them and then it's not the other person that gets into trouble, it's me' (Jean A, Coruisk School).

> The teachers shout at you for wee things, even if somebody else did it, they ken that you're always in trouble so they give you worse than what the other person got that's hardly ever in trouble. (Michael N, Lubnaig School)

Studies showed that the pupils concerned, like Michael N, were well aware of the consequences of 'getting a reputation', yet for some their behaviour was viewed as part of them and impossible to change. This passivity was quite striking. This might be interpreted as a way of absolving themselves from any responsibility for their actions – it was the teachers or school provision or organization which had to change. Alternatively it might be seen as a recognition that they were destined not to be a valued member of the school community, forever beyond the pale as it were, unable and maybe unwilling to accept school norms and values.

This latter interpretation is borne out to some extent by reports of feelings of low self-esteem, stupidity and general lack of worth by some excluded pupils. A number of psychological studies in the USA have shown the association between these feelings, aggressive behaviour and youth crime (see Goleman, 1996, pp. 234–7 for a useful overview; Cullingford and Morrison, 1995, p. 548). In the CRE (1996) study, some pupils were relieved to be excluded, perhaps because it removed one site in which such feelings were experienced. However, another theme emerging from the small number of studies which contain excluded pupils' voices is that of boredom, of missing school and of wanting to return.

These same studies report the stress which exclusion can cause in families. The CRE research (1996) involved interviews with 27 parents, 17 of whom used words such as stress, strain and worry, perhaps unsurprisingly, to describe the effects of exclusion. In a small number of extreme cases there were reports of illness, nervous breakdown and having to give up work. Other studies paint a similar picture, highlighting the other stresses often being experienced by families including poverty, bad housing, bereavement and illness (e.g. Cohen *et al.*, 1994; Lawrence and Hayden, 1997). Effects on the family are likely to be more intensely felt when the exclusion is permanent or long term and no alternative provision is made.

The impact of exclusion upon the generality of pupils is more difficult to gauge. Teachers' explanations of the purposes of exclusion often refer to their responsibilities for the general welfare of all the children in the class(es) as well as the individual welfare of troubled and troublesome pupils (Cullen *et al.*,

1996). Thus teachers contend that a 'cheer goes up from the silent majority of pupils' when a disruptive pupil is excluded. We might also speculate that exclusion sends messages about the kind of behaviour which would not be tolerated in school, reinforcing the existence of an unequal power relationship between teachers and pupils and the nature of the implied contract between them. More subtly, perhaps in terms of socialization, exclusion is sending messages about the nature of communities, their shared assumptive worlds of norms and values as a defining characteristic and, as far as schools are concerned, the importance of conforming to norms and values. A sense of belonging is thus premised on being alike rather than on understanding or even living with difference.

Conclusion

The current government is 'committed to promoting social inclusion and equality of opportunity in Scotland' (Scottish Office, 1999b, p. 3). It set up a social inclusion network in 1998 to 'improve co-ordination between relevant agencies and to help the government to develop its approach to social inclusion. The Network consists of representatives of Government and other national public and private sector organisations, alongside individuals with direct experience of tackling social exclusion' (Scottish Office, 1999b, p. 4). The Network has agreed three areas for priority attention:

- excluded young people;
- inclusive communities;
- the impact of local anti-poverty action.

The role of education features prominently in these areas. The role of schools in tackling exclusion has already featured in policy initiatives. For example, £23 million has been made available under the Excellence Funds for Schools to assist local authorities to develop strategies to reduce exclusion. This is in addition to the £3 million available through the Alternatives to Exclusion Grant Scheme which is allowing authorities to pilot innovative alternatives to exclusion. New Community Schools will bring together a team of professionals to provide integrated support to children and families, supported by £26 million of government investment. A significant feature of many of these schools is a commitment to zero exclusions. Such programmes are welcome as are the recently produced Guidelines on Exclusion from School (2/98) which emphasizes that exclusion should be a last resort and clarifies the legal framework. Will these initiatives succeed?

Schools may be understood as institutions driven by diverse and contested purposes, by the values of those who go there and by the practices which may or may not reflect purposes and values. Thus when it comes to decisions on exclusion, competing claims have to be weighed and compromises reached. Few people involved in exclusion from school, at whatever level, see it as straightforward and unproblematic.

It is only relatively recently that schools are being asked to publish figures on attendance, truancy and exclusion, thereby signalling national concern about these areas. The collection and publication of such statistics may affirm the values of those who regard the inclusive nature of schools as paramount. Unlike examination results, however, attendance and exclusions data are supplied by schools themselves with all the scope for 'massaging' the figures that such a system brings.

Even if headteachers do not massage the figures, a low exclusion rate may conceal poor quality provision for pupils in trouble, such as sitting in corridors or other forms of 'internal exclusion'.

This chapter has indicated that the numbers of children being excluded from school are a cause for concern and that such statistics as there are underestimate its extent. We know very little about the numbers of children in England and Wales on temporary exclusion and their characteristics in terms of age, gender, social class and ethnicity. Significant resources are now being invested to combat exclusions in Scotland as indicated above as part of the government's overall strategy to tackle social exclusion.

The chapter has also suggested that these well-intentioned policies, strategies and resources will have a better chance of success if schools seriously examine their ethos and recognize ways in which the beliefs and values of key staff drive the practice of exclusion. The chapter has not addressed the broader social policy context in which schools necessarily operate and may be read as giving greater weight to the agency of individual schools than is warranted in Britain at the end of the twentieth century. Yet the examples of minimizing exclusion come from real schools coping with the complicated and multifaceted job of teaching. These schools are tackling exclusion in a context in which there is:

- an increase in the psychosocial problems among young people (Rutter and Smith, 1995);
- an increased rate of family breakdown through divorce and a rise in the number of single parent families;
- a widening gap between the poor and others (EIS, 1998; Poverty Alliance, 1998; Mortimore and Whitty, 1999);
- a cultural response to alienating and alienated behaviour, which sees excluded pupils as culprits rather than victims (DfE, 1994; Blyth and Milner, 1994) or as having little entitlement to education (Lloyd-Smith, 1993; Abbotts and Parsons, 1993);

- a challenge to traditional notions of masculine and feminine identity which challenges traditional understandings of normative male and female behaviour (Weiner *et al.*, 1997);
- government policy to promote a quasi-market in schooling. Such policies include parental choice of school, devolved school management, the publication of comparative school performance in league tables and targets for schools in terms of specific improvements in pupil attainments. These policies are seen as producing a general climate in which schools are reluctant to admit or maintain pupils who threaten their image or performance (Munn *et al.*, 1998; Parsons, 1999).

If these low excluding schools were encouraged to share their practice and the aspects of their ethos underpinning their practice, we might be more confident that reductions in exclusion were being accompanied by the provision of a high quality curriculum in mainstream schools.

Note

1 We use headteachers as convenient shorthand for a sample that included headteachers, deputies and assistant headteachers. All school names, based on Scottish Lochs, are fictitious.

References

Abbotts, P. and Parsons, C. (1993). 'Children's rights and exclusion from primary school', *Therapeutic Care and Education*, 2, 2, 416–21.

Blyth, E. and Milner, J. (1994). 'Exclusion from school and victim-blaming', *Oxford Review of Education*, 20, 3, 293–306.

Cohen, R. and Hughes, M. with Ashworth, L. and Blair, M. (1994). *School's Out: The Family Perspective on School Exclusion*. London: Barnardo's and Family Service Unit.

Commission for racial equality (1996). *Exclusion From School – The Public Cost*. London: CRE.

Cullen, M. A., Johnstone, M., Lloyd, G. and Munn, P. (1996). *Exclusions from School and Alternatives: The Case Studies*. A Report to SOEID. Edinburgh: Moray House Institute of Education.

Cullingford, C. and Morrison, J. (1995). 'Bullying as a formative influence: the relationship between the experience of school and criminality', *British Educational Research Journal*, 21, 5, 547–60.

Department for Education (1994). *The Education of Pupils with Emotional and Behavioural Difficulties*. Circular 9/94. London: DfE.

Educational Institute for Scotland (1998). *Education and Poverty*. Edinburgh: EIS.

Gamoran, A., Nystrand, M., Berends, M. and Lepore, P. C. (1995). 'An organisational analysis of the effects of ability grouping', *American Educational Research Journal*, 32, 4, 687–715.

Goleman, D. (1996). *Emotional Intelligence*. London: Bloomsbury.

Gray, P. and Noakes, J. (1993). 'Reintegration of children with challenging behaviours into the mainstream school community'. In: Miller, A. and Lane, D. (Eds) *Silent Conspiracies, Scandals and success in the care and education of vulnerable young people*. Stoke: Trentham Books.

Harlen, W. and Malcolm, H. (1999). *Setting and Streaming: A Research Review*. Edinburgh: SCRE.

Lawrence, B. and Hayden, C. (1997). 'Primary school exclusions', *Educational Research and Evaluation*, 3, 1, 54–77.

Lloyd, G. (1999). 'Excluded girls'. In: Salisbury, J. and Riddell, S. (Eds) *Gender, Policy and Educational Change: Shifting Agendas in the UK and Europe*. London: Routledge.

Lloyd-Smith, M. (1993). 'Problem behaviour, exclusions and the policy vacuum', *Pastoral Care in Education*, 11, 4, 19–24.

Mortimore, P. and Whitty, G. (1999). 'School improvement: a remedy for social exclusion?'. In: Hayton, A. (Ed.) *Tackling Disaffection and Social Exclusion*. London: Kogan Page.

Munn, P., Johnstone, M. and Chalmers, V. (1992a). *Effective Discipline in Secondary Schools and Classrooms*. London: Paul Chapman.

Munn, P., Johnstone, M. and Chalmers, V. (1992b). *Effective Discipline in Primary Schools and Classrooms*. London: Paul Chapman.

Munn, P., Johnstone, M. and Sharp, S. (1998). 'Is indiscipline getting worse? Scottish Teachers' perceptions of indiscipline in 1990 and 1996', *Scottish Educational Review*, 30, 2, 157–72.

Munn, P., Lloyd, G. and Cullen, M. A. (2000). *Alternatives to Exclusion from School*. London: Paul Chapman.

Parsons, C. (1996). 'Permanent exclusions from school in England: trends, causes and responses', *Children and Society*, 10, 177–86.

Parsons, C. (1999). *Education, Exclusion and Citizenship*. London: Routledge.

Poverty Alliance (1998). *Social Inclusion in Scotland. A Framework for Development*. A response to the Scottish Office Consultation Paper 'Social Exclusion in Scotland'. Glasgow: Poverty Alliance.

Rutter, M. and Smith, D. (1995). *Psychosocial Disorders in Young People, Time, Trends and their Causes*. London: Wiley.

Sammons, P., Thomas, S. and Mortimore, P. (1997). *Forging Links, Effective Schools and Effective Departments*. London: Paul Chapman.

Scottish Office (1999). *Social Exclusion Strategy*. Edinburgh.

Slee, R. (1995). *Changing Theories and Practices of Discipline*. London: Falmer.

Sukhnandan, L. with Lee, B. (1998). *Streaming, Setting and Grouping by Ability: A Review of the Literature*. Slough: NFER.

Webster's (1986). *Third New International Dictionary*. London: Encyclopaedia Britannica.

Weiner, G., Arnot, M. and David, M. (1997). 'Is the future female? Female success, male disadvantage and changing gender patterns in education'. In: Halsey, A.H., Lauder, H., Brown, P. and Wells, A. S. (Eds) *Education, Culture, Economy, Society*. Oxford: Oxford University Press.

White, J. and Barber, M. (Eds) (1997). *Perspectives on School Effectiveness and School Improvement*. London: Institute of Education.

Chapter 6

'Behaviour support' from an external agency to mainstream schools: policy and practice

Bob Sproson

Introduction

The role of LEAs has come increasingly under the spotlight since the turn of the century. My interest lies specifically in what is expected of them in terms of enabling schools to be as inclusive as possible in their work with students seen by teachers as 'difficult to manage' (D2M). One part of my professional role for the last decade and a half has been the management of 'behaviour support' to secondary schools in a local education authority (LEA) in England. Teachers who work within that service have become used to threats to their existence and annual fears as to whether their work will be funded. More recently the whole question of whether they can be employed and paid as teachers has been brought into focus by the current pay structure and performance management systems in place for 'classroom teachers'. I do not intend to engage in the pay argument here, but I hope that in this chapter I present a case for the continued employment of skilled professionals to work in and with schools to develop their expertise in relating to D2M young people.

Differing perspectives on the role of school support services

Barrow (2002) describes his conversion from 'Mr Behaviour Man' who hurtled from school to school ready to 'cure' any young person deemed to be at risk of exclusion to a systems theorist who works with schools to enable them to develop a supportive learning environment in which the likelihood of a student being 'rejected' (excluded) is reduced to the minimal possible level. I have managed a support service to secondary schools for a decade and a half, at the same time as managing my LEA's provision for students educated 'other than at school'. Whilst I have never undergone any similar conversion, I do recognise the polarities which Barrow describes and acknowledge an obvious failing in any approach in which a support teacher simply steps in to re-model a young person's behaviour so that s/he is able to 'survive' within the mainstream context.

I remember very clearly, however, an article which appeared in the Times Educational Supplement during the early 1990s. Sadly I am not organised enough to have filed that article away or to have recorded its author, or indeed the date when it was published. The clarity with which I remember it some twelve or thirteen years later does, however, indicate its impact upon me. The article was written by a primary headteacher who had simply had enough of advisors, consultants, support teachers and the like coming into his school and telling him what they could and would do for him. He simply argued that he was the customer in this relationship – all of these 'experts' were actually providing him with a service. If he did not find that service to be what he wanted, then he wanted to refuse to have it or demand that it be changed. In the article he described a particularly pressured day in his school. He was coping with staff absence, the aftermath of a wet lunchtime, angry parents, sick children, an accident in a classroom and a particularly 'difficult to manage' class group in the early part of the afternoon when his behaviour support teacher arrived expecting to meet with him to discuss a small number of students with whom she was involved. She did not expect to do 'hands on' work with those students, but to monitor their progress. How, this headteacher raged, could sitting down and discussing the progress of a small group of students possibly help him at this particular moment in time? He was further aggrieved that the support teacher was unwilling to offer any alternative support. Maybe, he mused, she might have acted as a taxi driver to take the injured student to hospital and simply sat in the reception area throughout the afternoon. Eventually she left, having written a short note to the head asking him when he would be in a position to re-convene the meeting with her and expressing her regret that her time had been wasted because he had been insufficiently well organised to meet with her.

Personal experience of support service management

The reason that I found the article so powerful is that I was struggling at the time to understand what the support service which I had been appointed to manage was really supposed to do. Following a career as a mainstream teacher and special school teacher and headteacher, I had been appointed to manage this support service following the closure of my school (it was closed because the children's centre to which it was attached was being 'discontinued' by social services) and had been told very clearly, and accurately, that whilst I might know something about managing difficult to manage young people, I had no experience or knowledge of providing support to mainstream schools and therefore must acknowledge the greater experience of other members of the service and allow them to develop the service's approach.

Support services in the market place

Initial success rates pointed to a service more likely to expire than to expand. My view of the main reason for this is that the LEA failed to carry out any consultation with the customers of this service (schools) as to the style of service which they required.

Bowers (1992) consistently stressed the need for support services to take account of customer (school) requirements if they are to survive. Training courses, which I have been directed to attend by the LEA, provided by 'seasoned entrepreneurs' from the business world and aimed at turning me into a 'business unit manager' have stressed an essential element of marketing my service as being 'consultation', that is, finding what the market wants. My aim as a 'manager' should not be to convince my customers that what I have to offer is what they need; rather it should be to ensure that I know what their perception of what they need is and to tailor my product to meet that need. Diamond (1993) emphasised the undeniable dangers of such an approach, noting (p.92) that, 'if the language of the market place is allowed to dominate our transactions, it will inevitably permeate our thinking and influence our actions, ultimately divorcing them from their primary purpose, which is meeting children's needs'. Whilst I agree categorically with that statement, my experience leads me to believe that actually the relationship between a support service provider and his/her customer schools is more complex than either the 'give them what they want' or the purist 'I know what they need' models suggest.

Rôle and function of support teachers

To enter into the relationship, trust has to be built. To build that trust in the early days great cognisance has to be given to the requirements of the school as perceived by the senior managers; if that initial trust is created, then, through regular effective monitoring, a joint perception of need can be constructed within which both parties work with at least a degree of satisfaction. What I was faced with in 1989, although I did not really see it clearly, or understand it, at the time, was a situation whereby the policy makers within the authority wanted to move along the 'effective schools can cater for all students' (it's all the fault of the teachers?) road and had employed an advisory teacher who zealously promulgated a staff supervision model as the only way of achieving this aim. They now wanted to expand this approach throughout this new service. The policy makers saw this as a genuinely innovative move in the world of disruptive behaviour. As aforementioned, I was informed that my deputy, the advisory teacher who advocated the staff supervision model, had been given a brief to train the team in delivering a supervision model, and schools had been notified that support during that first year would be limited because of the need for team training.

The subsequent experience was a disaster. I had never come across a 'hard-line' supervision model which argued that to do any direct work with students could only de-skill teachers and provide a false hope of unlimited help for difficult students, and that, therefore, our work must be directed solely at supervising teachers' practice. Moreover I had neither experience nor understanding of a supervision model which argues that the supervisor needs no skills other than those of reflective listening and summarising, that the role is to act as a 'sounding board', thereby enabling teachers to clarify their own thoughts and develop practice accordingly. There is no requirement for the supervisor to be a skilful teacher of D2M students him/herself. The other aspect of the rôle, which disturbed me greatly, was that the support teacher (supervisor) might offer 'personal counselling' to the teacher involved, on the basis that a teacher who is 'together' about his/her own life is far more likely to be able to cope with the demands of potentially disruptive students. I absolutely adhere to the latter statement, but cannot subscribe to a view that making counselling-style supervision available to all teachers is the best way to achieve a high-esteem profession.

According to this model, strategies for work with students should not be suggested by the supervisor. That is inappropriate 'rescuing'. Rather, they should be generated by the supervisee, who is empowered so to do by the uplifting experience of the supervision. Faced with a complete unknown and being advised by my seniors that this had to be the way forward – although schools may not yet understand that – I, in extremely cowardly fashion, went along with the training for a term. It was only when the service began to take this model into schools and I to talk with the heads of those schools that reality, at least the reality of heads' views about such a model of support, genuinely dawned.

Reactions within the team were mixed, but I well remember the comment of one support teacher, that 'It's like trying to sell Christmas lights in the spring'.

Reactions from schools were, with a single exception, dire: a city head, who latterly became one of the staunchest supporters of the service, made it very clear that she perceived the approach as arrogant and useless: 'If you think that I am going to timetable my staff to sit and bare their souls to someone who hasn't got the faintest idea how to control kids, then ...' (quoted from memory from a personal conversation). In the light of responses such as these, the reality of the situation was crystallised for me with a most unpleasant sharpness and I determined to alter radically the service 'style', or, in the eyes of some of my staff, I 'bent like a straw in the wind' (staff meeting comment), betraying the right approach at the first sign of opposition and therefore ensured the failure of what should have been the answer to the behaviour management worries of all the schools in the LEA.

By January 1990, the service was moribund: there was dispute within the team as to the rôle of support teachers, we were making very little alternative provision, leading to serious complaints about availability of placements, and the vast majority of schools were extremely unhappy with the support available to them.

Challenges facing support teachers in schools

I am able to see now that my experience in that first year encapsulated the problems with which a support teacher or a co-ordinator of support services continually grapples. It is extremely difficult to take issue with the standpoint of Ainscow (1991) or Galloway and Goodwin (1987) that schools which provide students with appropriate curriculum experiences encounter few, at least fewer, 'behaviour management' difficulties than schools which do not. Whether the 'problem' is viewed from a 'what is taught' or a 'how it is taught / effective teacher–student relationship' standpoint, or a mixture of the two, it is blindingly obvious that schools need to examine their own practice. Even in the 'worst' of schools, some teachers and their students experience positive learning situations. If the other teachers practised in similar vein, then schools would improve.

The role of a support teacher must therefore be to enable teachers to become effective practitioners. This is easy to say!

Facilitating teacher continuing professional development (CPD)

Although the logic for supporting CPD is clear, experience rarely seems to match up to expectation. Schools are complex institutions full of equally complex human beings. During the last ten years I have delivered a substantial amount of in-service education for teachers (INSET) in schools throughout the country. Almost without fail heads or senior managers have discussed the problems of dealing with 'difficult' staff, staff who simply fail to enthuse students or staff who alienate or bully young people but 'never go beyond the limit of what would constitute unacceptable behaviour' – a 'polyquote' formed from numerous conversations with heads and deputies. Of course I have to ask whether bullying is acceptable behaviour. Staff groups have questioned me endlessly about the search for consistency. What has become clear to me is that within staff groups there is frequently such a range of deeply entrenched fundamental beliefs that consistency of practice seems unattainable. One staff member may believe that a young man is so damaged that the only way in which s/he can hope to help him improve is to take every opportunity to make positive comments to him whilst another is convinced that no such comment can or should be made until it has been 'earned'.

> Do you seriously expect me to tell him that he's done well to turn up and that I'm pleased to see him when he's late? He has to be punished, not rewarded.
>
> (response to my training at a Cardiff School)

Some staff members are hugely resentful of 'differentiating' their explicit curriculum or their behaviour management styles: again the notion of 'deserving' runs very deep.

> Why do we have to spend time on bad kids when there's lots of nice ones who deserve it?
>
> (response to my training at a Cambridge school)

Add to this the fact that staff groups are ever changing, what is agreed as 'the way forward' amongst a staff group of twenty or thirty may not be workable if staff changes run in double figures.

Tensions and contradicting in support teachers' rôles

Reflection upon my own experience together with evaluation of this research data leads me to the belief that a behaviour support teacher's job borders upon the impossible for the following reasons:

- theory suggests that their job is to create 'self managing schools' but the end product is unreachable within short time limits, possibly within longer ones;
- theory suggests consultancy – schools, whether rightly or wrongly, often want 'hands on' help;
- effective support teaching is viewed very differently by individual staff members – it is also viewed differently by different stakeholders, e.g. parents, students, teachers, governors, LEA officials;

- many teachers hold seemingly unchangeable beliefs about responses to 'bad' behaviour, which make it almost impossible for them to modify their practice.

Support teachers have to work within this complex reality – they have to work with the world as it is, in the school to which they are assigned.

When asked at a staff meeting by my most voracious opponents what the central components of the model I now intended to take into schools (if I intended to ditch the staff supervision only approach) were, I replied, 'flexibility and pragmatism', a response which horrified them, but which has proved to have some legitimacy. The work of the service which I manage has been aimed at closing the gap between 'what theorists and bureaucrats believe schools need' and 'what schools believe they want'.

Responding to schools' expressed needs

Throughout the 1990s I carried out research into the work of the support element of my service. I examined the work of support teachers and also surveyed the LEA's secondary headteachers to ascertain their perception as to what behaviour support might mean, or, at least, what they wanted from the service and, more particularly, if they were to become budget holders, what they would buy.

I found that much of the work being requested of support teachers was that of providing individual support to students who had presented staff with behaviour management difficulties, a rôle which schools often liked to describe as counselling. Although this indicates a notion of 'curing the student', schools clearly understood that their own practice is a significant factor in determining student behaviour, and senior managers in schools reflected the difficulties they met in dealing with 'difficult to manage teachers', that is, teachers who unerringly antagonise and alienate students. I looked in depth at interventions with two specific students. Both were successful, presuming that maintaining the student in mainstream school is the criterion used to indicate success.

The 'successes' appeared to be due to:

- the relationship formed between the support teacher and the student,
- the support teacher being directive (and honest, i.e. if this carries on, you're out) with the student at the outset,
- the support teacher using a range of intervention strategies,
- staff practice being influenced by the support teacher,
- subsequent misbehaviour on the part of the student being referred to or discussed with the support teacher (by the staff involved) rather than being 'taken' to the school's discipline hierarchy.

Throughout both of the case studies the findings were consistently checked back with a wider group of support teachers working throughout the southern area of the LEA. A very high degree of correlation was found.

To ascertain the views of the secondary heads within the county as to a support rôle which they would 'purchase', I interviewed the heads of the schools in which I had carried out the research and formulated a range of intervention styles from their described preferences. I then surveyed all the other secondary heads in the south of the county and produced a 'scored' list of rôles. They rated access to out-of-school provision as hugely important, indeed as absolutely essential, but also delineated an individual support role and rated that as equally vital. There was ample evidence again that schools fully understand the need for any work to influence the effectiveness of their own practice: the aspect of the work which was cited as most desirable by the heads was feedback from individual interventions with students which informs staff practice, i.e. 'tips' for staff on intervention strategies and building appropriate relationships with students.

My conclusion, therefore, was that there is a rôle wherein a support teacher provides individual support to a student, which can maintain potentially troublesome young people in mainstream schools because:

- it is valued by the schools,
- student behaviour is modified,
- staff (and whole institution) behaviour is modified.

The complexity of the link between the second and third factors runs throughout the research. I believe that the style of work described within the case studies goes some way to addressing the gap which may often be observed between school demands upon students and the behaviour of the staff group within the school.

The major themes which ran through the work are:

- the importance of forming appropriate relationships with adults for young people who are meeting difficulties in conforming to the demands which schools make upon them (probably for all young people),
- the importance of support teachers and classroom teachers having a range of appropriate and effective responses to behaviour available to them (rather than a pre-determined response),
- the need for students *and staff* to feel that they are listened to and 'valued',
- the effectiveness of creating an alternative referral route which obviates the need for senior staff involvement and overly punitive responses on the part of the school. Staff were discussing and generating management strategies themselves, rather than simply referring on to senior managers who

frequently have neither the time nor (sometimes) the inclination to respond in any manner other than punitive.

What was fascinating with regard to the last point is that senior staff presumed that students must be behaving far better because they were not constantly being 'referred' to them, and often went to find students to praise them for this, when, actually, there was little initial change in behaviour, just in the staff response to it.

Supporting individual students to prosper in mainstream

My own reflections upon Barrow's (2002) work, my own research and my continuing experience is that, although there are different starting points in our approaches, there is a huge area of agreement as to what it is that enables young people to survive and maybe even prosper in mainstream schools. I have found that going into schools, working pragmatically and flexibly with the institutions from the position they are at, no matter how you feel about that position as Murphy (2002) very persuasively argues in relation to individuals and, most usually, providing support to identified students, has enabled us to offer genuine support to schools and their students. A significant element of that work has always been the influence which the support teacher has been able to have upon the practice of staff, indeed upon the practice of the 'whole school'. Barrow has found that in going into schools and insisting that he and his staff work 'systemically' with the school, examining and evaluating its practices and approaches, they influence whole school practice and often provide support to individual and small groups of students as part of the newly developed systematic approach. Perhaps the debate is moribund. A member of my staff has long described the need for a 'shower and bidet' approach, that is, services must work from the bottom and the top at the same time. Thus the best of support teachers will feel equally at home making a presentation to the governing body or the senior management of a school and working with them to improve school processes and building a relationship with a group of 'disaffected' Year 9 students who are able to see little or no purpose in entering their remaining years of education.

Within my service we have come to talk about young people for whom education is a part of their 'quality world' (an expression taken from 'reality therapy' [Glasser, 1999]), that is, it is important to them, they value it by dint of their life experiences and therefore will engage successfully even if the way in which the fare is presented is not hugely appealing, and those for whom education is way outside their 'quality world'. It is the latter group with whom behaviour support services will engage. Whilst a knock-on effect of their work may well be that the learning experiences of all students are improved, that is not their raison d'être. In order to enable the students who do not have education as part of their 'quality world', someone has to enter their 'quality world' (Murphy, 2002), even if that quality world is 'murky' at the outset, and to lead them into some sort of engagement with education. That will take place through the building of trusting, appropriate relationships. Throughout my research I was quite staggered at the value which young people placed upon being listened to and I came to write about the 'listening key'. Listening is a core element to relationship building. One student talked 'quite crazily' (support teacher comment) at times but argued that he grew to trust the support teacher because she did not make him feel stupid for talking in this way. I am not advocating schools offering counselling services. In my experience such services often spend too much time reflecting upon what has gone wrong and, in offering confidentiality, can build barriers between support teachers and classroom teachers. I want focused discussion to be upon how things will improve, not to reflect upon why they 'got bad' in the first place.

I guess that within Barrow's model that work of relationship building is most likely to be carried out by school staff, with behaviour support staff working to develop systemic approaches which enable that work to happen, whereas within my world schools often expect their support teachers to provide much of that work. It may well be that the difference is simply a resourcing issue. If the support service is small and most of the funding sits with the school, then Barrow's model will have to operate. There could not be sufficient flexibility on the part of the support service to respond to need. For us, we are currently fortunate in holding some flexibility between in-school and out-of-school funding and being able to use this to develop support programmes in schools. I have, however, been telling my staff group for some time that the moment is likely to come when much of that funding passes straight into the hands of schools. That will be no disaster so long as they continue the relationship-building work which is essential to any notion of inclusive education.

Conclusion

Finally, to return to the 'quality world' notion, students who want what is on offer will tolerate an awful lot from teachers. I would be thrilled if behaviour support work meant that the daily experiences of those students improved, but the key for behaviour support work is engaging those students who do not place any value on education. That can be achieved by relationship building (mentoring?) with the student, but also by working to ensure that the package that is education makes some sense to the student: that it appears to them to offer some chance of success, some relevance to their life and some fun, and that it is offered to them by people who understand the need for the delivering of 'respect from a position of strength', i.e. they legitimately hold some power, but always treat the recipients of that power with absolute respect.

I believe above anything that education is about human interactions, that it involves adults modelling appropriate behaviour, specifically conflict resolution, for young people to experience. Schweitzer argued that example is not the best way of teaching, rather it is the only way. Effective support work ensures that schools understand the humanity of the education process and their role in 'teaching through example'. Support teachers able to facilitate that will always be 'in business', no matter where the funding for their work lies.

References

Ainscow, M. (1991) 'Effective Schools for All: An alternative approach to special needs in education', *Cambridge Journal of Education*, vol 21 no 3.

Barrow, G. (2002) *Delivering Effective Behaviour Support in Schools: A practical guide*. London: David Fulton.

Bowers, T. (1992) 'Planning for the Future', *Special Children*, November.

Diamond, C. (1993) 'A Reconsideration of the Role of SEN Support Services: Will they get in on the act?' *Support for Learning*, vol 8 no 3.

Galloway, D. and Goodwin, C. (1987) *The Education of Disturbing Children*. Harlow: Longman.

Glasser, W. (1999) *Choice Theory: a new psychology of personal freedom*. London: Harper-Collins.

Murphy, E. (2002) Seminar Address 'A Solution Focussed Approach – for all workers with "disaffected" young people'. London.

Schweitzer, A., quoted in Peter, L. (1978) *5000 Gems of Wit and Wisdom*. United Kingdom: Bath Press.

PART 2
Practitioner research issues

Chapter 7

Ethics, politics and research

Roger Sapsford and Pamela Abbott

The evaluation and planning of research is concerned with 'technical' questions. Beyond these, however, there is another important aspect of research evaluation: looking at the ethics and politics of particular research programmes and of the research process as a whole.

We need to look at ways in which what is taken for granted in our ordinary lives is also taken for granted in research (often thereby supporting one side of a 'political' issue at the expense of another) and how we can perhaps start to overcome our own 'cultural blinkers'. We need to look also at the relationship of researchers to the 'subjects' of the research and their interests and to the needs and interests of the wider society. When considering questions of 'harm to subjects', we need to bear in mind that research is embedded in people's real lives and it is *not* just the subjects of research who may be harmed, but those of whom they are taken as representative or typical, or even people who are not part of the research in any sense at all. Careful consideration needs to be given to the ways in which anyone whose interests are touched by the research might be harmed by it or by the dissemination of its conclusions.

Much of this chapter is about the ethical and political issues which appear in research to be technical ones: the ways in which the choice of measuring instruments and the selection of samples express assumptions which may not be neutral in respect of power relationships. Our examples are mostly drawn from fields where complex concepts are expressed in complex measuring instruments – intelligence, achievement, personality, social class. The points we want to make about them, however, also hold true for much simple concepts, and for concepts used in participant observation and 'unstructured' interviewing, as much as for the sort of highly structured research which calls for measuring instruments to be constructed. Ultimately, all research stands or falls by the way in which the researcher conceptualizes the field of study: in the design of the study, in the way that measures are defined and measuring instruments constructed, in how the data are coded or clustered or segmented for analysis and in the decisions the researcher makes about what it is important to report and what sense to make of it.

In the next section we look not at the measurements themselves, but at some of the purposes to which widely used measuring instruments have been put and at what kind of theory underlies them or is implicit in them. We look at the use of intelligence tests for purposes that would now be regarded as racist – or at least discriminatory in a pejorative sense – to declare some people unfit to be citizens, and indeed to exclude immigrants of certain nationalities. We look at the invisibility of gender in European and North American class theory up to the mid-1980s, as symptomatic of the way in which certain ideologies come to dominate even academic thought. We look at the use of concepts of intelligence and achievement, and the whole paraphernalia of measurement that goes with them, to help reproduce a particular type of social order and a set of taken-for-granted beliefs about the world.

Finally, we look briefly at the suggestions sometimes now made that ideological perspectives are reproduced not just by what we measure or how we measure it but by the overall 'style' in which we conduct research and what it takes for granted about the nature of the social world. Questions are raised about the normal relationship of researchers to the researched, about the ownership of data and about the status of knowledge and expertise. In other words, we look at the *politics of* research.

Ethics and research

A first principle of research ethics is that the subjects of the research should not be *harmed* by it. You might think this fairly obvious, but some quite startling breaches of it have been committed in the course of research. In 1969, for example, a United States medical doctor called Godzeiher established a study to test the side-effects of birth control pills which involved a control group receiving only a placebo (a sugar pill) without their knowledge; seven unwanted pregnancies ensued. Among projects which involved closer and more personalized interaction with the 'subjects', we might cite Milgram's (1974) work on conformity to authority, which involved subjects being in the position of apparently administering near-lethal electric shocks to students in a learning task, and Zimbardo's 'simulated prison' experiment, where he divided up a group of students into 'prisoners' and 'guards' and set up a mock prison in a university basement (Haney *et al.*, 1973). Milgram's experiment, as he reports himself, left students anxious and traumatized, and Zimbardo's had to be called off ahead of time because of the distress of some of the 'prisoners' and the behaviour of some of the 'guards'. Indeed, replication of Milgram's experiments by its members has been banned by the American Psychological Association.

The counter-argument which might be put forward (and was by Zimbardo, 1973) would be that the importance of the conclusions outweighed the pain caused by the research. Both Milgram and Zimbardo have justified their work by arguing that it was important to demonstrate in clear-cut and graphic terms the influence of situations on human behaviour. At a time when the atrocities of German and Japanese prison camps were being 'explained away' in terms of national character and the behaviour of some police and prison guards attributed to their character and/or rough working-class upbringing, Milgram and Zimbardo demonstrated in their different ways that ordinary, middle-class people will oppress inferiors, beat them up and even apply torture on the instruction of an authoritative other or in response to their perception of the situation and its demands.

Whatever your stance on these extreme studies, you ought to note that precisely the same ethical problems are faced by all experiments and many other research studies. We would generally agree that in 'ordinary' research the subject/informant/respondent should be protected from harm. It is for this reason, among others, that we generally promise informants confidentiality or anonymity in surveys or 'unstructured' interviewing projects. (As we are using the term, *confidentiality* is a promise that you will not be identified or presented in identifiable form, while *anonymity* is a promise that even the researcher will not be able to tell which responses came from which respondent.)

One ethical principle gaining increasing acceptance is that nothing should be done to the 'subjects' of research without their agreement, and that this agreement should be based on an adequate knowledge, supplied if necessary by the researcher, of what is implied by consenting. The concept of 'informed consent', however, is no easy answer to a set of moral dilemmas, because it is neither simple nor clear-cut itself. Very often, a researcher may be a practitioner within the area of social practice that is the target of the research and stands in a position of power or influence over the researched, or is identified with others who do so. The social worker, nurse, prison officer or teacher, researching his or her own clients, patients, prisoners or pupils, may have a direct power over the future of the people whom he or she wants as research informants. Even if not, there is an existing authority or dependency relationship such that the informants may feel bound to cooperate, however fairly the request is put. It is also not clear *whose* informed consent is required, in many cases.

There is also the question of how far the consent can ever be 'informed'. To what extent, lacking the researcher's knowledge and background, can the other parties to the research ever understand fully what it is to which they are committing themselves and what use will be made of it?

In some cases, the very process of giving information to researchers may itself cause people considerable distress and even long-term psychological problems. This may be the case, for example, if we want to research sensitive subjects. Re-living distressing and painful experiences may be a very potent experience and could cause long-term psychological distress in some informants. There is also the issue of whether the gender of the interviewer is problematic.

A further problem concerns those in whose lives we do *not* intervene. In a well-known educational experiment (Rosenthal and Jacobson, 1968), the researchers picked children from a range of school classes at random and convinced the teachers that these had been identified as people likely to show a spurt of intellectual growth in the near future. Surely enough, some of these children did indeed do so, and the experiment is used as an example of the self-fulfilling prophecy in education. No one was directly harmed by the research; children were either advantaged or left alone. If you were one of the 'control' children, however, and you read about the experiment afterwards, might you not feel that you too could have shown a spurt if you had been picked for the experimental sample?

We should also note that even in qualitative research such as participant observation, often considered ethically 'cleaner' because there is no direct manipulation or interrogation of 'subjects', ethical problems remain. The most difficult of these concern the relationships formed with participants and the use which is made of them. We tend to characterize participant observation and relatively unstructured interviewing as styles which give the participants a chance to express their own views and which treat them as people in their own right. In practice, however, the conduct even of ethnographic research can be quite Machiavellian. In Jack Douglas' book *Investigative Social Research* (1976) – which you will find refreshingly cynical or surprisingly realistic, depending on your expectations – the chapter on tactics of investigative research has as sub-headings 'Infiltrating the setting', 'Building friendly trust and opening them up', 'Setting them up' and 'Adversary discombobulation tactics'. In the first three of these, he points out how ethnographers and social anthropologists slip into the setting like spies, building relationships for the purpose of using them to extract information.

> the right use of friendly and trusting relations is not only a necessity of research, but also a powerful one … the extensive cultivation of friendly and trusting relations with people in all kinds of settings has been vital … In building affection and trust it does not matter whether the researcher is honest or merely doing presentational work … But he must be convincing.
>
> (Douglas, 1976: 134–7)

Further ethical problems are raised by the extent to which a research project is rooted in the deception of those involved. It is clearly less reactive, for example, to measure people's lives in unobtrusive ways than to make them the subjects of a formal and public experiment; it may even be less harmful to them, to the extent that the knowledge of being watched or studied might cause distress or anxiety. However, another way of putting the term 'unobtrusive measures' is 'spying on people without their knowledge and consent'. Secrecy in research can be an issue in any style, but it is most evident and therefore most discussed in participant observation. Here the 'classic' project would be a covert one, with a researcher joining the social setting as a participant (or, indeed, already being there as one) or passing as a genuine participant, and conducting the research while trying to change the setting as little as possible – again, 'spying out the land' in a very real sense. The alternative is to do the research openly, declaring one's role as researcher, which is more reactive and therefore sometimes less effective, particularly when it is a disapproved behaviour which is the topic of research, such as industrial corruption or racist discrimination. Nor is it clear that perfect openness occurs even in 'open' research. On the one hand, the researcher will not want to tell the actors how to behave or what to say in order to confirm the researcher's theories, and, on the other, it is not clear that the aims of research can necessarily be explained to those who do not share the researcher's training and background (see the discussion of 'informed consent' above).

Less discussed are wider ethical problems to do with the selection of problems and of samples. By studying girls at school, do we disadvantage boys? By looking for ways to make community care more effective for those who are receiving it, might we be doing a disservice to relatives or professionals? Studying youth's behaviour in public, do we distract attention from their economic circumstances or the institutionalized behaviour of the police and the criminal justice system? People may be harmed if their interests are not reflected in research, perhaps sometimes as surely as if they were physically or psychologically damaged. It was argued at one time, for example, that the tendency for sociological research to concentrate on the behaviour and attitudes of working-class people was just one more facet of social control.

Another problem is the use to which our research findings are put – often completely unintended by the researchers themselves. Findings may be interpreted in ways that are much to the disadvantage of the researched. Some research on poverty, for example, intended by the researchers to demonstrate the hardships and difficulties of living on low incomes, has been interpreted by others as demonstrating that the problem is not insufficient income but the ways in which the income is spent. In other words, if we say that our research should not harm anyone, we have to be very clear about what we mean by harm.

Politics and research

Intelligence and the politics of 'race'

Intelligence tests are often portrayed as imperfect but *in principle* relatively neutral measures of an underlying quality inherent in people. However, the decision to measure a quality of people – expressing the concept that people differ in important ways with respect to that quality – is not a neutral act but one with political significance. Intelligence tests form a particularly obvious example of the political masquerading as the scientific, because their origins are blatantly political and embody the assumptions of particular periods of history.

The concept of 'intelligence' – general mental ability – and the desire to measure it, and classify the population with respect to it, predate the invention of the tests which are the means by which the measurement may be made. From the mid-nineteenth century, there was growing neo-Darwinist concern about the deterioration of the 'national stock' – the notion that the physical and mental quality of the population was systematically declining. This was fuelled by military defeats abroad (for example, the defeat of Gordon at Khartoum), the poor physical condition of army recruits at the time of the Boer War, and the increasingly successful encroachment of Germany and the USA into areas of commerce and industry which had been seen as a British preserve.

'Deterioration' was seen as a multi-faceted condition of the disreputable poor: physical unfitness, 'mental inferiority', 'pauperism', prostitution, insanity, crime and delinquency were all seen as elements in a single 'weakening of the stock' with a common genetic origin. As the middle classes and the 'respectable' poor were beginning to limit family size, while the disreputable poor still bred without constraint, it was posited that bad hereditary traits were driving out good ones and the nation as a whole was declining in the same way that poorly bred cattle decline. A particular worry came to be people of low intelligence – 'feeble-minded' was the term used at the time – whose numbers became apparent with the introduction of universal schooling at the end of the nineteenth century.

The first IQ test, in 1905, was designed to pick out those children who were considered unteachable from those who were just badly taught, and it was a relatively pragmatic and untheorized object. It came into a social world which was very ready for it, however; a world in which the identification of 'defectives' and the monitoring and control of their rate of breeding was seen as of very great importance. The first promise of the test, to North American and British eyes, was that it at last provided a way of identifying 'borderline defectives', those with intelligence not much below the norm but who in the eyes of eugenic scientists were seen as fast and irresponsible breeders, likely to pollute and dilute the national stock, the gene pool.

in the near future intelligence tests will bring tens of thousands of these high-grade defectives under the surveillance and protection of society. This will ultimately result in curtailing the reproducing of feeble-mindedness and in the elimination of an enormous amount of crime, pauperism and industrial inefficiency.

(Terman, 1916: 16–17)

Thus the tests were welcomed as the first defence against what was seen as a very real 'threat from within'. Another group who welcomed them were those responsible for defence against the 'threat from outside' – the officials responsible for immigration control in the USA, where the problem of 'contamination of the national stock' was seen as even more severe than in the UK. *Within* the USA, eugenicists identified pockets of 'bad stock' where it was claimed that the inbreeding of 'degenerates' was spreading the disease of mental deficiency, pauperism, prostitution and crime. Immigration was the other problem, for it was firmly believed that 'races' differed in their innate ability. It was claimed that borderline mental deficiency

> is very common among Spanish-Indian and Mexican families of the Southwest and also among Negroes. Their dullness seems racial, or at least inherent in the family stocks from which they come … The whole question of racial differences in mental traits will have to be taken up again … The writer predicts that when this is done there will be discovered enormously significant racial differences which cannot be wiped out by any scheme of mental culture.

(Terman, 1916: 91–2)

When the same methods of investigation were applied to the different kinds of European who were attempting to migrate to the USA, it turned out that white Northern Europeans of protestant stock stood at the peak of the intellectual pyramid, and other (e.g. Mediterranean) nationalities some way behind them. This gave a scientific method and a scientific justification for regulating immigration to preserve the quality of the population. Official control over immigration began with an Act of 1875 barring 'coolies, convicts and prostitutes', but 'lunatics' and 'idiots' were added to the list in 1882, 'epileptics' and 'insane persons' in 1903, 'imbeciles' and 'feeble-minded persons' in 1907, and 'persons of constitutional psychopathic inferiority' in 1917 – demonstrating, among other things, the changes that were occurring in psychological terminology.

There arose a public clamour for some form of 'quality control' over the inflow of immigrants. This at first took the form of a demand for a literacy test; but it could scarcely be doubted that the new science of mental testing, which proclaimed its ability to measure innate intelligence, would be called into the nation's service. The first volunteer was Henry Goddard, who, in 1912, was invited by the United States Public Health Service to administer the Binet test and supplementary performance tests to representatives of what he called 'the great mass of average immigrants'. The results were sure to produce grave concern in the minds of thoughtful citizens. The test results established that 83 per cent of the Jews, 80 per cent of the Hungarians, 79 per cent of the Italians and 87 per cent of the Russians were 'feeble-minded'. By 1917 Goddard was able to report:

> that the number of aliens deported because of feeble-mindedness ... increased approximately 350 per cent in 1913 and 5670 per cent in 1914 ... This was due to the untiring efforts of the physicians who were inspired by the belief that mental tests could be used for the detection of feeble-minded aliens.
>
> (Kamin, 1977: 31)

The same tests, and others developed later, were very widely administered within the USA during and after the First World War, and it was their results that provided the first 'scientific evidence' for the alleged racial inferiority of Americans of African origin, something which was not of concern at the time but has since been elevated to a major scientific and political controversy. Carl Brigham, then an assistant professor at Princeton, developed a theory of races which paralleled and borrowed from what was being written in Germany at the time. He distinguished between people of 'Nordic', 'Alpine' and 'Mediterranean' origin, characterizing Nordics as rulers and aristocrats and Alpines as peasants and serfs. These ideas were widely taken up for a time, and they naturally allied themselves with the same sort of gratuitous anti-Semitism that characterized similar writing in Germany:

> we have no separate intelligence distribution for Jews ... [but] our army sample of immigrants from Russia is at least one half Jewish ... Our figures ... tend to disprove the popular belief that the Jew is intelligent ... he has the head form, stature and colour of his Slavic neighbours. He is an Alpine Slav.
>
> (Brigham, 1923: 190)

The point we are trying to make is not only that the tests were employed for political purposes, but also their use was scientifically illegitimate – a fact that was pointed out at the time but had little impact in the contemporary political climate. The employment of intelligence for this purpose was grounded in the discovery that certain populations tended on average to score less than 'native Americans' (by which term the proponents of the theory would have meant white settlers, not 'American Indians'); the differences were of the order of 10–15 score points, or one standard deviation. The plain fact is, however, that the tests of the time were not sufficiently precise for a difference of this order to be meaningfully attributed to genetic inferiority (and nor are current tests), for a number of reasons:

1. Although some attempt was made to overcome the problem, there can be no doubt that those for whom English was not a first language were at a disadvantage. Those who were functionally illiterate in American English

will have included a disproportionate number of people from impoverished homes, including immigrants and citizens of African origin.

2. The items of which the tests were made up were selected as representing the familiar and common-sense world – but the familiar world of British and white North American people, not of Mexicans or Spaniards or Greeks.

3. The whole notion of test-taking, as we shall see below, is tied up with a certain approach to schooling. Those who came from other cultures may well not have learned this particular skill. (Few modern-day testers put the effects of practice at 'intelligence tests in general' at less than 10–15 score points.)

4. The best marks on tests go to those who are fundamentally motivated towards individual competition and keyed up to show themselves at their best (without being disruptively over-anxious). This state of mind, and the rules of the 'game' which demand it, are characteristic of people in advanced capitalist societies and much less characteristic of peasant ones.

5. Tests generally have a time-limit within which the items have to be completed. This expresses and draws on a cultural norm of getting things done in a set time, which is much more common in advanced industrial societies, where time dominates the day's activities, than in non-industrial societies, where precise timing has less meaning.

In other words, the observed differences are as likely as not to be cultural, due to environment and upbringing rather than innate condition. Beyond this, the use of the tests for this purpose betrays the political stance of the scientists who advocated it, if only by their use or misuse of evidence. Sometimes the misuse is wilful. Brigham, for example, somehow managed to cling on to a 'racial' theory of intelligence even in the teeth of evidence that immigrants who had been in the USA some while scored no worse than 'native' Americans. Sometimes the misuse is more subtle, but it still constitutes misuse. The tests of the 1930s showed a gender difference, for example. This was not hailed as a great discovery, but identified as a fault in the tests at a time when gender differences were not acceptable in this respect, and eliminated by re-selection of items. When a 'racial' difference was found, however, it was hailed as a great discovery. Both reflect what was politically acceptable at the time.

The point remains that the concept of intelligence emanates from a particular period of history in response to the perceived problems of that period. Historically, its development has been much bound up with inequalities of race and, as we shall see later, with inequalities of class. Whether the concept would have been thought useful in a history where these particular inequalities were not crucial elements of social structure remains open to question. The need for the test, the concepts out of which it grew and the perceived social problems which these concepts addressed grew up together to yield the tests and the concepts that we now employ. These concepts and this way of looking at people is now more or less taken for granted, part of the 'cultural stock of knowledge'.

Intelligence, achievement and the politics of class

So far in this chapter we have looked at 'individualistic' ethics – the responsibility of the researcher for the 'subjects' of the research. We have examined the patent use of research concepts and their operationalized measures for political purposes. (It is the existence of the operationalized measure which makes the political action possible; if there were no tests of intelligence, groups could not be segregated or excluded on the basis of it.) Now we return to the measurement of intellectual potential and actual attainment, to look at a yet more subtle aspect of the way that research is grounded in politics.

We have seen that intelligence tests have been used for political purposes, though this use may perhaps not be inherent in their theory and construction. Achievement tests, by comparison, appear politically neutral; they simply test whether a form of teaching has 'taken' and a content been 'delivered'. There is a sense, however, in which both kinds of test play their part in the essentially political process whereby a form of society reproduces itself. Both can be seen as elements in a discourse that is prevalent in our society – a discourse that defines people as necessarily having a place on a continuum of intelligence. Even if intelligence tests are not used, people are judged and classified on this criterion, and the attributed intelligence of a child is used to define the type of education to which he or she is exposed.

(There is considerable confusion about the terms 'discourse' and ideology'. As used here, an 'ideology' might be described as a coherent set of propositions about what people and/or social institutions are like and how they ought to be – generally presenting to one group of people that certain behaviours are in their own interests and concealing the fact that they are also (or more!) in the interests of another and more powerful group. The term 'discourse', on the other hand, is used here to mean the general framework or perspective within which ideas are formulated. Thus the view that it is natural, necessary and right that mothers should put their children's and other dependants' interests before their own, and should want to devote their major energies to home-making and child-rearing, is an expression of an ideology: it presents a certain form of domestic and work organization, which is in the interests of men, as also in the interests of women and the natural and inevitable way in which they should view their lives. The ideology is framed within a discourse which defines certain terms – 'mother', 'child', 'family' – in ways which make certain conclusions easy and others apparently paradoxical or difficult to defend.)

Intelligence testing grew up initially in reaction to fears about people seen as inherently 'feeble-minded', stoked by the introduction of mass schooling, which made it possible to count their numbers. Binet originally denied that the test he devised in 1905 was suitable for anything other than this specific purpose, but by 1908 it was being used to calibrate the development of 'normal' children, and the concept of the intelligence quotient as a measure standardized for chronological age was developed two years later. The measurement of intelligence as a routine way of identifying potentially able pupils took a little longer to become established, but eventually it became a standard feature of the schooling system.

Schools became an important part of the state/societal mechanism for maintaining order and discipline as the UK became increasingly an industrial society. Schooling which had previously been denied to working-class children began sometimes to be available, in one form or another, during the eighteenth century, but without any evidence of intent to gather up and socialize a whole social class; this was distinctively a nineteenth-century phenomenon. The factory system undermined the traditional family to some extent – the family of agriculture or cottage industry, with children socialized to production at home – and the traditional skills that might have been learned at home became increasingly inappropriate in an era of rapidly changing methods. Schools came to be seen as necessary, therefore, for the teaching of new skills, including basic literacy and numeracy. More important to those who were active in establishing schooling for working-class children, the school was a medium of socialization, including gender differentiation. It taught 'habits of industry' and accustomed male children to the discipline necessary for factory work, while giving female children the skills needed for domestic labour. It accustomed children to systematic, routine and often dull work and brought them to regard it as a normal part of life. It was also a chance to convey the moral precepts of the work ethic, directly through instruction or indirectly by example. In other words, it was a site of power in the sense in which Foucault (for example, 1982) often uses the term – a place where people can be moulded into understanding the world in the way in which the shaper wants them to understand it and behaving habitually in accordance with that view of the world. Schools may inculcate critical enquiry, but while doing so they also set the parameters of the society within which this enquiry is to take place.

This is not to suggest that schooling became some sort of monolithic repressive mechanism, aimed at the working class. Indeed, the same period was one of working-class struggle *for* education and access to schooling. Education was not just something imposed from above; its value was well realized by working-class people, and there was considerable individual and collective striving to make it more available to working-class children. Education became a major means of upward mobility for working-class children and made a wide range of occupations available to them which would previously have been beyond their reach. However, none of this changed the basic structure of the society. It changed the likelihood of particular people filling particular positions within it, and constructed thereby a fundamentally more open society, but the broad pattern of social structures and social relations remained unchanged.

Perhaps even more important, both for mobility and for the preservation of the social structure, education became a 'site of classification' – a mechanism whereby emerging adults could be assigned their place in the scheme of things. Testing is inseparable from our concept of schooling; one important function of schooling is the rank-ordering of children with regard to their abilities, by teachers' informal reports and by public examination. More insidiously, school plays a part in assigning some children to higher-grade occupations and others to lower ones by a process of self-shaping. Perceiving themselves as succeeding or failing in the tasks which schools set them and which are necessary for the successful completion of public examinations, children come to think of themselves as able or less able, suitable or not suitable for the higher reaches, as successes or failures. This process may occur even in schools which have a conscious rhetoric and policy of encouraging all children. Despite the efforts of teachers, some children succeed in the system and some fail in it; it is in the nature of the schooling system that children have to be located on a success/failure dimension. Because middle-class children have an advantage over working-class children in the 'schooling game' – they come into school 'knowing the rules', or at least some of them – the process of education is not a politically neutral one. Middle-class children are more familiar with the objects and procedures relevant to schooling – books, pencils, reading, counting, drawing, perhaps even computers. Middle-class parents tend to worry more, and to more effect, about how their children are labelled at school, to interact more with teachers to secure their children's advantage, and to have the resources to supply additional schooling when the child appears 'not to be thriving' during the regular school day. They also tend to have more freedom to direct their children to schools according to their standing and more knowledge or access to knowledge on which such decisions can be based.

The development of intelligence testing in the first two decades of the twentieth century opened up the way to further stratification and the direction of children to types of school 'consonant with their needs and abilities' rather than just according to their parents' ability to pay. By about 1925 the division of schooling into 'academic' and 'vocational' was well advanced, and intelligence tests were well established as a way of determining which track should be followed. This process reached its most visible form in the tripartite system of grammar, technical and secondary modern schools which most Local Education Authorities established following the Education Act of 1944; here, intelligence testing came into its own as a means of selecting the best children irrespective of parents' ability to pay. There is research evidence that working-class children were still less likely to enter grammar schools than middle-class children of the same measured ability, but the tests acted in a more 'class-fair' manner than, for example, head teachers' recommendations. While we have retreated to some extent from this extreme separation over the past 30 years, vocational tracking still occurs in school practices (streaming and setting), in the nature of the curricula and in the nature of the examinations for which children 'of different abilities' are entered.

Achievement testing acts similarly to intelligence testing to differentiate, classify and assign pupils. The examination (and continuous assessment is included in this concept) provides documentation on the person and his or her abilities. The outcome of school practice – differential curricula, examining, profiling, testing – is therefore to produce a well-divided and ordered society. It does not necessarily preserve the status quo in the sense that only the children of advantaged parents finish up in advantaged positions – though there is a strong element of this – but it does tend to maintain the general shape and hierarchical nature of the society within which it is set. The existence of these divisions and the importance of correct allocation is the justification for a whole range of professional experts – teachers, lecturers, educational psychologists, sociologists of education. They in their turn have a stake in what these divisions shall be and some measure of power in determining what sort of people shall finish up in each of them.

School tests and examinations may be seen as arising out of, and at the same time reinforcing and reproducing, a particular discourse or way of viewing people and their social relations – one inherently typical of and adaptive for capitalist forms of social organization. Individuals are posited as truly individual rather than social, making their own decisions and 'naturally' in competition. They are seen as variously endowed, and it is this endowment which is seen as determining where they will finish up in the power hierarchy (but the fact that social background – class of origin – is part of this 'endowment' tends to be glossed over). The individual, in turn, is seen as being made up of – 'possessing' – qualities which are measurable and which enable us to compare one individual with another. During the period of industrialization, a new 'knowledge-base' grew up around this increasingly dominant view of human nature – what eventually became the disciplines of 'individual' and 'social' psychology. Terms developed which described the human subject, and concepts developed in these terms which allowed the measurement of the subject's 'interior state'.

This leads us to the most important feature of the discourse: that it is aimed at the *management* of individuals. Mostly, it posits human beings as perfectible or changeable or curable by manipulation of their qualities or attributes. At the same time, it assigns them their place in society by reference to these qualities or attributes. Thus the activity of testing, however scientific its form, is far from neutral politically. It may form a ladder by which the few transcend their class position, but for the majority it reproduces the structure of society unchanged.

To say this is not necessarily to criticize it or denounce it as unjust, but to identify one of its functions, as an institution which permits upward mobility but tends on the whole to maintain the stability of the social system. The same point may be made about a much wider range of research areas – the criminal justice system, health, community care, income maintenance – all of which are grounded in existing social institutions which generate and are maintained by particular discourses, particular models of what people and the social order are like and what may be taken for granted about them.

Politics, ideology and 'research style'

We have just looked at how theory, concepts and operationalized measures can embody ideologies or discourses, models of the world and of how questions about it are legitimately framed. Thus a line of research can be so imbued with a particular (unacknowledged) world view that its conclusions must fall within that world view and reinforce or validate it. In this section we shall look at the whole way in which research is conducted. It has been argued, as we shall see, that the 'stance' adopted in research itself expresses (and serves to validate) a particular model of how the social world is and should be.

It has been argued that to adopt one research style or 'stance' in preference to another is an implicitly political act, because research styles are not neutral or interchangeable: they embody implicit models of what the social world is like or should be like and of what counts as knowledge and how to get it.

In this section we shall explore a common criticism of 'conventional' research in the form in which it has been developed by feminist scholars and researchers. We should point out that the critique is by no means specific to feminism; elements of it have been expressed over the past 20 years by researchers in a number of quite disparate disciplines. (For a developed version emanating from humanistic psychology, for example, see Reason and Rowan, 1981.) Nor are we arguing here that there is a distinctive 'feminist research methodology'; indeed, we take rather different positions from each other on this issue. Feminist scholarship is one place, however, where issues of politics and power in research have been particularly sharply developed, and the discussion that follows owes a great deal to it. Two concepts of power are involved in our discussion of this scholarship: the direct power of the researcher over those researched, and the power of the researcher to 'set the agenda' of the research and declare and disseminate the results.

The arguments that feminists have put forward have tended to involve two separate (though related) issues. First, there is the criticism of quantitative research which conceives of itself as 'scientific', objective, value-free – the criticism of positivism. Feminists (and others) have argued that such research does not discover what the social world is like, but rather imposes its own conceptual schema on to the social world. A case in point would be the social mobility research briefly discussed above, which *declared* women unimportant both for examining rates of social mobility over time and for theorizing about social mobility (rather than *discovering* that they were unimportant). Sociological theory defined women as dependent on male heads of households and therefore outside the concerns of class theory. Conversely, accepting that the social differences between men and women were natural (biological) and inevitable, sociology did not see sexual divisions as an area of sociological concern and defined the work that women did in the domestic sphere as of no sociological interest. When Ann Oakley wanted to start research on house-work in the late 1960s, for example, she found it very difficult to find a supervisor and have the topic accepted, because housework was seen quite simply as something trivial, not something that constituted any sort of sociological problem. It was a very common experience of women sociology and psychology students in the 1960s and 1970s (and often still is today) to find a disjuncture between 'experience of the world … and the theoretical schemes available to think about it in' (Smith, 1974: 7); large areas of their lives and much of what really concerned them were declared non-existent, trivial, peripheral, not on the agenda for research or theory.

Feminists and others have argued that methods whose strength lies in the testing of theory are not suitable tools for research intended to develop *new* theory. Quantitative research is designed to obtain answers to researchers' questions; it does not yield an understanding of people's lives in depth nor, generally, leave space for them to indicate what *they* regard as the important questions. Quantitative methods typically isolate 'variables' for study, independent of the context in which they make sense and the sense which is made of them in that context: 'Concepts, environments, social interactions are all simplified by methods which lift them out of their context, stripping them of the very complexity that characterizes them in the real world' (Parlee, 1979: 131). Such criticism led to a call for relatively unstructured, qualitative methods which will 'take women's experience into account', explore the basis of women's everyday knowledge, let women 'speak for themselves' without the prejudgement and prestructuring of prior theory.

Positivistic science itself may reasonably be seen as expressing a discourse, a model of what truth is and how it is to be ascertained. The 'rules' of scientific discourse are that disputes are settled on the basis of evidence and logic – evidence in the form of careful, repeatable measurements whose relevance to the dispute can be readily justified, and logical argument from that evidence to a conclusion. These are the dominant 'rules of truth' in our current culture – the 'respectable' grounds on which arguments may be won. To say that something expresses a discourse is not to say that it is wrong; everything expresses some discourse, is framed according to some set of rules. The force of the scientific discourse, however, is to divert problematic issues from the arena of political debate – to 'depoliticize' them. 'Science' is not just a body of knowledge acquired for its own sake, but the basis of techniques which are used to solve problems. By accepting that certain kinds of issue are amenable to scientific solution – 'matters of fact' – we empower experts both to act on our behalf and ultimately to determine what our 'best interests' are. A part of the control, which this establishment of expertise exerts, is achieved:

> by taking what is essentially a political problem, removing it from the realm of political discourse, and recasting it in the neutral language of science. Once this is accomplished the problems have become technical ones … the language of reform is, from the outset, an essential component … Where there [is] resistance or failure … this [is] construed as further proof of the need to reinforce and extend the power of experts.
>
> (Foucault, 1982: 196)

The second criticism that feminists (and others) have raised is that much research is exploitative and oppressive – that it consists in a researcher with power controlling and manipulating 'subjects' for whom a better term might be 'objects'. Ann Oakley has raised as political/ethical the issue of the treatment of respondents in survey research – asking them identical questions in a set order and not being able to respond to issues they raise for fear of disturbing the standardized nature of the proceedings – in other words, treating human beings as like the objects of, e.g., research in physics or chemistry. This criticism is not confined to quantitative research, however; conventional participant observation research and 'unstructured' interview studies also come under fire. The process of research has been likened by some feminist scholars to the process of rape:

> the researchers take, hit, and run. They intrude into their subjects' privacy, disrupt their perceptions, utilize false pretences, manipulate the relationship, and give little or nothing in return. When the needs of the researchers are satisfied, they break off contact with the subject.
>
> (Reinharz, 1979: 95)

Thus research is criticized for the way it exercises power over its 'subjects'. A further criticism, however, might concern the power of the researcher to determine what is important in the situation, what needs researching, what the problem is. Here again the 'conventional' researcher has near-total autonomy and those who are researched may have little input (particularly in quantitative research).

These two criticisms have led some feminists and other researchers to call for fully collaborative research and the displacement of 'the researcher' from the control of the research process – or even, sometimes, for the abandonment of research in favour of participation in social action. As Maria Mies (1983) argues:

> The vertical relationship between researcher and 'research objects', the *view from above*, must be replaced by the *view from below* ...
>
> ... the hierarchical research situation as such defeats the very purpose of research: it creates an acute distrust in the 'research objects' ... It has been observed that the data thus gathered often reflect 'expected behaviour' rather than real behaviour ...
>
> [However,] Women, who are committed to the cause of women's liberation, cannot stop at this result. They cannot be satisfied with giving the social sciences better, more authentic and more relevant data. The ethical-political significance of the view from below cannot be separated from the scientific one ...
>
> The contemplative, uninvolved 'spectator knowledge' must be replaced by *active participation in actions, movements and struggles* ... Research must become an integral part of such struggles.
>
> (Mies, 1983, in Hammersley, 1993: 68–9)

Four problems occur to us:

1. We are inclined to think that adoption of a fully collaborative stance as an ethical imperative would abolish research into 'theory' and the use of research as an aid to scholarship and the development of ideas. If researchers are to avoid 'using' people for the researchers' purposes and confine their attention to helping to solve participants' problems, then all research becomes applied research. It is not clear, even, whether the researcher can initiate the research, or whether he or she has to wait to be 'commissioned'.

2. The adoption of a fully collaborative stance probably abolishes the role of researcher altogether. If the researcher is in no 'privileged' position – has no particular say in the planning of the research, no particular 'ownership' of the data, no special rights to use the material for publication – then it is difficult to see what he or she brings to the situation other than technical knowledge. Now, one may argue that researchers make their name and their living from studying the problems and miseries of others, and that the abolition of the role would be no bad thing, but one has to be clear that this *is* one possible consequence of this line of argument. We cannot take an authoritative position on this issue; as academics, we find it difficult to argue for the abolition of the academic role.

3. Most important of all, it is not clear that full power-sharing is possible, even in principle. In the extreme version of the collaborative stance, all

participants are to be equal, and the researcher's knowledge gives him or her no special position but has to be shared. 'Informed consent', in this position, involves the sharing of knowledge and experience so that all participants have the same power of understanding. Arguably, however, this would mean putting all participants through the same history of academic and research training and experience as the researcher has undergone, which is impractical and would not be desired by the participants. To the extent that it is not done, the power of knowledge necessarily remains with the researcher.

4. There is also the question of whom the researcher is collaborating with and who has given 'informed consent'. Research often involves several groups, where interests may not be the same; collaborating with one group may even reinforce power relationships, even if the research is intended to benefit all groups involved. For example, collaborative research with social workers into their practice still leaves the clients as research 'objects'.

We raise these objections not to decry the collaborative stance – we think that those who advocate it have alerted us to some very important ethical considerations, and that research should be strongly influenced by them – but to suggest that there are no easy answers to ethical and political dilemmas in research as in most walks of life.

Conclusion

We began this chapter with a discussion of research ethics, and this is where we have also finished up, but a lot of ground has been covered in between. We started with important questions of 'individualistic' ethics – for example, the design of research so that subjects/respondents/informants/participants are not harmed by it. We then went on, however, to look beneath the surface of the theories that are researched and the measures that are derived from them. It is easy to work as if qualities such as 'intelligence', 'achievement' or 'class' 'exist' in some sense which is difficult to define but unproblematic, so that the problems lie in how to measure them. However, we looked at the background, history and usage of these variables to examine how the concepts have grown up, not as academic abstractions but as ways of describing the social world for particular purposes. We discovered that social construction is an aspect of their 'existence': that they arise from certain theories or ideologies or discourses/world models and incorporate the assumptions implicit in their origins. The 'grand abstractions' of social science are not 'existent things', but ways of describing and abstracting from and characterizing the real 'existent things' – people and their social relations – and the notion that they might be constructed for a purpose, and deliberately or unwittingly incorporate theories about the social world, should come as no surprise. Going on to look at our own usual way of conceptualizing research as an activity, we found that even here taken-for-granted assumptions about the nature of the social world and the proper ('natural', 'inevitable') way that power and knowledge are distributed are built into the way the enterprise is conducted and can shape the outcomes.

In other words, in looking at research papers or conducting your own research you need to be sensitive to the 'taken-for-granted'. Taken-for-granted ways of conceptualizing a problem area (or even taken-for-granted ways of conceptualizing aspects of social behaviour as 'belonging' to certain problem areas) shape how the problem is formulated, which restricts what can conceivably come out as results of any study undertaken. (Even more interesting, perhaps, is the way that disciplines and applied areas declare some questions to be 'real' problems and others as peripheral, trivial or 'not on the agenda'. Some selection *has* to be made – not everything can be researched – but we have shown that the omissions sometimes add up to a systematic exclusion of some set of interests or points of view.) In a sense, this is not a criticism, because it is a general statement about all conceivable research projects and all conceivable research reports. It is not possible to work in a vacuum; at the same time as some aspects of a situation are problematized, others must be taken for granted. However, an important aspect of the conduct of research, and an even more important aspect of reading research reports, is thinking about precisely *what* has been taken for granted and how it affects the conclusions.

The point has also been made that the use of existing and accepted methods of research, grounded in the 'knowledge base' of a discipline, may sometimes amount to taking sides in a potential dispute. We have used intelligence and attainment as examples of implicit and (sometimes) unconscious prejudgement of issues related to 'race' and social class. It is inevitable that most research will proceed along established lines and within established paradigms – we cannot for ever question *everything* – and it is true that to use 'unconventional' methods and theoretical bases is equally to take sides. We need where possible, however, to identify what is being taken for granted in the methods we use and the disciplinary knowledge in which they are grounded.

This chapter has used a fairly small range of examples – research into social class, intelligence and achievement – to make its points. The overall 'message', however, is that all research can be viewed from this kind of perspective and is open to this kind of critique. A major debate in research on the criminal justice system, for example, has been the ways in which social class is ignored or hidden or taken for granted in its analyses. Research on families, health and community care is rightly, some would say, attacked for the way in which it tends to take for granted a particular set of relations between the genders and across the generations. Feminist research into the position of women is attacked for its tendency to ignore the important dimension of ethnic origins. It is always a relevant form of critique to uncover the buried assumptions taken for granted by a piece of research, if only to show that they make no difference to the credibility of the conclusions. In other words, we need to be careful that something that is a *political* problem associated with the research is not turned into a *technical* problem, or indeed taken for granted as solved because of the research methods and design that are employed.

References

Brigham, C. C. (1923) *A Study of American Intelligence*, Princeton, NJ, Princeton University Press.

Douglas, J. D. (1976) *Investigative Social Research: Individual and Team Field Research*, Beverly Hills, CA, Sage.

Foucault, M. (1982) 'The subject and power', in H. Dreyfus and P. Rabinow (eds), *Michel Foucault: Beyond Structuralism and Hermeneutics*, Brighton, Harvester.

Hammersley, M. (ed.) (1993) *Social Research: Philosophy, Politics and Practice*, London, Sage.

Haney, C., Banks, C. and Zimbardo, P. G. (1973) 'Interpersonal dynamics in a simulated prison', *International Journal of Criminology and Penology*, vol. 1, pp. 69–97.

Kamin, L. (1977) *The Science and Politics of IQ*, Harmondsworth, Penguin.

Mies, M. (1983) 'Towards a methodology for feminist research', in M. Hammersley (ed.) (1993), *Social Research: Philosophy, Politics and Practice*, London, Sage.

Milgram, S. (1974) *Obedience to Authority: An Experimental View*, London, Tavistock.

Parlee, M. (1979) 'Psychology and women', *Signs*, vol. 5, pp. 123–33.

Reason, P. and Rowan, J. (1981) *Human Inquiry: A Sourcebook of New Paradigm Research*, Chichester, Wiley.

Reinharz, S. (1979) *On Becoming a Social Scientist*, San Francisco, Jossey Bass.

Rosenthal, R. and Jacobson, L. (1968) *Pygmalion in the Classroom*, New York, Holt, Rinehart and Winston.

Smith, D. (1974) 'Women's perspective as a radical critique of sociology', *Sociological Enquiry*, vol. 44, pp. 7–13.

Terman, L. M. (1916) *The Measurement of Intelligence*, Boston, MA, Houghton Mifflin.

Zimbardo, P. G. (1973) 'On the ethics of intervention in human psychological research', *Cognition*, vol. 2, pp. 243–356.

Chapter 8

Educational action research

Ken Zeichner

The difficult thing about doing action research is that you have to override most of what you've learned about research as an activity. In a traditional research culture you begin by framing a question, setting up a situation which might provide some information, collecting data which bears on the question, then writing up the results. Action research isn't like that at all. The research activity begins in the middle of whatever it is you're doing – something happens you didn't expect … and you begin wondering what's going on … The hardest part of beginning an action research project is developing the discipline to keep a written account of what's happening, particularly when you have no idea of what you're looking for. For unlike traditional research, action research begins not with a research question but with the muddle of daily work, with the moments that stand out from the general flow …

(Newman, 1998: 2–3)

Last year I noticed that the children in my class were creating groups segregated by gender, and I wrote about it in my journal as I wrote about other issues and events. What I did not do last year was to start out by saying, 'I'm going to study gender issues in my classroom,' and to limit my observations and notes to that.

(Streib, in Threatt *et al.*, 1994: 237)

My question emerged out of what I understood to be problematic classroom dynamics that surfaced immediately at the beginning of the year. For one thing, eight boys … dominated the classroom especially during all class discussions. A second interesting pattern emerged. Whenever I asked the class to voluntarily form groups, line up, or make a circle, they did so in exactly the same fashion – sorting themselves neatly first by gender, then by ethnic and racial affiliation. My questions were: How can I increase participation in all class discussions by those less willing or able to share? How can I help the students in my classroom feel comfortable working with diverse groupings of classmates and ultimately overcome, at least part of the time, their desire to always be with their friends?

(Coccari, 1998: 2–3)

These excerpts from the action research reports of teachers in the USA illustrate some of the variety that exists in the ways that teachers[1] have conducted action research. In the first two cases, the teachers began by keeping journals on many aspects of their practice and eventually, for the second teacher, the issue of gender segregation in small-group work emerged for further study. This teacher's documentation was broad-ranging, focusing on many issues simultaneously and the inquiry did not necessarily follow the action research spiral of plan, act, observe and reflect (Kemmis and McTaggart, 1988). In the third case, the teacher began with a specific focus on two questions and the research proceeded, as do most studies in this school district-based programme, according to the action research spiral.

This chapter will examine some of the variety that has come to exist in educational action research in English-speaking countries. We will begin with an examination of the different traditions of action research that have exerted much influence on the emergence of educational action research in many different countries. Then, after a discussion of the different ways in which educational action research is conceptualized, organized and supported in North America, we will examine educational action research both as a professional development activity and as a form of knowledge production.

Traditions of action research in education

There are five major traditions of educational action research in English-speaking countries that have exerted influence, in conjunction with local factors, on the development of action research in the educational systems of many countries. First, there is the action research tradition in the USA that developed directly out of the work of Kurt Lewin and was brought into US schools by Stephen Corey and others at the Horace Mann-Lincoln Institute at Columbia University. Secondly, there is the British teacher-as-researcher movement that evolved in the 1960s and 1970s out of the curriculum reform work of British teachers and the support provided by several academics like Lawrence Stenhouse and John Elliott. Thirdly, there is the Australian participatory action research movement, supported by the work of Stephen Kemmis and Robin McTaggart at Deakin University and other Australian academics, that was greatly influenced by educational action research in the UK but that also developed in response to indigenous factors within Australia. Fourthly, there is the contemporary teacher researcher movement in North America that has been developed since the 1980s primarily by teachers, often with the support of their university colleagues and subject matter associations. Finally, there is the recent growth of self-study research by college and university educators who inquire into their own practice as teachers and teacher educators. Educational action research has also been influenced by the tradition of participatory research which developed in Africa, Latin America and Asia with oppressed groups and later was adapted to community-wide research in North America. This explicitly political form of action research often includes attention to the education sphere, but usually goes beyond it.

The action research tradition in the USA

In the 1940s and 1950s Stephen Corey, head of the Horace Mann-Lincoln Institute for School Experimentation at Columbia University, and his colleagues drew directly upon the work of social psychologist Kurt Lewin and brought action research into education. The Institute was formed in 1943 to improve the rate of curriculum change in schools and to reduce the gap between research knowledge and practice in classrooms (Olson, 1990). Corey (1953) believed that teachers would make better decisions in the classroom if they conducted research to determine the basis for their decisions.

Corey and his associates at the Institute worked cooperatively with teachers, principals and supervisors in school districts across the USA in the late 1940s and 1950s on a variety of group research efforts in what was referred to as the 'cooperative action research movement' (e.g., Cunningham and Miel, 1947; Foshay, Wann and Associates, 1954).

Like Lewin, Corey saw action research as a cyclical process with each cycle of research affecting subsequent ones. Corey (1953) outlined several distinct phases of the action research process: (1) the identification of a problem area; (2) the selection of a specific problem and formulation of a hypothesis or prediction that implies a specific goal and a procedure for reaching it; (3) the careful recording of actions and accumulation of evidence to determine if the goal has been achieved; (4) the inference from this evidence of generalizations regarding the relation between actions and the desired goal; and (5) the continuous retesting of these generalizations in action (pp. 40–1).

Corey's understanding of the action research process was generally similar to Lewin's in terms of the focus on the research being conducted in a group and the emphasis on the recursive nature of the action research process where researchers need to allow their initial understandings of a problem to shift to remain relevant to changing situations. Corey's view of the action research process differed from Lewin's, however, because of his emphasis on hypothesis formulation and testing. For Corey's students and those who followed him on the faculty at the Institute, action research increasingly became a linear problem-solving process as opposed to the recursive cyclical process that it had been for Lewin and Corey (e.g., Taba and Noel, 1957). It also increasingly became identified as a form of inservice teacher education as opposed to a methodology for knowledge production in education (e.g., Shumsky, 1958).

Corey spent much effort in defending action research as a legitimate form of educational inquiry (e.g., Corey, 1949) against attacks from the mainstream academic research community, but he was largely unsuccessful in doing so. Action research was severely attacked by academic researchers (e.g., Hodgkinson, 1957) and largely disappeared from the USA education literature until the 1980s when a new North American teacher research movement appeared.

The teacher-as-researcher movement in the UK

Following the decline of action research in the USA by the early 1960s, the idea of action research in the field of education emerged in the UK in the context of school-based curriculum development in the 1960s. According to John Elliott (1991, 1997), who was one of the central players in this movement, both as a secondary school teacher and university academic, this teacher-led movement arose in response to large-scale student disaffection in British secondary schools. In Elliott's view, it was from the attempts by teachers in some innovative secondary modern schools to restructure and reconceptualize the humanities curriculum that the ideas of teacher-as-researcher, teaching as a reflexive practice, and teaching as a form of inquiry emerged.

Another influence on the development of educational action research in Britain during this period was the Tavistock Institute of Human Relations which had been set up in 1947 to develop further practices that psychologists had used during the Second World War to train officers and resettle prisoners. There were strong parallels between the work of this institute and the Research Center for Group Dynamics that Lewin had set up in the USA (Wallace, 1987). According to Bridget Somekh (February 1998, personal communication), two other influences on the development of the teacher-as-researcher movement in Britain were the Educational Priority Area Programme that involved teachers and academics in collaborative research and the US social studies curriculum, 'Man: a Course of Study'.

The bottom-up curriculum reform work initiated by British teachers and later conceptualized and documented by academics like Lawrence Stenhouse, John Elliott, Jean Ruddick and others involved many different initiatives designed to make the curriculum more relevant to the lives of students, such as restructuring the content of the curriculum around life themes, transforming the instructional process from a transmission mode to a more interactive and discussion-based mode, using multiage grouping patterns, and so on.

A number of major curriculum reform projects were initiated in the 1960s and 1970s by Stenhouse, Elliott and others, which employed and further developed the idea of action research as curriculum development. These included the 'Humanities Curriculum Project', which dealt with the teaching of controversial issues (Stenhouse, 1968), the 'Ford Teaching Project', which dealt with implementing an inquiry/discovery approach to teaching (Elliott, 1976/77) and the 'Teacher–Student Interaction and Quality of Learning Project' which focused on the problems of teaching for understanding within the context of a system of public examinations (Elliott and Ebutt, 1986).

All of these projects involved university academics working with teachers and represented a rejection of a standards- or objectives-based approach to curriculum development in favour of one that is based on a pedagogically driven conception of curriculum change as a process dependent on teachers' capacities for reflection. According to this view, the act of curriculum theorizing is not so much the application in the classroom of theory learned in the university as it is the generation of theory from attempts to change curriculum practice in schools (Elliott, 1991; Stenhouse, 1976).

The efforts of John Elliott, Peter Holly, Bridget Somekh and many others in the UK led to the establishment of the Collaborative Action Research Network (CARN), an international network that has sponsored conferences and published action research studies and discussions of action research methodology. This network was instrumental in establishing the journal *Educational Action Research* which is the major international journal for action research in education today.

Participatory action research in Australia

Grundy (1997) describes a number of political, social and economic conditions that fostered a receptivity within Australia to the idea of teachers as producers of educational knowledge. Among these were three projects in the 1970s funded by the Commonwealth Schools Commission, 'The Innovative Grants Project', 'The Language and Learning Project' and the 'Curriculum Development Centre'. These projects, as well as changing conceptions of inservice teacher education at the state level, and the growth of action research in the education units of tertiary institutions, stimulated a lot of school-based curriculum development and evaluation, and teachers studying their own practices in Australian schools.

Australian educational action research developed with close ties to the British teacher-as-researcher movement because Stephen Kemmis, one of the leading proponents of educational action research in Australia, as well as other Australian academics, had spent time working with Elliott and his colleagues at the University of East Anglia. Grundy (1997) argues, though, that despite this link, the Australian movement developed its own practices and epistemology that distinguished it from the British movement.

Kemmis and his colleagues at Deakin University built on a strong movement among teachers for school-based curriculum development and for grass-roots involvement in policy-making (Grundy and Kemmis, 1988) and developed a view of 'emancipatory action research' based in critical theory (Carr and Kemmis, 1986) that challenged other models of action research as conservative and positivistic. The 'Deakin group', as well as other university academics across Australia (e.g., Tripp, 1990), articulated a methodology for educational action research in the form of an action research spiral (plan, act, observe and reflect) that was linked with an intent to promote greater equity and social justice in schools and the society (Kemmis and McTaggart, 1988). Although a number of projects of the critical emancipatory type are described in various publications (e.g., Kemmis and Grundy, 1997), there is some question as to the degree to which teachers throughout Australia who became engaged in action research took on the critical emancipatory purposes advocated by university academics (Grundy, 1982).

The North American teacher research movement

In the 1980s a new teacher research movement emerged in North America that was not derivative of the British teacher-as-researcher movement or a re-emergence of the co-operative action research movement of the 1950s. Anderson, Herr and Nihlen (1994) identify a number of influences on the development of this new emphasis on educational action research: (1) the growing acceptance of qualitative and case study research in education which more closely resembles the narrative forms of inquiry used by practitioners to communicate their knowledge; (2) the highly visible work of a number of teachers of writing like Nancy Atwell (1987), who conducted case studies of the teaching of writing; (3) the increased emphasis on action research in university teacher education programmes (e.g., Cochran-Smith and Lytle, 1993); and (4) the reflective practitioner movement in teaching and teacher education that recognized and valued the practical knowledge of teachers (e.g., Zeichner, 1994).

Cochran-Smith and Lytle (1999) also discuss other influences on teacher research in North America such as the National Writing Project, Breadloaf School of English, the National Council of Teachers of English, the Prospect School in Bennington, Vermont and the North Dakota Study Group (e.g., Carini, 1975; Goswami and Stillman, 1987; Mohr and Maclean, 1987; Perrone, 1989).

This emerging teacher research movement followed a number of years of 'interactive research and development' and other forms of collaborative research in education involving university academics and teachers (e.g., Oja and Smulyan, 1989). These collaborative projects involved teachers in some aspects of the research process but were not owned and controlled by teachers.

Currently, although some teachers engage in action research in the context of university courses, projects and degree programmes (e.g., Freedman *et al.*, 1999; Gitlin *et al.*, 1992) many others have formed teacher research communities that, although they may involve collaboration with academics, are controlled by teachers (e.g., Gallas, 1998a).

The tradition of self-study research

Although most of the action research conducted within all of the traditions discussed so far has involved elementary and secondary school staff in studying their practice, there has also been a growing tradition in which college and university faculties have conducted research on their own teaching within the academy. In the 1990s there has been a growing acceptance of action research as a method for self-study within colleges and universities, especially among teacher educators.

Recently there has been a tremendous growth in the publication of self-study research by teacher educators (e.g., Hamilton, 1998; Loughran and Russell, 1997; Russell and Korthagen, 1995) and calls for the academy to recognize the legitimacy of high-quality self-study research in tenure and promotion decisions (Adler, 1993). In 1992 a special interest group 'Self-Study of Teacher Education Practices' was formed in the American Educational Research Association and it has become one of the largest interest groups in the association.

The self-study research of college and university faculties has employed a variety of qualitative methodologies and has focused on a wide range of substantive issues. For example, some studies in this genre have employed narrative life history methods and describe the connections between teacher educators' life experiences and their current teaching practices (e.g., Cole and Knowles, 1995; Zeichner 1995). Some self-study research has involved inquiries about the use of particular strategies (e.g Grimmett, 1997; Richert, 1991) or of the implementation of particular educational philosophies in teacher education programmes (e.g., Ahlquist, 1991; Macgillivray, 1997). Many recent studies focus on the struggles of teacher educators with issues of race, class and gender (e.g., Ahlquist, 1991; Cochran-Smith, 1995; Martin, 1995).

Dimensions of variation in educational action research

Currently, there is a wide variety of approaches to conceptualizing, organizing and supporting educational action research. The dimensions along which action research in education have varied include the purposes and motivations of those who engage in the research, the conceptions of the action research process and the form and content of action research studies, the ways in which the findings of the research are represented by researchers to others, the relation of action research to externally produced research, the sponsorship and organizational location of the research, the structures in place to support the research, and the assumptions about knowledge and teacher learning that are reflected in particular research programmes. The following framework, based largely on educational action research as it exists today in North America, is presented as a starting-point for better understanding the varieties of educational action research throughout the world.

Noffke (1997) has outlined three different motivations that have existed for teachers who have conducted research about their own practices. First, there is the motivation to understand better and improve one's own teaching and/or the contexts in which that teaching is embedded. Here the main interest is in how the research can contribute to the betterment of one's own individual situation as a teacher and life in a classroom, school and community. Secondly, there is the motivation to produce knowledge that will be useful to others, either in the same setting or other settings. Here action researchers are interested in sharing their research with others through seminars, conference presentations and publications. Finally, consistent with the 'democratic impulse' that was originally associated with the emergence of action research in the US in the 1940s (Foshay, 1994), there is the motivation to contribute to greater equity and social justice in schooling and society. Here there is an explicit agenda by educational action researchers to work for social change by working on issues of equity within the classroom and beyond (Anderson, Herr and Nihlen, 1994).

A second dimension along which educational action research has varied is in terms of the sponsorship of the research. Here there have been many different sponsors of research, including teachers themselves (e.g., Gallas, 1998a, 1998b), school districts and local professional development centres (e.g., Caro-Bruce and McReadie, 1995; Richert, 1999), teacher unions (e.g., The British Columbia Teachers' Federation), colleges and universities, school/university partnerships (e.g., Troen, Kamii and Boles, 1999), professional subject matter associations (e.g., The National Council of Teachers of English), and local and national governments. Among the colleges and universities that have been involved in sponsoring educational action research are those that offer specific courses on action research, support action research masters theses and doctoral dissertations, and those like the University of California-Davis, that support educational action research on a broad scale for teachers in area school districts (Wagner, 1995).

Educational action researchers have conducted their inquiries under a variety of contextual arrangements. For example, they have conducted research alone, as part of small collaborative groups composed of peers, or in school faculty groups that involve everyone in a particular school (Calhoun, 1993). Most of the time educators voluntarily participate in conducting research, but in the case of some school-wide action research programmes, participation by all staff members is compulsory. When the research has been done in connection with a group, the groups have varied according to their size, the basis for their formation, and whether there is an external facilitator and/or university involvement. Some action research groups involve educators from the same team, department or school, and others mix together people from different schools. There have been a variety of external incentives provided to educators for participating in action research, including time away from their schools to think together with their colleagues, money, and university and professional advancement credits. Some action research programmes involve teachers for a year or less and others enable them to continue working on their research for several years.

Within the research programmes themselves, there is much variation in the form and content of action research studies. For example, Cochran-Smith and Lytle (1993) have described four different forms of systematic and intentional inquiry by teachers in North America: (1) journals which provide analyses of classroom life over time; (2) oral inquiries which consist of teachers' oral examinations of their practice in a group setting; (3) studies which represent teachers' explorations of their work using data based on observations, interviews and document analysis; and (4) essays which represent extended interpretations and analyses of various aspects of schooling. Cochran-Smith and Lytle (1993) argue that this broad view of practitioner inquiry in education accounts for some of the ways that educators inquire about their practice that do not fit with university models for doing research or with standard conceptions of action research.

As was indicated by the three brief vignettes at the beginning of this chapter, some educational action research involves the investigation of specific research questions and follows some variation of the well-known action research spiral: plan, act, observe and reflect (e.g., Elliott, 1991; Kemmis and McTaggart, 1988; McNiff, 1997). This is what Cochran-Smith and Lytle (1993) refer to as 'studies'. Other educational action research is more holistic and focuses simultaneously on a variety of questions (e.g., Gallas, 1998b).

Educational action researchers have investigated a variety of questions and issues in their inquiries. The following framework generated from an analysis of action research studies in the Madison, Wisconsin school district is illustrative of the nature and scope of the questions that are addressed in educational action research studies (Zeichner, 1999a). This framework shows that the action research of educational practitioners includes studies that focus within the educators' immediate domain of the classroom, beyond the classroom but within the school, and on issues that extend beyond the school. In the Madison school district's classroom action research programme over

400 studies have been done by educators since 1990. These studies have investigated a variety of questions and issues designed to:

1. Improve practice – e.g., How can I hold better discussions in my classroom and have a more learner-centred class?
2. Better understand a particular aspect of practice – e.g., Do I conduct my classes in a manner where students feel free to express different opinions and even to disagree with me? How does my school's behaviour management system affect students from different ethnic groups?
3. Better understand one's practice in general – e.g., What is going on in my third period biology class?
4. Promote greater equity – e.g., How can I help the girls in my mathematics class feel more confident about their abilities in maths and to participate more in classroom activities?
5. Influence the social conditions of practice – e.g., How can I get the school district to reallocate funding to support teacher-initiated professional development work?

In addition to the different kinds of questions and issues investigated by educational action researchers, their studies also vary in the ways that they relate to externally generated knowledge, including academic educational research and studies done by other practitioners. Troen, Kamii and Boles (1997) describe three patterns that emerged when they examined teachers' research studies in their Brookline, Massachusetts teacher inquiry community. Some teachers used concepts, questions and ideas from external research as the starting-point for their research. An example here would be a teacher who studies the ways in which multiple intelligence theory helps explain student learning within her classroom. Others consulted external research later on in the research process, but did not do so at the onset of the research. Finally, some researchers deliberately did not consult external research because they felt that it would not be helpful to do so.

Educational action research programmes also differ in terms of the structural conditions that are set up to support the work of researchers. These differences include the rituals and routines that are established in action research groups (e.g., what group facilitators do to help researchers think more deeply about their practice), the resources that are provided to researchers (e.g., materials to read, literature searches, publication support), the opportunities that are provided for researchers to interact with others about their work (e.g., local action research conferences), and the ways in which researchers are encouraged, supported or required to represent their research to others (e.g., as papers, on videos, through conference presentations).

Finally, one of the most significant dimensions along which educational action research varies is in terms of the philosophical orientations towards knowledge, teachers and their learning that are embedded in the structures, human interactions and organization of action research programmes. Some action research efforts, despite a rhetoric of teacher empowerment, replicate the hierarchial patterns of authority and dim view of teachers' capabilities that is characteristic of dominant forms of teacher professional development, while others display a deep respect for teachers and their knowledge and seek to break down authority patterns which limit teacher autonomy and control (Zeichner, 1999a).

Educational action research as professional development

Many educators who have engaged in action research have done so for reasons of professional development rather than out of a desire to publish or in other ways disseminate their findings to others. Over the years, many claims have been made about the benefits of teachers engaging in research about their own practices. For example, it has been asserted that doing self-study research helps teachers to become more flexible and open to new ideas (Oja and Smulyan, 1989), makes them more proactive in relation to external authority (Holly, 1990), boosts teachers' self-esteem and confidence levels (Dadds, 1995), narrows the gap between teachers' aspirations and realizations (Elliott, 1980), helps develop an attitude and skills of self-analysis which are applied to other situations (Day, 1984), changes patterns of interaction among teachers to more collegial interactions (Selener, 1997), alters teacher talk about students from a focus on student problems to an emphasis on student resources and accomplishments, and leads to more learner-centred classrooms (Cochran-Smith and Lytle, 1992).

Despite the growing testimony in the literature about the positive outcomes associated with teachers doing action research, there are a number of problems with drawing conclusions from these statements alone about the value of action research as a professional development activity. First, many of the references in the literature to the value of action research are anecdotal in nature and are not the result of systematic and intentional explorations of educators' research experiences. Secondly, even if we accept the accuracy of the claims that have been made about the value of action research, we are often provided with little or no information about the specific characteristics of the research experience and/or research context that would enable us to explain the particular conditions responsible for the positive impact. Given the tremendous variety in the conceptionalizations and arrangements for organizing and supporting educational action research described above, it is important to begin to identify the particular conditions of the action research experience that are associated with the kind of positive outcomes for teachers and their students that are so frequently cited in the literature.

There have been relatively few cases where the professional development process associated with educational action research has been systematically studied. In the few cases that do exist (Allen and Calhoun, 1998; Burgess-Macey and Rose, 1997; Calhoun and Allen, 1996; Dadds, 1995; Gallas, 1998a; Joyce *et al.*, 1996; Richert, 1996, 1999; Troen, Kamii and Boles, 1997, 1999; Zeichner, Caro-Bruce and Marion, 1998), researchers, often in collaboration with those doing the action research, collected data over time to examine the conditions under which the action research was organized and supported, and its impact on teachers, pupils and schools. In addition to analyses by others of teachers' action research experiences, some work has been done by Kemmler-Ernst in examining a wide variety of cases of teachers' self-reports of the learning that occurs while doing action research. Drawing on the published personal narratives of teacher researchers and their contributions to electronic mailing lists, Kemmler-Ernst (1998) discusses the ways in which action research may contribute to changes in teachers' thinking, practice and collegial relationships by examining the reports of teachers who participated in research through graduate university classes or organized teacher collaboratives and networks.

In an analysis of both systematic studies of the nature and impact of educational action research and Kemmler-Ernst's investigation of teachers' self-reports, Zeichner (1999a) concluded that under certain conditions, action research seems to promote particular kinds of teacher and student learning that teachers find very valuable and transformative. Specifically, there seems to be evidence that under particular conditions the experience of engaging in self-study research helps teachers to become more self-confident about their ability to promote student learning, to become more proactive in dealing with difficult issues that arise in their teaching, and to acquire habits and skills of inquiry that they use beyond the research experience. Zeichner (1999a) also cites evidence of links between conducting action research under these conditions and a movement towards more learner-centred instruction and improvements in student learning.

The particular conditions that appear to be related to these positive outcomes for teachers and students are:

1. The creation of a culture of inquiry that respects the voices of teachers and the knowledge that they bring to the research experience. This does not mean a romanticization of teachers' voices and an uncritical acceptance of everything that emerges from their research because it is asserted by a teacher. It does mean, though, that teacher knowledge is taken as seriously as other forms of knowledge and is evaluated according to both moral and educational criteria (Zeichner and Noffke, in press). A balance is achieved between honouring teachers' voices and expertise and asking them to critique what they know (Gallas, 1998b).

2. There is an investment in the intellectual capital of teachers which results in teachers having control over most aspects of the research process, including whether to participate or not, the research focus and the methods of data collection and analysis.
3. There is intellectual challenge and stimulation in the work and teachers are helped to think more deeply about their practice rather than given 'solutions' for their problems.
4. The research takes place over a substantial period of time (at least a year) in a safe and supportive environment. Predictable rituals and routines are established in groups of teacher researchers that help build community.
5. Participation in the research is voluntary.

There are other aspects of the action research process (e.g., whether or not teachers are required to write a research report at the end of the experience) where the connection to the kind of teacher and student learning described above is less clear. At this point in time, given the limited study of educational action research as professional development, the conditions identified above represent only a place from which to begin more in-depth investigations.

Educational action research as knowledge production

Although most teachers who have done action research have been uninterested in sharing their inquiries with others beyond their local research communities, an increasing number of teachers have published their work and/or presented it at local, regional and national conferences. Also, as academics have become involved in doing self-study research, increased acceptance of this work has developed as part of the tenure and promotion process. Generally, there has been increased citation of action research studies in educational research publications and an explosion of courses in colleges and universities that deal with action research as a legitimate form of educational inquiry (see Cochran-Smith and Lytle, 1999; Zeichner and Noffke, in press). There has also been an increased presence of educational action research and writing about educational action research at academic professional conferences such as the annual meetings of the American Educational Research Association (Zeichner, 1999b).

This increased acceptance of action research as a legitimate form of inquiry that can potentially inform practitioners, policy-makers, researchers and teacher educators has not been without controversy. For example, Cochran-Smith and Lytle (1999) discuss two critiques of educational action research that question its existence as a legitimate form of educational inquiry and the value of the knowledge that it produces. Huberman (1996) has questioned the claim that action research is a distinctive form of educational inquiry that provides unique insights into schooling and has argued that it needs to be judged according to standards applied to traditional academic interpretative inquiry. Fenstermacher (1994) has questioned the idea that teachers can generate knowledge valuable to others through their self-study research and also argues that action research needs to be governed by epistemological standards that are applied to academic research. On the other hand, many have argued that educational action research is a distinctive form of educational inquiry that should be judged by its own set of standards (e.g., Anderson, Herr and Nihlen, 1994). A literature has emerged in recent years that examines various aspects of the question of whether educational action research is a legitimate form of educational inquiry and if so, by which standards it should be judged (see Anderson and Herr, 1999; Whitehead, 1989; Zeichner and Noffke, in press). In many ways, these issues are just beginning to be debated and discussed in both academic and practitioner research communities.

Conclusion

Most of the literature discussed in this chapter has been written in English and was generated by academics in the USA, Canada, the UK and Australia. The discussion of educational action research traditions, dimensions of variation in conceptualizations and patterns for organizing action research programmes, and of literature on action research as professional development and knowledge production, has not included the growing literature on educational action research in other languages and in other parts of the world (e.g., Barabtarlo y Zedansky and Poschner, 1998; Hollingsworth, 1997; McTaggart, 1997; Walker, 1995). This chapter also has not included more than a few voices of teachers about the methodology of educational action research. Despite recent progress in the accessibility of educational action research studies, it still remains very difficult to access this work beyond, and even at the local level, and teachers have not been active participants in the public dialogue about action research as a research methodology in education. Ways must be found to make educational action research studies more easily available to others and to involve teachers actively in the important discussions about the role of action research in educational research, policy-making and teacher education. The conceptual frameworks and analyses presented in this chapter need to be examined and critiqued from a broader perspective that takes into account the work on action research that has been done in other parts of the world not included within the scope of this review.

Some of the most ambitious work in educational action research today is being done in developing countries in Latin America and Africa. For example, in Namibia, action research has been used since independence in 1990 as a major strategy in a comprehensive educational reform programme that has sought to transform teaching and teacher education from autocratic to more learner-centred forms (Dahlstrom, Swarts and Zeichner, 1999). Throughout Namibia, student teachers, teachers and teacher educators have been conducting action research that has focused on such things as increasing the participation of learners in the classroom and promoting greater understanding of content through more interactive teaching approaches, and so on.

As action research has come to be used in education within developing countries, concern has arisen about the colonialist implications in the importation of action research models developed in the USA, the UK and Australia to the developing world, and arguments have been made about the importance of adapting external models and developing indigenous forms of educational action research that take into account the particular cultures and traditions in the contexts in which it is used (Zeichner and Dahlstrom, 1999). Although educational action research can potentially be a liberating and emancipatory force, there is also the danger that it can slip into becoming another form of oppression in the developing world.

Note

1. The term 'teacher' will be used to refer to secondary educators (e.g., classroom teachers, principals, counsellors) and the term 'academic' will be used to refer to faculty and staff in colleges and universities. The term 'educator' will be used to refer to both teachers and academics.

References

Adler, S. (1993) 'Teacher education: research or reflective practice', *Teaching and Teacher Education*, 9 (20): 159–67.

Ahlquist, R. (1991) 'Position and imposition: power relations in a multicultural foundations class', *Journal of Negro Education*, 60 (2): 158–69.

Allen, L. and Calhoun, E. (1998) 'Schoolwide action research: findings from six years of study', *Kappan*, 79 (9): 706–10.

Anderson, G. and Herr, K. (1999) 'The new paradigm wars: is there room for rigorous practitioner knowledge in schools and universities?', *Educational Researcher*, 28 (5): 12–21.

Anderson, G., Herr, K. and Nihlen, A. (1994) *Studying Your Own School: an Educator's Guide to Qualitative Practitioner Research*. Thousand Oaks, CA: Corwin Press.

Atwell, N. (1987) *In the Middle: Writing, Reading, and Learning with Adolescents*. Portsmouth, NH: Boyton Cook/Heinemann.

Barabtarlo y Zedansky, A. and Poschner, T. (1998) 'Participatory action research in teacher education: a methodology for studying the everyday reality of teaching in Latin America', in G. Anderson and M. Montero-Sieburth (eds), *Educational Qualitative Research in Latin America*. New York: Garland.

Burgess-Macey, C. and Rose, J. (1997) 'Breaking through the barriers: professional development, action research, and the early years', *Educational Action Research*, 5 (1): 55–70.

Calhoun, E. (1993) 'Action research: three approaches', *Educational Leadership*, 52 (2): 62–5.

Calhoun, E. and Allen, L. (1996) 'The action research network: action research on action research', in B. Joyce and E. Calhoun (eds), *Learning Experiences in School Renewal: an Exploration of Five Successful Programs*. Eugene, OR: ERIC Center on Educational Management, University of Oregon. pp. 136–74.

Carini, P. (1975) *Observation and Description: an Alternative Methodology for the Investigation of Human Phenomena*. Grand Forks, ND: University of North Dakota Press.

Caro-Bruce, C. and McReadie, J. (1995) 'What happens when a school district supports action research?', in S. Noffke and R. Stevenson (eds), *Educational Action Research*. New York: Teachers College Press. pp. 154–64.

Carr, W. and Kemmis, S. (1986) *Becoming Critical: Education, Knowledge, and Action Research*. London: Falmer Press.

Coccari, D. (1998) 'We want to work with our friends', in C. Caro-Bruce (ed.), *Assessment and Health and Wellness Classroom Action Research*. Medison, WI: Madison Metropolitan School District.

Cochran-Smith, M. (1995) 'Uncertain allies: understanding the boundaries of race and teaching', *Harvard Educational Review*, 65 (4): 541–70.

Cochran-Smith, M. and Lytle, S. (1992) 'Communities for teacher research: fringe or forefront?', *American Journal of Education*, 100 (3): 298–324.

Cochran-Smith, M. and Lytle, S. (1993) *Inside-Outside: Teacher Research and Knowledge*. New York: Teachers College Press.

Cochran-Smith, M. and Lytle, S. (1999) 'The teacher research movement: a decade later', *Educational Researcher*, 28 (7): 15–25.

Cole, A. and Knowles, G. (1995) 'Methods and issues in a life history approach to self-study', in T. Russell and F. Korthagen (eds), *Teachers Who Teach Teachers*. London: Falmer Press. pp. 130–51.

Corey, S. (1949) 'Action research, fundamental research, and educational practices', *Teachers College Record*, 50: 509–14.

Corey, S. (1953) *Action Research to Improve School Practices*. New York: Teachers College Press.

Cunningham, R. and Miel, A. (1947) 'Frontiers of educational research in elementary school curriculum development', *Journal of Educational Research*, 40 (5): 365–72.

Dadds, M. (1995) *Passionate Inquiry and School Development*. London: Falmer Press.

Dahlstrom, L., Swarts, P. and Zeichner, K. (1999) 'Reconstructive education and the road to social justice: the case of post-colonial teacher education in Namibia', *International Journal of Leadership in Education*, 2 (3): 149–64.

Day, C. (1984) 'Professional learning and researcher intervention: an action research perspective', in R. Halkes and J. Olson (eds), *Teacher Thinking*. Lisse: Swets & Zwertlinger.

Elliott, J. (1976/77) 'Developing hypotheses about classrooms from teachers' practical constructs: an account of the Ford teaching project', *Interchange*, 7 (2): 2–22.

Elliott, J. (1980) 'Implications of classroom research for professional development', in E. Hoyle and J. Megarry (eds), *Professional Development of Teachers*. London: Kogan Page.

Elliott, J. (1991) *Action Research for Educational Change*. Milton Keynes: Open University Press.

Elliott, J. (1997) 'School-based curriculum development and action research in the UK', in S. Hollingsworth (ed.), *International Action Research: a Casebook for Educational Reform*. London: Falmer Press. pp. 17–28.

Elliott, J. and Ebutt, D. (eds) (1986) *Case Studies in Teaching for Understanding*. Cambridge: Cambridge Institute of Education.

Fenstermacher, G. (1994) 'The knower and the known: the nature of knowledge in research on teaching', in L. Darling-Hammond (ed.), *Review of Research in Education* (vol. 20). Washington, DC: American Educational Research Association. pp. 3–56.

Foshay, A. W. (1994) 'Action research: an early history in the US', *Journal of Curriculum and Supervision*, 9: 317–25.

Foshay, A. W., Wann, K. D. and Associates (1954) *Children's Social Values: an Action Research Study*. New York: Teachers College Press.

Freedman, S., Simons, E., Kalnin, J., Casareno, A. and the M-class teams (1999) *Inside City Schools: Investigating Literacy in Multicultural Classrooms*. New York: Teachers College Press.

Gallas, K. (1998a) *Teacher Initiated Professional Development: the Lawrence School Teacher Study Groups*. Chicago, IL: The Spencer and MacArthur Foundations.

Gallas, K. (1998b) *Sometimes I Can Be Anything: Power, Gender, and Identity in a Primary Classroom*. New York: Teachers College Press.

Gitlin, A., Bringhurst, K., Burns, M., Cooley, V., Myers, B., Price, K., Russell, R. and Tiess, P. (1992) *Teachers' Voices for School Change*. New York: Teachers College Press.

Goswami, D. and Stillman, P. (eds) (1987) *Reclaiming the Classroom: Teacher*

Research as an Agency for Change. Portsmouth, NH: Boyton Cook/
Heinemann.

Grimmett, P. (1997) 'Breaking the mold: transforming a didactic professor into a
learner-focused teacher educator', in T. Carson and D. Sumara (eds), *Action
Research as a Living Practice*. New York: Peter Lang. pp. 121–36.

Grundy, S. (1982) 'Three modes of action research', *Curriculum Perspectives*, 2
(3): 23–34.

Grundy, S. (1997) 'Participatory action research in Australia: the first wave,
1976–1986', in R. McTaggart (ed.), *Participatory Action Research: International
Contexts and Consequences*. Albany, NY: State University of New York Press.
pp. 125–49.

Grundy, S. and Kemmis, S. (1988) 'Educational action research in Australia:
the state of the art', in S. Kemmis and R. McTaggart (eds), *The Action
Research Reader* (third edition). Geelong, Vic: Deakin University Press.
pp. 321–35.

Hamilton, M. L. (ed.) (1998) *Reconceptualizing Teaching Practice: Self-study in
Teacher Education*. London: Falmer Press.

Hodgkinson, H. (1957) 'Action research: a critique', *Journal of Educational
Sociology*, 31 (4): 137–53.

Hollingsworth, S. (ed.) (1997) *International Action Research: a Casebook for
Educational Reform*. London: Falmer Press.

Holly, M. L. (April, 1990) 'Teachers' theorizing: research and professional
growth'. Paper presented at the annual meeting of the American Educational
Research Association, Boston, MA.

Huberman, M. (1996) 'Moving mainstream: taking a closer look at teacher
research', *Language Arts*, 73: 124–40.

Joyce, B., Calhoun, E., Carran, N., Simser, J., Rust, D. and Halliburton, C. (1996)
'The university town program: exploring governance structures', in B. Joyce
and E. Calhoun (eds), *Learning Experiences in School Renewal: an Exploration of
Five Successful Programs*. Eugene, OR: ERIC Clearinghouse on Educational
Management, University of Oregon. pp. 52–93.

Kemmis, S. and Grundy, S. (1997) 'Educational action research in Australia:
organizations and practice', in S. Hollingsworth (ed.), *International Action
Research: a Casebook for Educational Reform*. London: Falmer Press. pp. 40–8.

Kemmis, S. and McTaggart, R. (1988) *The Action Research Planner* (third edition).
Geelong, Vic: Deakin University Press.

Kemmler-Ernst, A. (April, 1998) 'Collaborative inquiry as a catalyst for change'.
Unpublished paper, Harvard University Graduate School of Education.

Loughran, J. and Russell, T. (ed.) (1997) *Teaching about Teaching: Purpose, Passion,
and Pedagogy in Teacher Education*. London: Falmer Press.

Macgillivray, L. (1997) 'Do what I say, not what I do: an instructor rethinks her
own teaching and research', *Curriculum Inquiry*, 27 (4): 469–88.

Martin, R. (ed.) (1995) *Practicing What We Preach: Confronting Diversity in Teacher Education*. Albany, NY: State University of New York Press.

McNiff, J. (1997) *Action Research: Principles and Practice*. London: Routledge.

McTaggart, R. (ed.) (1997) *Participatory Action Research: International Contexts and Consequences*. Albany, NY: State University of New York Press.

Mohr, M. and Maclean, M. (ed.) (1987) *Working Together: a Guide for Teacher Researchers*. Urbana, IL: National Council of Teachers of English.

Newman, J. (1998) *Tensions of Teaching*. New York: Teachers College Press.

Noffke, S. E. (1997) 'Professional, personal and political dimensions of action research', in M. Apple (ed.), *Review of Research in Education*, 22: 305–43.

Oja, S. and Smulyan, L. (1989) *Collaborative Action Research: a Developmental Approach*. London: Falmer Press.

Olson, M. W. (1990) 'The teacher as researcher: a historical perspective', in M. W. Olson (ed.), *Opening the Door to Classroom Research*. Newark, DE: International Reading Association. pp. 1–20.

Perrone, V. (1989) *Working Papers: Reflections on Teachers, Schools, and Communities*. New York: Teachers College Press.

Richert, A. (1991) 'Case methods in teacher education: using cases to teach reflection', in B. R. Tabachnick and K. Zeichner (eds), *Issues and Practices in Inquiry-oriented Teacher Education*. London: Falmer Press. pp. 130–50.

Richert, A. (1996) 'Teacher research on school change: what teachers learn and why that matters', in K. Kent (ed.), *Breaking New Ground: Teachers Action Research, a Wealth of New Learning*. Redwood City, CA: Bay Area IV Professional Development Consortium.

Richert, A. (April, 1999) 'The learning teacher for the changing school: teacher research as a methodology of change'. Paper presented at the annual meeting of the American Educational Research Association, Montreal.

Russell, T. and Korthagen, F. (ed.) (1995) *Teachers Who Teach Teachers: Reflections on Teacher Education*. London: Falmer Press.

Selener, D. (1997) *Participatory Action Research and Social Change*. Quito, Ecuador: Global Action Publications.

Shumsky, A. (1958) *The Action Research Way of Learning: an Approach to Inservice Education*. New York: Teachers College Press.

Stenhouse, L. (1968) 'The humanities curriculum project', *Journal of Curriculum Studies*, 23 (1): 26–33.

Stenhouse, L. (1976) *An Introduction to Curriculum Research and Development*. London: Heinemann.

Taba, H. and Noel, E. (1957) *Action Research: a Case Study*. Washington, DC: Association for Curriculum and Supervision.

Threatt, S., Buchanan, J., Morgan, B., Streib, L., Sugarman, J., Swenson, J., Teel, K. and Tomlinson, J. (1994) 'Teachers' voices in the conversation about teacher research', in S. Hollingsworth and H. Sockett (eds), *Teacher Research*

and *Educational Reform*. Chicago, IL: University of Chicago Press.
   pp. 223–33.

Tripp, D. (1990) 'Socially critical action research', *Theory into Practice*, 29 (3): 158–66.

Troen, V., Kamii, M. and Boles, K. (April, 1997) 'From carriers of culture to agents of change: teacher-initiated professional development in the learning/teaching collaborative inquiry seminars'. Paper presented at the annual meeting of the American Educational Research Association, Chicago, IL.

Troen, V., Kamii, M. and Boles, K. (April, 1999) 'Transformative professional development: teacher research, inquiry, and the culture of schools'. Paper presented at the annual meeting of the American Educational Research Association, Montreal.

Wagner, J. (1995) 'Research universities, schools of education, and the schools: a case of implementing cooperative research and extension in education', *Educational Policy*, 9 (1): 24–53.

Walker, M. (1995) 'Context, critique, and change: doing action research in South Africa', *Educational Action Research*, 3 (1): 9–27.

Wallace, M. (1987) 'A historical review of action research: some implications for the education of teachers in their managerial role', *Journal of Education for Teaching*, 13 (2): 97–115.

Whitehead, J. (1989) 'Creating a living educational theory from questions of the kind: how do I improve my practice?', *Cambridge Journal of Education*, 19 (1): 41–52.

Zeichner, K. (1994) 'Conceptions of reflective practice in teaching and teacher education', in G. Harvard and P. Hodkinson (eds), *Action and Reflection in Teacher Education*. Norwood, NJ: Ablex.

Zeichner, K. (1995) 'Reflections of a teacher educator working for social change', in T. Russell and F. Korthagen (eds), *Teachers Who Teach Teachers: Reflections on Teacher Education*. London: Falmer Press. pp. 11–24.

Zeichner, K. (1999a) *Action Research as Professional Development for P-12 Educators*. Washington, DC: US Department of Education.

Zeichner, K. (1999b) 'The new scholarship in teacher education', *Educational Researcher* 28 (9): 4–15.

Zeichner, K., Caro-Bruce, C. and Marion, R. (1998) *The Nature and Impact of Action Research in One Urban School District*. Chicago, IL: Spencer & McArthur Foundations.

Zeichner, K. and Dahlstrom, L. (eds) (1999) *Democratic Teacher Education Reform: the Case of Namibia*. Boulder, CO: Westview Press.

Zeichner, K. and Noffke, S. (in press) 'Practitioner research', in V. Richardson (ed.), *Handbook of Research on Teaching* (fourth edition). Washington, DC: American Educational Research Association.

Chapter 9

Addressing power and control issues in educational research[1]

R. Bishop and T. Glynn

Introduction

The general trend of research into indigenous people's lives in Aotearoa/New Zealand has been for the 'research storyteller' to be an outsider who gathered the stories of 'others', and made sense of them in terms of perceived patterns and commonalities. As a result, individuals' stories were subsumed within those of the researcher as storyteller. The researcher has been the storyteller, the narrator and the person who decides what constitutes the narrative. Researchers in the past have taken the stories of research participants and have submerged them within their own stories, and re-told these reconstituted stories in a language and culture determined by the researcher. As a result, power and control over research issues such as initiation, benefits, representation, legitimation and accountability have been traditionally decided by the imposition of the researcher's agenda, interests and concerns on the research process.

Such imposition is no longer acceptable to indigenous people such as the Maori of Aotearoa/New Zealand, who have been the focus of much research into their lives. Maori people strongly reject the continuance of researcher hegemony over Maori people's lives through the methods, methodologies and the very projects being controlled by the researcher.

This rejection of hegemony has major implications for researchers and the methods they employ. For example, when researching in Maori contexts, simply listening and recording stories of other people's experience is not acceptable. As Connelly and Clandinin (1990) point out, it is impossible for us as researchers to still our 'theorising voices'. As researchers we are constantly reflecting and seeking explanations for our experiences and the experiences of others, and to suppress this facility would distort the outcomes. Simply telling our own stories as subjective voices is not adequate either. This ignores the impact that the stories of the other research participants have had on our stories or vice versa. Instead, as researchers we need to acknowledge our participatory connectedness with the other research participants. We need to promote a means of knowing that denies distance and separation and promotes commitment and engagement. In short, questions as to how we address issues of initiation, benefits, representation, legitimation and accountability all focus on past and current practices of imposition by the researcher over all of these areas. Our question, then, is how do we address concerns about researcher imposition?

The search for a method

A major issue is the need to attempt to identify the current positioning of researchers in relation to those with whom they are working. Qualitative researchers may be less impositional, as Elliot Eisner (1991) argues, in that qualitative inquiry is concerned with sets of principles, arrays of heuristics, critical reflections and expressions that allow complexity and diversity to be acknowledged and examined. This is in contrast with the concerns of quantitative inquiry, for example about establishing a procedure, a formula or a set of rules. In qualitative inquiry, the researcher does not follow a set of how-to rules, but rather creates opportunities for the voice of the research participant to be heard for others to reflect on. This reflection will be complex and involve a variety of levels, abstractions of the reader's own consciousness. A qualitative research study may engage the reader in reflections on similar experiences of their own, in critical reflections and questioning assumptions about their own approaches to research, or in their own interpretations of the research narratives.

Qualitative research will engage the researcher in considerations of disclosure, advocacy, subjectivity, consciousness, participation, identification, positionings, and agency.

Methodologically, Eisner (1991), Reinharz (1992) and Haig-Brown (1992), who represent a range of qualitative researchers, characterise this stance in terms of there being a paucity of prescriptions in qualitative methodology, in contrast to the prescriptive, testable approach of quantitative methodology. They all argue that this distinction reflects a number of factors. These include:

1. Rather than seeking standardisation, uniformity and normalisation, qualitative inquiry seeks an idiosyncratic focus on the relationships between

individuals' strengths, ideas, aptitudes and ideologies and the cultural context within which they are located.

2. The form of the research process is influenced by style, and style is seen as personal and subjective. Far from trying to minimise personal style in order to ensure replicability, as does positivism, the individual researcher is seen as inextricably part of the work, where 'the whole self is the instrument of research' (Haig-Brown, 1992).

3. It is impossible to predict the flow of events that will unfurl, nor is it possible to predict how long a project may take; therefore, 'qualitative inquiry works best if researchers remain aware of the emerging configurations and make appropriate adjustments accordingly' (Eisner, 1991).

4. The power of individuals in the research relationship is granted recognition in that the end product of any research project is the result of the reciprocal interactions between researcher and researched. 'As in a good conversation, one listens to the other, and how, when and what one says depends upon what the other has to say' (Eisner, 1991). In this sense, conversation is a metaphor for reciprocity.

5. As Reinharz (1992) suggests, qualitative inquiry focuses 'on interpretation, relies on the researchers' immersion in social settings and aim(s) for intersubjective understanding between researchers and the person(s) studied'.

6. Qualitative inquiry rejects the idea of an external 'discoverable reality' independent of the researcher. Instead, it is necessary for researchers, by participation, to acknowledge 'that they interpret and define reality' (Reinharz, 1992).

These six factors illustrate that in qualitative inquiry there is a considerable and ongoing shift from the dominant positivist paradigm by researchers. Integral to this movement has been the realisation of the importance of meaning and interpretation of people's lives within their cultural contexts. As Thomas (1993) explains, people in their contexts are 'engaged in attempts at relating and communicating: are making efforts to understand and interpret their own behaviour and that of others in their community, context or milieu' (p. 232). Thomas suggests that one of the implications of these 'strivings and activities' is that there is a possibility of developing 'shared or negotiated meanings and shared and negotiated interpretations of both behaviours and thoughts' (p. 232). Such a stance diverts the focus of attention away from an exclusive focus on information and data and on to ideas, thoughts, perceptions and especially meanings by substituting organic, holistic metaphors for mechanistic ones.

Shifting paradigms for research: challenges from indigenous peoples

It is important to note, however, that the preceding analysis is the result of a paradigm shift within Western social science. It is also significant to note that both this research approach to constituting and defining knowledge, as well as the approach to improving its methodologies by shifting the research paradigm, is challenged by indigenous peoples. This challenge rejects the binary dialectic implied in simply replacing quantitative research with qualitative research. This challenge is focused on the impositional tendencies of all research processes that embody artificial and hegemonic power relationships (distances) between the researchers and researched. This challenge is directed at the domination of agenda-setting by researchers. Both quantitative and qualitative researchers need to address the problem of researcher imposition in their enterprises and to critique research methodologies that are rooted within the ideologies of dominant cultures.

Paradigm-shifting (after Kuhn, in Lather, 1991) need not result in any change in the relationship between the researcher and those they research. Paradigm-shifting may still perpetuate researcher domination through maintaining control of agenda-setting within the domain of the researcher.

Whatever the research method used and regardless of the methodological framework within which such a method is developed, there is the need for the theoretical framework to address Maori cultural aspirations for power and control over the issues of initiation, benefits, representation, legitimation and accountability. This needs to occur in such a way as to create a power-sharing process in the research. In other words, methods that have been selected and applied from and within the interests of the dominant discourse will have limited success in addressing Maori people's concerns about research into their lives. Neither does it follow that quantitative methods per se are inevitably linked to researcher imposition on Maori people. Given Maori people's ownership over the initiative, representation and legitimacy dimensions of a research project, the choice of a positivistic approach, embodying quantitative analysis, may be appropriate and effective for answering some research questions. Nevertheless, in this chapter we wish to examine a very popular qualitative research tool and demonstrate how it can be modified in order to address Maori priorities.

The interview as a tool for addressing researcher imposition

The interview is a very common tool used by researchers in attempts to address researcher imposition. However, interviews carry much 'cultural baggage' and assumptions from their very ubiquity. The interview itself can be a strategy, controlled by the researcher, and repressive of the position of the informant/participant. This underlies the position taken by Oakley (1981) in a critical review of the literature of the previous decades. She concluded that:

> the paradigm of the social science research interview promoted in the methodological textbooks does, then, emphasise (a) its status as a mechanical instrument of data collection; (b) its function as a specialised form of conversation in which one person asks the questions and another gives the answers; (c) its characterisation of interviewees as essentially passive individuals; and (d) its reduction of interviewers to a question-asking and rapport-promoting role (p. 36).

This approach essentially reproduces positivistic research approaches (Ballard, 1994b) which reduce both interviewer and interviewee to the status of 'depersonalised participants in the research process' (Oakley, 1981). Oakley is also critical of those who suggest that the interview be conducted in a 'non-directive' manner. Researchers in this hierarchical, 'expert-client' relationship use non-directive comments such as 'tell me more', 'why?', 'isn't that interesting' or 'uh-huh' to encourage a free association of ideas in order to reveal the 'truth' that the research has been designed to uncover in the first place.

Oakley concludes that both of these approaches to interviewing see the interviewer-interviewee relationship as one which can be defined in terms of binary relationships where:

> interviewers define the role of interviewee as subordinate; extracting information is more to be valued than yielding it; the convention of interviewer-interviewee hierarchy is a rationalisation of inequality; what is good for the interviewers is not necessarily good for the interviewees (p. 40).

Developments in interviewing have been toward mediating the tensions identified by Oakley and developing what could be termed an 'enhanced research relationship'. Oakley (1981) suggested that finding out about people through interviewing 'is best achieved when the relationship of interviewer and interviewee is non-hierarchical and when the interviewer is prepared to invest his or her own personal identity in the relationship'. The need to encourage disclosure on the part of the researcher is also elaborated by Burgess (1984), Lather (1991) and Haig-Brown (1992), researchers who work in widely divergent fields. Reinharz develops this notion of reciprocity further and suggests an orientation that is 'interviewee guided' so that subtleties are identified and reacted to, and that the meaning being expressed/sought by the interviewees becomes paramount and mutual trust is developed. Reinharz (1992) also suggests that the interview process needs to explore people's views of reality, and needs to encourage openness, trust between participants, engagement and development of potentially longlasting relationships (also in

Oakley, 1981) in order to form strong bonds between interviewer and interviewee.

Sequential, semi-structured, in-depth 'interviews as conversations'

Semi-structured or unstructured interviews (Reinharz, 1992), 'interviews as conversations' (Burgess, 1984), 'in-depth' interviews (Patton, 1990) and co-structured interviews (Tripp, 1983) are procedures designed for interviewing research participants in order to operationalise the 'enhanced research relationship'. To Reinharz (1992), semi-structured interviews offer access to people's ideas, thoughts and memories in their own words. To Burgess (1984), Oakley (1981) and Haig-Brown (1992), among others, this type of interview offers the opportunity to develop a reciprocal, dialogic relationship based on mutual trust, openness and engagement. In this relationship self-disclosure, personal investment and equality are promoted. This in effect defines a symmetrical relationship. Further, Lather (1991) suggests in-depth interviews offer a means of constructing what experiences mean to people. Tripp (1983) adds that these meanings can be constituted in terms of what people mean to say rather than simply the words they said.

The analogy of an in-depth interview as a conversation is suggested by Burgess (1984). However, Patton (1990) warns that conversation should not be taken too literally because in everyday conversations

> questions lack clarity. Answers go unheard. The sequence of questions and answers lacks direction. The person asking questions frequently interrupts the person responding (p. 108).

Therefore, conversation is best seen as a metaphor for this type of interview, which focuses on depth, detail and 'probes beneath the surface, soliciting detail and providing a holistic understanding of the interviewee's point of view (p. 108).

Semi-structured, in-depth interviews promote free interaction and opportunities for clarification and discussion between research participants through the use of open-ended questions rather than closed questions. In-depth interviews will 'more clearly reveal the existing opinions of the interviewee in the context of a world-view than will a traditional interview where the interviewer's role is confined to that of question-maker and recorder' (Tripp, 1983), as in survey research (Burgess, 1984; Eisner, 1991). Further, reflection of meaning rather than asking an interviewee to choose from a range of options predetermined and presented by an interviewer will better promote an interaction of ideas between the people participating in the interview. Tripp (1983) specifies that 'for the interviewer it is as important to learn what questions are important to the interviewee as it is to learn what questions are considered important by the interviewer' (p. 34). Hence, allowing for reciprocal design and co-joint responsibility for structuring the interview partly addresses the impositional power of the researcher to deny a symmetrical relationship.

However, 'finding out about people', 'self-disclosure' and the 'development of long-term relationships', even through a series of in-depth interviews as 'conversations' focusing on developing an 'enhanced research relationship', do not address researcher imposition so long as the interview remains a data-gathering exercise.

If the orientation of qualitative interviewing remains 'a research approach whereby the researcher plans to ask questions about a given topic but allows the data-gathering conversation itself to determine how the data is obtained' (Reinharz, 1992), the researcher's agenda is still promoted. This is so because the agenda of the interview, that of data-gathering for use by the researcher, remains the focus of the exercise. No manner of researcher disclosure, engagement, or development of long-term relationships will necessarily address what happens to the data if the focus of the interview remains solely on data collection. How those data are interpreted and used is usually implicitly, if not explicitly, out of the hands of the research participants.

As Tripp (1983) suggests, the crucial question becomes 'who controls what happens to the data and how?' (p. 34). In other words, what considerations are given to the processing of the information, the sense-making processes and the means of constructing meaning/seeking explanations? In order to address the imposition of the researcher in processing the information, we need to question what happens to data beyond the gathering stage. Perhaps more importantly, we need to address issues of representation and legitimation by questioning who writes the account of the research interview and who judges it to be fair?

Who controls what happens to the data?

When deciding how to present an analysis of data, 'the problem of finding a focus and selecting and organising what to say is crucial' (Eisner, 1991). How do you reduce events occurring in 'real time' to a 'portrait' that represents the salient features of an experience? Eisner suggests the use of an inductive approach similar to that of Glaser and Strauss's (1967) 'Grounded Theory'[2] which is described in Burgess (1984), Delamont (1992) and further developed in Strauss and Corbin (1994). This process assumes that qualitative research, by relying on induction rather than deduction, will necessarily address issues of imposition, participation and power-sharing by the formulation of themes, those recurring messages construed from the events observed and the interviews transcribed.

In the process of formulating themes, researchers are required to 'distil the material they have put together' (Eisner, 1991). The notes, interviews, ideas, comments, recollections and reflections can be used to 'inductively generate thematic categories' (p. 189).

However, an approach that leaves to the researcher the categorisation of themes and the subsequent sense and meaning construction (as Eisner suggests, the development of *a summary account of the story*) does not address the impositional tendencies inherent in this activity. Inductive development of themes may well come from the author's ideas alone. Data can be selected to fit the preconceptions of the author and data can also be selected to construct theories. Tripp (1983) suggests that the fundamental question being addressed by Eisner regarding the processing of data or, as he puts it, 'making people's views public', is really of a political (with a small 'p') nature. In this sense, then, Eisner's original 'How to?' questions render this process a quasi-positivistic search for prescription in the name of pragmatism. Instead, Tripp (1983) suggests a return to those structural issues of authority and representation: 'who controls what happens to the data, and how?' and 'in the research interview, who writes the account and judges it fair?' as being of primary concern. The approach that Eisner (1991) suggests perpetuates the imposition of the researcher's interpretation and editorial analysis and therefore locates ownership of the information with the researcher. This outcome obtains despite methods being employed which might facilitate the 'voice' of the researched person to be heard.

Tripp (1983) warns of qualitative accounts that intersperse interview quotations from the interviews of a dozen informants among the author's own narrative. The danger is that this approach may impose 'particular interpretations over which any one interviewee has absolutely no control' (p. 35). Qualifying or countering statements may be omitted, statements may be taken out of context and used to support the views, assumptions and aspirations of the author. There may be an opportunity later in the research project when the researcher sets out what has been learned from the research experience. However, to claim this is a strategy promoting power-sharing and self-determination is leaving too much to chance.

In addressing the problem of researcher control over what happens to the 'data', Opie (1989) describes a common practice that has emerged in recent years:

> In order to minimise appropriation through misrepresentation and stereotype, to expand the researcher's appreciation of the situation as a result of discussion and reworking the text with the participants, and to realign the balance of power in the research relationship, a practice has developed, which crosses disciplinary boundaries, of giving a draft of the report to participants and asking them to comment on its validity (pp. 8–9).

For example, commonly researchers will interview their subjects, then categorise these interviews, identifying themes which are developed inductively by the researcher, who then theorises, i.e. suggests explanations for the patterns that emerge inductively from earlier interviews.

However, Opie (1989) suggests that this procedure may not be sufficient. Problems may develop when disagreements arise over interpretation. Opie suggests that, should there be such disagreements, rather than engaging in further time-consuming negotiations, the researcher may subordinate their position or simply eliminate contentious material.

Further, this approach raises the issue of benefits again. The person who receives the (often huge) transcript is obliged to spend a considerable amount of time interacting with the text. The arrival of a vast colour-coded transcript in the mail, assuming recipients are interested enough to interact at the level of concentration practised by the researcher, raises the issue of the 'response cost' in terms of the 'cost of non-compliance', that is, the cost of resistance in terms of time and effort required may be too great for them to engage in, particularly if what they are asked to engage with is the analysis undertaken by the researcher rather than their being asked to reflect on what they said in terms of their own analysis. The problem may be compounded in cases of cross-cultural translation of meaning as Urion addresses (1990, in Te Hennepe, 1993). In all, a high degree of unanticipated compliance with the researcher's analysis and constructions may result in an invalid outcome. Nevertheless, returning the script to the co-participant is a necessary part of the ongoing dialogue. However, it is emphasised that engagement should be with the text and not with the analysis done by the researcher. This is to maximise opportunities for reciprocal negotiation and a collaborative construction of meaning by the participants.

Furthermore, depiction of the actual words of the research participant is often insisted upon. However, there is a danger that this strategy may replace the search for meaning through engagement in sequential discourse with a concentration on literal representation. Often, the actual words used at a particular time may not convey the full meaning that the person wanted to express. They may be able, on reflection, to express themselves in a manner that further explains or advances their position and understanding. This highlights the importance of sequential interviews that are, in Lather's (1991) terms, conducted within a framework of 'dialogic reflexivity'. This method insists that the theory generated (i.e. the meaning constructed/the explanations arrived at), must be a product of the interaction between the interview and interviewee, researcher/researched – in other words, to ensure the fair representation of the participant's views, 'negotiation of the account of meaning is essential' (Tripp, 1983).

How to convey the 'intensity of the speaking voice' (Opie, 1989) in a written text and how to identify the non-verbal factors are further complex considerations. Tripp (1983) argues that the interviewee's intended meaning may be lost in the transfer from an oral to a written account. Within the oral interview each participant is aware of their relationship with the other, assumptions are made about prior knowledge of the topic under discussion, references may be made to shared experiences, and dialogue may take the form of incomplete utterances interspersed with body language as the two attempt to clarify their understanding of the topic under discussion. Taken out of the interview context, and read by others who may not share the initial perspective and topic knowledge, the transcript may be read without the aid of visual prompts such as facial expression and body language, and as such may not convey the intended meaning. As such, Tripp views the interview (and subsequent written transcripts) as being tools useful to help the participants to reflect, modify and reflect again on their ideas in order to present the meaning they sought in a form understandable to the reader.

Therefore, the research participants are attempting to talk to the reader directly. What does this mean for the position of the researcher? If we as researchers abrogate the function of interpreter of gathered data, what is our function? Beyond participating in the research story, it would appear that our function is to act as a 'secretary' for the group, to write an account of the events as directed by the deliberations of the group of which we are a part. In the process of developing a collaboratively constructed story, we collaboratively draw out highlights, conclusions and considerations. Such 'coding' is revisited in further interviews.

Arguments may be put up for evaluation, probing and responding, positions may be challenged by suggesting the other person is wrong, that they have misconceptions, clouded views, blurred vision and so on. The aim of this approach is to explore the assumptions and the implications of the positions taken by the research participants (including the researcher as participant).

Two examples of collaborative construction of meaning

Case one: researching Canadian First Nation students' experiences with anthropology classes

Sheila Te Hennepe (1993), when reporting on researching Canadian First Nation students' experiences with anthropology classes, indicated how such an approach could be developed. At first she divided the research process into a series of phases that were distinct as to process, knowledge revealed, and limitations and problems encountered. Initially there was the phase of participating in conversations, which she describes as 'we discuss what you heard [experienced] and what it meant to you' (p. 213). This was followed by her 'analysis of what we said' (p. 214). During this second phase she coded the transcripts into 'general categories that emerged from the transcripts as topics of conversation in the stories I had been told' (p. 214). These categories were used to identify the common themes which were then used to recode the transcripts in order to generate questions from a central theme, in this case authority.

However, on reflection, Te Hennepe raised two concerns about her approach. She acknowledged that the typed script 'is the beginning of the research participants' loss of control over their words and over ways their words will be manipulated. Some might say that the speaking of the words was the beginning of the loss' (p. 218). The second concern she raised was that her coding of the interviews created a representational problem. Although she was familiar with these First Nation people's perceptions, she was outside of their actual lived experiences. The categories employed were her categories, based on her perceptions. On reflection, she suggested that 'only collaborative coding would be legitimately representational' (p. 218). Te Hennepe considers that she could have sought to create a representational language that spoke with the voices of those involved. Her concern was that by removing segments of conversation from their sense-making context, she was removing the individual from their cultural context – that cultural complexity which gives an individual 'voice'. She therefore questions how researchers, especially those from a different culture, can position themselves as creators of space where those directly involved, and with actual lived experience, 'can act and speak on their own behalf' (after Lather, 1989, in Te Hennepe, 1993). Te Hennepe suggests that in light of these considerations, the first two phases of analysis, interviewing and coding should be collapsed into one approach, seeking the authentic voice unconstrained by the categories developed by the researcher.

The third phase of Te Hennepe's research has further culturally appropriate messages for New Zealand. She said that this final phase was where 'I create a text to represent what I learned' (p. 206). This locates the researcher in a whanau (extended family) context, as teina, a learner, as a participant who is working for the good of the group and who is stating what they have learned from their tuakana (older) in the whanau.

Case two: a collaborative meta-study of five research projects conducted within Maori contexts

In a recent collaborative meta-study of five research projects conducted within Maori contexts, an attempt was made to develop and implement such an approach (Bishop, 1995, 1996). The meta-study sought to ascertain in what ways the researchers, in each of the five projects, were addressing Maori people's concerns about traditional patterns of research. The overall framework of the projects and the meta-analysis was Kaupapa Maori research, which is collectivistic and oriented toward benefiting all the research participants and their collectively determined agendas. Kaupapa Maori research is based on a growing consensus that research involving Maori knowledge and people needs to be conducted in culturally appropriate ways, that fit Maori cultural preferences, practices and aspirations in order to develop and acknowledge existing culturally appropriate approaches in the method, practice and organisation of research. The meta-study examined how a group of researchers addressed the importance of devolving power and control in the research exercise in order to promote self-determination (tino Rangatiratanga) of Maori people, i.e. to act as educational professionals in ways consistent with Article 2 of the Treaty of Waitangi. The first author talked with researchers who had accepted the challenge of positioning themselves or more probably being repositioned by and within the discursive practice that is Kaupapa Maori.

The first author's interest in investigating how other researchers addressed Maori people's concerns about research developed as the result of critical reflection on the process of conducting research within his own Maori family (Bishop, 1991b, 1994).

> However, my objective was not to judge other researchers or their projects against a set of criteria that I had established while conducting and/or critiquing my own study. Further, to ignore my own role in the process of investigation was not acceptable because I was also a participant in the projects with views, experiences and interests of my own. Hence, it seemed that a more realistic approach was to facilitate a joint construction of meaning.
>
> (Bishop, 1997b: 40)

As a result, negotiations were conducted and agreements reached to carry out a series of formal, in-depth, co-structured interviews (after Tripp, 1983; Burgess, 1984; Patton, 1990; Eisner, 1991; Reinharz, 1992). An interview schedule, which underwent constant modification, was used to guide researcher reflections on how the research community operationalises the issues of initiation, benefits, representation, legitimation and accountability within a culturally appropriate context. The interviews were to establish what extent the power to define and protect the knowledge created by the research participants was constituted within the research process. In addition, a sequence of informal 'interviews as chat' (after Haig-Brown, 1992) took place. Both formal and informal interviews were conducted within the context of co-joint participation in the projects.

The meta-study sought to investigate the first author's own position as a researcher within a co-joint reflection on shared experiences and co-joint construction of meanings about these experiences, a position where the stories of the other research participants merged with his own to create new stories. Such collaborative stories go beyond an approach that simply focuses on the cooperative sharing of experiences and focuses on connectedness, engagement, and involvement with the other research participants within the cultural world-view/discursive practice within which they function. This study sought to identify what constitutes this engagement and what implications this has for promoting self-determination/agency/voice in the research participants by examining concepts of participatory and cultural consciousness and connectedness within Maori discursive practice.

The stories that the researchers told demonstrated how they have located themselves within new 'story-lines' that address the contradictory nature of the traditional researcher/researched relationship. The language used contains the key to the new story-lines; the metaphor and imagery are those located within the research participant's domain and the researchers either were or have moved to become part of this domain. The researchers had positioned themselves or had been positioned by the use of contextually constituted metaphor within the domain where others can constitute themselves as agentic. Within this domain there are discursive practices which provide researchers with positions that enable us to carry through our negotiated lines of action.

Mishler (1986) explains this idea further by suggesting that in order to construct meaning it is necessary to appreciate how meaning is grounded in, and constructed through, discourse. Discursive practice is contextually (for example, culturally) and individually related. Meanings in discourse are neither singular nor fixed. Terms take on 'specific and contextually grounded meanings within and through the discourse as it develops and is shaped by speakers' (p. 65). A 'community of interest' between researchers and participants or among participants (call them what you will) cannot be created unless the interview is constructed so that:

> interviewers and respondents, strive to arrive together at meanings that both can understand. The relevance and appropriateness of questions and responses emerges through and is realised in the discourse itself. The standard process of analysis of interviews abstracts both questions and responses from this process. By suppressing the discourse and by assuming shared and standard meanings, this approach short-circuits the problem of meaning (p. 65).

This therefore suggests a trade-off between two extremes. The first position claims 'the words of an interview are the most accurate data and that the transcript of those words carries that accuracy with negligible loss' (Tripp, 1983). Such a position moves on from that where a narrative is recorded by a researcher. In other words, what people say should be presented unaltered and not analysed in any way beyond that which the respondent undertook. The second position maximises researcher interpretation, editorial control and ownership. This book suggests a third position where the 'coding' procedure is established and developed by the research participants as a process of 're-storying', that is the co-joint creation of further meaning. In other words, there is an attempt within the interviews and within a sequence of interviews through a process of spiral discourse to actually co-construct a mutual understanding by means of sharing experiences, thoughts and reflections.

In this meta-study, an agreed-to agenda was derived from the Kaupapa Maori research context. This agenda was used by the research participants to identify issues, descriptions, analyses and conclusions that became part of a narrative and also to identify issues that needed clarification and consideration in the next interview. Further, from this position the participants' words themselves are flexible, being of less importance than the collaboratively constructed views and meanings of the research participants. The narratives become 'co-authored statements', an agreed-upon account of the discussions that employs a 'cycle of negotiation, discussions and writing … an accurate record of the actual words spoken is of less importance than the effective transformation by the researcher of what was actually said into what the participants want written about what they said' (Tripp, 1983).

This further suggests there is the need to develop a way to conduct interviews so that the 'coding' exercise, as a product of shared meanings, becomes part of the process of description and analysis. It is suggested that sequential, semi-structured, in-depth 'interviews as conversations' conducted in a dialogic, reflexive manner need to be developed in order to facilitate ongoing collaborative analysis and construction of meaning/explanations about the experiences of the research participants. This process is termed 'spiral discourse'.

Consequently, rather than needing to reduce the distance between researcher and researched in quantitative terms (as suggested by Troyna and Carrington, 1989), spiral discourse provides a means of effecting a qualitative shift in terms of how participants relate to each other. One way of achieving this shift is by focusing on stories and narratives of these stories. Narrative inquiry requires a shift in the relationship between those traditionally constituted as researchers and those traditionally constituted as researched.

In such ways the researchers in the meta-study participated in a process that facilitated the development in people of a sense of themselves as agentic and of having an authoritative voice. This is not a result of the researcher 'allowing' this to happen nor of the researcher 'empowering' participants. It is the function of the cultural context within which the research participants position themselves, negotiate and conduct the research, that is the interactions. The cultural context positions the participants by constructing the storylines, and with them the cultural metaphors and images, as well as the 'thinking as usual', the talk/language through which research participants are constituted and researcher/researched relationships are organised. Thus the joint development of new story-lines is a collaborative effort. The researcher and the researched together rewrite the constitutive metaphors of the relationship. What makes the enterprise Maori is that it is done using Maori metaphor within a Maori cultural context.

One of the major understandings that such a process demonstrates is that whakawhanaungatanga (establishing relationships in a Maori context) is used metaphorically to give voice to a culturally positioned means of collaboratively constructing research stories in a 'culturally conscious and connected manner'. There are three major overlapping implications of whakawhanaungatanga as a research strategy. The first is that establishing and maintaining relationships is a fundamental, often extensive and ongoing part of the research process. This involves the establishment of 'whanau of interest' through a process of 'spiral discourse'. The second is that researchers understand themselves to be involved somatically in the research process; that is, physically, ethically, morally and spiritually and not just as a 'researcher' concerned with methodology. Such positionings are demonstrated in the language/metaphor used by the researchers in the stories described in this study. The third is that establishing relationships in a Maori context addresses the power and control issues fundamental to research, because it involves participatory research practices – in this context termed 'participant driven research' (Bishop, 1995, 1996) – and calls for 'researcher commitment' and not simply for removing research bias.

The researchers in the meta-study employed a number of other Maori metaphors to explain their involvement in the research process. These included hui take, koha, whitiwhiti korero, mauri, raranga korero, tuakana/teina, tino rangatiratanga, taonga tuku iho, waka and kawa. One example of how Maori metaphor sets the scene for different interaction patterns and how these interactions address the five issues of power and control is seen when researchers explain the meaning constructed of their experiences of hui and powhiri.

A hui includes a formal welcome, a powhiri, a welcome rich in cultural meaning and imagery, and cultural practices which fulfil the enormously culturally important task of recognising the relative tapu (potentiality for power) and mana of all the participants.[3] Salmond (1975) and Irwin (1992a) both detail the ritualised coming together of hui participants. Symbolically this is of enormous importance for establishing research agendas, for it is here that the relationship is established and the interaction patterns that are determined by the kawa of the marae are invoked. Full participation in the research requires the researcher to be able to engage meaningfully in the powhiri process, and to understand the power and control issues represented and addressed and their own part in this process. Once the formal welcome is complete and once the participants have been ritually joined together by the process of the powhiri, hui participants move on to the discussion of the 'take', or the matter under consideration. This usually takes place within the meeting house, a place designated for this very purpose that is free of distractions and interruptions. It is also significant that such deliberations take place within a house that is symbolically the embodiment of an ancestor, further emphasising the normality of a somatic approach to knowing in such a setting and within these processes. The participants address the matters under consideration under the guidance of kaumatua (respected elders), whose primary function is to create and monitor the correct spiritual and procedural framework within which the participants can discuss the issues before them. The 'take' is laid down, as it were, in front of all. Then people get a chance to address the issue without fear of being interrupted.

Generally the procedure at a hui is for people to speak one after another, either in sequence of left to right or of anyone participating as they see fit. People get a chance to state and restate their meanings, to revisit their meanings, and to modify, delete and adapt their meanings according to local tikanga. The discourse spirals, in that the flow of talk may seem circuitous, opinions may vary and waver, but the seeking of a collaboratively constructed story is central. The controls over proceedings are temporal in the form of kaumatua, and spiritual, as in all Maori cultural practices. The procedures are steeped in metaphoric meanings, richly abstract allusions being made constantly to cultural messages, stories, events of the past and aspirations for the future. They are also highly effective in dealing with contemporary issues and concerns of all kinds.

Rose Pere (1991) describes the key qualities of a hui as:

> respect, consideration, patience, and co-operation. People need to feel that they have the right and the time to express their point of view. You may not always agree with the speakers, but it is considered bad form to interrupt their flow of speech while they are standing on their feet; one has to wait to make a comment. People may be as frank as they like about others at the hui, but usually state their case in such a way that the person being criticised can stand up with some dignity in his/her right of reply. Once everything has been fully discussed and the members come to some form of consensus, the hui concludes with a prayer and the partaking of food (p. 44).

The aim of a hui is to reach consensus, to arrive at a jointly constructed meaning. But the decision that this has or has not been achieved rests within the Maori culture, i.e. in the kaumatua. This takes time, days if need be, or sometimes a series of hui will be held in order that the kaumatua monitoring proceedings can tell when a constructed 'voice' has been arrived at. At the departure from a hui, a process of poroporoaki takes place and is often a time when new agendas or directions are set or laid out. Again used metaphorically, poroporoaki (ritual farewells) can well be part of a research process.

Hui as a metaphor for collaborative storying

Just as storytelling is a culturally located and culturally legitimated process, so the process of collaborative story construction can be understood within Maori cultural practices. Metaphorically, the concept of a Maori hui (ceremonial meeting) describes the interactions between the participants within the interviews and the process of arriving at an agreed story/write-up of the narratives.

The situation of two or three people collaboratively constructing a story about their experiences within a particular research context can be understood within Maori cultural practices. Metaphorically, the concept of the hui (meeting) describes the interactions between the participants within the interviews and the process of arriving at an agreed collaborative story. The interviews for the meta-study were conducted within a context where there had already been a ritual of encounter, a metaphoric 'powhiri' (welcome) process in which there had already been an expression of the 'take' (subject) under discussion. These 'take' had been 'laid down' as it were, and there had already been participation by the interviewer in the activities of the researched. This was not a case where interviews were conducted with people selected by the researcher for the likelihood that they would contribute to the researcher's agenda. These interviews were a useful part of an already existing and ongoing exercise. The procedure of arriving at a collaborative consensual 'story' at a hui was replicated in the sequence of formal semi-structured, in-depth interviews and the informal 'interviews as chat' within the agreed agenda of Kaupapa Maori framework of research that were the ways in which the collaborative stories constituted the bulk of the research (see Bishop, 1996).

Conclusion

In this chapter we have suggested that in indigenous research contexts, rather than the interview being a research tool primarily used by the researcher to gather data for subsequent processing, interviews should be developed to position the researcher within co-joint reflections on shared experiences and co-joint construction of meanings about these experiences, a position where the stories of the research participants merge with that of the researcher in order to create new stories. Thomas (1993) terms this position as being part of a 'collaborative narrative construction'. Tripp (1983) refers to this as creating 'co-authored statements'. Connelly and Clandinin (1990) term it 'collaborative stories'; that is, the co-joint construction of what Ballard (1994a), terms 'research as stories'.

Interviews as collaborative storying goes beyond an approach that simply focuses on the cooperative sharing of experiences and focuses on connectedness, engagement, and involvement with the other research participants. However, what is crucial for researching in indigenous contexts is that it necessarily will take place within the cultural world-view and discursive practice within which the research participants function, make sense of their lives and understand their experiences. Both quantitative and qualitative researchers have been slow to acknowledge the importance of culture and cultural differences as key components in successful research practice and understandings.

This chapter has argued that the interview can be a means of constituting such engagement. The tendency in traditional research has been to initiate and conduct research within frameworks established by the concerns and interests of the researcher. However, promoting self-determination/agency/voice in the research participants by restructuring the research relationship and its interaction patterns offers a powerful means of addressing issues of power and control from within the domain of the participant.

In other forms of narrative inquiry, Connelly and Clandinin (1987, 1990) suggest that the research participants need to first tell their story. Therefore, in attempts at collaboration, it is the researcher as manuhiri (the visitor) who needs to be quiet/silent and attentive so that the person who has long been silenced in the research relationship has the time and space to tell their story. This contributes to removing the traditional dominance of the researcher. Note the parallel here with the role of manuhiri in relation to tangata whenua in a powhiri where the manuhiri have to wait to be called. Attentiveness in this sense as in a state of abeyance means that the researcher is waiting and willing to participate, and that their agenda, concerns and intents do not swamp the voice of the research participant. However, the 'researcher in abeyance' is willing and able to participate in a 'conversation' that is more directly related to the intents, concerns and agendas of the research participants. Such a position is respectful and means the researcher is disallowing the dominance of the self, becoming fully attentive to the other people. This allows other participants' stories to gain the authority and the validity that the researcher's story has had for so long. This initiation sets the scene and the pattern for subsequent interactions where the research participants (termed as such to remove the discursive distance established by the conceptualisation of researcher and researched) engage in an interactive, complex, holistic approach to research. This involves mutual telling and re-telling of stories by people who are living those stories. In such an approach to narrative inquiry, research participants are engaging in a discourse where meanings are contextually grounded and shift as the discourse develops and is shaped by the speakers (Mishler, 1986). In this way, research participants tell others of their experiences and relive their experiences and their stories of their experiences, their stories of their stories and so on, which is exactly what goes on in the wharenui after the whaka noa. The researcher becomes involved in the process of collaboration, of 'mutual story-telling and re-storying as the research proceeds ... a relationship in which both stories are heard' (Connelly and Clandinin, 1990). This relationship creates a setting in which the researcher becomes an inextricable part. Such an approach is similar to other contexts where the other research participants relate their story, for example at a lecture or in a wharenui (meeting house), for they have made decisions and selections regarding what and how it will be told, according to who is the listener. What is their culture? What is their status? What is their age? What is their kaupapa (agenda)? What parts of the story will be important to them? What parts will be safe to tell them? The restorying can then proceed on this basis once the relationships involved have been identified and acknowledged.

Heshusius (1994) suggests that researchers need to acknowledge their participation and attempt to develop a 'participatory consciousness'. This means becoming involved in a 'somatic, non-verbal quality of attention that necessitates letting go of the focus of self' (p. 15). Heshusius (1994) questions what we, as researchers, do after being confronted with 'subjectivities'. 'Does one evaluate them and try to manage and to restrain them? And then believe one has the research process once again under control?' (p. 15). Both these positions address 'meaningful' epistemological and methodological questions of the researcher's own choosing. Instead, Heshusius suggests researchers need to address those questions that would address moral issues, such as 'what kind of society do we have or are we constructing?' (p. 20). For example, how can racism be addressed unless those who perpetuate it become aware through a participatory consciousness of the lived reality of those who suffer? How can the researcher become aware of the meaning of Maori schooling experiences if they perpetuate an artificial 'distance' and objectify the 'subject', dealing with issues in a manner that is of interest to the researcher, rather than of concern to the subject? The message is that you have to 'live' the context in which it happens.

Rather than there being distinct stages in a research project, of 'gaining access', 'data-gathering' to 'data processing' to 'theorising', in this approach the image of a spiral, a koru (an opening fern frond) is presented as one that describes the process of continually revisiting the kaupapa (agenda) of the research. As Heshusius (1994) suggests, this is a process where 'reality is no longer to be understood as truth to be interpreted, but as mutually evolving' (p. 18). From the very first meeting, total involvement by both researcher and participant is developed. Decisions about access, description, involvement, initiation, interpretation and explanations are embedded in the very process of storytelling and re-telling where 'interviews are conducted between researcher and participant, transcripts are made, the meetings are made available for further discussion, and they become part of the ongoing narrative record'

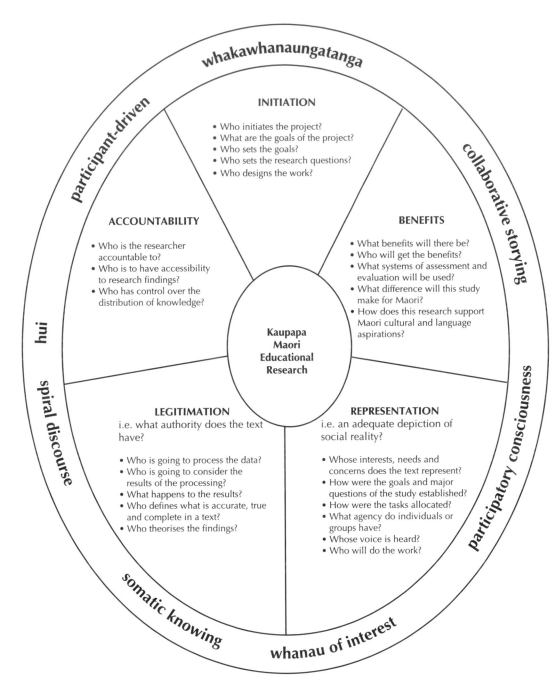

Figure 9.1 Evaluation model: research in Maori contexts

(Connelly and Clandinin, 1990). We believe that this process which describes an ongoing symmetrical relationship between researchers and participants is very applicable to the ongoing relationship between teachers and learners in classrooms.

Figure 9.1 identifies how the five issues of power and control are addressed by this approach to research. The model identifies how a researcher positioned at the centre of this diagram as the expert who participates in the process of truth-seeking known as paradigm-shifting will address these questions from a monocultural, impositional stance. The model also shows that when a researcher is repositioned within a research culture constituted by Maori cultural processes (as represented in the outer circle), then these questions must be addressed in entirely different ways and will have entirely different outcomes.

Notes

1. Much of this chapter has previously been published in Bishop, 1997b.
2. Nevertheless, Delamont (1992) describes the development of 'grounded theory' in 1967 as 'ground-breaking', in that it provided the major intellectual justification for not using statistical sampling techniques.
3. Salmond, A. (1975); Irwin, K. (1992a); Shirres, M. (1982). All detail the ritualised coming together of hui participants. Symbolically this is of enormous importance for establishing research agendas, for it is here that the relationship is established and the interaction patterns that are determined by the kawa of the marae are invoked.

References

Ballard, K. (ed.) (1994a). *Disability, family, whanau and society*. Palmerston North: Dunmore Press.

Ballard, K. (1994b). 'Inclusion, paradigms, power and participation'. In A. Dyson, C. Clark, and A. Millward, (eds). *Organisational change and special needs: school improvement or dilemma management?* London: David Fulton Publishers.

Bishop, R. (1991). 'He whakawhanaungatanga tikanga rua'. Unpublished M. A. thesis. Dunedin: Education Department, University of Otago.

Bishop, R. (1994). 'Initiating empowering research'. *New Zealand Journal of Educational Studies*, 29 (1), 1–14.

Bishop, R. (1995). 'Collaborative Research Stories: Whakawhanaungatanga'. Unpublished PhD thesis. Dunedin: Education Department, University of Otago.

Bishop, R. (1996). *Collaborative research stories: Whakawhanaungatanga.* Palmerston North: Dunmore Press.

Bishop, R. (1997). 'Interviewing as collaborative storying'. *Education Research and Perspectives.* 24, (1) 28–47.

Burgess, R. G. (1984). *In the field: An introduction to field research.* New York: The Falmer Press.

Connelly, F. M. and Clandinin, D. J. (1987). 'On narrative method, biography and narrative unities in the study of teaching'. *The Journal of Educational Thought*, 21 (3), 130–139.

Connelly, M. and Clandinin, J. (1990). 'Stories of experience and narrative inquiry'. *Educational Researcher*, June-July, 2–14.

Delamont, S. (1992). *Fieldwork in educational settings: Methods, pitfalls and perspectives.* London: The Falmer Press.

Eisner, E. W. (1991). *The enlightened eye: qualitative inquiry and the enhancement of educational practice.* New York: Teachers' College Press.

Glaser, B. and Strauss, A. (1967). *The discovery of grounded theory: strategies for qualitative research.* Chicago: Aldine.

Haig-Brown, C. (1992). 'Choosing border work'. *Canadian Journal of Native Education*, 19 (1) 96–115.

Heshusius, L. (1994). 'Freeing ourselves from objectivity: Managing subjectivity or turning toward a participatory mode of consciousness?' *Educational Researcher.* 23 (3) 15–22.

Irwin, K. (1992). 'Towards theories of Maori feminisms'. In R. Du Plessis with P. Bunkle (eds). *Feminist voices: women's studies texts for Aotearoa/New Zealand.* Auckland: Oxford University Press.

Kuhn, T. (1970). *The structure of scientific revolutions.* Chicago: University of Chicago Press.

Lather, P. (1991). *Getting smart: Feminist research and pedagogy within the postmodern.* London: Routledge.

Mishler, E. (1986). *Research interviewing: Context and narrative.* Cambridge: Harvard University Press.

Oakley, A. (1981). 'Interviewing women: A contradiction in terms'. In H. Roberts (ed.). *Doing feminist research.* London: Routledge (pp. 30–61).

Opie, A. (1989). 'Qualitative methodology, deconstructive readings, appropriation of the 'other' and empowerment'. A paper presented at the SAA Conference, Victoria University of Wellington. November.

Patton, M. (1990). *Qualitative evaluation and research methods* (2nd ed.). Newbury: Sage Publications.

Pere, R. (1991). *Te Wheke: A celebration of infinite wisdom*. Gisborne: Ao Ako.

Reinharz, S. (1992). *Feminist methods in social research*. Oxford: Oxford University Press.

Salmond, A. (1975). *Hui: A study of Maori ceremonial greetings*. Auckland: Reed and Methuen.

Shirres, M. (1982). *Tapu. Journal of the Polynesian Society*, 91 (1) 29–52.

Strauss, A. and Corbin, J. (1994). 'Grounded theory methodology'. In N. K. Denzin and Y. S. Lincoln (eds). *Handbook of qualitative research*. London: Sage Publications. (pp. 273–285).

Te Hennepe, S. (1993). 'Issues of respect: Reflections of First Nation Students' experiences in postsecondary anthropology classrooms'. *Canadian Journal of Native Education*, 20 (2), 193–260.

Thomas, D. (1993). 'Treasonable or trustworthy text: Reflections on teacher narrative'. *Journal of Education and Teaching*. 19 (4&5) 231–249.

Tripp, D. H. (1983). 'Co-authorship and negotiation: The interview as act of creation'. *Interchange*, 14 (3), 32–45.

Troyna, B. and Carrington, B. (1989). ' "Whose side are we on?": Ethical dilemmas in research on "race" and education'. In R. G. Burgess (ed.). *The Ethics of Educational Research*. New York: The Falmer Press.

PART 3
Cultural issues

Chapter 10

Culture, mind and education

J. Bruner

Fundamental changes have been altering conceptions about the nature of the human mind in the decades since the cognitive revolution. These changes, it now seems clear in retrospect, grew out of two strikingly divergent conceptions about how mind works. The first of these was the hypothesis that mind could be conceived as a computational device. The other was the proposal that mind is both constituted by and realized in the use of human culture. The two views led to very different conceptions of the nature of mind itself, and of how mind should be cultivated. Each led its adherents to follow distinctively different strategies of inquiry about how mind functions and about how it might be improved through 'education.'

The first or *computational* view is concerned with *information processing:* how finite, coded, unambiguous information about the world is inscribed, sorted, stored, collated, retrieved, and generally managed by a computational device. It takes information as its given, as something already settled in relation to some pre-existing, rule-bound code that maps onto states of the world.[1] This so-called 'well-formedness' is both its strength and its shortcoming, as we shall see. For the process of knowing is often messier, more fraught with ambiguity than such a view allows.

This brings us directly to the second approach to the nature of mind – call it *culturalism*. It takes its inspiration from the evolutionary fact that mind could not exist save for culture. For the evolution of the hominid mind is linked to the development of a way of life where 'reality' is represented by a symbolism shared by members of a cultural community in which a technical-social way of life is both organized and construed in terms of that symbolism. This symbolic mode is not only shared by a community, but conserved, elaborated, and passed on to succeeding generations who, by virtue of this transmission, continue to maintain the culture's identity and way of life.

Culture in this sense is *superorganic*.[2] But it shapes the minds of individuals as well. Its individual expression inheres in *meaning making*, assigning meanings to things in different settings on particular occasions. Meaning making involves situating encounters with the world in their appropriate cultural contexts in order to know 'what they are about.' Although meanings are 'in the mind,' they have their origins and their significance in the culture in which they are created. It is this cultural situatedness of meanings that assures their negotiability and, ultimately, their communicability. Whether 'private meanings' exist is not the point; what is important is that meanings provide a basis for cultural exchange. On this view, knowing and communicating are in their nature highly interdependent, indeed virtually inseparable. For however much the individual may seem to operate on his or her own in carrying out the quest for meanings, nobody can do it unaided by the culture's symbolic systems. It is culture that provides the tools for organizing and understanding our worlds in communicable ways. The distinctive feature of human evolution is that mind evolved in a fashion that enables human beings to utilize the tools of culture. Without those tools, whether symbolic or material, man is not a 'naked ape' but an empty abstraction.

Culture, then, though itself man-made, both forms and makes possible the workings of a distinctively human mind. On this view, learning and thinking are always *situated* in a cultural setting and always dependent upon the utilization of cultural resources.[3] Even individual variation in the nature and use of mind can be attributed to the varied opportunities that different cultural settings provide, though these are not the only source of variation in mental functioning.

Like its computational cousin, culturalism seeks to bring together insights from psychology, anthropology, linguistics, and the human sciences generally, in order to reformulate a model of mind. But the two do so for radically different purposes. Computationalism is interested in any and all ways in which information is organized and used – information in the well-formed and finite sense mentioned earlier, regardless of the guise in which information processing is realized. In this broad sense, it recognizes no disciplinary boundaries, not even the boundary between human and non-human functioning. Culturalism, on the other hand, concentrates exclusively on how human beings in cultural communities create and transform meanings.

I want to set forth in this chapter some principal motifs of the cultural approach and explore how these relate to education.

Let me set out some tenets that guide a psycho-cultural approach to education. In doing so I shall commute back and forth between questions about the nature of mind and about the nature of culture, for a theory of education necessarily lies at the intersect between them. We shall, in consequence, constantly be inquiring about the interaction between the powers of individual minds and the means by which the culture aids or thwarts their realization. And this will inevitably involve us in a never-ending assessment of the fit between what any particular culture deems essential for a good, or useful, or worthwhile way of life, and how individuals adapt to these demands as they impinge on their lives. We shall be particularly mindful of the resources that a culture provides in making this fit possible. These are all matters that relate directly to how a culture or society manages its system of education, for education is a major embodiment of a culture's way of life, not just a preparation for it.[4]

Here, then, are the tenets and some of their consequences for education.

1. The perspectival tenet. First, about meaning making. The meaning of any fact, proposition, or encounter is relative to the perspective or frame of reference in terms of which it is construed. A treaty that legitimizes the building of the Panama Canal, for example, is an episode in the history of North American imperialism. It is also a monumental step in the history of inter-ocean transportation, as well as a landmark in man's effort to shape nature to his own convenience at whatever cost. To understand well what something 'means' requires some awareness of the alternative meanings that can be attached to the matter under scrutiny, whether one agrees with them or not.

Understanding something in one way does not preclude understanding it in other ways. Understanding in any one particular way is only 'right' or 'wrong' from the particular perspective in terms of which it is pursued.[5] But the 'rightness' of particular interpretations, while dependent on perspective, also reflects rules of evidence, consistency, and coherence. Not everything goes. There are inherent criteria of rightness, and the possibility of alternative interpretations does not license all of them equally. A perspectival view of meaning making does *not* preclude common sense or 'logic.' Something that happens a century after an event cannot be taken as a 'cause' or 'condition' of that event.

Interpretations of meaning reflect not only the idiosyncratic histories of individuals, but also the culture's canonical ways of constructing reality. Nothing is 'culture free,' but neither are individuals simply mirrors of their culture. It is the interaction between them that both gives a communal cast to individual thought and imposes a certain unpredictable richness on any culture's way of life, thought, or feeling.

Life in culture is, then, an interplay between the versions of the world that people form under its institutional sway and the versions of it that are products of their individual histories. It rarely conforms to anything resembling a cookbook of recipes or formulas, for it is a universal of all cultures that they contain factional or institutional interests. Nonetheless, any particular individual's idiosyncratic interpretations of the world are constantly subject to judgment against what are taken to be the canonical beliefs of the culture at large. Such communal judgments, though often governed by 'rational' and evidentiary criteria, are just as often dominated by commitments, tastes, interests, and expressions of adherence to the culture's values relating to the good life, decency, legitimacy, or power.

An 'official' educational enterprise presumably cultivates beliefs, skills, and feelings in order to transmit and explicate its sponsoring culture's ways of interpreting the natural and social worlds. And as we shall see later, it also plays a key role in helping the young construct and maintain a concept of Self. In carrying out that function, it inevitably courts risk by 'sponsoring,' however implicitly, a certain version of the world. Or it runs the risk of offending some interests by openly examining views that might be taken as like the culture's canonically tabooed ones. That is the price of educating the young in societies whose canonical interpretations of the world are multivocal or ambiguous. But an educational enterprise that fails to take the risks involved becomes stagnant and eventually alienating.

It follows from this, then, that effective education is always in jeopardy either in the culture at large or with constituencies more dedicated to maintaining a status quo than to fostering flexibility. The corollary of this is that when education narrows its scope of interpretive inquiry, it reduces a culture's power to adapt to change. And in the contemporary world, change is the norm.

In a word, the perspectival tenet highlights the interpretive, meaning-making side of human thought while, at the same time, recognizing the inherent risks of discord that may result from cultivating this deeply human side of mental life. It is this double-facing, Janus-like aspect of education that makes it either a somewhat dangerous pursuit or a rather drearily routine one.

2. The constraints tenet. The forms of meaning making accessible to human beings in any culture are constrained in two crucial ways. The first inheres in the nature of human mental functioning itself. Our evolution as a species has specialized us into certain characteristic ways of knowing, thinking, feeling, and perceiving. We cannot, even given our most imaginative efforts, construct a concept of Self that does not impute some causal influence of prior mental states on later ones. We cannot seem to accept a version of our own mental lives that denies that what we thought before affects what we think now. We are obliged to experience ourselves as invariant across circumstances and continuous across time. Moreover, to pick up a theme that will concern us later, we need to conceive of ourselves as 'agents' impelled by self-generated intentions. And we see others in the same way. In answer to those who deny this version of selfhood on philosophical or 'scientific' grounds, we reply simply, 'But that's how it is: can't you *see?*'

Our legal system takes it as a given and constructs a *corpus juris* based upon notions like 'voluntary consent,' 'responsibility,' and the rest. It does not matter whether 'selfhood' can be proved scientifically or whether it is merely a 'fiction' of folk psychology. We simply take it as in the 'nature of human nature.'

Such intrinsic constraints on our capacities to interpret are by no means limited only to subjective concepts like 'selfhood.' They even limit our ways of conceiving of such presumably impersonal, 'objective' matters as time, space, and causality. We see 'time' as having a homogeneous continuity – as flowing evenly whether measured by clocks, phases of the moon, climatic changes, or any other form of recurrence. Discontinuous or quantal conceptions of time offend common sense to such an extent that we come to believe that continuous time is the state of nature that we experience directly. And this despite the fact that Immanuel Kant, one of the most highly honored philosophers in the Western tradition, made so strong a case for time and space as categories of mind rather than facts of nature. Faced with the fact, adduced by anthropologists, that there are local cultural variations in conceptions of time and space, and that these have practical implications in a culture's ways of life and thought,[6] we tend to 'naturalize' them by labeling them exotic. It seems to be a human universal that we nominate certain forms of interpreted experience as hard-edged, objective realities rather than 'things of the mind.' And it is widely believed, both among lay people and scientists, that the 'nominees' for such objective status reflect certain natural or native predispositions to think and interpret the world in a particular way.

These universals are generally considered to constitute the 'psychic unity of mankind.' They can be considered as limits on human capacity for meaning making. And they require our attention because they presumably reduce the range of the perspectival tenet discussed in the preceding section. I think of them as constraints on human meaning making, and it is for that reason that I have labeled this section 'the constraints tenet.' These constraints are generally taken to be an inheritance of our evolution as a species, part of our 'native endowment.'

But while they may reflect the evolution of the human mind, these constraints should not be taken as man's *fixed* native endowment. They may be common to the species, but they also reflect how we represent the world through language and folk theories. And they are not immutable. Euclid, after all, finally altered our way of conceiving of, even looking at, space. And in time, doubtless, Einstein will have done the same. Indeed, the very predispositions that we take to be 'innate' most often require shaping by exposure to some communally shared notational system, like language. Despite our presumably native endowment, we seem to have what Vygotsky called a Zone of Proximal Development,[7] a capacity to recognize ways beyond that endowment.

The educational implications that follow from the foregoing are both massive and subtle. If pedagogy is to empower human beings to go beyond their 'native' predispositions, it must transmit the 'toolkit' the culture has developed for doing so. Obviously, not everybody benefits equally from instruction in the culture's toolkit. But it hardly follows that we should instruct only those with the most conspicuous talent to benefit from such instruction. That is a political or economic decision that should never be allowed to take on the status of an evolutionary principle. Decisions to cultivate 'trained incompetencies' will concern us presently.

I mentioned *two* constraints on human mental activity at the start of this discussion. The second comprises those constraints imposed by the symbolic systems accessible to human minds generally – limits imposed, say, by the very nature of language – but more particularly, constraints imposed by the different languages and notational systems accessible to different cultures. The latter is usually called the Whorf-Sapir hypothesis[8] – that thought is shaped by the language in which it is formulated and/or expressed.

As for the 'limits of language,' not much can be said with any certainty – or with much clarity. It has never been clear whether our ability to entertain certain notions inheres in the nature of our minds or in the symbolic systems upon which mind relies in carrying out its mental operations.

As for the Whorf-Sapir hypothesis, its power and reach are also still not clearly understood.[9] But as with the 'limits of language' question, it poses an interesting question for the cultural psychology of education. All that is known for sure is that consciousness or 'linguistic awareness' seems to reduce the constraints imposed by any symbolic system.[10] The real victims of the limits of language or of the Whorfian hypothesis are those least aware of the language they speak.

The pedagogical implications of the foregoing are strikingly obvious. Since the limits of our inherent mental predispositions can be transcended by having recourse to more powerful symbolic systems, one function of education is to equip human beings with the needed symbolic systems for doing so. And if the limits imposed by the languages we use are expanded by increasing our 'linguistic awareness,' then another function of pedagogy is to cultivate such awareness. We may not succeed in transcending all the limits imposed in either case, but we can surely accept the more modest goal of improving thereby the human capacity for construing meanings and constructing realities. In sum, then, 'thinking about thinking' has to be a principal ingredient of any empowering practice of education.

3. The constructivism tenet. This tenet has already been implied in all that has gone before. But it is worth making explicit. The 'reality' that we impute to the 'worlds' we inhabit is a constructed one. Reality construction is the product of meaning making shaped by traditions and by a culture's toolkit of ways of thought. In this sense, education must be conceived as aiding young humans in learning to use the tools of meaning making and reality construction, the better to adapt to the world in which they find themselves and to help in the process of changing it as required. In this sense, it can even be conceived as akin to helping people become better architects and better builders.

4. The interactional tenet. Passing on knowledge and skill, like any human exchange, involves a subcommunity in interaction. At the minimum, it involves a 'teacher' and a 'learner' – or if not a teacher in flesh and blood, then a vicarious one like a book, or film, or display, or a 'responsive' computer.

It is principally through interacting with others that children find out what the culture is about and how it conceives of the world. Unlike any other species, human beings deliberately teach each other in settings outside the ones in which the knowledge being taught will be used.

It is customary to say that this specialization rests upon the gift of language. But perhaps more to the point, it also rests upon our astonishingly well developed talent for 'intersubjectivity' – the human ability to understand the minds of others, whether through language, gesture, or other means.[11] It is not just words that make this possible, but our capacity to grasp the role of the settings in which words, acts, and gestures occur. We are the intersubjective species par excellence. It is this that permits us to 'negotiate' meanings when words go astray.

Our Western pedagogical tradition hardly does justice to the importance of intersubjectivity in transmitting culture. Indeed, it often clings to a preference for a degree of explicitness that seems to ignore it. So teaching is fitted into a mold in which a single, presumably omniscient teacher explicitly tells or shows presumably unknowing learners something they presumably know nothing about. Even when we tamper with this model, as with 'question periods' and the like, we still remain loyal to its unspoken precepts. I believe that one of the most important gifts that a cultural psychology can give to education is a reformulation of this impoverished conception. For only a very small part of educating takes place on such a one-way street – and it is probably one of the least successful parts.

So back to the innocent but fundamental question: how best to conceive of a subcommunity that specializes in learning among its members? One obvious answer would be that it is a place where, among other things, learners help each other learn, each according to their abilities. And this, of course, need not exclude the presence of somebody serving in the role of teacher. It simply implies that the teacher does not play that role as a monopoly, that learners 'scaffold' for each other as well. The antithesis is the 'transmission' model first described, often further exaggerated by an emphasis on transmitting 'subject matter.' But in most matters of achieving mastery, we also want learners to gain good judgment, to become self-reliant, to work well with each other. And such competencies do not flourish under a one-way 'transmission' regimen. Indeed, the very institutionalization of schooling may get in the way of creating a subcommunity of learners who bootstrap each other.

Consider the more 'mutual' community for a moment. Typically, it models ways of doing or knowing, provides opportunity for emulation, offers running commentary, provides 'scaffolding' for novices, and even provides a good context for teaching deliberately. It even makes possible that form of job-related division of labor one finds in effective work groups: some serving pro tem as 'memories' for the others, or as record keepers of 'where things have got up to now,' or as encouragers or cautioners. The point is for those in the group to help each other get the lay of the land and the hang of the job.

One of the most radical proposals to have emerged from the cultural-psychological approach to education is that the classroom be reconceived as just such a subcommunity of mutual learners, with the teacher orchestrating the proceedings. Note that, contrary to traditional critics, such subcommunities do not reduce the teacher's role nor his or her 'authority.' Rather, the teacher takes on the additional function of encouraging others to share it. Just as the omniscient narrator has disappeared from modern fiction, so will the omniscient teacher disappear from the classroom of the future.

There is obviously no single formula that follows from the cultural-psychological approach to interactive, intersubjective pedagogy. For one thing, the practices adopted will vary with subject: poetry and mathematics doubtless require different approaches. Its sole precept is that where human beings are concerned, learning (whatever else it may be) is an interactive process in which people learn from each other, and not just by showing and telling.

5. The externalization tenet. A French cultural psychologist, Ignace Meyerson,[12] first enunciated an idea that the main function of all collective cultural activity is to produce 'works' – *oeuvres*, as he called them, works that, as it were, achieve an existence of their own. In the grand sense, these include the arts and sciences of a culture, institutional structures such as its laws and its markets, even its 'history' conceived as a canonical version of the past. But there are minor oeuvres as well: those 'works' of smaller groupings that give pride, identity, and a sense of continuity to those who participate, however obliquely, in their making. These may be 'inspirational' – for example, our school soccer team won the county championship six years ago, or our famous Bronx High School of Science has 'produced' three Nobel Laureates. Oeuvres are often touchingly local, modest, yet equally identity-bestowing, such as this remark by a 10-year-old student: 'Look at *this* thing we're working on if you want to see how *we* handle oil spills.'[13]

The benefits of 'externalizing' such joint products into oeuvres have too long been overlooked. First on the list, obviously, is that collective oeuvres produce and sustain group solidarity. They help *make* a community, and communities of mutual learners are no exception. But just as important, they promote a sense of the division of labor that goes into producing a product: Todd is our real computer wonk, Jeff's terrific at making graphics, Alice and David are our 'word geniuses,' Maddalena is fantastic at explaining things that puzzle some of the rest of us.

I can see one other benefit from externalizing mental work into a more palpable oeuvre, one that we psychologists have tended to ignore. Externalization produces a *record* of our mental efforts, one that is 'outside us' rather than vaguely 'in memory.' It is somewhat like producing a draft, a rough sketch, a 'mock-up.' 'It' takes over our attention as something that, in its own right, needs a transitional paragraph, or a less frontal perspective there, or a better 'introduction.' 'It' relieves us in some measure from the always difficult task of 'thinking about our own thoughts' while often accomplishing the same end. 'It' embodies our thoughts and intentions in a form more accessible to reflective efforts.

All viable cultures, Ignace Meyerson noted, make provisions for conserving and passing on their 'works.' Laws get written down, codified, and embodied in the procedure of courts. Law schools train people in the ways of a 'profession' so that the *corpus juris* can be assured for the future.

Obviously, a school's classroom is no match for the law in tradition-making. Yet it can have long-lasting influence. We carry with us habits of thought and taste fostered in some nearly forgotten classroom by a certain teacher. I can remember one who made us relish as a class 'less obvious' interpretations of historical happenings. We lost our embarrassment about offering our 'wilder' ideas. She helped us invent a tradition.[14] I still relish it. Can schools and class-rooms be designed to foster such tradition-inventing? Denmark is experimenting with keeping the same group of children and teachers together through all the primary grades – an idea that goes back to Steiner. Does that turn 'work' into 'works' with a life of their own? Modern mobility is, of course, the enemy of all such aspirations. Yet the creation and conservation of culture in shared works is a matter worth reflecting upon.

Externalizing, in a word, rescues cognitive activity from implicitness, making it more public, negotiable, and 'solidary.' At the same time, it makes it more accessible to subsequent reflection and metacognition. Probably the greatest milestone in the history of externalization was literacy, putting thought and memory 'out there' on clay tablets or paper. Computers and e-mail may represent another step forward. But there are doubtless myriad ways in which jointly negotiated thought can be communally externalized as oeuvres – and many ways in which they can be put to use in schools.

6. The instrumentalism tenet. Education, however conducted in whatever culture, always has consequences in the later lives of those who undergo it. Everybody knows this; nobody doubts it. We also know that these consequences are instrumental in the lives of individuals, and even know that, in a less immediately personal sense, they are instrumental to the culture and its various institutions (the latter are discussed in the following tenet). Education, however gratuitous or decorative it may seem or profess to be, provides skills, ways of thinking, feeling, and speaking, that later may be traded for 'distinctions' in the institutionalized 'markets' of a society. In this deeper sense, then, education is never neutral, never without social and economic consequences. However much it may be claimed to the contrary, education is always political in this broader sense.

There are two pervasive considerations that need to be taken into account in pursuing the implications of these hard-edged facts. One has to do with *talent*; the other with *opportunity*. And while the two are by no means unrelated, they need to be discussed separately first.

About talent, it is by now obvious that it is more multifaceted than any single score, like an IQ test, could possibly reveal. Not only are there many ways of using mind, many ways of knowing and constructing meanings, but they serve many functions in different situations. These ways of using mind are enabled, indeed often brought into being, by learning to master what I earlier described as a culture's 'toolkit' of symbolic systems and speech registers. There is thinking and meaning making for intimate situations different in kind from what one uses in the impersonal setting of a shop or office.

Some people seem to have great aptitude in using certain powers of mind and their supporting registers, others less. Howard Gardner has made a good case for certain of these aptitudes (he calls them 'frames of mind') having an innate and universal basis – like the ability to deal with quantitative relations, or with linguistic subtleties, or with skilled movement of the body in dance, or with sensing the feelings of others.[15] And he is engaged in constructing curricula for fostering these differing aptitudes.

Beyond the issue of differing native aptitudes, however, it is also the case that different cultures place different emphasis upon the skilled use of different modes of thought and different registers. Not everybody is supposed to be numerate, but if you occupy the role of engineer, you're something of a queer duck if you're not. But everybody is supposed to be passingly competent in managing interpersonal relations. Different cultures distribute these skills differently. And these very rapidly get 'typed' and consolidated through training and schooling: girls used to be considered more 'sensitive' to poetry, were given more experience in it, and more often than not *became* more sensitive. But this is a harmless example of the kinds of considerations that affect the *opportunity* young people have for developing the skills and ways of thinking that they will later trade for distinctions and rewards in the larger society.

There are many uglier features of opportunity that blight lives far more profoundly. Racism, social-class entitlements, and prejudice, all of them amplified by the forms of poverty they create, have powerful effects on how much and how we educate the young. Indeed, even the so-called innate talents of children from 'socially tainted' backgrounds are altered before they ever get to school – in ghettos, barrios, and those other settings of poverty, despair, and defiance that seem to suppress and divert the mental powers of the young who 'grow up' in them. Indeed, it was principally to counteract these early blighting effects of poverty (and, of course, racism) that Head Start was founded. But schools themselves, given that they are locally situated, also tend to continue and perpetuate the subcultures of poverty or defiance that initially nipped or diverted children's 'natural' talents of mind in the first place.

Schools have always been highly selective with respect to the uses of mind they cultivate – which uses are to be considered 'basic,' which 'frills,' which the school's responsibility and which the responsibility of others, which for girls and which for boys, which for working-class children and which for 'swells.' Some of this selectivity was doubtless based on considered notions about what the society required or what the individual needed to get along. Much of it was a spillover of folk or social class tradition. Even the more recent and seemingly obvious objective of equipping all with 'basic literacy' is premised on moral-political grounds, however pragmatically those grounds may be justified. School curricula and classroom 'climates' always reflect inarticulate cultural values as well as explicit plans; and these values are never far removed from considerations of social class, gender, and the prerogatives of social power.

Nothing could be more expressive of a culture than the conflicts and compromises that swirl around quasi-educational questions of this order. What is striking in most democratic states is that the compromises that emerge initially get buried in the rhetoric of official blandness, after which (and partly as a result of which) they become candidates for bitter and rather poorly considered attack. All children should have the same curricula? Of course. With increased community awareness, formerly innocent issues like curriculum soon become political ones – and quite appropriately so. The trouble, of course, is that purely political debate specializes in oversimplification. And these are not simple issues.

So the 'underground curriculum' continues to loom larger – a school's way of adapting a curriculum to express its attitudes toward its pupils, its racial attitudes, and the rest. And in the community's politicized reaction, political slogans become at least as determinative of educational policy as do theories about the cultivation of the multiple powers of mind.

Surely one of the major educational tenets of a cultural psychology is that the school can never be considered as culturally 'free standing.' *What* it teaches, what modes of thought and what 'speech registers' it actually cultivates in its pupils, cannot be isolated from how the school is situated in the lives and culture of its students. For a school's curriculum is not only *about* 'subjects.' The chief subject matter of school, viewed culturally, is school itself. That is how most students experience it, and it determines what meaning they make of it.

This, of course, is what I mean by the 'situatedness' of school and school learning. Yet, for all its pervasiveness, there is little question that, with thought and will, it can be changed. Change can occur even by little symbolic innovations – like creating a chess club in a ghetto school, and providing real coaching. But bits of symbolism scarcely touch the problem at large.

None of this is new. What does the cultural psychologist have to say about such matters? Certainly one general thing: education does not stand alone, and it cannot be designed as if it did. It exists in a culture. And culture, whatever else it is, is also about power, distinctions, and rewards. We have, in the laudable interest of protecting freedom of thought and instruction, officially buffered schools against political pressures. School is 'above' politics. In some important sense, this is surely true – but it is a threadbare truth. Increasingly, we see something quite different. For, as it were, the secret is out. Even the so-called man in the street knows that how one equips minds matters mightily later in our postindustrial, technological era. The public, to be sure, has a rather unformed sense of this – and certainly the press does. But they are aware. The *New York Times* carried as front-page news in the spring of 1995 that achievement levels had gone up in the city's schools; and Dublin's *Irish Times* in the summer of that same year carried on its front page the news that Irish students had scored 'above the average' in a comparative study of reading ability in European schools.

Why not, then, treat education for what it is? It has always been 'political,' though cryptically so in more settled, less aware times. There has now been a revolution in public awareness. But it has not been accompanied by a comparable revolution in our ways of taking this awareness into account in the forging of educational policies and practices. All of which is not to propose that we 'politicize' education, but simply that we recognize that it is already politicized and that its political side needs finally to be taken into account more explicitly, not simply as though it were 'public protest.' I will return to this issue in more detail later in this chapter.

7. The institutional tenet. My seventh tenet is that as education in the developed world becomes institutionalized, it behaves as institutions do and often must, and suffers certain problems common to all institutions. What distinguishes it from others is its special role in preparing the young to take a more active part in other institutions of the culture. Let us explore now what this implies.

Cultures are not simply collections of people sharing a common language and historical tradition. They are composed of institutions that specify more concretely what roles people play and what status and respect these are accorded – though the culture at large expresses its way of life through institutions as well. Cultures can also be conceived as elaborate exchange systems,[16] with media of exchange as varied as respect, goods, loyalty, and services. Exchange systems become focalized and legitimized in institutions which provide buildings, stipends, titles, and the rest. They are further legitimized by a complex symbolic apparatus of myths, statutes, precedents, ways of talking and thinking, and even uniforms. Institutions impose their 'will' through coercion, sometimes implicit as in incentives and disincentives, sometimes explicit as in restriction backed by the power of the state, such as the disbarring of a lawyer or the refusal of credit to a defaulting merchant.

Institutions do the culture's serious business. But for all that, they do so through an unpredictable mix of coercion and voluntarism. I say 'unpredictable' because it remains perpetually unclear both to participants in a culture and to those who observe it from 'outside' when and how the power of enforcement will be brought to bear by those delegated or otherwise thought privileged to use it. So if it can be said that a culture's institutions do 'serious business,' it can equally be said that it is often ambiguous and uncertain business.

It is also characteristic of human cultures that individuals rarely owe allegiance to any single institution: one 'belongs' to a family of origin and one by marriage, an occupational group, a neighborhood, as well as to more general groups like a nation or a social class. Each institutional grouping struggles to achieve its distinctive pattern of rights and responsibilities. This adds further to the inherent ambiguity of life in culture. As Walter Lippmann and John Dewey long ago pointed out,[17] how any given individual forms his interpretation on issues of public concern will usually involve him in a conflict of interests and identities. For while institutions may complement each other functionally, they also compete for privilege and power. Indeed, the power of a culture inheres in its capacity to integrate its component institutions through a dialectic of conflict resolution.

Institutions, as Pierre Bourdieu has suggested,[18] provide the 'markets' where people 'trade' their acquired skills, knowledge, and ways of constructing meanings for 'distinctions' or privileges. Institutions often compete in getting their 'distinctions' prized above those of others, but the competition must never be 'winner take all,' for institutions are mutually dependent upon each other. Lawyers and businessmen need each other as much as patients and doctors do.

While all this may at first seem remote from schools and the process of education, the remoteness is an illusion. Education is up to its elbows in the struggle for distinctions. The very expressions *primary, secondary*, and *tertiary* are metaphors for it. It has even been argued recently that the 'new' bourgeoisie in France after the Revolution used the schools as one of their principal tools for 'turning around' the system of prestige and distinction previously dominated by the aristocracy and gentry of the *ancien régime*.[19] Indeed, the very concept of a meritocracy is precisely an expression of the new power that schools are expected to exercise in fixing the distribution of distinctions in contemporary bureaucratic society.

It was the 'tug' of institutional competition that mainly concerned us in the preceding section, often converted into a more conventionalized political form. I commented there that there had been an 'evolution in awareness' about education. Let me pursue that now. Few democracies today are short of cultural critics who bring educational issues before the public, sometimes vividly: a Paulo Freire in Latin America, a Pierre Bourdieu in France, a Neil Postman in America, or an A. H. Halsey in Britain. There is lively public discussion of education in virtually every developed country of the world. Despite that, most countries still lack public forums for informed consideration of educational issues.

But there is more to the matter than public opinion and the need to inform it. For, as I remarked at the outset, educational systems are themselves highly institutionalized, in the grip of their *own* values. Educators have their own usually well informed views about how to cultivate and how to 'grade' the human mind. And like other institutions, education perpetuates itself and its practices: by establishing graduate schools of education, *grandes écoles* like the École Normale Supérieure in France, even elite academies like the chartered National Academy of Education in America and the informal All Souls Group in Britain. And, as often happens, it invents durable ways of distributing skills, attitudes, and ways of thinking in the same old unjust demographic patterns. A reliable example of this can be found in procedures for examining students that, somehow, long outlive exposés of their unfairness to less privileged groups in the population. In consequence, the goodness of fit between school practices and society's demands comes increasingly under scrutiny.

Yet, in a sense, the public discussions that occur in consequence of this scrutiny are by no means strictly about 'education.' It is not simply that we are trying to reevaluate the balance between schools as a fixed Educational Establishment, on the one side, and a set of well-established needs of the culture, on the other. The issues are much broader than that. They have to do with the emerging role of women in society, with the vexing problem of the ethnic loyalties of the children of guest workers, with minority rights, with sexual mores, with unmarried mothers, with violence, with poverty. The Educational Establishment, for all its fingertip expertise in dealing with educational routines, has little by way of established doctrine for dealing with such problems. Nor do other institutions within the culture, though they nonetheless seem always tempted to 'blame education' for its particular set of troubles – whether it be the falling competitiveness of the auto industry, the increase in births out of wedlock, or violence on the streets.

It is astonishing how little systematic study is devoted to the institutional 'anthropology' of schooling, given the complexity of its situatedness and its exposure to the changing social and economic climate. Its relation to the family,

to the economy, to religious institutions, even to the labor market, is only
vaguely understood.[20]

I must conclude this discussion of 'institutionalization' on a more homely
note. Improving education requires teachers who understand and are
committed to the improvements envisioned. So banal a point would scarcely be
worth mentioning were it not so easily overlooked by many efforts at
educational reform. We need to equip teachers with the necessary background
training to take an effective part in reform.[21] The people who run them make
institutions. However thoughtful our educational plans may become, they must
include a crucial place for teachers. For ultimately, that is where the action is.

8. The tenet of identity and self-esteem. I have put this tenet late in the list. For it
is so pervasive as to implicate virtually all that has gone before. Perhaps the
single most universal thing about human experience is the phenomenon of
'Self,' and we know that education is crucial to its formation. Education should
be conducted with that fact in mind.

We know 'Self' from our own inner experience, and we recognize others as
selves. Indeed, more than one distinguished scholar has argued that self-
awareness requires as its necessary condition the recognition of the Other as a
self.[22] Though there are universals of selfhood – and we will consider two of
them in a moment – different cultures both shape it differently and set its limits
in varying ways. Some emphasize autonomy and individuality, some
affiliation;[23] some link it closely to a person's position in a divine or secular
social order,[24] some link it to individual effort or even to luck. Since schooling is
one of life's earliest institutional involvements outside the family, it is not
surprising that it plays a critical role in the shaping of Self. But I think this will
be clearer if we first examine two aspects of selfhood that are regarded as
universal.

The first is *agency*. Selfhood, most students of the subject believe, derives
from the sense that one can initiate and carry out activities on one's own.[25]
Whether this is 'really' so or simply a folk belief, as radical behaviorists would
have us believe, is beyond the scope of this inquiry. I shall simply take it as so.
People experience themselves as agents. But then too, any vertebrate
distinguishes between a branch *it* has shaken and one that has shaken *it*.[26] So
there must be something more to selfhood than the recognition of simple
sensorimotor agentivity. What characterizes human selfhood is the construction
of a conceptual system that organizes, as it were, a 'record' of agentive
encounters with the world, a record that is related to the past (that is,
'autobiographical memory,' so-called)[27] but that is also extrapolated into the
future – self with history and with possibility. It is a 'possible self' that
regulates aspiration, confidence, optimism, and their opposites.[28] While this
'constructed' self-system is inner, private, and suffused with affect, it also
extends outward to the things and activities and places with which we become

'ego-involved.'[29] Schools and school learning are among the earliest of those places and activities.

But just as important as the inner psychodynamics of selfhood are the ways in which a culture institutionalizes it. All natural languages, for example, make obligatory grammatical distinctions between agentive and patientive forms: *I hit him; he hit me.* And even the simplest narratives are built around, indeed depend upon, an agent-Self as a protagonist with his or her own goals operating in a recognizable cultural setting.[30] There is a moral aspect to selfhood as well, expressed simply by such ubiquitous phenomena as 'blaming yourself' or 'blaming another' for acts committed or outcomes that result from our acts. At a more evolved level, all legal systems specify (and legitimize) some notion of *responsibility* by which Self is endowed with obligation in regard to some broader cultural authority – confirming 'officially' that we, our Selves, are presumed to be agents in control of our own actions.

Since agency implies not only the capacity for initiating, but also for completing our acts, it also implies *skill* or *know-how.* Success and failure are principal nutrients in the development of selfhood. Yet we may not be the final arbiters of success and failure, which are often defined from 'outside' according to culturally specified criteria. And school is where the child first encounters such criteria – often as if applied arbitrarily. School judges the child's performance, and the child responds by evaluating himself or herself in turn.

Which brings us to a second ubiquitous feature of selfhood: *evaluation.* Not only do we experience self as agentive, we evaluate our efficacy in bringing off what we hoped for or were asked to do. Self increasingly takes on the flavor of these valuations. I call this mix of agentive efficacy and self-evaluation 'self-esteem.' It combines our sense of what we believe ourselves to be (or even hope to be) capable of and what we fear is beyond us.[31]

How self-esteem is experienced (or how it is expressed) varies, of course, with the ways of one's culture. Low esteem sometimes manifests itself in guilt about intentions, sometimes simply in shame for having been 'found out'; sometimes it is accompanied by depression, even to the point of suicide, sometimes by defiant anger.[32] In some cultures, particularly those that emphasize achievement, high self-esteem increases level of aspiration;[33] in others it leads to status display and standing pat. There may even be an individual temperamental component in how people deal with threatened self-esteem – whether one blames oneself, others, or circumstances.[34]

Only two things can be said for certain and in general: the management of self-esteem is never simple and never settled, and its state is affected powerfully by the availability of supports provided from outside. These supports are hardly mysterious or exotic. They include such homely resorts as a second chance, honor for a good if unsuccessful try, but above all the chance for discourse that permits one to find out why or how things didn't work out as planned. It is no secret that school is often rough on children's self-esteem, and we are beginning to know something about their vulnerability in this area.[35] Ideally, of course, school is supposed to provide a setting where our performance has fewer esteem-threatening consequences than in the 'real world,' presumably in the interest of encouraging the learner to 'try things out.' Yet radical critics, like Paulo Freire,[36] have argued that school often metes out failures to those children the society would later 'exploit.' And even moderate critics, like Roland Barthes and Pierre Bourdieu, make the provocative case that school is principally an agent for producing, say, 'little Frenchmen and French-women' who will conform to the niche where they will end up.[37]

Obviously there are other 'markets' where even school children can 'trade' their skills for distinctions, to use Bourdieu's interesting terms again. And these 'markets' often compensate for sensed failure in school – as when 'street smarts' are traded on the market of petty crime, or when defiance of the majority community earns black teenagers respect among their peers. School, more than we have realized, competes with myriad forms of 'anti-school' as a provider of agency, identity, and self-esteem – no less at a middle-class suburban mall than on the ghetto streets.

Any system of education, any theory of pedagogy, any 'grand national policy' that diminishes the school's role in nurturing its pupils' self-esteem fails at one of its primary functions. The deeper problem – from a cultural-psychological point of view, but in workaday common sense as well – is how to cope with the erosion of this function under modern urban conditions. Schools do not simply equip kids with skills and self-esteem or not. They are in competition with other parts of society that can do this, but with deplorable consequences for the society. America manages to alienate enough black ghetto boys to land nearly a third of them in jail before they reach the age of thirty.

More positively, if agency and esteem are central to the construction of a concept of Self, then the ordinary practices of school need to be examined with a view to what contribution they make to these two crucial ingredients of personhood. Surely the 'community of learners' approach mentioned earlier contributes to both. But equally, the granting of more responsibility in setting and achieving goals in all aspects of a school's activities could also contribute – everything from maintenance of a school's physical plant to a share in decisions about academic and extracurricular projects to be undertaken. Such a conception, earlier so dear to the progressive tradition in education, is also in the image of the constitutional principle that (in a democracy) rights and responsibilities are two sides of the same coin. If, as I noted at the outset, school is an entry into the culture and not just a preparation for it, then we must constantly reassess what school does to the young student's conception of his own powers (his sense of agency) and his sensed chances of being able to cope with the world both in school and after (his self-esteem). In many democratic cultures, I think, we have become so preoccupied with the more formal criteria of 'performance' and with the bureaucratic demands of education as an institution that we have neglected this personal side of education.

9. The narrative tenet. I want finally to leapfrog over the issue of school 'subjects' and curricula in order to deal with a more general matter: the mode of thinking and feeling that helps children (indeed, people generally) create a version of the world in which, psychologically, they can envisage a place for themselves – a personal world. I believe that story making, narrative, is what is needed for that, and I want to discuss it briefly in this final tenet.

I shall begin with some basics. There appear to be two broad ways in which human beings organize and manage their knowledge of the world, indeed structure even their immediate experience: one seems more specialized for treating of physical 'things,' the other for treating of people and their plights. These are conventionally known as *logical-scientific* thinking and *narrative* thinking. Their universality suggests that they have their roots in the human genome or that they are (to revert to an earlier tenet) givens in the nature of language. They have varied modes of expression in different cultures, which also cultivate them differently. No culture is without both of them, though different cultures privilege them differently.[38]

It has been the convention of most schools to treat the arts of narrative – song, drama, fiction, theater, whatever – as more 'decoration' than necessity, something with which to grace leisure, sometimes even as something morally exemplary. Despite that, we frame the accounts of our cultural origins and our most cherished beliefs in story form, and it is not just the 'content' of these stories that grip us, but their narrative artifice. Our immediate experience, what happened yesterday or the day before, is framed in the same storied way. Even more striking, we represent our lives (to ourselves as well as to others) in the form of narrative.[39]

The importance of narrative for the cohesion of a culture is as great, very likely, as it is in structuring an individual life. Take law as an illustration. Without a sense of the common trouble narratives that the law translates into its common law writs, it becomes arid.[40] And those 'trouble narratives' appear again in mythic literature and contemporary novels, better contained in that form than in reasoned and logically coherent propositions. It seems evident, then, that skill in narrative construction and narrative understanding is crucial to constructing our lives and a 'place' for ourselves in the possible world we will encounter.

It has always been tacitly assumed that narrative skill comes 'naturally,' that it does not have to be taught. But a closer look shows this not to be true at all. We know now, for example, that it goes through definite stages,[41] is severely impaired in brain damage of certain kinds,[42] fares poorly under stress,[43] and ends up in literalism in one social community while becoming fanciful in a neighboring one with a different tradition.[44] Observe law students or young lawyers preparing their final arguments for litigation or mock court and it will quickly be plain that some people have the knack more than others – they have simply learned how to make a story believable and worth thinking about.

Feeling at home in the world, knowing how to place oneself into self-descriptive stories, is surely not made easier by the enormous increase in migration in the modern world. It is not easy, however multicultural your intentions, to help a ten-year-old create a story that includes him in the world beyond his family and neighborhood, having been transplanted from Vietnam to the San Fernando Valley, from Algeria to Lyons, from Anatolia to Dresden. If school, his *pied-à-terre* outside the family, can't help him, there are alienated countercultures that can.

None of us know as much as we should about how to create narrative sensibility. Two commonplaces seem to have stood the test of time. The first is that a child should 'know,' have a 'feel' for, the myths, histories, folktales, and conventional stories of his or her culture (or cultures). They frame and nourish an identity. The second commonplace urges imagination through fiction. Finding a place in the world, for all that it implicates the immediacy of home, mate, job, and friends, is ultimately an act of imagination. So, for the culturally transplanted, there is the imaginative challenge of the fiction and 'quasi-fiction' that takes him or her into the world of possibilities—.

Obviously, if narrative is to be made an instrument of mind on behalf of meaning making, it requires work on our part – reading it, making it, analyzing it, understanding its craft, sensing its uses, discussing it. These are matters much better understood today than a generation ago.[45]

All of which is not intended to undervalue the importance of logical-scientific thinking. Its value is so implicit in our highly technological culture that its inclusion in school curricula is taken for granted. While its teaching may still be in need of improvement, it has become strikingly better since the curriculum reform movements of the 1950s and 1960s. But it is no secret that for many of the young now in school, 'science' has come to seem 'inhuman' and 'uncaring' and 'off-putting' – despite the first-class efforts of science and mathematics teachers and their associations.[46] Indeed, the image of science as a human and cultural undertaking might itself be improved if it were also conceived as a history of human beings overcoming received ideas. We may have erred in divorcing science from the narrative of culture.

A summary is hardly necessary. A system of education must help those growing up in a culture find an identity within that culture. Without it, they stumble in their effort after meaning. It is only in the narrative mode that one can construct an identity and find a place in one's culture. Schools must cultivate it, nurture it, cease taking it for granted. There are many projects now in the making, not only in literature but also in history and social studies, that are following up interesting leads in this field. We will have an opportunity in later chapters to consider them in more detail.

More as a postscript than as a general conclusion, I offer one last reflection on the set of tenets I've put forth in the spirit of a cultural-psychological perspective on education. I realize, reading back over them, to what degree they emphasize the powers of consciousness, reflection, breadth of dialogue, and negotiation. In all systems that depend on authority, even duly constituted and representative authority, all of these factors seem to pose risks by opening discussion of currently institutionalized authority. And they are risky. Education *is* risky, for it fuels the sense of possibility. But a failure to equip minds with the skills for understanding and feeling and acting in the cultural world is not simply scoring a pedagogical zero. It risks creating alienation, defiance, and practical incompetence. And all of these undermine the viability of a culture.

Let me revert finally to the theme with which this chapter opened. I tried to show at the start that education is not simply a technical business of well-managed information processing. It is a complex pursuit of fitting a culture to the needs of its members and of fitting its members and their ways of knowing to the needs of the culture.

Notes

1. Though I use the expression 'the computational view,' there are in fact two such models, one based upon the idea of the mind as a set of computational devices that operate in parallel and without benefit of a central processing system, the other on the idea of a central processing unit that controls the sequential order of computational operations that must be performed to achieve solutions to particular problems. Though the differences between these two models are profound in many ways – particularly in their conceptions of the role of 'rationality' and 'experience' – that difference need not concern us. Compare, for example, David E. Rumelhart and James L. McClelland, eds., *Parallel Distributed Processing: Explorations in the Microstructure of Cognition*, vols. 1 and 2 (Cambridge, Mass.: MIT Press, 1986), with Philip N. Johnson-Laird, *The Computer and the Mind: An Introduction to Cognitive Science* (Cambridge, Mass.: Harvard University Press, 1988).
2. Alfred L. Kroeber, 'The Superorganic,' *American Anthropologist*, 19(2) (1917): 163–213.
3. Some representative works in this cultural-psychological tradition are: Jerome Bruner, *Acts of Meaning* (Cambridge, Mass.: Harvard University Press, 1990); Michael Cole, *The Cultural Context of Learning and Thinking: An*

Exploration in Experimental Anthropology (New York: Basic Books, 1971); Barbara Rogoff, *Apprenticeship in Thinking: Cognitive Development in Social Context* (New York: Oxford University Press, 1990); Richard A. Shweder, *Thinking through Cultures: Expeditions in Cultural Psychology* (Cambridge, Mass.: Harvard University Press, 1991); James V. Wertsch, *Voices of the Mind: A Sociocultural Approach to Mediated Action* (Cambridge, Mass.: Harvard University Press, 1991). Its ancestry traces back to writers like Vygotsky, Durkheim, Schutz, and Max Weber: Lev S. Vygotsky, *Thought and Language* (Cambridge, Mass.: MIT Press, 1962); Emile Durkheim, *Elementary Forms of the Religious Life: A Study in Religious Sociology* (Glencoe, Ill.: Free Press, 1968); Alfred Schutz, *On Phenomenology and Social Relations: Selected Writings* (Chicago: University of Chicago Press, 1970); Max Weber, *Theory of Social and Economic Organization* (Glencoe, Ill.: Free Press, 1947).

4. Bruner, *Acts of Meaning*; Carol Fleisher Feldman and David A. Kalmar, 'Some Educational Implications of Genre-Based Mental Models,' in David Olson and Nancy Torrance, eds., *Handbook of Education and Human Development* (Oxford: Blackwell, 1996), pp. 434–460.

5. For a fuller discussion of this point, see Goodman, *Ways of Worldmaking*; Richard Rorty, *Philosophy and the Mirror of Nature* (Princeton, N.J.: Princeton University Press, 1979).

6. Stephen C. Levinson and Penelope Brown, 'Immanuel Kant Against the Tenejapans: Anthropology as Empirical Philosophy,' *Ethos*, 22(1) (1994): 3–41.

7. Vygotsky, *Thought and Language*.

8. Benjamin L. Whorf, *Language, Thought, and Reality: Selected Writings* (Cambridge, Mass.: Technology Press of MIT, 1956).

9. For a good summary of these debates, see Bradd Shore, *Culture in Mind* (New York: Oxford University Press, 1996).

10. Alison F. Garton and Chris Pratt, *Learning to Be Literate: The Development of Spoken and Written Language* (Oxford: Basil Blackwell, 1989).

11. Colwyn B. Trevarthen, 'Form, Significance, and Psychological Potential of Hand Gestures of Infants,' in Jean-Luc Nespoulous, Paul Perron, and Andre Roch Lecours, eds., *The Biological Foundations of Gestures: Motor and Semiotic Aspects* (Hillsdale, N.J.: Erlbaum, 1986), pp. 149–202; Alison Gopnik, 'How We Know Our Minds: The Illusion of First-Person Knowledge of Intentionality,' *Behavioral and Brain Sciences*, 16 (1993): 1–14; Alison Gopnik and Andrew N. Meltzoff, 'Minds, Bodies, and Persons: Young Children's Understanding of the Self and Others as Reflected in Imitation and Theory of Mind Research,' in Sue Taylor Parker, Robert W. Mitchell, and Maria L. Boccia, eds., *Self-Awareness in Animals and Humans: Developmental Perspectives* (Cambridge: Cambridge University Press, 1994), pp. 166–186.

12. Ignace Meyerson, *Les Fonctions Psychologiques et les Oeuvres* (Paris: J. Vrin, 1948); Meyerson, *Écrits, 1920–1983: Pour une Psychologie Historique* (Paris: Presses Universitaires de France, 1987). An appreciation of Meyerson's work is contained in Françoise Parot, ed., *Les Oeuvres d'Ignace Meyerson: Un Hommage* (Paris: Presses Universitaires de France, in press), in which is included Jerome Bruner's 'Meyerson aujourd'hui: Quelques Reflexions sur la Psychologie Culturelle.'

13. This is a verbatim remark made to me by a ten-year-old in one of the Oakland classrooms, commenting on the plan his class was devising to deal with disasters like the oil spill from the *Exxon Valdez* two years earlier – a class project in ecology.

14. For a more general discussion of this process, see Eric Hobsbawm and Terence Ranger, eds., *The Invention of Tradition* (Cambridge: Cambridge University Press, 1983).

15. Howard Gardner, *Frames of Mind: The Theory of Multiple Intelligences* (New York: Basic Books, 1983).

16. Claude Lévi-Strauss, *Structural Anthropology* (New York: Basic Books, 1963).

17. Walter Lippmann, *Public Opinion* (New York: Harcourt, Brace, 1927); John Dewey, *The Public and Its Problems* (Chicago: Swallow Press, 1954).

18. Pierre Bourdieu, *Language and Symbolic Power* (Cambridge, Mass.: Harvard University Press, 1991).

19. Harry Judge, Michel Lemosse, Lynn Paine, and Michael Sedlek, *The University and the Teachers: France, the United States, England* (Wallingford: Triangle, 1994).

20. There have of course been notable exceptions. One need only cite the work of Lawrence A. Cremin, *Popular Education and Its Discontents* (New York: Harper & Row, 1990); Theodore W. Schultz, *The Economic Value of Education* (New York: Columbia University Press, 1963); Neil Postman, *Conscientious Objections: Stirring Up Trouble about Language, Technology, and Education* (New York: Knopf, 1988); Pierre Bourdieu, *Language and Symbolic Power* (Cambridge, Mass.: Harvard University Press, 1991); Shirley Brice Heath, *Ways with Words: Language, Life, and Work in Communities and Classrooms* (Cambridge: Cambridge University Press, 1983); and most recently, Harry Judge *et al.*, *The University and the Teachers: France, the United States, England* (Wallingford: Triangle, 1994). There has also been a recent and lively growth of studies in what has come to be called the 'ethnography of the classroom,' such as Hugh Mehan's *Learning Lessons: Social Organization in the Classroom* (Cambridge, Mass.: Harvard University Press, 1979), which, though limited to self-contained school communities, have shed much light on how broader authority and affiliative patterns within the culture mirror themselves in classroom practices.

21. See Peter B. Dow, *Schoolhouse Politics: Lessons from the Sputnik Era* (Cambridge, Mass.: Harvard University Press, 1991); Dorothy Nelkin, *Science Textbook Controversies and the Politics of Equal Time* (Cambridge, Mass.: MIT Press, 1977); Comptroller General of the United States, *Report to the House Committee on Science and Technology: Administration of the Science Education Project – Man: A Course of Study*, October 14, 1975.

22. George H. Mead, *Mind, Self, and Society from the Standpoint of a Social Behaviorist* (Chicago: University of Chicago Press, 1962); Paul Ricoeur, *Oneself as Another* (Chicago: University of Chicago Press, 1992); Nicholas Humphrey, *Consciousness Regained: Chapters in the Development of Mind* (Oxford: Oxford University Press, 1983); Robert Jay Lifton, *The Life of the Self: Toward a New Psychology* (New York: Basic Books, 1983).

23. Hazel Rose Markus and Shinobu Kitayama, 'Culture and the Self: Implications for Cognition, Emotion, and Motivation,' *Psychological Review*, 98(2) (1991): 224–253.

24. Jean Pierre Vernant, *Myth and Society in Ancient Greece* (Sussex: Harvester Press, 1980); Vernant, *The Origins of Greek Thought* (Ithaca, N.Y.: Cornell University Press, 1982); Vernant, *Myth and Thought among the Greeks* (London: Routledge, 1983); Vernant, *Myth and Tragedy in Ancient Greece* (Cambridge, Mass.: MIT Press, 1988).

25. John Campbell, *Past, Space, and Self* (Cambridge, Mass.: MIT Press, 1994).

26. Erich von Holst, *The Behavioural Physiology of Animals and Man: The Collected Papers of Erich von Holst* (Coral Gables, Fla.: University of Miami Press, 1973).

27. David Rubin, ed., *Remembering Our Past* (Cambridge: Cambridge University Press, 1996).

28. Markus and Kitayama, 'Culture and the Self'; Kurt Lewin, Tamara Dembo, Leon Festinger, and Pauline Snedden Sears, 'Level of Aspiration,' in J. McV. Hunt, ed., *Personality and the Behavioral Disorders: A Handbook Based on Experimental and Clinical Research* (New York: Ronald Press, 1944), pp. 333–378; J. W. Atkinson, 'Motivational Determinants of Risk-Taking Behavior,' *Psychological Review*, 64 (1957): 359–372; J. W. Atkinson and N.T. Feather, eds., *A Theory of Achievement Motivation* (New York: Wiley, 1966).

29. Muzafer Sherif and Hadley Cantril, *The Psychology of Ego-Involvements, Social Attitudes, and Identification* (New York: John Wiley, 1947).

30. Bruner, *Acts of Meaning*; Vladimir Propp, *Morphology of the Folktale*, 2nd ed., rev. (Austin: University of Texas Press, 1968); William Labov and Joshua Waletzky, 'Narrative Analysis: Oral Versions of Personal Experience,' in June Helm, ed., *Essays on the Verbal and Visual Arts: Proceedings of the 1966 Annual Spring Meeting of the American Ethnological Society* (Seattle: American Ethnological Society), pp. 12–44). We'll return to this topic in a later section.

31. For a pioneering disucssion of competence, see R. W. White's classic 'Motivation Reconsidered: The Concept of Competence,' *Psychological Review*, 66 (1959): 297–323.
32. See Ruth F. Benedict, *Patterns of Culture* (Boston: Houghton Mifflin, 1959).
33. Pauline S. Sears and Vivian S. Sherman, *In Pursuit of Self-Esteem: Case Studies of Eight Elementary School Children* (Belmont, Calif.: Wadsworth, 1964).
34. Saul Rosenzweig, *Aggressive Behavior and the Rosenzweig Picture-Frustration Study* (New York: Praeger, 1978).
35. See Norman Garmezy and Michael Rutter, eds., *Stress, Coping, and Development in Children* (New York: McGraw–Hill, 1983); Jon Rolf, ed., *Risk and Protective Factors in the Development of Psychopathology* (Cambridge: Cambridge University Press, 1990); Marc Zimmerman and Revathy Arunkumar, 'Resiliency Research: Implications for Schools and Policy,' *Social Policy Report*, 8(4) (1994): 1–17.
36. Paulo Freire, *Pedagogy of the Oppressed*, new rev. 20th-anniversary ed. (New York: Continuum, 1994).
37. Pierre Bourdieu, *Distinction: A Social Critique of the Judgment of Taste* (Cambridge, Mass.: Harvard University Press, 1984); Roland Barthes, 'Toys,' in his *Mythologies* (New York: Hill and Wang, 1982), pp. 53–55.
38. See Jerome Bruner, 'Narrative and Paradigmatic Modes of Thought,' in Elliot Eisner, ed., *Learning and Teaching the Ways of Knowing: Eighty-fourth Yearbook of the National Society for the Study of Education* (Chicago: University of Chicago Press, 1985), pp. 97–115.
39. Jerome Bruner, 'Life as Narrative,' *Social Research*, 54(1) (1987): 11–32.
40. Ronald M. Dworkin, *Law's Empire* (Cambridge, Mass.: Harvard University Press, 1986); James Boyd White, *Heracles' Bow: Essays on the Rhetoric and Poetics of the Law* (Madison: University of Wisconsin Press, 1985).
41. Carol F. Feldman, Jerome Bruner, David Kalmar, and Bobbi Renderer, 'Plot, Plight, and Dramatism: Interpretation at Three Ages,' *Human Development*, 36(6) (1993): 327–342.
42. Jerome Bruner and Carol Feldman, 'Theories of Mind and the Problem of Autism,' in Simon Baron-Cohen, Helen Tager-Flusberg, and Donald J. Cohen, eds., *Understanding Other Minds: Perspectives from Autism* (Oxford: Oxford University Press, 1993), pp. 267–291; Oliver Sacks, 'A Neurologist's Notebook: An Anthropologist on Mars,' *The New Yorker*, 69(44) (1993): 106–125.
43. Bruno Bettelheim, *The Uses of Enchantment: The Meaning and Importance of Fairy Tales* (New York: Random House, 1989); Donald E. Polkinghorne, *Narrative Knowing and the Human Sciences* (Albany: State University of New York Press, 1988).

44. Shirley Brice Heath, *Ways with Words: Language, Life, and Work in Communities and Classrooms* (Cambridge: Cambridge University Press, 1983).

45. See Bruner, 'Narrative and Paradigmatic Modes of Thought'; Shelby Anne Wolf and Shirley Brice Heath, *The Braid of Literature: Children's Worlds of Reading* (Cambridge, Mass.: Harvard University Press, 1992); Carole Peterson and Allyssa McCabe, *Developmental Psycholinguistics: Three Ways of Looking at a Child's Narrative* (New York: Plenum, 1983); Allyssa McCabe and Carole Peterson, eds., *Developing Narrative Structure* (Hillsdale, N.J.: Erlbaum, 1991); *Journal of Narrative and Life History* (Hillsdale, N.J.: Erlbaum); Theodore R. Sarbin, ed., *Narrative Psychology: The Storied Nature of Human Conduct* (New York: Praeger, 1986); Richard J. Gerrig, *Experiencing Narrative Worlds: On the Psychological Activities of Reading* (New Haven, Conn.: Yale University Press, 1993).

46. Both the National Council of Teachers of Mathematics and the National Science Teachers Association are actively involved in such efforts. See, for example, *Curriculum and Evaluation Standards for School Mathematics* (Reston, Va.: National Council of Teachers of Mathematics, 1989), and *Professional Standards for School Mathematics* (Reston, Va.: National Council of Teachers of Mathematics, 1991). A report on the progress of these efforts is contained in Mary M. Lindquist, John A. Dossey, and Ina V. S. Mullis, *Reaching Standards: A Progress Report on Mathematics* (Princeton, N.J.: Policy Information Center, Educational Testing Service, undated [appeared 1995]).

Chapter 11

Racism, policy and the (mis)education of Black children

David Gillborn

> Whereas the Queen's majesty, tendering the good and welfare of her own natural subjects, greatly distressed in these hard times of dearth, is highly discontented to understand the great number of Negroes and blackamoors which (as she is informed) are crept into this realm … who are fostered and relieved here, to the great annoyance of her own liege people who want the relief which these people consume … hath given especial commandment that the said kind of people shall be with all speed avoided and discharged out of this her majesty's dominions …
>
> *Royal Proclamation of 1601* (File and Power 1981, pp. 6–7)

There is a common assumption that Britain was somehow ethnically homogeneous before the major post-war migrations from the Caribbean and Indian subcontinent in the mid twentieth century. In fact, Britain has *always* been ethnically diverse and, as the quotation above demonstrates, racism has a long history too. In this chapter, my focus is upon the most recent part of that history; specifically, how has education policy sought to respond to Britain's ethnically diverse population?[1] My aim is to identify broadly the changing landscapes of education policy: unfortunately, the continuities are strong. Indeed, I will argue that despite changes in terminology, even the most recent policy moves give little or no cause for optimism that racism is finally to be addressed seriously in education policy.[2]

Sally Tomlinson (1977) produced the first serious attempt to chart the position of 'race' issues in British education policy. Since then numerous writers have produced their own versions, almost all borrowing terms from Tomlinson's original.[3] This approach typically categorises changing perspectives and actions via a series of 'models' or 'phases'. This has its dangers, not least glossing over contradictions and resistance in an attempt to describe (create?) neat categories. The problem is visible in the wide variety of terms used by authors, sometimes choosing to highlight different trends and periods. As with previous attempts, my policy map is necessarily incomplete: the start/end dates are not precise and there are points of opposition and counter-developments where national trends contrasted dramatically with local practice in some areas. My hope is that by looking back, we can better understand current approaches and future possibilities.

History of post-war issues of race and education

Ignorance and neglect (1945 to the late 1950s)

The term 'ignorance and neglect' is James Lynch's (1986: 42) description of the early post-war period. The initial education policy response to migration from the Caribbean and Indian subcontinent was to do nothing. Others have variously referred to the same period as one of 'laissez-faire' disregard (Massey 1991: 9) or 'inaction' (Rose *et al.* 1969 in Massey, 1991).

Assimilation (late 1950s to the late 1960s)

In 1958 'riots' in Nottingham and Notting Hill, London, saw white racist attacks on migrant communities misrepresented in the press as demanding action on the 'colour problem', while politicians on both sides of the House of Commons sought to excuse the actions of convicted whites (Ramdin 1987: 208–10). 'Racial' diversity was, therefore, presented as a threat to order and the migrant communities (victims of white racist violence) were projected as a 'problem'. Policy responses at this point were characterised first, by action to severely restrict Black and Asian migration; and second, by the policy goal of assimilationism. Tomlinson, for example, points to the view of the Commonwealth Immigrants Advisory Council, who in 1964, stated that 'A national system cannot be expected to perpetuate the different values of immigrant groups' (Tomlinson 1977: 3). This view fuelled attempts to assimilate minorities into the majority culture (or at least the official version of it) and can be seen most clearly in the policies that prioritised teaching the English language and the physical dispersal of 'immigrant' children to minimise their numbers in any single class/school – a policy that left many children and young people especially vulnerable to racist attacks (cf. Dhondy 1982).[4] The overriding policy objective here was to protect the stability of the system and placate the 'fears' of white racist communities and parents: a circular from the then Department of Education and Science (DES) makes explicit the priorities of the period:

> *It will be helpful if the parents of non-immigrant children can see that practical measures have been taken to deal with the problems in their schools, and that the progress of their own children is not being restricted by the undue preoccupation of the teaching staff with the linguistic and other difficulties of immigrant children.*
>
> (DES circular 7/65, quoted in Swann 1985: 194, original emphasis)

Integration (1966 to late 1970s)

Roy Jenkins (then Labour Home Secretary) famously advocated, in a 1966 speech, 'not a flattening process of assimilation but equal opportunity, accompanied by cultural diversity, in an atmosphere of mutual tolerance' (quoted in Mullard 1982: 125). This was important symbolically for acknowledging the contemporary existence of marked *in*equalities of opportunity, and for apparently withdrawing support for assumptions of white cultural superiority that had argued the need to 'absorb'/destroy ethnic differences. This period saw some important steps forward, not least the passing of the Race Relations Act (1976) and establishment of the Commission for Racial Equality (CRE). Nevertheless, educational work tended to assume a patronising and exoticised approach to teaching about 'race' and assumed the need to build 'compensatory' programmes to make good the supposed cultural deficits of minority pupils (Massey 1991: 11–12). It has been said that during this period 'emphasis was on life *styles* rather than life *chances*' (Lynch 1986: 41, emphasis added), a statement that draws attention to the publication of curricular materials that frequently reflected and reinforced crude stereotypes of minorities as at best exotic and strange, at worst as backward and primitive, and always as alien. The 'problem', therefore, was still seen as residing in the minority communities themselves; a position that continued to absolve the education system of responsibility. 'Tolerance' and 'diversity' emerged as new watchwords (that are still in vogue today) but essentially, protection of the status quo remained the key driving force in policy (just as in assimilationism).

Cultural pluralism and multiculturalism (late 1970s to late 1980s)

This period saw the rhetoric of cultural pluralism assume widespread support (across political parties). Like the other 'phases' there was a borrowing (in more or less altered forms) of some of the key concepts and terms of previous periods. So, for example, 'diversity' and 'tolerance' continued to feature prominently in the discourse, but importantly notions of liberal pluralism were at their height and began to find expression in official policy. An official committee of inquiry was established to examine the education of ethnic minority pupils (cf. Rampton 1981; Swann 1985) and its analysis traded on a 'radical' or 'strong' perspective that used differences in group outcome as indicative of inequalities of opportunity. The recommendations of the Rampton and Swann reports were highly criticised, from the political right and left. Nevertheless, the reports marked something of a watershed in public policy on 'race' and education in Britain by first, rejecting IQist notions of innate intellectual differences between 'races', and second, stating that teachers (in their expectations and actions toward pupils and parents) might actively be implicated in the creation of 'race' inequality. These advances, however, were highly constrained: not only did the Conservative government of the day reject the committee's most important recommendations (see below) but its chairman, Lord Swann, prepared a personal summary that barely even mentioned 'racism'.

Despite the changed nature of the public policy debate at this time, in education much work continued to trade on superficial 'positive images' stereotypes of the type Barry Troyna devastatingly described as the *3S's* – saris, samosas and steel bands (see Troyna and Carrington 1990: 20). As the phrase encapsulated, the concern was with a shallow 'celebration' of difference, in a context where issues of power and racism were conspicuously ignored or silenced. This was the very point pursued by anti-racists who sought to place issues of power at centre stage.

Anti-racist counter-cultural developments

I noted earlier that a danger of labelling the past via a series of 'phases' is that counter trends and points of resistance can be glossed over. One of the most important such 'moments' in British education policy concerns the development of anti-racist analyses and pedagogies. Against the wider thrust of public policy, this period saw key developments on the anti-racist front, symbolised by the establishment of several prominent pressure groups (including the National Antiracist Movement in Education and All London Teachers Against Racism and Fascism: see Gaine 1995: 42–4; Massey 1991: 15–17). Despite its presentation in the media and parts of academia as a Marxist ideology of revolution (cf. Flew 1984; Palmer 1986), anti-racism was never tightly defined as a single theory or pedagogic approach. Much anti-racist work traded on a critique of previous approaches, only rarely venturing into the realms of suggested classroom practice. Godfrey Brandt's *The Realization of*

Anti-racist Teaching (1986) stood out as a distinctive attempt to synthesise anti-racist critique and pedagogy. Brandt's work, as much as anyone's, captured the spirit of anti-racism at this point. He positioned liberal multiculturalism (with its fascination for 'positive images' and curricular change) as 'the Trojan horse of institutional racism' (p. 117) and argued that anti-racism differed fundamentally. In particular he argued that anti-racism should accord a central role to the 'experience and articulations of the Black community' (p. 119) and be characterised by an oppositional form. This involved an analysis that focused on power and the need to challenge dominant conceptions of knowledge and pedagogy. Nevertheless, anti-racism took a dynamic and varied form such that 'there was no body of thought called anti-racism, no orthodoxy or dogma, no manual of strategy and tactics, no demonology' (Sivanandan 1988: 147).

In many ways anti-racism reached a zenith, so far as education policy was concerned, with the work of the Inner London Education Authority (ILEA). Several local authorities, mostly serving large metropolitan areas, adopted anti-racist policies but the Greater London Council (GLC) and the ILEA (London's education authority) were at the forefront of public campaigns to advance anti-racist issues. In hindsight it is certainly true that the GLC and ILEA made mistakes. This version of 'municipal anti-racism' (Gilroy 1987) has subsequently been subject to numerous critiques, including those of left intellectuals who question both the conceptualisation and execution of public anti-racism for trading on essentialised notions of difference and for oversimplifying the complex politics of 'race' and racism (cf. Gilroy 1987, 1990; Modood 1992; Modood *et al.* 1996). Nevertheless, the GLC and ILEA led the way so far as anti-racist public policy was concerned; ILEA's Research and Statistics branch, for example, made concerted efforts to analyse and understand racialised patterns of success and failure in the capital's schools. Ultimately both the GLC and ILEA paid the price for their counter-cultural stance in their abolition at the hands of a Thatcher government.

An inquiry into a racist murder at Burnage High School in Manchester (Macdonald *et al.* 1989) also became entangled in the wider racialised politics of the time. The report's authors, all active in combating racism, argued publicly that 'the work of all schools be informed by a policy that recognises the pernicious and all-pervasive nature of racism in the lives of students, teachers and parents, black and white, and the need to confront it' (Macdonald *et al.* 1989: xxiv). Nevertheless, this message was lost amid a torrent of distorted press coverage that misrepresented the particular criticisms that the panel had made of anti-racism as practised at Burnage. Rather than being recognised as a vital step forward in the attempt to identify workable and critical anti-oppressive strategies, the report was falsely presented as an attack on anti-racism *per se*; as 'signalling the failure of the anti-racist project in education'

(Rattansi 1992: 11). Although anti-racist school practice is far from dead, therefore, the late 1980s and early 1990s witnessed many attacks on anti-racism (from left as well as right) and it undoubtedly suffered a retreat in many areas (cf. Gillborn 1995).

Although anti-racist initiatives were a vital part of this time period they never reached a widespread position of citation (let alone genuine influence). While multiculturalist and anti-racist advocates fought it out in meetings, on committees and in the pages of books and journals, it was only ever a modest version of multiculturalism that achieved the status necessary for characterising the period as a whole. The peak for liberal pluralist multiculturalism was the publication of the Swann Report (1985) which, despite attempts to integrate anti-racist sensitivities, remained largely wedded to (and stands as an exemplar for) the cultural pluralist/multicultural sensibilities of the period. Even as this period reached its peak, however, its destruction was in sight: signalled most obviously in the dismissive response of the Conservative government of the day. Speaking as the Swann Report was presented to Parliament, the then Secretary of State for Education, Keith Joseph, repeated the historic refusal of British governments to take serious targeted action on the inequalities endured by minority communities and their children:

> under-achievement is not confined to the ethnic minorities ... [Our] policies apply to all pupils irrespective of ethnic origin. As they bear fruit, ethnic minority pupils will share in the benefit.
>
> (quoted in Gillborn 1990: 166)

It was Joseph's rejection of the report's principal recommendations, rather than the Swann Report itself, that set the tone for future policy in this field.

Thatcherism: The new racism and colour-blind policy (mid 1980s to 1997)

This period was dominated by what Martin Barker (1981) characterised as 'the new racism'; a perspective that asserts a strong cultural homogeneity among the majority population as a basis for privileging the views, needs and assumptions of that group over minority communities. The focus on '*race*' and *superiority* of older times was replaced by a discourse that stressed *culture* and *difference*:

> You do not need to think of yourself as superior – you do not even need to dislike or blame those who are so different from you – in order to say that the presence of these aliens constitutes a threat to our way of life.
>
> (Barker 1981: 18)

This strand in Conservative ideology is strongly associated with Margaret

Thatcher but as an overriding policy force it did not come to dominate until well into her reign as Prime Minister. However, elements of this same perspective outlived her occupancy of No. 10 Downing Street and could still be seen in the speeches and policy programmes of both main parties as they fought the 1997 general election (cf. Gillborn 1999a). The period was characterised by ferocious individualism; as a prop for the pursuit and acquisition of individual wealth and power, but also as a refusal of wider state responsibilities and diversity around class and ethnic interests. The tone of the period is perhaps best captured by Thatcher's statement that there is 'no such thing as society' (cf. Thatcher 1993: 626).

The period witnessed a strong assertion of national homogeneity, where the interests of the majority *have* to come first, not through any supposed superiority (as in the assimilationist phase) but simply because *we* are 'different' and, after all, it's *our* country (cf. Ansell 1997; Barker 1981; Gillborn 1995).[5] In education, this phase is characterised by two events: first, its rise is clear in the rejection of the Swann Report (above), and second, the subsequent publication of the initial consultation on the National Curriculum, in 1987, which made no mention of cultural diversity. The period ended with the Tories' election defeat in May 1997.

Education policy in this period was characterised by *equiphobia* (Myers 1990) wedded to market economics and the tyranny of 'standards' discourse. This was seen most graphically in the sweeping education reforms of the decade (e.g. the introduction of the National Curriculum, testing regimes, and opting out of local authority control), each one pursued vigorously, with no reference to cultural diversity and with complete disregard (often contempt) for the likely consequences for minority pupils, parents and communities. 'Colour-blindness' (an obstinate refusal to consider ethnic diversity despite a wealth of evidence that minorities are *not* sharing equally) became the officially sanctioned approach. During his final year as Prime Minister, for example, John Major openly fixed colour-blindness as official government policy:

> Few things would inflame racial tension more than trying to bias systems in favour of one colour – a reverse discrimination that fuels resentment. An artificial bias would damage the harmony we treasure. Equality under the law – yes; equality of opportunity and reward – yes. These promote harmony.
> Policy must be colour blind – it must just tackle disadvantage. Faced by British citizens, whatever their background might be.
>
> (Major 1997: 7)

And what would this look like in education? More of the same market policies:

> But how do you achieve equality of opportunity?
> It begins with education.
> Over the last few years we've opened up our schools so parents – and taxpayers – can

see how well they're performing. That hasn't always made comfortable reading. Too often bad schools are found where we need good schools the most – in areas where education is a life line of hope … Testing children on the basic skills, and giving parents the results. Inspecting schools on a regular basis. And, when it's really necessary, closing down failing schools … Specialist schools, grant-maintained schools, city technology colleges and – yes, if parents want them – grammar schools. This is the choice we're opening up.

(ibid.: 7–8)

Under successive Conservative administrations, therefore, 'race' inequalities were removed from the agenda; subsumed amid other issues; and denied legitimacy as a topic for concerted action.

During this period, of course, there was also a running contest for influence between different factions *within* right-wing ideology, most obviously between the neo-liberals and the neo-conservatives (cf. Whitty 1992, 1997). The influence of both factions can be detected in the overall shape of the Tories' reforms, with the neo-liberal pursuit of market-driven reform somewhat tempered by the neo-conservative requirement to retain a core entitlement and 'National' Curriculum. The latter strand of neo-conservative thought was also apparent in the Tories' repeated refusal to grant state funding to Islamic schools. The latter area is one where an incoming Labour administration made an immediate difference (see below); but just how different is New Labour's approach to 'race' and education policy?

Naive multiculturalism: new labour, old inequalities (1997–)

At the time of writing, Tony Blair's self-styled 'New' Labour has not yet enjoyed a full term in office; it is early to be talking about a new phase in the politics of 'race' and education in Britain. Nevertheless, the first Labour government for eighteen years quickly established an approach very different (in some ways) from that of its Conservative predecessors. In other, quite fundamental respects, the parallels with previous approaches are distressingly strong.

Equality of opportunity and the naming of ethnic diversity

Once in office New Labour's first White Paper, *Excellence in Schools* (published just 67 days after the general election), proclaimed 'the Government's core commitment to equality of opportunity and high standards for all' (DfEE 1997: 3). The ritual concern with 'standards' (measured in a crude form) was a clear legacy from the previous policy phase, but the focus on equality of opportunity contrasted sharply with the Conservatives' open hostility to equity (see Gillborn 1995: 32). A further significant break with Tory education discourse was Labour's readiness openly to acknowledge *ethnic* inequalities in attainment and opportunity. The 1997 White Paper, for example, included several discreet references to inequalities of experience and outcome by ethnicity. The main body of the document carried a section entitled 'Ethnic minority pupils' that referred, among other things, to inequalities in achievement and offered modest commitments to consult on ethnic monitoring and 'best practice' in multi-ethnic schools (DfEE 1997: 34–5). In a document of more than 80 pages, the provision of a few paragraphs is, at best, a small beginning. In fact, *Excellence in Schools* set a pattern that was repeated later by another flagship policy document, the first report of the new Social Exclusion Unit (SEU) which, once again, took education as its first theme. Like the White Paper, the SEU's first report acknowledged the importance of racialised inequalities: in this case, the massive over-representation of Black students among those expelled from school.[6] Additionally, a wider review of academic research (Gillborn and Gipps 1996) was cited, including the view that white teachers might actively be involved in producing the inequalities via a range of differential expectations and responses to pupil behaviour.

These moves represented a significant break with previous policy but, in isolation, they proved inadequate. In both documents, the discussions of ethnic inequalities were separate from the rest of the analysis and did not impinge on the arguments feeding into the wider formulation of policy. Consequently, an understanding of racism and 'race' inequality remained almost completely absent from how the principal policy issues were conceived. As a result, policy continued to pursue colour-blind targets. This is important because the lessons of education policy since 1988 are clear: where equity is not monitored, and crude notions of league table 'standards' are prioritised, the outcome is frequently a *worsening* of existing inequality. In the decade following the 1988 Act, for example, there was a dramatic rise in the proportion of young people ending compulsory schooling with five or more higher grade (A*–C) passes in their General Certificate of Secondary Education (GCSE) examinations: from around 30 per cent in 1988 to just over 46 per cent in 1998. At the same time, however, the inequality in attainment between white and Black pupils worsened. In 1985 only 7 per cent of Black students attained five or more higher grades, compared with 21 per cent of whites (a gap of 14 percentage points). By 1996 the gap had grown to 22 percentage points, with 23 per cent of Black, and 45 per cent of whites attaining the same level (Commission for Racial Equality 1998; Drew 1995; Gillborn and Youdell 1998 p. 226).

Funding separate schools: equality of access or state-sponsored segregation?

New Labour's commitment to 'equality of opportunity' was important, in view of the Conservatives' disdain for the notion, but their actions on 'race' and education remained firmly locked into a superficial and weak understanding of equity.[7] Although inequalities in experience and attainment have been openly acknowledged and described as unacceptable (see above on Black attainment and exclusions), the only binding targets established were those dealing in colour-blind terms; there were no specific targets for raising minority attainment nor reducing Black exclusions per se. In contrast, there was early action on the question of access and entitlement. After a decade of refusals by successive Conservative governments, within a year of its election Labour had granted state funding to Islamic schools: the Islamia primary in London (which first applied for state support in 1986) and the Al Furqan primary in Birmingham (which began moves in 1994). In granting the applications the Secretary of State for Education and Employment reportedly emphasised the technical merit of the applications, rather than any ideological points:

> Mr Blunkett said the schools had demonstrated that they 'will comply with the statutory provisions governing all maintained schools, such as delivering the national curriculum and offering equal access to boys and girls'.
>
> (Lepkowska 1998: 18)

It is interesting that equal opportunities, in terms of gender and access, were mentioned but not, apparently, any of the related issues that the decision raised concerning religious segregation. This is especially surprising in view of the controversy that had, until then, dogged these debates. For example, the last major inquiry into relevant issues, as part of the Rampton/Swann committee's work, could not agree a unanimous view. The committee argued that:

> The establishment of 'separate' schools would fail to tackle many of the underlying concerns of the communities and might exacerbate the very feelings of rejection which they are seeking to overcome.
>
> (Swann 1985: 519)

They saw 'a situation in which groups of children are taught exclusively by teachers of the same ethnic group' as undesirable for 'the children, the minority community' and 'society as a whole' (ibid.). Furthermore, a majority of the committee argued that existing anomalies in the funding of certain religious schools in Britain should be reconsidered as part of a review of the relevant sections of the 1944 Education Act (Swann 1985: 514). Six members of the committee, however, dissented from this position. They argued that:

it is unjust at the present time not to recommend that positive assistance should be given to ethnic minority communities who wish to establish voluntary aided schools in accordance with the 1944 Act.

(Swann 1985: 515)

Labour's decision on this issue went almost completely unremarked. There is insufficient space here to debate the pros or cons of any particular position in the separate schools debate; rather, for our purposes, it is significant that such a pivotal change passed without any explicit commentary by the government. It may be that the decisions were made purely on technical grounds of adequacy of teaching, management, curriculum, etc. Alternatively (or additionally) the decisions may have been an attempt to extend formal equality of opportunity (of access and provision) to previously excluded minority communities. In any case, it is highly significant that such precedents were set without any attempt publicly to debate the implications in terms of social/educational policy, 'race' inequality and ethnic diversity. It is in this way that New Labour's approach can be characterised as 'naive multiculturalism'. There is a concern with a weak notion of equal opportunity (in terms of access) but a failure to engage with deeper structural forms of inequality. A further element of naive multiculturalism can be seen in Labour's response to the Stephen Lawrence inquiry, which presented an opportunity for anti-racist change, but was finally used in education as a platform for limited curricular moves.

The Stephen Lawrence Inquiry

The publication of the Stephen Lawrence Inquiry (Macpherson 1999) heralded a brief but highly significant period when the issue of racism in public institutions was placed high on the political and media agenda. Although the police service was at the centre of the Lawrence inquiry itself, other public services (especially education) were also implicated in its findings. The Department for Education and Employment (DfEE)'s response was quick and disappointing. There were strong echoes of Keith Joseph's dismissal of Swann (see above) in the department's assertion that steps were already being taken to address the issues. On the day that the report was published a DfEE press statement quoted David Blunkett on social justice in education:

> This is about how we treat each other and, importantly, how we learn to respect ourselves and one another as citizens … That is why we are promoting the teaching of citizenship at school, to help children learn to grow up in a society that cares and to have real equality of opportunity for all.

(DfEE 1999: 1)

The prominence given to citizenship education was a worrying sign. Citizenship emerged as a key curricular issue during the years of Conservative reform and, for a while, became an area around which much multicultural and anti-racist work seemed to coalesce (Taylor 1992). Unfortunately, citizenship education, with its traditional emphasis on formal notions of pluralism and 'tolerance', does not necessarily provide a sound home for critical anti-racist developments (Gillborn 1995). Certainly, there is no evidence that work on citizenship can actually penetrate the school as a whole (see Whitty 1992). Nevertheless, David Blunkett's emphasis on citizenship was retained and strengthened in the government's formal response to the Lawrence inquiry (Home Office 1999). As the *Times Educational Supplement* noted, 'in practice the plan will mean few changes in schools' (*TES*, 26 March 1999, p. 4). In fact, the education-related parts of the 'action plan' involved little or no new action; they simply repackaged existing provision and policies. In relation to suggested changes in the National Curriculum, for example, it stated:

> The Department [for Education and Employment] has taken a number of actions to date. The National Curriculum addresses and values the diverse nature of British society.
>
> (Home Office, 1999)

The arrogance of this assertion is breathtaking. Macpherson had questioned the adequacy of the National Curriculum for a multi-ethnic society but was met simply with an apparent reassurance that things were fine. The section continued with explicit references to a few none-core subject areas (history; geography; music; art; personal, social and health education) before stating that teachers had already been granted sufficient 'flexibility':

> all subject documents are designed to provide teachers with flexibility to tailor their teaching to stimulate and challenge all pupils, whatever their ethnic origin or social background.
>
> (ibid.)

The section continued with heavy emphasis on citizenship education, talking about diversity and understanding but making no reference at all to racism or anti-racism:

> *we will ensure that citizenship has a prominent place in the revised National Curriculum and that provision builds on existing good practice* ... developing pupils' knowledge and understanding of different beliefs and cultures, including an appreciation of diversity.
>
> (ibid., original emphasis)

The potential for a return to the worst kind of multiculturalism (characteristic of earlier phases) was clear: racism was left unexamined and unopposed, substituting for any anti-racist intent, a concern with 'understanding'. This theme continued in the department's talk of 'mutual respect and tolerance' in relation to guidance on good behaviour, and a restatement of policies already in place (prior to Macpherson) such as measures on truancy and exclusion, including provision for more on-site units. Finally, the government trumpeted 'the new *"Excellence in Cities"* initiative' which it claimed 'will bring enormous benefits to children living in inner city areas, including those from minority ethnic communities'. Again, note the way that Black students were subsumed into another category (inner-city children) almost as an afterthought.

Conclusions

> *Those who cannot remember the past are condemned to repeat it.*
>
> George Santayana (1863–1952)

The late 1980s, the 1990s and the start of the twenty-first century witnessed a succession of education reforms that left no publicly funded school untouched. In terms of ethnic diversity and racism, however, little of substance has changed. Although there are pockets of good anti-racist practice, at the national level it is clear that 'race' equality has never been a major concern. Despite its renewed commitment to 'equality of opportunity' and the fine words that met the publication of the Lawrence Inquiry, for example, New Labour has failed to break decisively with the traditional policy neglect in this field. Perhaps the one area where ethnic diversity *has* been addressed differently, in relation to funding for minority religious schools, is also the area where little or no public debate has taken place.

If national policy makers are serious about race equality they should consider moving away from some of the tried and failed approaches of the past. In this chapter, several have emerged. The approach that subsumes 'race' beneath other categories of action was clear in Keith Joseph's rejection of the Swann Report (in 1985) and the same tactic emerged in the DfEE's response to the Lawrence Inquiry (1999). A concern for 'tolerance' and 'understanding' has long been a feature of policy discourse but, without clear and targeted anti-racist action, the lessons of the past are that such an approach is at best limited, at worst tokenistic. The marketising zeal of recent Conservative administrations has been replaced by New Labour's programme of social inclusion, but both have refused to set specific targets for minority attainment while prioritising crude and exclusionary 'standards' that appeal to tabloid sensitivities but leave ethnic inequalities to worsen. Racism and 'race' inequality are long established traits of the British education system; there is little reason for optimism that they will remain anything except a minority concern for the foreseeable future.

Notes

1. Parts of this argument have been developed elsewhere, including Blair *et al.* (1999) and Gillborn (1999b). In this paper the word 'race' is presented in inverted commas to denote its socially constructed nature (cf. Gillborn 1990).
2. Throughout this paper I use 'racialised' to refer to patterns of experience and outcome that are strongly associated with differences in ethnic origin. The term 'racism' is used here to denote social processes and differences in outcome that result in the disproportionate disadvantage of one or more minority ethnic groups.
3. The most frequently cited addition to this literature is undoubtedly Chris Mullard's essay 'Multicultural Education in Britain: from Assimilation to Cultural Pluralism' (Mullard 1982).
4. Dispersal was again embraced as a policy tool, in the late 1990s, by a Labour government keen to placate popular racist sentiments about asylum seekers.
5. Interestingly, similar themes of the rights and sensitivities of natural (white) subjects can be seen in the proclamation of 1601 quoted at the beginning of this chapter.
6. One study revealed that children of Black Caribbean ethnic origin were almost six times more likely to be expelled than their white counterparts (Gillborn and Gipps 1996: 52–3).
7. There have been many attempts to formulate definitions of equality of opportunity in education. Briefly, 'weak' versions tend to stress questions of access (concerning formal conditions) rather than substantive differences in attainment and experience, which are central to 'strong' versions of the concept: see Foster, Gomm and Hammersley 1996; Gillborn and Youdell 2000; Halsey, Heath and Ridge 1980; Valli, Cooper and Frankes 1997).

References

Ansell, A. E. (1997) *New Right, New Racism: Race and Reaction in the United States and Britain*, London: Macmillan.

Barker, M. (1981) *The New Racism: Conservatives and the Ideology of the Tribe*, London: Junction Books.

Blair, M., Gillborn, D., Kemp, S. and MacDonald, J. (1999) 'Institutional racism, education and the Stephen Lawrence Inquiry', *Education and Social Justice*, 1, 3, pp. 6–15.

Brandt, G. L. (1986) *The Realization of Anti-racist Teaching*, Lewes: Falmer.

Commission for Racial Equality/Runnymede Trust (1993) 'The debate so far', Conference paper 9, *Choice, Diversity, Equality: Implications of the Education Bill*, A Working Conference, 30 January.

Commission for Racial Equality (1998) *Education and Training in Britain*, London: CRE.

Commonwealth Immigrants Advisory Council (1964) *Second Report*, Cmd 2458, London: HMSO.

Department for Education and Employment (DfEE) (1997) *Excellence in Schools*. Cm 3681. London: The Stationery Office.

Department for Education and Employment (DfEE)(1999) 'Ethnic minority pupils must have the opportunity to fulfil their potential – Blunkett', *Press Release 90/99*, London: DfEE.

Dhondy, F. (1982) 'Who's afraid of ghetto schools?', in Dhondy, F., Beese, B. and Hassan, L. (eds) *The Black Explosion in British Schools*, London: Race Today Publications.

Drew, D. (1995) *'Race', Education and Work: the Statistics of Inequality*, Aldershot: Avebury.

File, N. and Power, C. (1981) *Black Settlers in Britain 1555–1958*, London: Heinemann.

Flew, A. (1984) *Education, Race and Revolution*, London: Centre for Policy Studies.

Foster, P., Gomm, R. and Hammersley, M. (1996) *Constructing Educational Inequality*, London: Falmer.

Gaine, C. (1995) *Still No Problem Here*, Stoke on Trent: Trentham.

Gillborn, D. (1990) *'Race', Ethnicity and Education: Teaching and Learning in Multi-Ethnic Schools*, London: Routledge.

Gillborn, D. (1995) *Racism and Antiracism in Real Schools: theory. policy. practice*, Buckingham: Open University Press.

Gillborn, D. (1999a) 'Race, nation and education: New Labour and the new racism', in Jack Demaine (ed.) *Education Policy and Contemporary Politics*, London: Macmillan, pp. 82–102.

Gillborn, D. (1999b) 'Fifty years of failure: "race" and education policy in Britain', in Annette Hayton (ed.) *Tackling Disaffection and Social Exclusion: Education Perspectives and Policies*, London: Kogan Page, pp. 135–55.

Gillborn, D. and Gipps, C. (1996) *Recent Research on the Achievements of Ethnic Minority Pupils*, Report for the Office for Standards in Education, London: HMSO.

Gillborn, D. and Youdell, D. (1998) ' "Raising standards" and deepening inequality: league tables and selection in multi-ethnic secondary schools', Paper presented at the annual meeting of the American Educational Research Association, 13–17 April, San Diego.

Gillborn, D. and Youdell, D. (2000) *Rationing Education: Policy, Practice, Reform and Equity*, Buckingham: Open University Press.

Gilroy, P. (1987) *There Ain't No Black in the Union Jack*, London: Hutchinson.

Gilroy, P. (1990) 'The end of anti-racism', *New Community*, **17**, 1, pp. 71–83.

Halsey, A. H., Heath, A. F and Ridge, J. M. (1980) *Origins and Destinations: Family, Class, and Education in Modern Britain*, Oxford: Clarendon Press.

Home Office (1999) *Stephen Lawrence Inquiry: Home Secretary's Action Plan*, London: Home Office. Available at http://homeoffice.gov.uk/ppd/oppu/slpages.pdf

Lepkowska, D. (1998) 'Muslims gain equality of funding', *Times Educational Supplement*, 16 January, p. 18.

Lynch, J. (1986) *Multicultural Education: Principles and Practice*, London: Routledge and Kegan Paul.

Macdonald, I., Bhavnani, R., Khan, L. and John, G. (1989) *Murder in the Playground: The Report of the Macdonald Inquiry into Racism and Racial Violence in Manchester Schools*, London: Longsight.

Macpherson, W. (1999) *The Stephen Lawrence Inquiry*, CM 4262-I, London: The Stationery Office.

Major, J. (1997) *Britain – The Best Place in the World*, text of a speech to the Commonwealth Institute, 18 January. London: Conservative Central Office.

Massey, I. (1991) *More Than Skin Deep*, London: Hodder and Stoughton.

Modood, T. (1992) *Not Easy Being British: Colour, Culture and Citizenship*, Stoke-on-Trent: Runnymede Trust and Trentham Books.

Modood, T., Banton, M., Cohen, P., Gillborn, D. and Shukra, K. (1996) 'The changing context of "race" in Britain: a symposium', *Patterns of Prejudice*, **30**, 1, pp. 3–42.

Mullard, C. (1982) 'Multiracial education in Britain: from assimilation to cultural pluralism', in Tierney, J. (ed.) (1982) *Race, Migration and Schooling*, London: Holt, Rinehart and Winston, pp. 120–33.

Myers, K. (1990) 'Review of "Equal Opportunities in the New Era" ', *Education*, 5, October, p. 295.

Palmer, F. (ed.) (1986) *Anti-Racism – An Assault on Education and Value*, London: Sherwood Press.

Ramdin, R. (1987) *The Making of the Black Working Class in Britain*, Aldershot: Westwood House.

Rampton, A. (1981) *West Indian Children in Our Schools*, Cmnd 8273, London: HMSO.

Rattansi, A. (1992) 'Changing the subject? racism, culture and education', in Donald, J. and Rattansi, A. (eds) (1992) *'Race', Culture and Difference*, London: Sage, pp. 11–48.

Rose, E. J. B., Deakin, N., Abrams, M., Jackson, V., Peston, M., Vanags, A. H., Cohen, B., Gaitskell, J. and Ward, P. (1969) *Colour and Citizenship*, Oxford: Oxford University Press.

Sivanandan, A. (1988) 'Left, Right and Burnage', *New Statesman*, 27 May, Reprinted in Sivanandan, A. (1990) *Communities of Resistance: Writings on Black Struggles for Socialism*, London: Verso, pp. 145–52.

Swann, Lord (1985) *Education for All: Final Report of the Committee of Inquiry into the Education of Children from Ethnic Minority Groups*, Cmnd 9453, London: HMSO.

Taylor, M. J. (1992) *Multicultural Antiracist Education after ERA: Concerns, Constraints and Challenges*, Slough: National Foundation for Educational Research.

Thatcher, M. (1993) *The Downing Street Years*, London: Harper Collins.

Times Educational Supplement (1999) 26 March: 4.

Tomlinson, S. (1977) 'Race and education in Britain 1960–77: an overview of the literature', *Sage Race Relations Abstracts*, 2, 4, pp. 3–33.

Troyna, B. and Carrington, B. (1990) *Education, Racism and Reform*, London: Routledge.

Valli, L., Cooper, D. and Frankes, L. (1997) 'Professional development schools and equity: a critical analysis of rhetoric and research', in Apple, M. W. (ed.) *Review of Research in Education*, Volume 22, Washington DC: American Educational Research Association, pp. 251–304.

Whitty, G. (1992) 'Education, economy and national culture' in Bocock, R. and Thompson, K. (eds) *Social and Cultural Forms of Modernity*, Oxford: Polity.

Whitty, G. (1997) 'Creating quasi-markets in education: a review of recent research on parental choice and school autonomy in three countries', in Apple, M. W. (ed.) *Review of Research in Education*, Volume 22, Washington DC: American Educational Research Association, pp. 3–47.

Chapter 12

Future prospects – towards inclusive education for all

C. Wright, D. Weekes and A. McGlaughlin

Introduction

This chapter summarises a study in five schools that explored the impact of race, class and gender on the interactions of pupils and teachers in the classroom setting and school in general. The research sought to investigate the processes involved that help to explain the differential rates of school exclusion between pupils of different ethnic backgrounds, social class and gender. The research has focused on the often delicate balance between power and resistance.

The research undertaken built on previous research findings on school exclusion and broadened it by examining how changing policies can affect the school processes which lead to exclusion. To provide an adequate explanation for differential rates of exclusion, school processes have been explored in relation to the nature of interactions between schools, teachers and pupils. The study has also sought to disentangle how race, gender and class impact on these interactions. The after-effects of exclusion have also been studied and how school exclusion can exacerbate a variety of forms of social exclusion. The research has also attempted to build on recent work on masculinity (Mac an Ghaill, 1994; Sewell, 1997) which is particularly important given the disproportionate number of males excluded. The research also suggests that the simplistic view of antagonistic relationships between pupils and teachers is in fact structured within the recent changes in educational policy.

The intention of this chapter is to review the findings of the study and by so doing look at ways in which the negative social consequences of school exclusion can be avoided. This involves the formulation of recommendations and initiatives based on the experiences of pupils and teachers involved in the research. Initiatives relate to in-school interventions as well as wider policy interventions. The findings and recommendations of the MacPherson Report (1999) will also be addressed, in so far as they relate to schooling, education and 'institutional racism'.

Changing policy considerations

At the outset of the study it was clear that the relationship between exclusion and race can be situated within the wider context of educational policy and the need for schools to have 'desirable' pupils in order to enhance or maintain their status. This is particularly significant when considering the rapid increase in school exclusions over recent years.

The increased marketization of education and the resulting publication of league tables of school performance has made it apparent that, in order for positions to be maintained, schools treat some pupils as more desirable than others. Where it operates, parental choice primarily enables parents to avoid schools with substantial numbers of pupils who are different from themselves. Indeed, it is difficult to separate the effect of the Education Reform Act (ERA) from the increasing number of school exclusions, especially of African-Caribbean males. The issue is not just one of parents choosing schools but of schools choosing pupils, thereby redefining their population. Thus in practice, through a variety of entrance measures and selection procedures, it is frequently the case that it is the school choosing the pupils rather than vice versa.

It is possible to regard exclusion as one of the ways in which schools choose pupils. The large increase in the rate of school exclusions in recent years may be part of the process whereby schools are selecting and deselecting pupils. For schools, the marketability and desirability of pupils operates through social class, race and gender. Not all groups are equally desirable in terms of their potential impact on school 'performance' and league table position. Within a context that has become increasingly consumerist and competitive it is not surprising to find that the school processes of pupil selection and deselection have a disproportionately adverse effect on some groups of pupils. The marketability of pupils may be related to their ability to give the school the qualities it is looking for.

One effect of the ERA has been to encourage the media, government and OFSTED to concentrate on the overall performance of schools, as evidenced through measures of performance in national tests and examinations. This focus leads to the neglect of what schools are doing for individual pupils or disadvantaged groups of pupils. Teachers face increasing pressure to produce a performance for a class group or subject that is easily measured. They therefore have less time to spend with individual pupils who may exhibit behavioural or learning difficulties. The pressure and stress on teachers to produce a measurable performance is not compatible with meeting the needs of all groups of children equally.

The 1998 School Standards and Framework Act has a focus on school exclusion, but it is still essentially blind to the differentials of race and class as they impact on school exclusions. The importance of racial stereotypes held by those working in schools and selecting/deselecting pupils is not addressed in recent education policies. It has been left to a government-sponsored report, the MacPherson Report (1999), which is not specifically concerned with education, to focus on racial stereotypes that are held throughout public institutions.

In addition to processes emanating from outside the school and impinging on school procedures and practices, there are other processes internal to the school. It is these internal procedures and practices that are determining the disproportionately high percentage of pupils of African-Caribbean origin who are being excluded from school. At the heart of this is the long recognized observation that relations between White teachers and Black pupils are far too often characterized by conflict. Bound up with this is the perception of Black pupils' attitudes towards authority. In addition, there is the contestation and resistance by Black pupils to teacher authority and their perception of their treatment by teachers. This has resonances with accounts of how schools treat their working-class pupils (Willis, 1977).

Black pupils, to an increasing extent, do not fit the concept of the 'ideal pupil'. This is with respect to both their marketization/desirability and their perceived reaction to authority, especially school authority. It is through both internal school practices and external policies that some groups of pupils become increasingly regarded as potential liabilities.

Empirical implications

The empirical work undertaken as part of this investigation has revealed the way in which exclusion largely results from the nature of the relationship between schools and their pupils. These relationships are often bound up with the nature of the schools' response to the issue of discipline. Schools vary in their exclusion policies and practices. School policies were found to vary from what might be termed 'zero tolerance', which involved a relatively quick recourse to fixed-term exclusion, to policies where there were either no clear guidelines or sanctions were simply left to the discretion of individual members of staff. This range of policies resulted in varying exclusion rates and different attitudes by schools towards the use of exclusion. Therefore, pupils at different schools varied in their likelihood of experiencing sanctions.

Schools had a variety of types of ethos and these were expressed through the views of headteachers and senior staff, particularly in relation to their 'disruptive minorities'. Sanctions were seen to be needed in order to reinforce the type of behaviour the schools found acceptable and as the means of reinforcing teacher/school authority. Where schools were adamant as to the importance of the latter, there tended to be higher rates of exclusion, especially where headteachers and senior staff regarded the use of exclusion as inevitable, and regretted the loss of physical punishment as a sanction. Discipline was found to relate to ideas about punishment, with the assumption that this would have a positive outcome for pupils. Schools frequently emphasized the division between the well-behaved majority and the poorly-behaved minority. This division was often perceived by teachers, senior staff and headteachers and created a climate of conflict between staff and pupils.

The conflict that occurs between pupils and schools has a relationship with the extent to which schools resort to sanctions as a response to pupil resistance. When the conflict involves African-Caribbean and Asian pupils, it is important to examine the nature of the conflict in relation to the resistance these groups are exhibiting and the extent to which this derives from their racialized positions. Most Black people are aware of the value of education. What is being resisted and contested is the nature of the power and control expressed by the schools. This is coupled with the extent to which pupils feel or experience discrimination and how this permeates through to the way in which teachers perceive their behaviour. Black pupils are contesting and resisting the nature of the knowledge the school is reproducing and the nature of the authority and power used by the schools.

The nature of the school ethos was found to be important in the extent to which pupils' responses and behaviour could be regarded as resistant. Resistances were also found to vary with the extent to which pupils perceived sanction policies as fair and/or their ability to get staff to listen to them. It was also clear that the extent to which pupils considered treatment to be fair was influenced by their perception as to whether incidents with and attitudes of teachers were racist. Where Black pupils perceived White pupils as misbehaving without experiencing sanctions, they would place their strategies of resistance within a racial context. Variations in experiences of exclusion by pupils were perceived as indicative of racism. When teachers were unwilling to address accusations of racism levelled at them by pupils, conflict was often exacerbated. However, suggestions in the March 1999 OFSTED report of institutional racism in schools have been met with denials by teachers and their unions.

Pupils resisted teacher control in a variety of ways. Although teachers often recognized the nature of this and the reasons behind it, they varied in their attitudes to addressing it. Pupil 'disaffection' was clearly identified as a background factor, but some teachers felt powerless in assisting pupils. This was particularly evident when they disagreed with the sanction policies of senior staff.

Pupils resistance to schooling and school processes and their responses to the use of sanctions, was found not merely to be a matter of school policy and ethos, but how the practice of these was mediated through the racialized and gendered positions of the pupils. The schools in the study had a variety of complex ways in which they were involved in the production of masculinities and femininities. The disproportionate involvement of Black males in exclusion has been known for some time and there is an interrelating of race and gender involved in this outcome. It is important to know how schools perceive and respond to Black masculinity. However, it is also important to include Black femininities here, as young Black women also perceive and experience the influence of 'race' in their response to school sanctions.

The research has examined how masculinity, femininity and 'race' intersect to produce complex responses to school sanctions. It is Black pupil masculinity that has received the greatest attention in theorizing. The research here shows how schools and teachers can produce attitudes that lead to the perception of Black male pupils as being more aggressive. In a response to this, some teachers wish to (re-)gain control through more physical means. In fact to make control become more heavily masculine. Teachers were more likely to see Black male pupils as a threat. This involved an attendant disproportionate involvement of those pupils in school sanctions.

Teacher perception of pupils' behaviour could also lead to Black male pupils finding themselves placed in lower sets and pupil referral units. Exclusion from higher status academic knowledge could in turn lead to Black masculinity being defined in terms of sporting prowess. However, this was not always the case. Black male pupils respond in complex ways to their perception of teacher attitudes. This may involve both conforming to dominant stereotypes and a rejection of them.

In terms of the experience of school sanctions, there is no equality of outcome when similar behaviours by White/Black female and male pupils involve different experiences. Black males have been known for some time to be disproportionately involved in school exclusions.

It is also important to analyse whether male and female pupils respond to sanctions differently and how any differences are related to the ways in which schooling produces definitions of masculinity and femininity. For many African-Caribbean male pupils, schooling involves confrontation to the consequent neglect of a focus on academic achievement. Black female pupils were also seen to be involved in confrontation, but the academic outcome for them is generally more positive. However, these pupils don't respond to the threat of school sanctions in a clearly identical way.

This study found that few Black females saw differences between themselves and their male peers in how they responded to school sanctions. Indeed, male pupils often did respond to the power of teachers in ways not specifically defined as masculine. The gendered background of teachers was also shown to be important in how different definitions of pupils are produced. Male teachers appeared more likely to use stereotypical notions of masculinity to exert influence and control over male pupils.

Black females are known to assert that their ethnicity is of greater importance than their gender in its effect on their economic and social positions. Indeed, Black female pupils were found to be responded to by teachers in similar ways to Black male pupils. The response of these pupils to sanctions and exclusion was partially mediated through gendered positions. Many pupils, irrespective of racial background, attempted to resist teacher power. African-Caribbean and Asian pupils were also seen to do this, but it was mediated through concerns related to gender and racial background. Black female pupils were seen to be more likely to stress their lack of power and this may be related to their feelings of helplessness in the face of teacher authority.

The greatest differentials in the ways in which pupils adapted and responded to school were based on 'race'. Teachers did sometimes consider Black male pupils to pose more discipline problems and this is related to images of Black males. However, it is 'race' that is the dominant dimension in this process. Teachers tend to regard African-Caribbean pupils as an homogeneous group, which is more likely to be disruptive, whereas White pupils were likely to be heterogenized.

The nature of teacher perception of Black pupils is part of the process involved in creating high rates of exclusion. However, schools do exclude pupils at different rates. Therefore schools do have an effect on exclusion rates and this can be related to their 'ethos'. This ethos is developed under a range of complex influences. On the one hand, internal policies, structures and attitudes of senior staff are involved. On the other, there is also a range of external pressures and factors. The latter have, in recent years, appeared primarily as competition between schools, and performance as indicated in school league tables. As a result, schools pay greater attention to improving performance, as shown on measured outcomes, and less attention to the needs of the disaffected. This change has been accompanied by the spreading culture of managerialism in schools. Managerialism results in an emphasis on such factors as economy and efficiency, which in the school setting means a greater stress on indicators such as examination results and less stress on trying to meet the needs of less motivated pupils. The high rates of exclusion of African-Caribbean pupils should be placed within this climate of change.

Superimposed on a culture which emphasizes the importance of measurable performance indicators, is the way in which some schools exhibit a lack of sensitivity and understanding in meeting the needs of African-Caribbean children. Hence Black pupils and their parents often feel as though White children are treated more favourably. This does, however, vary by school. Schools with policies applied coherently and consistently are more successful in dealing with disruptive behaviour. Less effective schools have practices that are less supportive. Such schools tend to blame the pupils, with the implication that exclusion is meeting the needs of the school. Even in schools with clear policies, the practice was often seen by Black pupils and parents as divisive. This was particularly evident in how they saw disciplinary practices as disadvantaging Black children. Practices that aim at resolving conflict, rather than stressing harmony, may be the more successful and less discriminating in outcome. Where there is an inability to solve problems and little commitment to equality, exclusion rates are higher.

As noted earlier, changes brought about by the ERA have resulted in less tolerance towards aberrant student behaviour, with the increasing probability of exclusion being used to solve the problem. Black parents and students still see too many teachers ignoring racist behaviour and being less than sensitive to the needs of ethnic minority pupils. If Black pupils see that teachers are not addressing their needs and not dealing with the racism they experience, it creates a climate where disobedience occurs. Disobedience is the main reason leading to exclusion. Therefore, it happens that Black pupils are sometimes excluded for reacting to the racism they experience.

When Black pupils perceive or feel that teachers have low expectations of them, or are treating them unequally, they are more likely to express their reaction through aberrant behaviour. Black students frequently felt that in being excluded they were treated unfairly by schools. One consequence of unequal and unfair treatment by White teachers is that pupils and parents emphasize the need for Black teachers. This is because the White teachers involved lack the necessary sophistication to understand the effects of racism on students. One indication of this is that when Black pupils confront racism in school they are often seen by teachers as having behavioural problems.

African-Caribbean parents place great importance on academic success and achievement through education. It is in this context that we explain the strong feelings of Black parents and children when exclusion happens, particularly as they know that it is likely to have a lasting effect on the pupil. This also makes them more suspicious of teachers. Despite this, the parents of excludees want their children to return to schooling as soon as possible. This is seen as particularly important, given that excludees are at a much greater risk of longer-term social exclusion.

A constantly recurring theme for Black parents and pupils is how Black students, especially boys, should confront racism and racist abusers, when in the process they are likely to be seen by teachers as the perpetrators of problems and so risk exclusion. Also frequently stressed is how teacher assumptions about Black people may lead to confrontation. They do not feel that teachers deal with them fairly. The high rate of exclusion is seen as testament to this.

This study has examined the complex interaction of teacher-pupil relations, teacher perceptions and expectations and, superimposed on these, structural processes operating at the policy level. It is this complex interaction that leads to the differential experience of school sanctions by African-Caribbean pupils as compared with other pupil groups. It can be argued that what is at work here and is leading to disproportionately high rates of exclusion is institutional racism (Sasson, 1993). Sasson refers to anecdotal evidence that, 'when White youngsters are turned off schools and the curriculum, they truant. Black youngsters are forced by their parents to go to school where they become disruptive and in due course expelled' (p. 11). However, when this disruptive behaviour is exhibited, Black pupils still have a different experience of school sanctions than other groups. When Black pupils experience racism in school from whatever source, they react. However, it appears that their reaction is regarded as the problem, rather than the racism they have experienced. The unfairness that Black pupils identify refers to the fact that they see sanctions being applied more stringently to their reaction to racism than they see them being applied to the racism itself.

Converging views: Runnymede (1998), MacPherson (1999) and OFSTED (1999)

Recently, the Chairman of the CRE has commented on the low priority given to combating racism in schools and three recent reports have highlighted this problem: Runnymede (1998), MacPherson (1999) and OFSTED (1999).

The Runnymede Trust Report (1998)

The first of these reports stems from research undertaken by the Runnymede Trust and is focused on the general problem of raising the achievement of African-Caribbean pupils. Central to this problem is the need to address the high rate of exclusion. The two, however, are regarded as inseparable and hence the report recommends what it refers to as a 'whole school approach'. The report stresses a no-blame approach in that teachers and others need to work together in a variety of community initiatives. Teachers need to know that they are not being singled out for blame or criticism as they are intricately and vitally involved in solutions to the problem of disproprotionate exclusion rates. Genuine partnerships need to be developed, but the report emphasizes that, currently, these are rare.

It is in this context that the report recommends collaboration and dialogue between schools, community, parents and pupils as the key to raising African-Caribbean pupil achievement. Initiatives must target those pupils at risk from exclusion and focus on raising motivation, self-esteem and teacher expectation. Having more Black teachers and mentors is seen as important in this. The report goes on to recommend a large number of initiatives and measures to reduce exclusion and raise achievement. The difficulties that Black pupils have at school should be addressed in a specific and targeted way. Initiatives should therefore avoid being 'colour blind' and instead must target pupils most at risk of exclusion.

Measures must have the support of senior staff to prevent the issue of school exclusion being seen as marginal. Headteacher commitment is also vital. It is important that a positive school ethos is created, in which teachers listen to and respect pupils, and in which teachers are given support to reach each target relating to achievement and exclusion. In this respect, initiatives to reduce exclusion must incorporate the views of those pupils who have been excluded as to how they think exclusions could be reduced. Targets should be set within schools in relation to the behaviour management of pupils and involve subject staff. Targets for behaviour must also be closely tied to academic achievement.

In relation to pupils at risk of exclusion or having been excluded, the report suggests that support for these pupils should be integrated, with the aim of raising pupil motivation and achievement. Pupils excluded should be given home-based work to undertake to reduce problems of falling behind.

Schools should establish conflict resolution techniques for pupils. Teachers need to examine the underlying causes of disputes between pupils, and between themselves and pupils, rather than only concentrating on the immediate effects of confrontation. Teachers also need to recognize that racist name calling and abuse are real problems. There must also be an agreed procedure for dealing with racist incidents, as it is these that can lead to Black pupils reacting in ways that result in sanctions being applied to them. Important in this is that teachers must be consistent in allocating sanctions and with giving praise.

In relation to the whole school approach suggested by the report, schools are asked to consult with community groups, youth workers, parents and pupils. Initiatives to raise Black pupil achievement, recognizing that reducing the exclusion problem is part of this, should be integrated into schools' plans. At the national level the report goes on to suggest that the government should set national targets to reduce the number of African-Caribbean pupils excluded. In-service and initial teacher training should provide teachers with the skills to address issues of teacher stereotyping and low expectations, particularly of African-Caribbean boys.

The MacPherson Report (1999)

A very large number of initiatives involving school and community are described and recommended by the Runnymede Report. These received national media attention. Receiving much greater media, national and government attention has been the publication of the MacPherson Report (1999), investigating the murder of Stephen Lawrence. This report did not have a specific remit on education or school exclusion, but related primarily to the handling of the investigation into the racist murder of Stephen Lawrence. However, the report produced a wide ranging set of recommendations not confined to the issue of policing. The report identified many issues to do with racism working in society at large. In this regard the report did suggest action that needed to be undertaken in schools and by the education system, in order to address racism. The report did indicate that some schools have resisted antiracist policies, and even where they do exist these policies are largely ineffective. There was a need identified to combat racism in pupils, in order to reduce racist incidents which affect the behaviour of black pupils.

The report produced a number of recommendations for schools in relation to combating racism. The one particular measure relating to school exclusions was that schools should publish data on exclusions broken down by ethnic group. There should also be a league table of pupils excluded. A number of other measures were recommended that have a bearing on school exclusion, including that schools should record all racist incidents and report them to pupils' parents, governors and the LEA. The number of such incidents should be published annually by schools. The report identified it as important that the national curriculum be amended, by incorporating issues of preventing racism and valuing cultural diversity. Hence, the national curriculum should reflect a diverse multi-ethnic society. The necessity to teach anti-racism as part of the national curriculum was also recommended. Racial awareness should also be provided in the classroom.

The OFSTED Report (1999)

Following soon after the MacPherson Report came the OFSTED Report: *Raising the Attainment of Ethnic Minority Pupils* (1999). The focus of this report is the performance of ethnic minority pupils in schools. It examines the strategies that schools use and could use to raise attainment, along with policies for tackling stereotyping and ensuring high expectations. All of these are vital ingredients in tackling the problem of school exclusion among African-Caribbean pupils. The report finds that this group of pupils 'make a sound start in primary schools but their performance shows a marked decline at secondary level'. This suggests that the major problems are at this level.

The report finds limited evidence of schools having positive strategies to address the problems faced by African-Caribbean pupils. Few schools monitor initiatives to raise attainment or have clear procedures for monitoring the implementation of Equal Opportunity policies. There is limited use of ethnic monitoring in schools and few schools review their curriculum and pastoral strategies to ensure that they are sensitive to ethnic minority pupils. In those schools which have been successful in raising the attainment of ethnic minority pupils, senior managers make it clear that underperformance is not acceptable and they challenge staff to make it clear what they intend to do about it. Schools in which ethnic minority pupils do well, understand the 'hostility' the pupils face. These schools develop successful strategies for countering stereotyping and this can have a positive effect on confidence and self-esteem. Schools with successful race relations have an ethos where pupils can express their concerns and play a part in their resolution.

In relation to exclusion, few schools analyse data by ethnicity or consider the causes of exclusion. Some schools have discovered that African-Caribbean pupils involved in fights and confrontation had experienced racist abuse prior to the incidents. 'Those minority ethnic pupils who react angrily to racist insults often find themselves at the sharp end of sanctions. Schools must make it explicit that racist behaviour is wrong and will not be tolerated' (OFSTED, 1999: 38). The research undertaken in the present study has emphasized the role of unfairness in the perception of the lives of Black pupils. Approaches and strategies to deal with this are vital in tackling the problem of excessive school exclusions of these pupils.

The OFSTED Report echoes the Runnymede Report in that it emphasizes whole school policies. It stresses that schools should monitor pupil achievement, behaviour, attendance and exclusion by ethnic group and use this data to set targets for improvement. Schools must counter harassment and stereotyping by having policies that are clear and include practical guidance on how to deal with racist behaviour. An open school ethos is part and parcel of this. LEAs need to set targets to reduce the exclusions of African-Caribbean pupils and should also collect and collate data on exclusion and behaviour by ethnic group.

Conclusion

These three reports resonate clearly with the investigations and findings discussed in the previous chapters. The emphasis must involve a change of school culture from exclusion to inclusion. It must be remembered that school exclusion infringes the rights of children to education. Those pupils who are excluded often find it difficult to regain entry to formal education. When faced with exclusion, parents must have the ability to exercise their right to places for their children in other schools. The increased marketization of schooling and competition between schools is leading to a situation where exclusion is more and not less likely. Rather than seeing exclusion as a means of solving problems, schools need to adopt approaches that aim at keeping and retaining pupils they may perceive as less desirable. They need to move to a position where they regard all pupils as potential high achievers.

It is not sufficient simply to eschew overt acts or words of racism. We have to recognize that Black pupils are not expected to do as well as White students and/or are expected to be louder or less well-behaved than White children. It is possible to improve pupils' achievements by treating them as if they will succeed or behave well. So, if others are treated as if they will perform badly or fail, we must bear responsibility for this. Pupils can live down to the school's expectations of them. Strategies and an ethos must be put in place, whereby Black students have high self-esteem if they are to do themselves justice. Others' perceptions of Black pupils can be changed, along with their own perceptions of themselves.

These perceptions are inextricably linked to the over-representation of African-Caribbean pupils in school exclusion statistics. This problem has to be tackled in conjunction with an overall school policy of raising achievement. As such, a whole school approach is vital and should incorporate a large number of interconnected measures. Headteachers must take a strong lead on equal opportunities. If necessary, appropriate further training may be required. Both in-service and initial teacher training have to incorporate anti-racism training and all that it involves, in relation to teacher expectations and stereotypes. Black pupils frequently stress the importance of having Black teachers in their schools. Black mentor programmes are also known to assist in increasing self-esteem and raising pupils' expectations of themselves. Underpinning the success of such programmes is the building of strong links between schools and the communities they serve.

It is impossible to measure improvements without monitoring. It is vital for schools to monitor achievement, exclusion and behaviour incidents by ethnic group. Accompanying this monitoring must be the setting of targets with all school staff involved, together with a clear commitment from senior staff to improvement. Target setting is inseparable from having a clear strategy for preventing exclusion. Part and parcel of a clear strategy is to listen to and learn from both pupils and parents. There must be incorporated in this strategy clear targeting and tracking of pupil achievement and behaviour by ethnic group.

Schools and teachers must be seen to be intolerant of racism. Every school must have a clear procedure for responding to racist incidents and treat them as a potential source of poor behaviour, rather than responding to pupils' behaviour which is itself the reaction to racism. Schools have to investigate grievances and be vigilant in those relating to racism. Strategies for dealing with stereotyping need to be linked to the role of developing a curriculum that is truly multi-cultural and anti-racist.

It is not simply a matter of policies for schools. A lead needs to be taken by LEAs and government. In this respect the present government has already given its response to the MacPherson Report (1999). Schools will be required to log all racist incidents and report patterns and the frequency of racism to the LEA. Parents have the right to know what action schools will take to tackle racism. The government has also stated that it agrees with the MacPherson Report call to include anti-racism in the national curriculum. However, it believes that the national curriculum already addresses the diverse nature of British society and schools will not have to publish league tables of racist behaviour as recommended in the report. Rather, the government believes that this would penalize those schools which are open and honest about racism. However, as noted in the OFSTED Report (1999), such schools are relatively rare.

Concluding implications

So, what implications should finally be drawn from this study? First, we must acknowledge the importance placed on education by African-Caribbean parents and their children. Because of this, many disaffected Black pupils remain in school and want to be educated, instead of which they frequently end up excluded. Their disaffected White peers more often simply stay away from school and, thus, are no longer seen as a problem.

As well as wanting to be educated, indeed in order to be educated, Black pupils need to have the differentiated recognition and respect that their White peers attract. Colour blind treatment is unacceptable. Pupils need racially aware teachers, who interact with them, taking account of their colour and culture, and who encourage diversity, not unthinking conformity. Likewise, class and gender cannot be ignored.

Treating any group of pupils as if they are homogeneous is a mistake; and treating all Black pupils alike, without reference to their class, gender or other individual characteristics, is both racist and insulting. White pupils are far more likely to be treated in a differentiated way. We also have to accept that schools that are run on competitive lines, sensitive to the market in which they operate and their position in the performance league tables, are likely to succumb to a managerialist culture. In turn, this will further marginalize or even ignore the needs of disaffected pupils, rather than provide the positive and supportive ethos that they require. In such a culture teachers are more likely to ignore racism and thereby further alienate and incite their black pupils. They will certainly lose respect and encounter a lack of co-operation. But when those same Black pupils refuse to accept racism and instead react to it, their behaviour may very well be seen as the problem. Punishing understandable responses to racism, whilst ignoring the racism itself, is hardly the way to engage Black pupils in the education enterprise. Black people, whether parents or pupils, are not going to ignore racism. Having already fought and overcome slavery and segregation, exclusion from school is not going to be accepted without complaint, where it is imposed for reacting to racist taunts, slurs, insults or other racist behaviour. Schools and their communities have to recognize the inter-connectedness of race, class, gender and power and then act together to ensure that cultural diversity is both respected and valued. Exclusion from school has to be recognized as indicative of a problem yet to be solved, not as one that has been resolved.

References

Mac an Ghaill, M. (1994) *The Making of Men: Masculinities, Sexualities and Schooling*, Milton Keynes: Open University Press.

MacPherson Report (Home Office) (1999) 'The Report of the Stephen Lawrence Inquiry chaired by Lord MacPherson', London: HMSO.

OFSTED (Office for Standards in Education) (1999) *Raising the Attainment of Minority Ethnic Pupils: School and LEA Responses*, London: OFSTED Publications Centre.

Runnymede Trust (1998) *Improving Practice: A Whole School Approach to Raising the Achievement of African-Caribbean Youth*, London: The Runnymede Trust.

Sasson, D. (1993) 'The price of banishment', *Education* 181(6): 111.

Sewell, T. (1997) *Black Masculinities and Schooling: How Black Boys Survive Modern Schooling*, Stoke-on-Trent: Trentham Books.

Willis, P. (1977) *Learning to Labour: How Working Class Kids Get Working Class Jobs*, Aldershot: Saxon House.

Chapter 13

Moral education in victim offender conferencing

Francis J. Schweigert

Introduction

If every crime represents a failure in moral learning – on the part of the offender, his/her community, and possibly the surrounding society – then every crime also presents an opportunity for moral learning. Just as the child accepting a treat is caught before running away and admonished to say 'thank you,' the offender is caught in the act of turning away from moral and legal norms and punished. The analogy holds over a broad range of aims in criminal justice: correcting the offender, restoring social order and security, repairing harm to the victim, re-affirming moral values or rectifying a moral imbalance, and reminding all observers of the public will. All these aims are moral, for morality includes both person and society, intention and act, correcting and healing, and values and goods.

This chapter argues that victim offender conferencing offers an opportunity to reevaluate and expand the educational potential of criminal justice. If victim offender conferencing offers more effective educational practice than does punishment alone, then the aims listed above can be reaffirmed more clearly as *educational* aims. That is, moral learning can have more priority as an outcome of the criminal justice system.

Victim offender conferencing and restorative justice

Victim offender conferencing is part of the larger movement of restorative justice, which draws its inspiration from a wide variety of responses to conflict, all of which aim above all to restore what the conflict has damaged or threatened, to the extent possible. Thus, divorce mediation cannot restore the marriage, but it can restore the ability of parents to cooperate for the good of their children. Likewise, victim offender conferencing cannot completely erase the trauma of crime, but it can restore a sense of physical and emotional security, replace the value of material goods, and provide a pathway for reintegrating offenders.

As Aristotle says, justice is a complex term meaning several things: complete virtue, legal order, transactional equity, political equality, proportional distribution of goods, rectification of harms, and equity as a modification where the letter of law would be too rigid.[1] Responding to crime with the aim of restorative justice incorporates elements of all of these. Crime is addressed as a violation of the legal order, but also as a violation of persons. Political equality and rights are reaffirmed, but in a context of personal conversation and even confrontation. The proportion between crime and consequences is maintained, but according to the perceptions of those most directly involved more than by the impersonal hand of the state. Harms are rectified in proportion to the damage done but especially in light of what is important to those harmed. Contracts are negotiated by consensus. Above all, crime is addressed in a manner consistent with what Aristotle calls complete justice: an overall sense of what is right and good for individuals as well as the commonwealth, the combination of all the virtues of public life in the good person. It is this element of justice that especially marks the various forms of victim offender conferencing.

Victim offender conferencing is a process of dialogue, negotiation, and problem solving involving those most directly affected by the crime. Four versions of conferencing are in common use. *Victim offender mediation* (also called victim offender dialogue) involves three parties directly – the offender, the victim, and a mediator – although supporters may be present. *Family group conferencing* typically includes a conference facilitator, the victim, the offender, and members of their respective families and support networks. *Community conferencing* includes a convener/facilitator, victims, offenders, and members or representatives of the local community, sometimes in addition to family members or personal supporters. *Circle sentencing* is open to the public and can include as many as one hundred persons, including victims, offenders, family members, personal supporters, and concerned members of the community – all participating in an orderly pattern of conversation guided by a circle keeper. Increasingly, these processes appear in combinations and with variations that reflect the on-going experimental nature of the conferencing movement.

All four versions of victim offender conferencing share similar assumptions and purposes and follow similar formats, ensuring that all participants are respected, heard, and permitted to contribute to the solution: (a) the facilitator opens the session with introductions of participants and of the process; (b) the victim, offender, and other participants describe the incident from their points of view; (c) together, participants identify the issues and interests at stake and explore possible ways to solve the problems that have been raised; (d) participants agree to a settlement by consensus, which may include financial reparation, personal service, community service, education or training or counseling for either party, or other possible actions jointly agreed-upon; (e) the facilitator closes the session by summarizing what has occurred in the process and the terms of the settlement; and (f) in the informal space that follows, the participants discuss what they have experienced, often share food and drink, and very often exchange profound gestures of apology, forgiveness, reconciliation, and reintegration.

The working of restorative justice is visible, creative, and open-ended in its concern for victims and offenders. The conference is a social space in which participants can tap into individual and communal strengths to design effective ways that injury and conflict can be converted into healing and community development.

These guiding principles are the distinguishing marks of restorative practices in all their forms. In this sense, restorative justice is more a philosophy or even a 'spirituality of practice' than it is a set of procedures, interventions, or programs. The principles provide direction for participants, but not all participants pursue this path with equal determination, creativity, or endurance. It is therefore important to recognize the limits assumed in the suggestions raised in this paper. Restorative practices are oriented to outcomes more than to procedures, but the outcomes are dependent upon the particularities of each situation, including the backgrounds, sensitivity, creativity, and enthusiasm of participants. Even so, there is a consistency between means and ends, such that the nature of the outcomes will be consistent with the nature of the interactions in the intervention.

Expanding the educational aim of criminal justice

The punishment of offenders already involves moral aims that are therefore educational aims, as noted above. To make this linkage between morality and education clearer, it is necessary to make explicit the assumptions involved. Education is always an intervention in the on-going process of social learning, to facilitate learning in a particular direction; the direction is embodied in the assumptions guiding the practice. The assumptions in the educative aim of criminal justice are well articulated by Jean Hampton.[2]

First, if moral education is a purpose of punishment, it entails a judgment of moral wrongdoing. The offender has not merely broken a law; he or she has done something morally wrong, and the state is acting through the criminal justice system to bring this wrong to the offender's attention. *Second*, by definition, moral acts are freely chosen; therefore a moral education theory of punishment entails a belief in human freedom. The offender is a free person, who could have chosen the right but chose instead the wrong. Punishment is imposed not merely as a behaviorist instrument, to curb wrongdoing by a conditioned response, but as an instructional instrument appealing to the offender's freedom, seeking to raise the offender's awareness of right and wrong so that he or she will make better choices in the future. *Third*, if moral education is the purpose of punishment, then the punishment is intended to benefit the offender directly. That is, it is intended to augment or correct the offender's knowledge of right and wrong. It would not be consistent with this purpose to punish the offender merely to demonstrate the state's determination to enforce the law or to display the power of the state over individual citizens. *Fourth*, a moral education theory of punishment is inconsistent with viewing crime as an illness that needs to be treated or as a handicap that requires rehabilitation. Rather, crime is evidence of ignorance, a lack of moral perception and knowledge; or crime is a result of weakness of will, a failure of moral judgment and character. In either case, crime is evidence of a problem whose remedy is learning, and hence can be addressed by education. *Fifth*, punishment as moral education always has a moral goal – to communicate moral truth in the face of wrong-doing. In this view, crime is miseducative, a departure from truth, a frustration of human freedom and growth, a denial of right understanding. The victim is wronged by the offender's imposition of moral falsehood. The punishment of the offender is therefore a declaration of the victim's moral innocence at the same time that it is a denunciation of the offender's moral culpability. The aim is not merely to uphold the law, but to uphold and affirm moral righteousness.

These five assumptions comprise a view of the individual as a social person and a moral person, accountable at once to a particular community and to an understanding of right and wrong – and since accountable, therefore both educable and capable of choice. Even more than in punishment, these assumptions are operative in restorative justice, and especially in victim offender conferencing, which is an intervention designed to facilitate moral learning, individually and communally, using the occasion of criminal apprehension as a teachable moment for all involved.

First, as in a moral education view of punishment, victim offender conferencing is designed to confront the offender with a judgment of wrongdoing, not merely lawbreaking. In conferencing, however, this judgment draws upon the moral authority of the community as well as that of the state.

As in punitive justice, one source of moral authority resides in the moral principles underlying the laws of the state – the system of inalienable rights articulated in the tradition of the Declaration of Independence and the Bill of Rights. These are the classic liberal moral principles of individual freedom and equality that comprise what John Rawls calls an 'overlapping consensus' in Western style democratic societies, providing a basis upon which to adjudicate public claims and coerce public conformity.[3] These rights parallel what Thomas Lickona calls 'universal values,' such as responsibility, respect, tolerance, fairness, honesty, and cooperation.[4] It is helpful to think of these as procedural values, specifying a manner of social cooperation without demanding agreement on substantive commitments and ways of life. Their moral authority is based on personal assent achieved through rational reflection and reasoned debate, which is also the ground for the state's judgment of moral wrongdoing in criminal justice. In victim offender conferencing, this judgment is embodied in the policeman who makes the arrest, in the judge who participates in the arraignment or sits in the sentencing circle, and in the facilitator of the conference who represents the public stake in this case and reinforces these values as the governing principles for interaction in the conference itself. All of these persons, as representatives of the state, also represent its moral authority. This moral consensus on equality and human dignity also guides the conference process of equal participation, shared responsibility, consensus decision-making, and – as a kind of background safety-net – the option of offenders and victims to withdraw from the conference and take their case to the court system.

Victim offender conferencing also introduces a second source of moral authority by incorporating informal social interaction into the process of justice and by including members of the families and/or communities of the victim and offender. Offenders are held accountable not only to the procedural values of the state but to family commitments to standards of behavior, good character, religious norms, cultural expectations, interpersonal trust, and familial loyalty and reputation. These are values that arise from a comprehensive view of the right and good, rooted in familial and cultural and religious traditions. These values do not necessarily appeal to reason; their authority may flow from divine command, interpersonal bonds, or cultural expectations.[5]

The conference provides a public space in which these communal values can be expressed, but it does not guarantee they will be incorporated into the outcomes. Rather, the procedural safeguards of the conference function as a kind of testing ground for family and community norms, sometimes supporting and sometimes challenging them. Three examples from recent conferences can serve as illustrations. In one instance, a parent demanded a rigid accountability from her son, linked with an ultimatum of rejection from the household; the ultimatum was challenged in the circle by other parents and was later withdrawn. In a second instance, a parent dismissed the seriousness of her daughter's offense; other circle members refused to accept this as a proper response. A third instance moved in the other direction when, in contrast to the harshness of parents and community members, the victim forgave the offenders and offered them a pathway to reintegration as respected young adults.

The educative aim of victim offender conferencing therefore moves in two directions: raising consciousness of the moral values underlying democratic society and embodied in its laws, and reinforcing – but also testing – the substantive moral values in families and communities. It is difficult to describe in simple terms the multiple directions in which learning moves in this kind of situation. Individuals are made more aware of certain values *and* more aware of roles they are expected to fulfill – including their role as citizens with rights and responsibilities. The moral authority of families and communities is reinforced *and* held accountable to liberal democratic values. Participants representing state institutions are given a platform from which to project societal norms *and* they are required to put these norms at the service of personal, familial, and communal goods.

Second, victim offender conferencing confronts the offender as one possessing freedom of will, who could have chosen to do otherwise in the past and who can be expected to choose to do otherwise in the future. In the *matter* of moral confrontation, restorative justice and punitive justice do not differ – both confront the offender in moral terms – but they do differ in the *manner* of confrontation. The conferencing process educates not merely by looking backward to wrong choices and forward to better choices, but also by requiring the offender to participate in good choices here and now. A convicted offender can passively accept punishment as imposed by the court, while refusing to accept responsibility for the offense or for his or her response to the offense. In conferencing, the offender must exercise freedom to gain access to the conference and must exercise freedom to complete the work of the conference. Furthermore, because the conference requires consensus on any agreements, the offender must actively participate in determining justice in this case. Individual moral autonomy is doubly assumed.

Third, both punitive justice and victim offender conferencing require that sanctions work to the benefit of the offender, toward his or her moral education. It is a hallmark of victim offender conferencing, however, that the sanctions and the process through which they are determined work first of all to the benefit of the victim as well and to the benefit of the community, if possible. To the extent that the benefit intended for the victim and community is educative, this intention might appear to imply that the victim and community need to learn something and thus bear some moral culpability that needs to be corrected. While this is certainly possible, it is not assumed in the design and purpose of victim offender conferencing. What *can* be assumed is that the manner of resolving crime in victim offender conferencing can be a moral lesson for all involved. Values are reinforced, commitments are affirmed, needs are clarified, and all participants are instructed and coached in a method of solving problems and resolving conflicts respectfully.

Fourth, victim offender conferencing is directed to learning rather than to treatment or rehabilitation, even more emphatically than in a moral education theory of punishment. Treatment and rehabilitation imply that the offender is at least temporarily disabled in fulfilling his or her responsibilities and hence must be subjected to a therapeutic regimen of some kind. In a conference, the offender is expected to participate fully, to be held accountable for the crime, and to take responsibility for restoring what the crime has damaged, to the extent possible and appropriate. This is one of the empowering dynamics of conferencing, since accountability implies the ability to fulfill one's responsibilities, and the conference supplies practical support in doing so. This does not preclude including therapeutic elements in the conference agreement, but it puts the offender in the position of having to participate in choosing the treatment program.

This dynamic of empowerment with support is extended to the victim and to the community as well. The victim is able to confront the offender and negotiate a solution from a position of moral strength rather than as one diminished by the crime. The community is given a forum through which it can exercise its responsibility for its members rather than suffer crime passively and depend entirely upon the coercive power of the state for protection and order.

Fifth, victim offender conferencing also has a moral goal, but its aim is more comprehensive than the goal of a moral education theory of punishment. In punitive justice, 'The state, as it punishes the lawbreaker, is trying to promote his moral personality; it realizes that "[h]is soul is in jeopardy as his victim's is not".'[6] Restorative justice aims not only to correct the offender but also to make the whole situation right, to the extent possible. The first priority morally is to heal the victim, the second to correct the offender. The process of victim offender conferencing aims to reinforce a moral commitment to the universal, procedural values of the state and to strengthen the communal values of empathy, compassion, healing, forgiveness, reconciliation, trust, fidelity, and loyalty.

In sum, then, rather than assuming that the offender is the sole focus of moral learning, victim offender conferencing includes family, friends, and community members within its educative aim. Rather than assuming that the process of criminal apprehension and adjudication will result in a changed offender who will be able to go forth and embody that learning alone, the conference aims to alter the patterns of interaction in the community of support to which the offender belongs. The whole community learns. Just as all who have suffered from the crime have a stake in restoring what has been damaged and lost, all have a stake in learning ways of interacting that will reinforce positive behavior and attitudes and reduce harmful behavior. Ultimately, the educative aim of criminal justice is to achieve more resilient and peaceful communities.

The educative dynamics in victim offender conferencing

In general, competing programs of moral education appeal to four basic methods for theoretical justification: behaviorism, values clarification, the cognitive-developmental approach, and character education.

A *behaviorist* methodology prescribes a carefully calibrated system of rewards and punishments – or incentives and disincentives – which, if consistently applied, will gradually shape the behavior and attitudes of learners. *Values clarification* distinguishes moral instruction, which is the responsibility of so-called private institutions such as families and churches, from public moral discourse, which is guided by public institutions such as schools. Hence, in this view, public educators presume that students already have moral values, either as innate capacities or as a result of previous training and experience. Therefore, the responsibility of public institutions such as schools is to help students clarify their values and to learn to articulate these values in the public arena, using procedural values such as respect and tolerance as a framework governing public moral discourse. The *cognitive-developmental* approach emphasizes the structural organization of moral thinking rather than the content of moral rules.[7] As children learn, they must continually reorganize their ways of thinking to take account of the increasing complexity of their experience. In regard to right and wrong, the direction of development is from moral judgments based on reward and punishment to moral judgments expressing universal moral principles based on reason. The educator's role is to stimulate this developmental process by presenting learners with vignettes of ethical conflicts and challenging them to use the more advanced styles of moral reasoning in determining a response. Abstract universal moral principles – however important to democratic participation – are seen as meaningless if individuals do not know what is good and are not committed to pursue it. Children need to learn what is right and good by observing those around them, by hearing the stories of heroic virtue in the past, and by practicing the right and pursuing the good until it is ingrained in their character.

These four methods are not mutually exclusive in practice, and all four play some role in victim offender conferencing. What seems particularly beneficial, from the perspective of victim offender conferencing, is the complementarity between the dynamics associated with each of these methods, in the particular circumstance of responding to crime.

Criminal justice, unlike other aspects of social order and public action, is peculiar in its determination to impose the public will on individuals. For the most part, by far, social order is maintained through informal social controls that operate cooperatively between the innate sociality of individuals and the implicit or explicit expectations of families, communities, and the larger society. Human freedom – as the capacity of each person to perceive, learn, and act as a self-determining yet other-regarding member of the group – is the essential linchpin of social order. The maintenance of social order in all the complexities of countless unique circumstances would be impossible without the exercise of human freedom, formed in accord with social obligations. To the formation of this individual conscience all moral education is aimed. It is therefore peculiar indeed that in situations of critical social concern – that is, crime – individual freedom is overwhelmed by the social determination to impose the public will. This peculiarity can easily be seen as a contradiction: education vs. punishment, restorative justice vs. punitive justice.

Punishment involves considerable social risk. The pain imposed can be miseducative as well as educative. The denial of freedom can provoke further alienation as well as greater desire for inclusion. The limit of toleration – always in some sense arbitrary and subject to political machination, and restricted by law to a kind of universal application – can be too severe for the case. Yet it is impossible to escape entirely the need for some socially determined limit; and it is difficult to imagine how such a limit – however it is symbolized – could function without similar risks. Punishment may not be an essential part of justice, but an equally potent symbol would be needed to replace it.

Moral education at this boundary therefore takes on urgency, calling for the proper exercise of human freedom lest the offender be lost to the group – with this loss being justified in advance by the loss already suffered by the victim. This creates a potent opportunity for learning. The argument so far suggests that punishment alone is not likely to be as effective as victim offender conferencing – always assuming that victim offender conferencing is being employed in a situation where the social limit of toleration has already been made clear. This argument can be extended by showing how the four methods of moral education identified above are enacted in the process of victim offender conferencing, with particular attention to the cognitive-developmental approach and character education.

A *behaviorist* understanding of moral education highlights the interplay of positive and negative reinforcements in victim offender conferencing. Punishment lies at the outside edge of the process, threatened but not imposed, while within the conference the conversation vibrates between disincentives and incentives: shame and invitation, guilt and positive engagement, confrontation with harm done and empowerment in problem solving.

Values clarification names the process through which the moral convictions of individuals and the moral assumptions underlying social institutions are articulated in a public space. Moral learning occurs when the demand to express these values in public brings clarity to the values, especially when participants must also integrate their personal convictions with societal expectations – as they must in victim offender conferencing.

The *cognitive-developmental* approach assumes that moral development is stimulated by wrestling with moral problems and conflicts, resulting in a natural – but not automatic – progress toward the higher stages of moral thinking. Victim offender conferencing appears to provide an excellent challenge to participants to rise to a higher level of moral thinking.

In a recent case of juvenile auto theft, for example, the following understandings of the moral conflict were expressed: the theft is wrong because I can be punished for it (stage one); the theft is wrong because it inconvenienced the owner/victim (stage two); the theft is wrong because nobody likes a thief (stage three); the theft is wrong because it broke the law (stage four); the theft is wrong because it violated the shared understanding of neighbors that their property would be respected by others (stage five); and the theft is wrong because stealing is a violation of human dignity and human rights (stage six). Whatever their stage of cognitive development, the conversation presented a challenge to rise to a higher level of moral thinking – a level more adequate for solving the problem. From the cognitive-developmental perspective, the educational power of victim offender conferencing lies in the process of moral dialogue, stimulating individual participants to comprehend and use higher levels of moral reasoning. The effects of this kind of learning tend to carry over into other situations. 'As people *can* comprehend higher moral concepts, they tend to *use* them in making moral decisions,' simply because these more developmentally advanced ways of thinking are more effective in organizing cooperation.[8]

Character education was defined 2300 years ago, when Aristotle noted that 'states of character arise out of like activities … for example, men become builders by building and lyre-players by playing the lyre; so too we become just by doing just acts, temperate by doing temperate acts, brave by doing brave acts.'[9] While human beings are 'adapted by nature to receive moral virtues,' virtues do not arise automatically; they have to be learned, and the only way to learn them is to practice them. Long years of practice will develop habits of thought, perception, desire, and action oriented toward pursuing what was really good for oneself – which is in accord with one's humanity. Thus the personal good will also be good for the community, for human beings are by nature social creatures and the personal good must therefore also be a social good, or it would be contrary to one's own nature.

The external goods of conferencing can include restitution paid to the victim, community service, victim satisfaction with the process, reintegration of the offender, healing of the victim, restoration of the community's sense of security, reduced recidivism rates among offenders, and increased interdependence among community members. These are the kinds of outcomes that can be measured and according to which the process can be judged successful. At the same time, conferencing requires internal goods – qualities of character that render participants able to achieve the external goods identified above: interpersonal sensitivity, fairness, honesty, respect, responsibility, willingness to listen, willingness to articulate one's beliefs and values, willingness to change, willingness to be held accountable, willingness to belong and to give and receive support, and willingness to repent and forgive. Without these qualities in some degree, conferences cannot achieve the desired outcomes. Thus, as stated earlier in this chapter, the quality of outcomes is dependent upon the capacities and character of participants. Yet the nature of the practice itself is educative, in the sense of demanding the exercise of these qualities of character – these virtues – and providing a public arena in which they can be displayed, appreciated, reinforced, strengthened, and extended.

Aristotle defines each virtue as a mean between two extremes: an excess and a deficiency. There is no formula for determining this mean; it is always an act of moral judgment, doing the right thing 'to the right person, to the right extent, at the right time, for the right reason, and in the right way.' Aristotle admits this is not easy, and for this reason good conduct is 'rare, praiseworthy, and noble.'[10] Also, for this reason, opportunities to practice this kind of moral judgment are essential to moral learning. Several of the virtues Aristotle highlights in the *Nicomachean Ethics* are central to the practice of victim offender conferencing; these can serve to illustrate the complementarity between qualities of character and moral decision-making.

Aristotle presents *generosity* as the mean between extravagance and stinginess, which are typically the kinds of excess and deficiency to avoid in working out terms of restitution in conferences. *Pride* is the mean between self-abasement and vanity, an accurate sense of the honor one has earned by what one has done. To discredit the good one has done is a vice, just as it is a vice to think better of one's actions than they deserve. Conferences often involve efforts on both sides of the mean. Offenders may fail to see the harm they have done and so must be shown the true effects of their deeds, to move them from false vanity toward an honest assessment. Conversely, offenders may be so shamed by their deeds that they see no good in themselves at all, and their deeds must be put in proper perspective so that they can rise above them to regain some sense of pride. Victims often feel debased by what they have suffered and need to be helped to see that the crime was not their fault, so they can regain a proper sense of self-esteem. *Good temper* is the mean between short temper and apathy. 'The man who is angry at the right things and with the right people, and further, as he ought, when he ought, and as long as he ought, is praised.'[11] This is the kind of 'instruction' in anger that occurs in conferencing. Anger is not in itself discouraged in victim offender conferencing; rather, anger can be an important source of energy in defense of what is right and good when it is expressed in a good way.

Aristotle devotes two entire books of the *Nicomachean Ethics* to the virtue of *friendship*. The crux of this virtue is that true friends support each other in doing what is right and in avoiding what is wrong. In this light, victim offender conferencing is a school in friendship: helping offenders turn from the misleading loyalties of a deviant peer group and toward real support which helps them become the best person they can become. Conferences also help community members and family members rise to their best hopes for one another and then commit to helping one another achieve it. *Shame*, according to Aristotle, is not a true virtue because it is more an affect than a characteristic. Yet he considers it close to being a virtue in young people, as a proper 'fear of dishonor' if their unworthy deeds were to become known by their elders.[12] Because of the fragmentation of contemporary American life, much that is done by youth may pass unnoticed or unconfronted by elders whose esteem they value. Victim offender conferencing provides an avenue for exactly this kind of check on juvenile offenders.

Justice, as noted earlier, is a complex term with many meanings. For Aristotle, however, the excess and deficiency in regard to justice is quite simple: the unjust person grasps for more than he or she deserves, creating some kind of inequality, while the just person seeks to match equal with equal or to restore equality where it has been taken away. This sense of equality is not rigid, however, for justice that cannot bend is not the best justice: this describes the kind of outcomes sought in conferencing. Because of the sensitivity to the facts by people who know the victim and offender very well, it is possible to shape a solution that truly fits the needs of those affected. Conferences can be faulted because, at least on the surface, they do not result in equal sentences for equal crimes. But this does not mean that conferences fail to achieve justice as the equitable, where legal justice fails on account of a lack of flexibiliy.

Practical wisdom is the ability to deliberate well, weighing the matter at hand and acting to bring about the best result. Aristotle sees this as an intellectual virtue, a seeking after truth, in the sense of trying to know what the facts of the situation are, what is truly at stake in the situation, and what good can be done in this situation. He is careful to point out, however, that there can never be the degree of certainty in these matters that one can achieve in mathematics and logic. Therefore practical wisdom is also a moral virtue, a wisdom that can be learned only through long effort at trying to achieve the good in all that one does. This virtue is required in every conference, as those seated in the circle try to find the good that can be done in this situation and then commit themselves to achieve it.

In sum, Aristotle points out that the practice of virtue is inseparable from moral reasoning, which is inseparable from the pursuit of pleasure and the avoidance of pain, which is inseparable from a conception of the good life as a whole and its constitutive goods. That is, the underlying social dynamics of the four methods of moral education identified in this paper are complementary in the informal, everyday practice of morality. They can also be seen as complementary in pedagogical practice, as long as the context of learning is sufficiently complex to require the exercise of all four methods. In many educational settings, the complexity of everyday life is eliminated in favor of conceptual clarity and simplicity; but this is not necessarily an advantage for learning.[13] Rather, the human brain is designed to learn in the complex situations of daily life, with particular attention to social demands and remedies.[14] Here, victim offender conferencing has an advantage over classroom moral education, because the social situation is complex and the stakes are actual rather than contrived. Positive and negative reinforcements abound. Values are expressed, challenged, clarified, and modified. Participation in moral decision-making is required as a precondition for inclusion in the process. The practice of virtues is required in order to achieve the outcomes explicitly projected.

Conclusion: a reevaluation of the educative aim of criminal justice

There is a growing body of evidence that conferencing meets the perceived needs of those who participate. Victims who have participated in victim offender conferencing report greater satisfaction and more fairness than victims who participate in court, while offenders participating in conferencing perceive greater fairness, 'extremely high' satisfaction, and possibly lower recidivism. Victims in conferences also experience reduced fear and anxiety, greater interpersonal respect, a desire to help offenders, opportunities to express feelings and ask questions, higher rates of completed restitution, and a sense that the process was helpful to them.[15] These high rates of satisfaction can be interpreted as indirect evidence of moral learning, to the extent that successfully completing the conference indicates rising to the demands of the situation and achieving the competence needed to solve the problem. These data would also indicate that the potential for moral education is being realized in conferencing to a greater extent than in court processes alone.

This is not evidence for simply replacing courts with conferences or replacing punishment with restoration, since all the conferencing studied occurred within a context presuming the possibility of courts and punishment. It is, however, evidence that the educative aim of criminal justice can be expanded – indeed, *is* being expanded – by victim offender conferencing. This, in turn, prompts a reevaluation of the priority of education in criminal justice. If the public response to crime *can* be made more effective educationally, it *should* be made more effective. Furthermore, there is no apparent limit to how far this effectiveness can be expanded. Apart from institutional conservatism or ideological loyalties, there appears to be no certain degree or frequency of punishment necessary in order to achieve its symbolic purpose as a signal of the social limit of tolerance. Moral learning is enhanced when the complementarity between the limit of tolerance and the teachable moment is realized. The way lies open for moral education to become a priority of the criminal justice system, not only in service of public safety and victim satisfaction, but in service of the good sense and good will upon which our democracy depends.

> My hope for my own town is that the thousands of children who have experienced participatory anti-bullying programs in our schools, the thousands of adults who have experienced restorative justice conferences in our police stations, will learn how to do justice restoratively and apply those lessons in the families, clubs and workplaces where they face their sharpest conflicts. Most especially I hope conferences are educating the police for democracy. ... My hope about conferences in my town is that citizens are learning in them how to deliberate respectfully in the face of the greatest of the provocations of daily life. If they can learn to deliberate wisely and respectfully in the most provocative contexts then they are citizens well educated for democracy.[16]

Notes

1. ARISTOTLE, THE NICOMACHEAN ETHICS bk V (trans. W.D. Ross 1925).
2. Hampton, *The Moral Education Theory of Punishment*, in PUNISHMENT 112, at 117–20 (ed. A. J. Simmons, M. Cohen, J. Cohen, & C. R. Beitz 1995).
3. Rawls, *The Idea of an Overlapping Consensus*, 7 OXFORD J. LEGAL STUD. 1 (1987).
4. T. LICKONA, EDUCATING FOR CHARACTER: HOW OUR SCHOOLS CAN TEACH RESPECT AND RESPONSIBILITY 38 (1991).
5. Kohlberg, *Stages of Moral Development as a Basis for Moral Education*, in MORAL DEVELOPMENT, MORAL EDUCATION, AND KOHLBERG 15 (ed. B. Munsey 1980). Kohlberg associates the universality of principled moral judgment with its increasing rationality and autonomy, 'independent of appeals to either authority or self-interest' (54).
6. *See* Hampton, *The Moral Education Theory of Punishment*, *supra* n. 2, at 119.
7. *See* Kohlberg, *Stages of Moral Development as a Basis for Moral Education*, *supra* n. 5, at 31.

8. Rest, *Developmental Psychology and Value Education*, in MORAL DEVELOPMENT, MORAL EDUCATION, AND KOHLBERG, *supra* n. 5, at 116 (emphasis in original).

9. ARISTOTLE, THE NICOMACHEAN ETHICS, *supra* n. 1, bk II, 1103a–b.

10. ARISTOTLE, THE NICOMACHEAN ETHICS, *supra* n. 1, bk II, 1109a.

11. *Id.* bk IV, 1125b.

12. *Id.* bk IV, 1128b.

13. *See* Cobb & Bowers, *Cognitive and Situated Learning Perspectives in Theory and Practice*, 28 (2) EDUCATIONAL RESEARCHER, 4 (1999).

14. Iran-Nejad & Marsh II, *Discovering the Future of Education* 114 EDUCATION, 249 (1993); J. LAVE, COGNITION IN PRACTICE: MIND, MATHEMATICS, AND CULTURE IN EVERYDAY LIFE (1988).

15. J. BRAITHWAITE, RESTORATIVE JUSTICE: ASSESSING AN IMMODEST THEORY AND A PESSIMISTIC THEORY (1997), available at <http:// ba048864.aic.gov.au/links/ braithwaite/abstract.html>.

16. *Id.* sec. II.O.

Chapter 14

Hei Āwhina Mātua: the development of a New Zealand bi-cultural home and school behaviour management programme

Mere Berryman and Ted Glynn

Introduction

Teachers are finding it increasingly difficult to meet the needs of individual students with behavioural and learning difficulties, especially when they come from different cultural backgrounds from those of their students. It is even more difficult when they try to meet students' needs independently of parents and caregivers in their school communities. Parents are finding it more and more stressful and frustrating to be held responsible for their children's behaviour and learning at school when they have neither the authority nor the strategies to intervene at school (Glynn, Fairweather & Donald, 1992). Parent involvement in their children's education more frequently embodies parents participating either in fund-raising, clerical assistance and other teacher-support activities or, alternatively, participating as elected representatives on school Boards of Trustees. Although important and worthwhile, these forms of participation do not provide an effective means of sharing information about the behaviour and learning of individual students. They do not provide the means for parents and teachers to co-operate and collaborate and to reinforce and build on learning that occurs in both home and school settings.

Consequently, students' learning and behavioural difficulties in one setting (home or school) are too easily attributed to the perceived inadequacies of the other. This is especially problematic when teachers belong to a different ethnic group from their students (Glynn, 1995).

Teachers too readily blame students' failure to learn at school on perceived inadequacies in students' home backgrounds, their cultural differences, their ethnicity and their parents' lack of motivation or commitment to help them achieve (Bishop, Berryman, Richardson & Tiakiwai, 2001). Parents may just as readily blame their children's low achievement and behavioural difficulties on teachers' ignorance of students' cultural and ethnic origins, and on teachers growing increasingly out of touch with the financial and emotional stresses and strains of contemporary parenting.

Over the last 25 years various different approaches have been introduced within the New Zealand education system to improve the quality of services for students with behavioural and learning difficulties. These have included Guidance and Learning units (modelled after the original Māngere Guidance Unit), short-term residential programmes with concurrent parent training – for example, The Glenburn Residence and School Support Teams for students with special needs – and imported overseas programmes and initiatives such as whole-school behaviour management programmes – for example, Assertive Discipline (Canter & Canter, 1992a, 1992b). These approaches have met with varying degrees of success. The Māngere Guidance Unit was able to provide on-site in-service support with instructional programmes and behavioural management strategies for teachers in the three Intermediate schools it served (Thomas & Glynn, 1976; Thomas, Pohl, Presland & Glynn, 1977; Thomas, Presland, Grant & Glynn, 1978; Glynn, Thomas & Wotherspoon, 1978). The Glenburn residential and school programmes combined the three elements of within-school instructional and behavioural programmes, residential behaviour management combined with social skills training and training parents in the skills needed to support the school and residential programmes when their children returned home each weekend (Glynn, 1983; Glynn, Seymour, Robertson & Bullen, 1983; Glynn & Vaigro, 1984; Glynn, Clark, Vaigro & Lawless, 1984). The Support Team approach also provided on-site in-service support for teachers who have students with special needs in their classes. The Support Team combines the services of an experienced teacher employed within a school who is released part-time to work strategically with other key staff within the school together with the services of outside itinerant peripatetic professionals – for example, educational psychologists. The Support Team works to provide indirect assistance for students with special needs by modifying curriculum delivery and allocating existing school resources to support individual teachers in meeting student needs within their regular classrooms. Where the Support Team model is clearly understood, it can contribute to incremental school-wide changes in the way a school responds to and accepts responsibility for its students who have learning and behavioural difficulties (Glynn, Moore, Gold & Sheldon, 1992; Moore, Glynn & Gold, 1993). All these approaches have built-in needs for focused and hands-on training of key personnel in a wide range of professional skills. These skills include behavioural assessment and intervention; they also include designing of individual instructional programmes that are consistent with the national curriculum, and consultative and collaborative skills to ensure effective working relationships with parents and other professionals.

However, across these different approaches, a vital element that was missing was partnership with parents in decision-making about how to improve student behaviour. The extent of parent involvement, apart from in the Glenburn programmes, was largely limited to attending meetings called by school staff or other professionals to elicit their assistance in implementing behaviour management strategies devised or selected by the school. Moreover, none of these approaches addressed the concerns of local communities about how the behavioural and learning needs of their children should be met. It is a particular concern for one community, Māori, who as an ethnic group continue to be over-represented in the proportion of students with learning and behaviour difficulties in New Zealand schools (Ministry of Education, 2003). Excluding Māori communities from sharing in planning and decision-making is a contravention of the principle of tino rangatiratanga (Māori autonomy and control), as embodied in the Treaty of Waitangi. This was an agreement negotiated between Māori tribal leaders and the British Crown in 1840, and since 1985 regarded as guiding and informing all future New Zealand legislation and government policy.

A recent New Zealand initiative that replaced Support Teachers is that of Resource Teachers of Learning and Behaviour (RTLB). RTLB have received an additional two years of postgraduate professional development in preparation for their role as agents of change within schools. RTLB provide support for teachers and school communities in inclusive teaching strategies and in managing students with mild to moderate behaviour difficulties (Anderson, Brown, Davies, Glynn, Jones, Medcalf, Moore, Thomson & Walker, 2001). A focus on improving behaviour and learning outcomes for Māori students is a crucial professional development component (Glynn, 1999; Macfarlane & Glynn, 1998).

What is needed is an approach that will capitalise on the strengths of parents and teachers, and enable them to take joint responsibility for students' behaviour and learning. This will require professionals trained in delivering behavioural and learning programmes for individual students and in working collaboratively with adults, parents, teachers and community members. An example of such a collaboration project is Hei Āwhina Mātua, described below.

Background to the Hei Āwhina Mātua project

In 1990 Māori teachers and elders from the Tauranga region expressed an urgent need for more positive and effective behaviour management strategies and educational resource materials focused specifically on the needs of young Māori children learning in Māori language settings. Teachers particularly sought strategies and resources to work with parents and children in their communities to improve student behaviour.

Local educational psychologists and special educators provided a professional development programme focused on how behaviour was learned and how to respond more appropriately to the most challenging student behaviours. The professional development programme was adapted from the Assertive Discipline programme (Canter & Canter, 1992a, 1992b) that was being widely used in many mainstream primary schools. Following the intensive three-day programme, oral and written evaluation from teachers expressed their need for further and continuing input into managing challenging student behaviours. It was clear that these teachers had previously received very little specific training in positive behaviour management principles and practices. It was also clear that some of them had previously believed that smacking was an appropriate and acceptable response to the challenging behaviours of some students. Most importantly, however, teachers had difficulty accepting the behavioural concepts, principles, rewards and sanctions as they were packaged in the Assertive Discipline programme, with no regard for the cultural values and preferences of Māori students and their whānau (extended family). The ignorance and/or misinterpretation by non-Māori educators and programme developers of Māori language and cultural values and preferred learning practices was identified as a key challenge to be addressed (Glynn & Bishop, 1995).

Taking up the challenge, this small group of teachers and special educators undertook to develop a behaviour management programme that reflected a Māori cultural perspective, and incorporating input from teachers, parents and family members throughout the entire research and development process. They identified Māori students of all ages in the local community who were experiencing behavioural and learning difficulties. These students were increasingly challenging parents at home and teachers at school. In this area, there was a marked increase in the proportion of Māori students being referred to special educators for behavioural and learning difficulties. Schools were requesting support and assistance for Māori students and their families and for their teachers. Growing concerns about the suspension and expulsion rates of Māori students focused the attention of the group onto mainstream primary (Years 1 to 6) and intermediate (Years 7 to 8) settings. There was an urgent challenge to develop culturally appropriate learning and behaviour resources for these students. Clearly there was also a need for more robust knowledge and training for the teachers of these students and their family members.

Poutama Pounamu: the research group

Effective solutions to these challenges were seen to lie within increased Māori ownership and control of the research and development of programmes to improve behavioural and learning outcomes for Māori students. A research group, centred on the former Specialist Education Services, *Poutama Pounamu* Education Research and Development Centre proposed the development of a behaviour management training programme for teachers and family members of Māori students. This research group operates as a whānau-of-interest (family-of-interest) (Bishop, 1994). Participation by kaumātua and kuia (respected male and female Māori elders) ensures that appropriate Māori cultural values, beliefs and practices are followed in all aspects of planning and decision making. The group also includes Māori special educators and researchers, and a tauiwi (non-Māori) researcher. Members of the group have responsibilities to support the wellbeing of the whānau (family/group), and to respect and uphold the cultural integrity and credibility of the research work. Members have rights to participate and contribute from within a kaupapa Māori (Māori agenda) framework. In these respects, the position of the tauiwi researcher is no different from that of any other member.

Adherence to kaupapa Māori principles ensures that the ownership and control of the research questions, methodology, procedures, the data they generate and how those data are understood and interpreted remain clearly within the whānau. Critical power issues between the researcher and researched related to control over questions of initiation, benefits, representation, legitimation and accountability (Bishop, 1996) are defined and resolved from a Māori worldview. This approach contrasts with the majority of educational research addressing the educational achievement of Māori students. In these studies resolutions of those critical issues are imposed from a Western European worldview, well outside that experienced by Māori students and their families or their teachers. The Hei Āwhina Mātua behaviour management project aimed to address these concerns.

Phase One: The development of the Hei Āwhina Mātua resources

The first task for researchers and School One teachers in the Hei Āwhina Mātua project was to develop three behavioural checklists to identify the:

(a) settings where students were getting into trouble,

(b) challenging behaviours that were occurring,

(c) positive behaviours that were most valued.

Data from the checklists in School 1 were used to produce the eleven behavioural scenarios in the Hei Āwhina Mātua video resource.

School One

School One was a large urban Intermediate, with over 300 students, aged from 11 to 13, of whom 30% were Māori. The school had a Māori language syndicate (grouping of teachers) and two mainstream English language syndicates. The Māori language syndicate comprised three classes. The first class (Māori immersion) had 20 students who received 80% of their teaching in Māori. A female teacher who was a fluent native Māori speaker taught this class. She was supported by a kuia (woman elder) who also was a fluent native speaker. Students needed to have high competency in Māori to enter this class. Most of them had previous experience in Māori immersion classes. The second class (bilingual) had 30 students who received 50% of their teaching in Māori, and was taught by a female teacher who was a second language learner of Māori. Entry into this class required previous experience in Māori language education. The third class was an enrichment class of 33 students who had previously had no background in Māori language education. These students were highly motivated to learn Māori and strove hard to be selected into this class. Their teacher was also still developing competence in Māori language.

Ninety percent of students in the three classes in this syndicate were Māori. The syndicate was supported by a male kaiāwhina (teacher aide). This person provided support for the boys, while the kuia provided support for the girls. The kaiāwhina was also responsible for maintaining tikanga (traditional beliefs and protocols) relating to the male disciplines such as haka (former war dance now an essential component of cultural performances), wero (formal challenge used during rituals of encounter), mau taiaha (traditional martial art involving hand-held wooden staff) and whaikorero (oratory).

Student participants as members of the research team

Inspecting the behavioural checklists provided students with their first opportunity to reflect on what was happening in the research and for the researchers to reflect on the power of the students. The checklists were trialed with 11- to 13-year-old students in School One, and their input was sought to verify the 'street credibility' of the language and item content. The seriousness and depth of the students' responses to this invitation impressed the researchers. Students affirmed and extended the colloquial language used in the checklists and the settings identified by the teachers and researchers. Students identified important behaviour settings omitted by the research team from the 'settings' checklist. Their suggestions were welcomed and adopted by the research team who soon came to appreciate that if they wanted to collect accurate information on student behaviour, they needed to continue consulting with the students, who, after all, were the 'experts' on their own behaviour. From this point on, students were fully recognised as part of the research team. Students in this school had a clear understanding of the role of the checklists:

> It all began with filling out the checklists. There were three different checklists. One was about when and where we might get into trouble, the next one was about behaviour that bothers us, and the last one was about behaviour that we like.
>
> (Troy)

Students, family members and teachers were all asked to complete these checklists. Family members responded to the checklists at a meeting called in the school hall to say farewell to one of their teachers. Students ensured a full turn-out of their family members by putting on a brief kapa haka (traditional Māori song and dance) performance. A large attendance of parents, kaumātua and other whānau members came to see their children perform, to say farewell to their teacher, to hear the Hei Āwhina Mātua project introduced by the research whānau, and to complete the three behavioural checklists. Student commitment to the project ensured a very high proportion of checklists was completed and accurately analysed. Each of the checklist items allowed responders to rate how frequently specific behaviours and contexts were of concern to them. They rated each item on a four-point scale (0, never; 1, sometimes; 2, often; 3, always). Responses to the checklists were collated separately for students, school staff and whānau members. From the individual responses to every item, a mean score for each responder group (students, school staff and whānau members) was calculated. Item mean scores were then ranked from highest to lowest, for each responder group.

The ten highest ranked items from each of the three checklists provided a framework for constructing the Hei Āwhina Mātua video and training manual.

> We found out what the checklists had identified as the problems. From here we talked about what would be in the skits and who would want to be in a video.
>
> (Troy)

> After the researcher listed the ten main problem areas, the teachers, parents and kids were asked their ideas about the different situations, what we thought of the wording and how everything happened.
>
> (Bronwyn)

Following this meeting skits were developed by a group of students and teachers. Teachers encouraged students to role-play various situations in order to clarify how specific behaviours occurred at home, at school and in the community, and how teachers, parents and other adults responded to these behaviours.

> We talked about the scripts and we were allowed to change whatever we thought didn't seem realistic … We asked if we were allowed to swear in the video. We suggested that we should be allowed because kids like swearing all the time as a bad habit.
>
> (Tara)

> We were allowed to change some of the parts that we thought didn't seem real.
>
> (Danielle)

This advice was listened to and heeded by the research team. It is reflected in the *'better but not perfect'* approach taken in all of the alternative response versions of the scripts. Although it was in the school holidays, the 'film week' in which the video was made saw an impressive voluntary attendance by students.

> It was our choice to decide to do this video because we held the meetings and did the acting during our holidays. And that was just hard luck giving that time up. But, I wanted to do the acting and all the hard work because I was excited about being a part of the skits.
>
> (Tama)

While not all students turned up at the time required for their assigned roles, there was always someone willing to step in. Students were given outlines of each skit just before the filming began. They were encouraged to put themselves into the role of their characters rather than be required to memorise and rehearse specific dialogue. What was more important was to convey the message contained within the skit. Students were free to ad-lib.

> When I started to act I was just being my usual self doing an everyday thing.
>
> (Tama)

> We were allowed to say whatever came naturally, so that it would be more realistic and therefore more helpful to those who would use it in the future.
>
> (Bronwyn)

The continuing process of consultation and collaborative production of the skits with the students ensured credible performances set in realistic scenarios.

Soon after, the first milestone report on Hei Āwhina Mātua was due for presentation to the Ministry of Education Advisory Committee. Five students volunteered to write about specific aspects of the research project that they had been directly involved with and presented their reports in person at the

Advisory Committee meeting. Their detailed presentations were delivered confidently and competently, and were well received by the Advisory Committee, so much so that the then Director of the Ministry of Education Research Division recommended additional funding to allow the five students to travel to the University of Otago to participate in the video editing process.

During the week of editing in Dunedin these students viewed all the taped material and identified the specific takes that were their preferred choices for use in each video skit. Their contribution was especially valuable in the editing of the interviews. Three of the students interviewed on the video were also in the editing team. While in Dunedin, the five students were interviewed by local newspapers and featured as a news item on Southern Television. Researchers talked with the students about what they had learned from the process of making this video. The discussion focused on the checklists, script writing, acting and filming.

> It was fun doing this video and it was a good learning opportunity to do something different. I hope this video will be helpful to others … The people who were in it now have a good idea about what it is like to make movies.
>
> (Danielle)

> I think the video was good to do because it shows problems and how they could be solved. Then we will not get into this sort of trouble any more. We will be using this video as a teaching video and to help parents solve problems with kids.
>
> (Tara)

The students made notes about each of the skits and considered what they hoped other people might learn from viewing them. These notes were incorporated into the second milestone report for the Ministry of Education and into the related Hei Āwhina Mātua resources. The students were justifiably very proud of their contribution to the Hei Āwhina Mātua video and training manual. The video incorporated eleven skits (scenarios) dealing with behaviours and settings ranked most problematic as well as behaviours ranked most desirable as identified by the checklist information. The training manual provided workshop materials around ten behavioural principles identified by these students as being best able to assist other Māori students, their families and school staff to consider ways to improve their own behavioural interactions.

A strong and productive working relationship was established between students and the research team. The distinction between researchers and researched had become blurred. Indeed, researchers had come to appreciate that the research whānau-of-interest included, and must continue to include, students. These students continued to offer their sound and constructive criticism throughout the project, and without a doubt the research project benefited from this.

Phase Two: Trialing the Hei Āwhina Mātua resources

Having developed the resources in School One the research team needed schools in which to apply the resources and evaluate their effect.

School Two

School Two was a small rural kura kaupapa Māori (a school where the agenda is grounded in Māori principles and the language of instruction is Māori) with approximately 100 students. This school had just recently acquired kura kaupapa Māori status and was the first and only school of its kind in the area. The school had a non-teaching principal and four classroom teachers supported by a kaiarahi i te reo (Māori language assistant) and a kaiāwhina. A caretaker and a clerical assistant made up the rest of the staff. Two teacher trainees from Te Rangakura (a Māori Teacher Education Programme) were also working in the school at the time of the study. Classes at this school ranged from Year 1 students to Year 8 students and all programmes were delivered in Māori.

Trialing the checklists in School Two required presenting the checklists in Māori. This was not simply a matter of straightforward translation. Wai Harawira, a fluent native speaker from the Tūhoe tribe, and a member of the SES Kaiwhakahaere (National Office Management Team Māori), undertook the challenging task of expressing the wide range of behavioural concepts in traditional Māori style using metaphors and images. For example, 'withdrawal' became te whakamōtu i a koe anō (to make an island of oneself), 'tagging' became tuhi paruparu (writing which makes things dirty).

As was the case of School One, a hui was called so that families and school staff could fill out the checklists at school. The hui began with a pōwhiri (formal ritual of encounter, now traditional welcoming ceremony) to welcome the research whānau and some new families into the school. After the pōwhiri the students performed. These performances demonstrated the positive achievement of students and staff alike as well as the pride and support of the community. Both Māori and English versions of the checklists were then provided for family members to fill out. Students from Years 6 to 8 had responded to the checklists earlier in the week. Checklists for students had been administered in Māori by one of the teachers. All students and school staff completed the Māori versions, while the majority of school family members chose to complete the English versions.

School Three

School Three was a small bilingual, semi-rural primary school with 64 students in three classes. Year 1 and Year 4 students were in a Māori immersion programme. Year 5 and Year 6 students were in a transition programme where English was introduced for one day of the week. After Year 6 students from this school moved on to the Intermediate School identified in this project as School One. School Three had a teaching principal, a 0.3 full-time-equivalent teacher who provided principal release time, two full-time primary teachers, a full-time kaiarahi reo (Māori language assistant), a part time kaiāwhina (teacher aide), a clerical assistant and a caretaker/cleaner. Three teacher trainees were also working in the school at the time of the study.

The checklists in School Three were trialed with the Year 5 and Year 6 students using the Māori version of the checklists but with instructions and clarifications given in English. Four recently enrolled students from mainstream English programmes were given the English version of the checklist. The researchers and the classroom teacher administered the checklists over two separate occasions.

Parents and school family members were invited by the Board of Trustees (B.O.T.) to an early evening meeting held at the school, to find out about the Hei Āwhina Mātua project and to fill out the checklists. The principal, kaumātua, family members and B.O.T. members attended and the checklists were completed. Some whānau members took checklists home for other members to fill out. These were returned completed, the next day. School staff members were given a week to complete their checklists.

In both Schools Two and Three the checklists were scored following the same procedure as described for School One. On each checklist the ten items with overall mean ranks above 0.9 on the 0 to 3 scale were identified for students, teachers and whānau members in each school (see Appendix 1, 2 and 3). The checklists showed the high similarity amongst the three schools in their responses to the checklists and also generated a great deal of useful information for developing resources and procedures for improving the existing behaviour management strategies that both school and family members were using.

Playground behaviour observations

Researchers developed a non-participant observation procedure to quantify the range of behaviours occurring on the playground. Each school playground was separated into two sections, one with two zones, the other with four. Within each section all zones listed were clearly visible. Researchers recorded, zone by zone, on a time-sample basis, antecedent information, (time, location (zone), number and gender of students present, number of teachers and adults present), behaviour information (categories of behaviour), and information on immediate consequences of the observed behaviour (if any).

Classroom behaviour observations

Researchers gathered time-sampled observation of ten randomly-selected students in each classroom, on two or three occasions pre- and post-implementation of the Hei Āwhina Mātua training. Definitions of on-task and off-task behaviour appropriate to the lesson observed were negotiated separately with each teacher. The time-sample procedure followed a ten-second observe, five-second record format, cycling across each of the students in a random sequence.

Assessments of academic behaviour

Assessments of reading, writing and maths performance were taken from samples pre- and post-programme. Reading and writing data were gathered in Māori. Reading achievement was assessed from an analysis of audiotaped three-minute oral reading samples. The three-minute taped oral reading samples were used to assess students' reading accuracy, reading rate, and comprehension (from their oral responses to recall questions and cloze items). Writing was assessed from an analysis of students' writing in Māori taken in a sample that involved writing for ten minutes and then proofreading for a further five minutes. These samples provided data on writing accuracy, writing rate (correct and incorrect rates per minute), and allowed for independent qualitative assessments of audience impact and language quality.

Mathematical achievement was based on the objectives from the Number Strand of the Pāngarau Mathematics Curriculum document (Ministry of Education, 1994). The number strand is intended to provide opportunities for students to:

- understand numbers, the way they are represented and the quantities for which they stand;
- calculate accurately, efficiently and confidently, mentally, on paper and with a calculator;
- estimate and approximate and be alert to the reasonableness of results and measurements.

School and home training

After baseline data had been gathered, the schools and their home communities met with the research team for an interactive evening and day training session held at the local marae and conducted according to Māori cultural protocol. Kaumātua (Māori elders), some of whom were grandparents of the students, helped researchers to run the sessions. The sessions trained groups of kaumātua, family members, students and teachers from Schools Two and Three. The eleven skits in the Hei Āwhina Mātua video were used to provide examples of problem behaviours and problem settings and to illustrate ways of responding to them. The most crucial element of training was the development of understanding about the ten *principles* underlying the specific procedures for changing behaviour in Hei Āwhina Mātua. This understanding was essential if parent, whānau and teachers' attitudes and behaviour were to change. It was the changes in attitude that ensured the occurrence of more effective behaviour change, as illustrated in the following incident that occurred when one of the kuia sat watching breakfast being cooked by the mothers. She remarked that even though the gas cookers had been in the *marae* kitchen for quite some time she had not yet learned to use them. One of the mothers picked up on the concept of 'modelling' that had been discussed the night before and quickly remarked *'Can't you see I'm modelling what you need?'* At which the kuia grinned and affirmed that the mother was indeed doing this. However, she had better keep on modelling because the kuia had not quite learned yet.

Throughout the training each of the principles was role-played in contexts where the problem situation and typical response was presented, followed by presenting an improved response based on the ten specific principles. Small groups presented their role-plays to the workshop as a whole and these were discussed with the whole group, which often generated even more effective and appropriate responses. For example, in one instance where a skit included inappropriate hitting, the wider group was able to note the impact of this behaviour being modelled for children, and in turn applied by them to their younger siblings. Following the Hei Āwhina Mātua workshop, parents and teachers returned to their homes and schools, ready to negotiate and plan for more informed and effective behaviour management. Parents at home and teachers at school would be implementing strategies based on the same ten principles. Further, teachers and parents planned to share information on students' behaviour more openly and regularly, with the encouragement and support of kaumātua.

Results

This paper presents the playground and classroom observation results only from School Two. The full set of behaviour and academic results for both

Table 14.1 Playground observation data

School 2	Pre		Post	
Section1	% students appropriately engaged	Teachers interacting with students	% students appropriately engaged	Teachers interacting with students
Zone 1: Netball courts	50		100	
Zone 2: Big field	81	2	98	7
Section 2				
Zone 3: Right of the quadrangle	92		85	
Zone 4: Back verandah	60		100	
Zone 5: Left of the quadrangle	93		100	
Zone 6: Front verandah	55	4	99	15

schools are presented in the final report (Glynn, Berryman, Atvars & Harawira, 1996).

As previously mentioned, each school playground was separated into two sections, one with two zones, the other with four zones. Within each section all zones listed were clearly visible from one observation point. Table 14.1 shows the percentage of students actively engaged in each zone and the number of teachers or adults present in each section, pre- and post-Hei Āwhina Mātua training. Data in Table 14.1 are mean data across three separate pre- and post-observation samples within the same zone.

Pre-intervention observation revealed a wide range of appropriate student engagement (50% to 93%). Three zones in particular showed low levels of appropriate student engagement, the netball courts (with 50%), the front verandah (with 55%) and the back verandah (with 60%). Higher rates were observed on the big field (with 81%) and at the right and the left of the quadrangle (92% and 93%). Over the pre-programme playground observations, only two teachers were observed interacting with students in section 1 and four in section 2.

Post-intervention data showed an improvement in student engagement across five of the six zones. In section one, on the netball courts, appropriate student engagement improved from 50% to 100% and on the big field it improved from 81% to 98%. Post-programme, there were more observed instances of teachers interacting with students: 7, in contrast with 2 at pre-programme.

In section two, appropriate student engagement in the back verandah zone increased from 60% to 100%, in the front verandah zone from 55% to 99% and in the left of the quadrangle from 93% to 100%. The zone to the right of the quadrangle was the only zone to show a reduction from 92% to 85%. From pre- to post-programme in section 2, as with section 1, there was an increase in the

Table 14.2 Classroom observation data School Two on-task behaviour

	Pre	*Post*
Classroom 1		
Class Mean	76	76
Target student 03	80	100
Classroom 2		
Class Mean	43	86
Target student 01	20	60
Classroom 3		
Class Mean	68	93
Target student 02	63	73
Classroom 4		
Class Mean	77	82
Target student 04	40	70
Target student 05	97	*60
Target student 06	60	67

* Student going through change of medication for epilepsy

number of instances of teachers interacting with students, from 7 at pre-programme to 15 at post-programme.

Table 14.2 presents results from the observations of on-task behaviour in each classroom. Data in Table 14.2 provide, for each classroom, a mean on-task behaviour level as well as an individual on-task level for particular target students from the time sample. Pre- and post-programme data have been averaged over three separate observation sessions.

Classroom 1 was a new-entrant class with a long-term relief teacher (supply teacher). A reasonably high level of on-task behaviour was maintained from pre- to post-programme in this classroom at a level of 76%. The mean on-task behaviour of target student 03, which was already above the class average at 80%, rose a further 20% to 100% at post-assessment.

Classroom 2 was a junior class with a Year One teacher. The low class average at pre-intervention indicates high levels of student off-task behaviour. The class average of 43% improved by post-intervention to 86%. The average on-task behaviour of target student 01 at pre-programme (20%) was half the class average. By post-intervention, despite the fact that this student was still operating below the class average, she showed a marked improvement from 20% to 60%.

Classroom 3 was a middle school class with a long-term relief teacher. The classroom at pre-intervention was operating at a reasonable level of on-task behaviour at 68%, which improved to 93% by post intervention. The on-task behaviour of target student 02 at pre-intervention was 63%, a little below the class average. At post-programme, although still below the class average, this student's on-task behaviour improved to 73% (a gain of 10%).

Classroom 4 was a senior school class with a mature long-term relief teacher. Students' on-task behaviour improved slightly from 76% (pre-programme) to 82% (post-programme). Target student 04's on-task behaviour was well below the class average at pre-programme but improved by 30% (from 40% to 70%) at post-programme. Target student 06 at pre-intervention was well below the class average and remained below the class average at post- intervention, but showed a small gain from 60% to 67%. The major decrease in on-task behaviour that occurred for Target 05 between pre- and post-programme is most likely explained because of a change in medication for epilepsy.

Conclusion

The implementation of the Hei Āwhina Mātua programme reported in this chapter demonstrates the effectiveness of teachers, parents, students and community working constructively and collaboratively to address challenging student behaviour at school. This implementation also demonstrates the power and the resources that are present within families and communities to identify and find solutions to learning and teaching problems centred around challenging behaviour. For the Māori students, whānau and teachers in School Two, it is clear that effective solutions stemmed from activating culturally-preferred values and practices for engaging school and community, and from establishing a more equitable sharing of responsibility, expertise and accountability between them. The design and delivery of the Hei Āwhina Mātua training programme took place in cultural locations and contexts in which Māori protocol prevailed. Locations and contexts allowed for kaumātua to exercise their traditional leadership roles, and for three generations to examine and reflect together on ways of managing behaviour that they judged to be culturally safe and effective.

These results show that as a result of parents, teachers and students in School Two exercising responsibility and ownership of the Hei Āwhina Mātua programme, a range of positive behaviour and achievement outcomes occurred. There were major gains in appropriate student behaviour in most zones of the school playground, that certainly appear to correlate with increased interaction between teachers and other adults and the students. Even though the mean pre-programme on-task behaviour levels varied considerably across the four classrooms in School Two, there were marked gains at post-programme in three classrooms, while maintaining at a reasonably high level in the fourth. On-task behaviour gains between pre- and post-programme were also observed for all but one of the target students. While this chapter reported only on behavioural data from School Two, The academic data from School Two and the behavioural and academic data from School Three also confirmed the effectiveness of the school collaborating with its Māori community to resolve behavioural challenges in a culturally competent and responsive manner.

In both of these schools, parents, whānau and teachers alike celebrated these positive data because they were seen as positive outcomes of the collaborative effort that went into designing and delivering the Hei Āwhina Mātua programme. Instead of looking to blame one other for the behaviour of students at school, these parents, whānau and teachers asserted collective ownership of both the problem and the solution, and in the process learned to show increasing respect for the level of expertise and commitment of the others.

References

Anderson, A., Brown, D., Davies, T., Glynn, T., Jones, L., Medcalf, J., Moore, D., Thomson, C. & Walker, J. (2001). Research teachers learning and behaviour: Collaborating to support inclusion. *Journal of Positive Behavioural Interventions* (submitted).

Bishop, R. (1994). Initiating empowering research. *New Zealand Journal of Educational Studies*, 29 (1), 1–14.

Bishop, R. (1996). *Collaborative Research Stories Whakawhanaungatanga*. Palmerston North: Dunmore Press.

Bishop, R., Berryman, M., Richardson, C. and Tiakiwai, S. (2001) *Te Kotahitanga: Experiences of Year 9 and 10 Māori Students in Mainstream Classrooms*. Final report prepared for ministry of Education, Wellington.

Canter, L. & Canter, M. (1992a). *Assertive Discipline: a Take-charge Approach for Today's Educator*. Santa Monica, CA: Lee Canter & Associates.

Canter, L. & Canter, M. (1992b). *Assertive Discipline: Positive Behaviour Management for Today's Classroom*. Santa Monica, CA: Lee Canter & Associates.

Glynn, T. (1983). *Development and initial evaluation of child and family programmes at Glenburn Centre*. Report to Research and Statistics Section, Department of Education, Wellington, New Zealand.

Glynn, T. (1995). Pause Prompt Praise: reading tutoring procedures for home and school partnership. In S. Wolfendale & K. Topping (Eds.) *Parental Involvement in Literacy – Effective Partnerships in Education* (ch. 4). London: Cassell.

Glynn, T. (1999). Māori and bi-cultural positions within the training programme for resource teachers (learning and behaviour). Paper presented at the Learning and Behaviour: Future Directions Conference, Waipuna Conference Centre, Auckland.

Glynn, T., Berryman, M., Atvars, K. & Harawira, W. (1996). *Hei Āwhina Mātua: a Home and School Behavioural Programme. Final report, book 1*. Wellington: Ministry of Education.

Glynn, T. & Bishop, R. (1995). Cultural issues in educational research: a New Zealand perspective. *He Pukenga Kōrero*, 1 (1), 37–43.

Glynn, T., Fairweather, R. & Donald, S. (1992). Involving parents in improving children's learning at school: policy issues for behavioural research. *Behaviour Change. Special Issue on Behavioural Family Intervention, 9(3)*, 178–185.

Glynn, T., Moore, D., Gold, M. & Sheldon, L. (1992). *Support Teams for Regular Education*. Report to Research and Statistics Division, Ministry of Education, Wellington.

Glynn, T., Seymour, F., Robertson, A. & Bullen, D. (1983). Glenburn child behaviour management procedures. *Behavioural Approaches with Children*, 7 (1), 17–32.

Glynn, E.L., Thomas, J. D. & Wotherspoon, A. T. (1978). Applied psychology in the Māngere Guidance Unit: implementing behavioural services in the school. *The Exceptional Child*, 25 (2), 115–126.

Glynn, T. & Vaigro, W. (1984). Accountability through systematic record keeping in a residential setting. *The Exceptional Child*, 31 (2), 142–150.

Glynn, T., Clark, B., Vaigro, W. & Lawless, (1984). A self-management strategy for increasing implementation of behavioural procedures by residential staff. *The Exceptional Child*, 31 (3), 209–222.

Macfarlane, A. & Glynn, T. (1998). Mana Māori in the professional development programme for resource teachers (learning and behaviour). Paper presented at NZARE, Dunedin.

Ministry of Education (1994). *Pāngarau Te Tauākī Marautanga He Tauira*. Wellington: Ministry of Education.

Ministry of Education (2003) Ministry of Education Statement of Intent 2003–2008. Wellington: Ministry of Education.

Moore, D. W., Glynn, T. & Gold, M. (1993). Enhancing teachers' skills in special education: support teams in New Zealand schools, establishment and practice. *International Journal of Disability, Development and Education*, 40 (3), 193–203.

Thomas, J D. & Glynn, E.L. (1976). *Māngere Guidance Unit: evaluation of behavioural programmes*. Report to the Director-General of Education, Wellington: Department of Education.

Thomas, J., Pohl, F., Presland, I. & Glynn, E.L. (1977). A behaviour analysis approach to guidance. *New Zealand Journal of Educational Studies*, 12 (1), 17–28.

Thomas, J., Presland, I. V., Grant, D. & Glynn, E.L. (1978). Natural rates of teacher approval and disapproval in Grade 7 and 8 classrooms. *Journal of Applied Behavior Analysis*, 11 (1), 91–94.

Appendix 1 PROBLEM CONTEXT RANKINGS

KEY
✓✓ top ten rankings
✓ 10–15 ranking
Scoring:
0 – never
1 – sometimes
2 – often
3 – always

Students

	Ranking	Mean Scores	School 1	School 2	School 3
Own classroom – inside	1	1.24	✓	✓✓	✓✓
Getting ready for school	2=	1.23	✓✓	✓	✓✓
Own classroom – whole class	2=	1.23	✓✓	✓✓	✓
At home after school, own thing	4	1.22	✓✓	✓✓	✓✓
At home after school, doing jobs	5	1.21	✓✓	✓✓	✓✓
Homework	6	1.17	✓	✓	✓✓
Going to bed	7	1.11	✓	✓✓	✓
Bus, travel to and from school	8	1.09	✓✓	✓✓	
Out with friends	9	1.08	✓✓	✓✓	
Walk, travel to and from school	10=	1.07	✓✓		✓✓
Own room – individual activities	10=	1.07	✓	✓✓	✓✓

Whānau Members

	Ranking	Mean Scores	School 1	School 2	School 3
At home after school, doing jobs	1	1.63	✓✓	✓✓	✓✓
Getting ready for school	2	1.30	✓✓	✓✓	✓✓
Getting up	3	1.28	✓✓	✓✓	✓✓
At home after school, own thing	4	1.20	✓✓	✓✓	✓✓
Going to bed	5	1.19	✓✓	✓✓	✓✓
Homework	6	1.17	✓✓	✓✓	✓✓
Breakfast	7	1.15	✓✓	✓✓	✓✓
Evening Meal	8	1.03	✓✓	✓✓	✓✓
Shopping Centre	9	1.00	✓	✓✓	✓✓
Family outings	10	0.97	✓✓	✓✓	✓

School Staff

	Ranking	Mean Scores	School 1	School 2	School 3
School sports & fitness	1	1.58	✓✓	✓✓	✓✓
Other classrooms	2	1.44	✓✓	✓✓	✓✓
Lunchtime / playtime	3=	1.35	✓	✓✓	✓✓
Own classroom – outside	3=	1.35	✓✓	✓✓	✓✓
School trips and outings	5	1.33	✓✓	✓✓	✓✓
Assemblies	6	1.26	✓✓	✓✓	✓✓
Own classroom – whole class	7	1.25	✓✓	✓✓	✓
Whole school activity	8	1.22	✓✓	✓	✓✓
Own classroom – inside	9	1.20	✓✓	✓✓	✓
Marae	10=	1.19	✓	✓✓	✓✓
Homework	10=	1.19	✓✓	✓	✓

Appendix 2   PROBLEM BEHAVIOUR RANKINGS

KEY
✓✓ top ten rankings
✓ 10–15 ranking
Scoring:
0 – never
1 – sometimes
2 – often
3 – always

Students

	Ranking	Mean Scores	School 1	School 2	School 3
Arguing with brothers & sisters	1	1.71	✓✓	✓✓	✓✓
Fighting with brothers & sisters	2	1.44	✓✓	✓✓	✓✓
Shouting and yelling	3	1.39	✓✓	✓✓	✓✓
Not listening	4	1.34	✓✓	✓✓	✓✓
Teasing / Taunting	5	1.29	✓✓	✓✓	✓✓
Spitting	6	1.24	✓✓	✓	✓✓
Hitting	7=	1.2	✓✓	✓✓	✓✓
Not following instructions	7=	1.2	✓✓	✓✓	✓✓
Interference	9=	1.12		✓✓	✓✓
Stirring	9=	1.12	✓✓		✓✓

Whānau Members

	Ranking	Mean Scores	School 1	School 2	School 3
Arguing with brothers & sisters	1	1.84	✓✓	✓✓	✓✓
Fighting with brothers & sisters	2	1.64	✓✓	✓✓	✓✓
Not listening	3	1.47	✓✓	✓✓	✓✓
Shouting / yelling	4	1.46	✓✓	✓✓	✓✓
Teasing / taunting	5	1.29	✓✓	✓✓	✓✓
Not following instructions	6	1.26	✓✓	✓✓	✓✓
Tantrums / packing a sad	7	1.14	✓✓	✓✓	✓✓
Attention seeking	8	1.11	✓✓	✓✓	✓✓
Verbal abuse	9	0.99	✓✓	✓✓	✓
Stirring	10	0.97	✓✓	✓✓	✓✓

School Staff

	Ranking	Mean Scores	School 1	School 2	School 3
Not listening	1	1.64	✓✓	✓✓	✓✓
Not following instructions	2	1.60	✓✓	✓✓	✓✓
Shouting / yelling	3	1.31	✓✓	✓✓	✓✓
Learning difficulties	4	1.27	✓✓	✓	✓✓
Teasing / taunting	5	1.26	✓✓	✓✓	✓✓
Interference	6=	1.18	✓✓	✓✓	✓✓
Attention seeking	6=	1.18	✓	✓✓	✓✓
Verbal abuse	8=	1.15	✓✓	✓	✓✓
Stirring	8=	1.15	✓✓	✓✓	✓✓
Bullying	10	1.08	✓✓	✓✓	

Appendix 3 MOST VALUED BEHAVIOUR RANKINGS

KEY
✓✓ top ten rankings
✓ 10–15 ranking
Scoring:
0 – never
1 – sometimes
2 – often
3 – always

Students

	Ranking	Mean Scores	School 1	School 2	School 3
Playing together	1	1.91	✓✓	✓✓	✓✓
Choosing friends carefully	2	1.69	✓✓	✓✓	✓✓
Sharing	3	1.68	✓✓	✓✓	✓
Caring	4	1.64	✓✓	✓✓	✓✓
Listening	5=	1.61	✓	✓✓	✓
Being prepared	5=	1.61	✓	✓✓	✓✓
Supporting	7=	1.59	✓✓	✓✓	✓
Good personal care	7=	1.59	✓✓	✓	✓✓
Being on time	9	1.55	✓✓		✓✓
Being responsible	10	1.54	✓✓		✓✓

Whānau Members

	Ranking	Mean Scores	School 1	School 2	School 3
Sharing	1=	2.12	✓	✓✓	✓✓
Caring	1=	2.12	✓✓	✓✓	✓✓
Showing respect for people	3	2.09	✓✓	✓✓	✓✓
Good personal care	4	2.08	✓✓	✓✓	✓✓
Being responsible	5	2.04	✓✓	✓✓	✓✓
Offering help	6	2.00	✓✓	✓✓	✓✓
Choosing friends carefully	7	1.96	✓✓	✓	✓✓
Respect for people's things	8	1.93	✓✓	✓✓	✓
Independence	9	1.92	✓✓	✓✓	✓✓
Respect for own things	10	1.90	✓✓	✓✓	

School Staff

	Ranking	Mean Scores	School 1	School 2	School 3
Caring	1	2.13	✓✓	✓✓	✓✓
Listening	2	1.98	✓✓	✓✓	✓
Good personal care	3	1.93	✓✓	✓	✓✓
Showing respect for people	4	1.90	✓✓	✓✓	✓
Sharing	5	1.86	✓✓	✓✓	✓✓
Playing together	6=	1.83		✓	✓✓
Being responsible	6=	1.83	✓✓		✓✓
Getting involved	8	1.82	✓	✓	✓✓
Offering help	9=	1.80	✓✓	✓✓	✓
Supporting	9=	1.80	✓✓	✓✓	

PART 4
Inclusive practices

Chapter 15

Inclusive education: a critical perspective

Geoff Lindsay

Introduction

Inclusive education is now firmly established as the main policy imperative with respect to children who have special educational needs (SEN) or disabilities (Department for Education and Skills, 2001a). It is championed as a means to remove barriers, improve outcomes and remove discrimination. Inclusion is, however, a complex and contested concept and its manifestations in practice are many and various. While some argue that only a proportion, if any, of these examples of inclusion in practice are 'true' inclusion, others propose a broader approach. Indeed, ironically, those who may be seen as less 'correct' with respect to 'true' inclusion may be considered more inclusive of the practices they are prepared to support, promote, foster and develop. Consideration of inclusion, therefore, must take account of conceptual and practical issues and the tensions within and between each domain.

In this chapter I intend to address what I consider to be one of the key distinctions, between rights and efficacy. I shall examine the arguments made for inclusive education and the evidence presented to persuade us that we should support it. In so doing, I shall consider the question of whether efficacy is a proper concern at all or whether, as a question of children's rights, the efficacy of inclusion is not and cannot be a justified or relevant concern. In addressing this issue I shall consider the nature of research, as well as the results of research.

Rights

The Salamanca Statement

A familiar statement of the rights basis for inclusion is the Salamanca Statement (UNESCO, 1994). This was proclaimed by delegates representing 92 governments and 25 international organisations in June 1994 for the World Conference on Special Needs Education. Paragraph 2 is the key statement of belief and comprises five clauses. The first states a view on children's rights:

- Every child has a fundamental right to education, and must be given the opportunity to achieve and maintain an acceptable level of learning.

The second point asserts each child's uniqueness:

- Every child has unique characteristics, interests, abilities and learning needs.

The third states a belief about how the education system should operate, as a consequence of this premise:

- Education systems should be designed and educational programmes implemented to take into account the wide diversity of these characteristics and needs.

The fourth clause develops this line, stating a requirement:

- Those with special educational needs must have access to regular schools which should accommodate them within a child-centred pedagogy capable of meeting these needs.

Finally, clause five provides a rationale for regular schools:

- Regular schools with this inclusive orientation are the most effective measures of combating discriminatory attitudes, creating welcoming communities, building an inclusive society and achieving education for all; moreover, they provide an effective education to the majority of children and improve the efficiency and ultimately the cost-effectiveness of the entire education system.

The Salamanca Statement, therefore, makes an explicit statement concerning children's rights and this refers to education and level of learning rather than a mechanism (inclusion). The moral imperatives embedded in this statement (should, must) are of two kinds. The first derives from an assertion that children's characteristics, interests, abilities and learning needs are unique to each child and collectively diverse. The second, access to regular schools, is based on the assertion in the fifth clause that this is the most effective form of school organisation, although we should note that the end of this clause refers to their providing the most effective education to the 'majority of children'.

It is difficult to argue with the first imperative, although the designation of each child as having *unique* characteristics, while true in an absolute sense, even for identical twins, ignores the large degree to which salient factors are common (see, for example, Norwich, 1996). However, my main concern is with the second moral imperative requiring access to 'regular' schools. Firstly, the term 'regular' is not uncontentious. Indeed, 'regular' may refer to an absolute definition (not provided in the statement) or be interpreted relative to the system in place in any country. What would a 'regular' school in the UK be characterised by? Consider a variety of factors such as size; nature of amenities; secular or religious; pupil catchment; levels of achievement; attendance; or rates of exclusion. Does 'regular' mean 'non-special'? If so, consider special schools that partner mainstream schools and those mainstream schools with designated special provision. The latter may range from schools with segregated units to highly inclusive, class-based provision (e.g. Lindsay, Dockrell, Mackie & Letchford, 2002). Secondly, this rationale is a statement of asserted empirical fact: 'regular schools … *are* the most effective'. Is this the case? If not, then the argument in favour of 'regular' schools is brought into question. Thirdly, if they are effective only for the majority, what are the implications for the minority?

The Framework for Action which accompanies the Statement develops the argument mainly by providing guidelines for action. However, the main point to be made here is that the Salamanca Statement is based on a combination of a view of children's rights; of moral imperatives for action which do not directly relate to the right that is proclaimed; and of an assertion of evidence. Also implicit is a tension between application of the proposed system for all children and a view that it may not be effective for all.

Inclusion in the UK

Within the UK the development of policy towards inclusion is well advanced, but is not all-encompassing. This is not a recent phenomenon but is the latest step in a trend which may be traced back at least three-quarters of a century. For example, the Wood Committee in 1928 stressed the unity of ordinary and special education and the debate on the Education Act 1944 also reveals a concern for normalisation. Chuter Ede, the Parliamentary Secretary, stated in the debate on the Bill:

> May I say I do not want to insert in the Bill any words which make it appear that the normal way to deal with a child who suffers from any of these disabilities is to be put into a special school where he will be segregated. Whilst we desire to see adequate

provision in special schools we also desire to see as many children as possible in the normal stream of school life.

The 1944 Act and the 1945 Regulations recognised that the majority of children requiring 'special educational treatment' would be in mainstream schools. Ironically, the post-war building regulations inhibited further inclusive practice, allowing new school buildings only on the basis of class sizes of 30 pupils in secondary and 40 in primary schools. This was seen as a constraint and led to the purchase of old manor houses and the like, so leading to the development of more separate special schools. This trend was later reversed, and smaller proportions of children entered separate special schools for many reasons. The most obvious was the impact of the Warnock Report (Department for Education and Science, 1978) which argued for integration, albeit with caveats.

But the Warnock Committee was not simply far-sighted. Rather, and this may not be so evident today, they were reflecting upon and reporting what they saw on visits and were told by those giving evidence. Indeed, there were local education authorities and schools already practising what the Warnock Committee promoted, even if somewhat cautiously. For example, a number of educational psychologists in the late 1960s and early 1970s, regarded as 'radical' at the time, promoted and practised an approach to children with SEN that challenged the use of special schools. The Movement of Practising Psychologists was one loosely organised group, not limited to educational psychology, who adopted radical perspectives. The Sheffield Psychology Service, at that time led by David Loxley, was challenging the system of special school placements as well as the practice of the profession of educational psychology (Loxley, 1978). This resulted in a realisation in the early 1970s that almost no child in Sheffield had been referred to what were then called ESN(M) schools (for the 'educationally subnormal') for almost a year. These schools realised that, if this continued, they would lose custom and, presumably, face closure. Other psychological services were also adopting different approaches to supporting children and schools, as part of the 'reconstructing educational psychology' movement (Loxley, 1978; Gillham, 1978; Burden, 1981).

These initiatives were guided by one main driving force: were the rights and educational opportunities of children with SEN being promoted or harmed by special schools? This concern was fuelled by evidence, unsystematic and anecdotal though much of it was, that children leaving special schools were not in an advantageous position. For example, in 1974 I assessed the school leavers for one ESN(M) school in a large county LEA and found that not only were reading levels equivalent only to those of seven to nine year olds, but there were young people whose records showed that these scores were *lower* than their reading ages on entry to the school when they were about eight or nine years old. Also, the Warnock Report noted that only 22% of teachers in special schools had special qualifications for the job (para 12.24). A third concern at that time involved the numbers of children from the Caribbean who had been inappropriately placed in ESN(M) schools (Coard, 1971), a finding confirmed by a systematic study of ESN(M) schools in Sheffield. These initiatives in the 1970s and 1980s accelerated the development of integration, as it was then called. It is important to note that they were energised by professionals at the front line, street-level practitioners who not only implemented, but also *formulated* policy by their practice.

The recent post-1997 Labour Government has accelerated the policy of inclusion through its Green Paper (Department for Education and Employment, 1997) and Special Educational Needs Action Programme (Department for Education and Employment, 1998), leading up to the revised Code of Practice and the guidance which explains the policy of inclusion and how it might be implemented (Department for Education and Skills, 2001a; 2001b). The guidance indicates when a child may not be included: that is, when he or she is a threat to others, or is taking up a disproportionate amount of teacher's time. Most recently, the Special Educational Needs and Disability Act 2001 has taken these developments another step further. This legislation is clearly moving towards an increasing emphasis on inclusion. For example, the three caveats dating back to the Warnock Report whereby non-inclusion may be justified have been reduced to two. The new Section 316 of the 1996 Education Act, as amended by the Special Educational Needs and Disability Act 2001, requires that a child who has SEN and a Statement *must* be educated in a mainstream school unless this would be incompatible with:

(a) the wishes of the parents, or
(b) the provision of efficient education of other children.

Note that the 'lost' caveat is that which has, since Warnock, referred to the protection of the interests of the child concerned, the implication being this is no longer an issue. Furthermore, clear evidence is necessary to show that (b) pertains in any particular case. Hence the promotion of inclusion is more advanced. However, a critical view of these developments might suggest that this promotion of a policy of inclusion is still insufficiently strong and that an absolute commitment to total inclusion is necessary. In this sense, inclusion not only refers to the mainstream but to the specific 'local' school (Armstrong & Barton, 1999).

Models of special educational needs and disability

Others argue that social justice and the right to inclusion is not so straightforward and that social justice, for example, is not a unitary or universally shared concept (Christenson & Dorn, 1997). Furthermore, differing views on social justice may underlie the apparent contradictions in the implementation of policies. The development of communitarian principles may promote common values, with negative impact on people with disabilities. Also, one line of argument is that non-inclusion is equivalent to discrimination and segregation which may occur as a result of sexism and particularly racism. This approach compares battles to promote inclusion as comparable to those challenging racist discrimination and segregation policies.

This approach is often referred to as the 'social model' and is distinguished from the 'medical model'. The social model is clearly in the ascendancy and was a necessary development from the worst aspects of previous practice, which was condition-related, categorical and deterministic to a very large degree. However, there is a need to analyse these models more critically (Lindsay, 1997). The so-called medical model in fact has at least two quite different elements. The first concerns the medical profession rather than educationists effectively running the system, as the key decision-makers in respect of need and necessary intervention and provision. There has been concern about the approach of those key medical practitioners who were criticised as promoting the worst excesses of mystification relating to their role as 'the expert'. Remember too that, up to the beginning of the 1980s, the rights of parents were very limited and they were less likely to challenge the opinions and decisions of these professionals. For a vivid personal account of this in practice see the autobiography of John Hawkridge (1991).

The second element is the focus in the medical model on 'within-child' factors, stressing the impairment and underplaying, even ignoring, the impact of environmental factors. The social model takes various forms (as indeed did the 'medical model') and I am always uncomfortable dealing with these concepts as though each were unitary and straightforward whereas operationally they have a variety or continuum of meanings. Nevertheless, I suggest that the general trend over the past 30 years has been away from a medical to a social model. I consider this to be entirely appropriate, as far as it goes, but there are two points I want to stress.

Firstly, the social model, as it is often presented, is illogical and unhelpful. For many, including myself, the need was to shift focus to acknowledge that the needs of children must be considered with respect both to their own relative strengths and weaknesses and to the nature of their environment, including the home and school, and their community. This approach was developed by one of Ron Gulliford's colleagues, Klaus Wedell. He proposed the concept of compensatory interaction to represent these two major influences of within-child and environmental factors, later supplemented by a third dimension of time (Wedell, 1978; Wedell & Lindsay, 1980; Lindsay, 1995a). This was an *interactive* model. Children's functioning, and hence their needs, were conceptualised as an interaction between their inherent characteristics and the supports, and barriers, of the environment. Time was added as a third influence since the pattern of these interactions could change, for example with a different teacher, or through the provision of an aid. It is important to note the significance of 'within-child' factors per se, whether these derive from an impairment to functioning, as with a profound hearing loss, or reflect the increasing evidence of a genetic component to a wide range of developmental difficulties (Plomin & Walker, in press).

The difficulty with the social model is that it plays down, or actively ignores, both the within-child factors and the issue of interaction. In its 'hardest' form, it is proposed that the only salient factor to consider is the external world which disables the individual. As Colin Low (2001) stated in his Insights lecture at City University, drawing in part on Oliver's statement (1996), disability is *wholly* and *exclusively* social (Low's emphasis):

> In a kind of reductionism, 'not *only* the individual' has become mistranslated as 'only social', and 'the individual is not everything' has become 'the social is everything'.

Low's paper, entitled 'Have disability rights gone too far?', is a most welcome critical review of the social model, carefully and persuasively indicating its logical and practical inadequacies, while stressing the importance of recognising the importance of the social dimension. At this time, perhaps despite its inadequacies, the social model has been influential in policy formulation, particularly in developing legislation based on 'rights' arguments, but he recognises the tension in practice.

Others have also offered critical perspectives on arguments based on rights. For a comprehensive overview of this area, which considers disability rights against those relating to ethnicity and race, and to gender, see Mithaug (1998), who argues that:

> by now it should be apparent that the inclusive society as conceived by policymakers of the 1960s and 1970s is not going to happen. There have been too many policy failures and unexpected negative consequences in the last decade.
>
> (p.5)

The reason for this failure is that inclusion is only one of several competing values that might be held. Mithaug, writing from an American perspective, offers freedom and equality as other values which 'Americans held as dearly'. Furthermore, there are several foundations for holding an inclusive view. Consider the two dimensions of the individual's capabilities and freedom *from* obstacles and *to* self-determine. In the first case, we might consider all children to have what Mithaug calls 'equal moral capacity', and so inclusion requires *opportunities* for individuals to participate in society. If, however, we consider that children have 'unequal natural capacity' then inclusion requires *protection* of 'helpless' individuals, a welfare model. However, these two positions, and the other two in Mithaug's four-cell matrix, are recognised as usually inaccurate and incomplete and the view of individuals derived from each position is inadequate.

These different conceptualisations of disability, rights and required action lead to different policies. These must, in turn, interact with policies for general education. Hence the post-1988 emphasis on standards, increasing freedom of choice and diversity promoted both by the Conservative and Labour Governments (Lindsay, in press), set a backdrop for the development of SEN policy. It is clear from documents such as the Green Paper (Department for Education and Employment, 1997) and Special Needs Action Plan (Department for Education and Employment, 1998) that these same concerns are indeed *central* to government's thinking on SEN. However, what is less clear is the relationship between these factors and evidence. It is to the latter that I now turn.

Research evidence

Before considering research evidence per se, I want to acknowledge the view that what I am about to present is all irrelevant. A number of authors have argued that empirical evidence is either inconclusive or unnecessary because the issue is one of rights not evidence (Gallagher, 2001). I shall return to this and other questions concerning methodology later.

Researching inclusion

Researching 'inclusion' is problematic. The primary difficulty is that it is not a simple, unambiguous concept and so operationalising inclusion as a variable is a necessary step in the research process. This is not unusual in educational research. It applies to topics as varied as reading difficulties, dyslexia, autism/autistic spectrum disorders, Headstart and Follow-through. There is a need to specify, in the absence of unambiguous definitions, the children (by type of disability and SEN, and age, for example) and the nature of the intervention. The former is increasingly problematic the more exceptional are the children, as comparability of samples becomes questionable. Evaluation of intervention becomes increasingly difficult as complexity increases. Compare, for example, evaluation of a reading programme with detailed specification such as Reading Recovery as against a policy of inclusion. Even within the former, and assuming that child variables can be satisfactorily specified, there still remain questions of fidelity – for example, was the programme actually implemented as intended?

There have been a number of studies that have reviewed the evaluation of inclusion. Overall, these reviews cannot be said to be ringing endorsements (Sebba & Sachdev, 1997; Madden & Slavin, 1983; Hegarty, 1993, Baker, Wang & Walberg, 1994; Tilstone, Florian & Rose, 1998). These overviews, reviews and meta-analyses fail to provide clear evidence for the benefits of inclusion, although Staub and Peck (1994) also suggest a lack of evidence for deceleration of academic progress among the other children, those without SEN, in the inclusive settings. For example, the review by Baker et al. (1994) of these meta-analyses found a positive but small effect size, mainly with academic achievement, but this was primarily in one of the three analyses (Table 15.1).

Further evidence is provided by a review of the educational achievement of deaf children. Powers, Gregory and Thoutenhoofd (1999) report that a number of studies indicate higher achievement among deaf pupils in mainstream, but that many have not taken into account confounding factors. Do these analyses provide support for inclusion as a policy? At best, the support is weak. It is not at the level implied in the Salamanca Statement.

Given that the policy development for over 75 years has been towards increasing inclusion, we might ask whether evaluating inclusion is appropriate at all (for example, Lindsay, 1989). I am not arguing, as for example has Gallagher (2001), that there is no need for empirical investigation, but I do challenge the usefulness of this research question. A more profitable route is that of examining effectiveness of particular aspects of inclusion. A number of studies have taken this approach and their findings provide useful information.

Manset and Semmel (1997) provide evidence of varying degrees of progress, and hence variable impact, of eight model programmes. Their conclusions are highly critical of inclusion as an overall policy:

> Inclusive programming effects are relatively unimpressive for most students with disabilities especially in view of the extraordinary resources available to many of these model programmes.

> (p. 177)

Table 15.1 Effects of inclusive placements: three meta-analytic studies (from Baker, Wang & Walberg, 1994)

	Carlberg & Kavale	*Wang & Baker*	*Baker*
Year published	1980	1985–6	1994
Time period	Pre-1980	1975–84	1983–92
No. of studies	50	11	13
Academic effect size	0.15	0.44	0.08
Social effect size	0.11	0.11	0.28

Table 15.2 Effect sizes for gains in three types of provision (From Mills et al., 1998)

Measure	Special education only	Integrated	Mainstreamed
McCarthy			
General Cognitive Index	0.36	0.40	–0.01
Verbal	–0.01	0.48	0.01
Perceptual	0.17	0.25	0.02
Memory	–0.10	0.29	–0.24
PLAI	0.78	0.64	0.60

Mills, Cole, Jenkins and Dale (1998) report the differntial effectiveness of three approaches with varying degrees of inclusion (Table 15.2). They found the greatest effect on several measures was provided by an 'integrated' resource rather than special school or mainstream. Marston (1996) also compared three models: inclusion only, 'pull-out' only and a combined service for children with mild disabilities, reporting significantly higher increases in reading for the combined service over the two alternative approaches. Such studies are not limited to academic progress. Vaughan and Klinger (1998) investigated student perceptions across eight studies, and concluded that, in general, the students preferred to receive assistance in a resource room rather than in the regular class. They reported they were better able to concentrate and that they learnt more, although there was also an age factor with the latter effect found among post-primary youngsters. On the other hand the study cited social benefits of the general education setting.

Investigation of individual schools as case studies has a substantial tradition and has produced a wealth of evidence. Hegarty, Pocklington and Lucas's (1981) study is in many ways a landmark in the UK, but many subsequent case studies have been presented to extend the range of material. As an example, the study of six schools by Dyson and Millward (2000) provides a rich description and analysis of inclusion, revealing the variety, tensions and conflicts to which I have previously alluded. However, no data on child outcomes are presented. Lee and Henkhuzens (1996) report a national study of LEAs plus case studies of secondary schools, but again offer little child progress data.

Towards the identification of success factors

What these studies provide is evidence in a number of different elements relevant to inclusion. They are essentially concerned with *implementation* and so help us with questions of *how* rather than *why*. Frederickson and Cline (2001) have summarised the evidence from a number of studies which they consider to indicate factors relevant to successful inclusion. These include, perhaps not unexpectedly, the quality of the programme, which of course needs to be operationalised, and the extent to which the general education system accommodates the academic and social needs of a diverse range of young people with disabilities and SEN. Such compilations provide a potentially useful resource, although they are only as valid as the rigour of the sources on which they are based. There is a danger of going the way of early school effectiveness work where research findings of *relationships* were interpreted as *causal* factors in effective schools.

Lipsky and Gartner (1998) report on the National Study of Inclusive Education which reviewed about 1,000 school districts and produced seven factors, congruent with those identified in a study of 12 inclusive schools conducted by the Working Forum on Inclusive Schools:

- visionary leadership;
- collaboration;
- refocused use of assessment;
- support for staff and students;
- funding;
- effective parental involvement;
- use of effective programme models and classroom practices.

Inspection of this list reinforces my earlier caution. These are general factors which require further, detailed explanation. For example, collaboration is relevant at levels from national policy down to classroom practice (Law, Lindsay, Peacey, Gascoigne, Soloff, Radford & Band, 2000). Support includes teaching assistants, for which there is an accumulating evidence base (Farrell, Balshaw & Polat, 1999; Riggs & Mueller, 2001), and non-educational support, for example speech and language therapists. The means by which these different professionals collaborate varies. An increasingly popular approach by speech and language therapists, which had been previously developed by educational psychologists and SEN support teachers, is that of consultation. However, this is not unproblematic in terms of its implementation (Forbes, 2001; Law, Lindsay, Peacey, Gascoigne, Soloff, Radford & Band, 2002; Lindsay et al., 2002) and its perception by teachers (Dockrell & Lindsay, 2001) and parents (Lindsay & Dockrell, in press). For example, what skills are required of a 'consultant'?

In the medical field, consultants will have had extensive training *and* experience in their specialities. Furthermore they will have continuing hands-on experience. They are consulted for their expertise. Compare this with the professionals who wish to take on the role of a 'consultant' immediately after initial training or after transferring from a school to support service. Consultancy is not just a style or a method. It should be based upon extensive experience. At a higher level there are also difficulties, exemplified by the problems of co-ordinating speech and language therapy input to the educational system, recently indicated as a major concern in responses to the Audit Commission's (2002) consultation document on statutory assessment and standards of SEN (Peacey, Dockrell & Peart, 2002).

Research and values

Gallagher (2001) has provided a trenchant critique of 'neutral' scientific approaches to inclusion. However, her argument is some way distant from the position I believe I am taking. Indeed, I am not sure her critique correctly identifies the position to which she is responding. She is dismissive of critics of full inclusion who, she asserts, argue that it should not be implemented in the absence of scientific evidence that it is effective. Gallagher then attacks scientific neutrality, arguing that a number of researchers who promote scientific enquiry hold the view that science is neutral:

> that it is possible to establish foundational knowledge about an independent existing reality and secondly that there is an assumption of methodological neutrality as a means for establishing fundamental knowledge.

> (p.639)

Gallagher's critique of research as a relevant factor in inclusion is not unrelated to the view that there is no need to consider the evidence, just rights. However, there are several problems with this position. Gallagher has arguably constructed a straw person. While there may be some researchers who hold the views she states, the research of which I have spoken is not of this kind. At least, I would argue that such an interpretation would be inappropriate. On the contrary, all empirical research needs to be conceptualised, planned, implemented, analysed and reported with full recognition that the research endeavour exists within a social, value-laden world, and that consideration of the implications is necessary at all of these points (Lindsay, 1995b).

A further perspective on the social model is provided by Moore, Beazley and Maelzer (1998) who argue that:

> Any research which is based on an individual model of disability will inevitably recycle individual-blaming images of disabled people and consequently inform relevant practical and policy issues in highly inauspicious ways. Such research is invariably oppressive and sweeps aside the generic and collective interests of disabled people.

> (pp.12–13)

Note the certainty again, the reference to inevitability of impact, of invariability. Note also that this critique concerns the individual model of disability, which is not defined, and so is presumably seen as uncontentious. Later the authors state what good disability research is *not* like. It should not be embedded in, or regulated by, medical model ideologies or '(attempts) to disregard the impact of oppression on disabled people's lives' (p.14). Again we have an undefined concept, this time called the 'medical model' which I have suggested is not uncontested. If the criterion is of a simple, simplistic even, approach to disability which focuses only on an individual's characteristics and ignores the social dimension, then I fully concur. But what does this mean in practice? Would this exclude studies that included only those with a particular type of disability, for example, profound hearing impairment? Low provides a strong critique of such thinking. Granted there is overlap and commonality, but there is also distinctiveness. The use of braille by some visually impaired children and cochlear implants for some hearing impaired children are two examples of factors where there is a clearly *specific* element. Hence, investigating the use of cochlear implants, for example, their benefits in terms of educational achievement and social relationships, seems to me to be worthwhile and necessarily focused (Bennett & Lynas, 2001). On the other hand, if cochlear implants were totally successful for all children with severe and profound hearing impairments, this would effectively remove a significant subset of our society, one with a history as a recognisable community. But is this oppression? It may be seen as such at a social level, but is it oppression of the individuals concerned? As Low argues, acting positively, not discriminating against a group such as the deaf, and recognising the value of all those concerned as members of society, is very different from saying that it is inappropriate to offer interventions that, arguably, will provide improved opportunities. Thus, the social *dimension* is surely key to research in this field, but oppression is not the only relevant factor.

Furthermore, research in a wide sense, as I am proposing, includes a variety of foci and methods. These include parental, teacher and child perspectives as much as evaluation of academic gains. The qualitative approach has much to offer to provide insight into the world of the researcher (Clough, 1995). Skidmore's analysis of a single case study of an English secondary school strikingly identifies competing discourses within the school. It also goes on to argue, on the basis of these findings and previous research on school improvement and inclusion, that the need for consensus among teaching staff may have been exaggerated (Skidmore, 1999). If this is true, there are clear implications for action.

On the other hand, there is also a need for studies of effectiveness and demonstrable impact. It is my contention that, with respect to inclusion, we have too few, not too many, good studies using quantitative methods, including quasi-experimental designs. For example, a recent study by Shield, Dockrell, Jeffrey and Tatchmatzidis (2002) has examined the effects of classroom noise on children's performance. The findings suggest a negative impact of noise on all pupils and, importantly, that the resultant decrement in performance is greater for the children in the sample who were designated as having SEN. Other studies comparing factors, whether placement types or intervention programmes, require experimental or, more practically, quasi-experimental designs in order to demonstrate not only an effect but its importance (Gersten, Baker & Lloyd, 2000). For example, the study by Mills et al. (1998) reported earlier indicates differential effects for three levels of inclusion. However, while higher functioning children with disabilities benefited more from integrated special education, relatively lower functioning children with disabilities benefited more from special education classes or mainstream. Hence we also need to identify the strengths of effects per se, and their relative impact on different children.

Research methods

The focus of the paper has been on the two issues of rights and efficacy with reference to the inclusion of children with SEN. I have argued that each is a complex and contested concept, and have rejected the position that focuses on one or the other. My view is that the only way we can progress is on both fronts. We need to be energised by a view of society and of the place of children and adults who have disabilities and difficulties. I am with Colin Low (2001) in rejecting the idea that we should focus *only* on the rights element. Although I have argued this position for some time, indeed all of my professional career, I was stung by Low's view of his being a lonely struggle, and by his challenge that 'if I do not speak as I find, nobody will' (p.18). Low speaks of his belief that 'the disability movement is a monolith, in that's it's not enough to be disabled to be a member – you have to think a certain way on pain of ex-communication' (p.18).

My view is that it is simply not good enough to ignore the question of within-child factors or the research evidence pertaining to *all* aspects of inclusion, including classroom practice, school organisation, LEA systems and government policies. Each is a justified and necessary element for research. However, I add two caveats. Firstly, the research should be rigorous within its own paradigm. It is for the research and professional community, in consultation with users and voluntary bodies, to design research appropriate to the question for which answers are sought and their responsibility to interpret findings for the benefit of other researchers, practitioners, parents and children. In this respect I welcome and support the use of qualitative approaches. Indeed, these methods were promoted by a number of us involved in the training of educational psychologists in the 1970s to address complex questions. However, along with Tooley and Darby (1998), I recognise that qualitative as well as quantitative research can be done badly.

Research, especially in the UK, has a number of limitations: a lack of empirical research, small samples, non-longitudinal designs and non-experimental approaches. The benefits of including teachers as researchers are clear, but practitioner research is usually too limited in scale and design to provide substantial additions to knowledge, although there are exceptions. The Doctor of Education (EdD) and its variants have allowed more educationists, including teachers, to undertake research of substance. The development of doctoral training for educational psychologists is also providing important results. This group is particularly pertinent as they have previous experience of research at undergraduate and Masters level. They have roles that may facilitate a wider research culture within LEAs, and allow the implementation and generalisation of research findings.

We must address a range of research questions and these need a range of methods. In many cases a 'mixed method' approach is to be advocated. For example, a comparison of different intervention approaches requires at least a quasi-experimental design (Gersten et al., 2000), but measures of academic achievement, for example, may be supplemented by qualitative interviews with the children and relevant adults. This approach produces a wider range of information to allow conclusions to be drawn about effects *and* their meanings.

My second caveat concerns time and action. I do not subscribe to a view that we need to wait to gather all the evidence before acting. Indeed, I know of nobody who does. Rather, we live in a real and changing world. The education of children with SEN is happening *now*. It must be provided within a general educational policy framework. This Government's avowed policy is to promote and develop an inclusive society, a policy concerned with broader issues than special educational needs. How to achieve this end is not 'obvious'. There are conflicts and tensions arising from conflicting values. There is also no one 'obvious' route to an inclusive society.

It is necessary, therefore, to develop an evidence base for action, a policy to which the Government and the Department for Education and Skills are committed. This requires the development of specific policies, which are based on evidence wherever possible, within this broad policy framework, followed by the evaluation of their implementation, modifying policy and implementation as a result. This is happening. As examples of this approach I offer some of our own work in CEDAR. My work with Julie Dockrell concerning children with specific speech and language difficulties (SSLD) has raised significant questions about inclusion for these children – most of our sample are in mainstream. For example, the teachers report a lack of knowledge and skills (Dockrell & Lindsay, 2001), a finding also reported more generally in the responses to the Audit Commission's consultation (Peacey et al., 2002). Parents are also concerned – they are torn between inclusion, with a belief that this will be correct in social terms, and a concern from their experience of the limitations of provision in mainstream (Lindsay & Dockrell, in press). Furthermore, some aspects of self-esteem were better developed among children in special schools than those in mainstream (Lindsay & Dockrell, 2000). In a separate study, we have identified a series of tensions experienced by LEAs, speech and language therapy services and schools in implementing inclusion for children with SSLD in England and Wales (Lindsay et al., 2002).

My colleagues Jonothan Neelands, Viv Freakley, Sue Band and I are evaluating the national Dance and Drama Awards scheme, which provides bursaries for over 800 students a year to undertake professional dance, drama and stage management training. Our evaluation has shown a consistently low number of students with self-reported disabilities, other than dyslexia. As a result, the Department for Education and Skills and the schools have taken action to support schools to develop their facilities and training (Neelands, Lindsay, Freakley & Band, 2002). Malcolm Maguire and I, together with colleagues from three Warwick research centres, examined the implications of the introduction of what was then called 'graduation' and more recently 'matriculation'. This is a broadly based qualification intended to acknowledge achievement not only within traditional academic domains (GCSE) but also with respect to citizenship, other skills and achievements (for example, music or sport). However, our study suggested that there was also a strong class bias in these other domains, except sport, as well as with GCSE. Consequently there was an even greater hurdle for young people with significant disadvantage or disabilities who not only had to gain more GCSEs post-16, but also demonstrate their other 'wider achievements'. Furthermore, they were less likely to have access to support and facilities than students remaining in schools for advanced level. The exceptions to the latter barrier were special school students who stayed on post-16. Hence a policy that was intended to help promote an inclusive society would be likely to provide further evidence of the relative lack of success of these young people, possibly reducing their motivation and *hindering* inclusion (Lindsay & Maguire, 2002).

There is also a need to respect economic reality, a clear message from the recent discussion document on access. Many LEAs and schools have responded on an individual basis to requests for building modifications. There is a clear conflict between providing resources for a child in the 'local' school, and providing resources in one school to serve a community. Given limited resources, the former, in practice, leads to a denial of equality of opportunity across a number of children in different schools, while one or two may benefit. The latter is more cost-effective, arguably more efficient, but is a restriction of meaningful choice. The recent guidance stresses a strategic approach to increasing the accessibility of schools (Department for Education and Skills, 2002).

Inclusion is the policy framework. What is at issue is the interpretation and implementation of inclusion in practice. We need to ensure that there is a dual approach focusing on both the rights of children and the effectiveness of their education. There is a need to develop beyond concerns about inputs and settings to a focus on experiences and outcomes and to attempt to identify *causal* relationships. We need research to inform policy and practice, but research that is rigorous. In addition to descriptive case studies of examples of 'good practice', useful though these can be, we need careful analysis to examine whether 'good' practice is an appropriate descriptor. In methodological terms, we need more highly developed, substantial studies using quasi-experimental approaches to examine the strengths, and relative impacts, of a range of factors, together with qualitative examination of the experiences of key participants. Rigorous, substantial research projects demonstrating effectiveness will enhance the process of addressing children's rights.

References

Armstrong, F. & Barton, L. (1999) 'Is there anyone there concerned with human rights? Cross-cultural connections, disability and the struggle for change in England', in F. Armstrong & L. Barton (eds) *Disability, Human Rights and Education: cross-cultural perspectives*. Buckingham: Open University Press.

Audit Commission (2002) *Statutory Assessments and Statements of SEN: In Need of Review?* Wetherby: Audit Commission Publications.

Baker, E. T., Wang, M. C. & Walberg, H. J. (1994) 'The effects of inclusion on learning', *Educational Leadership*, 52 (4), 33–5.

Bennett, E. & Lynas, W. (2001) 'The provision of local mainstream education for pupils who have cochlear implants', *Deafness and Education International*, 3 (1), 1–14.

Burden, R. (1981) 'The educational psychologist as instigator and agent of change in schools: some guidelines for successful practice', in I. McPherson & A. Sutton (eds) *Reconstructing Psychological Practice*. London: Croom Helm.

Christenson, C. A. & Dorn, S. (1997) 'Competing notions of social justice in special education reform', *Journal of Special Education*, 31 (2), 181–198.

Clough, P. (1995) 'Problems of identity and method in the investigation of special educational needs', in P. Clough & L. Barton (eds) *Making Difficulties: research and construction of SEN*. London: Paul Chapman Publishing.

Coard, B. (1971) *How the West Indian Child is Made Educationally Subnormal in the British School System*. London: New Beacon Books.

Department for Education and Employment (1997) *Excellence for All Children*. London: The Stationery Office.

Department for Education and Employment (1998) *Meeting Special Educational Needs: A Programme for Action*. London: DfEE.

Department for Education and Science (1978) *Special Educational Needs* (The Warnock Report). London: HMSO.

Department for Education and Skills (2001a) *Special Educational Needs Code of Practice*. London: DfES.

Department for Education and Skills (2001b) *Inclusive Schooling: children with special educational needs*. London: DfES.

Department for Education and Skills (2002) *Accessible Schools: planning to increase access to schools for disabled pupils*. London: DfES.

Dockrell, J. & Lindsay, G. (2001) 'Children with specific speech and language difficulties: the teachers' perspectives', *Oxford Review of Education*, 27 (3), 369–394.

Dyson, A. & Millward, A. (2000) *Schools and Special Needs*. London: Paul Chapman.

Farrell, P., Balshaw, M. & Polat, F. (1999) *The Management Role and Training of Learning Support Assistants*. London: DfEE.

Forbes, J. C. (2001) 'Teacher/therapist collaboration policy: an analysis', *Child Language Teaching and Therapy*, 17, 195–205.

Frederickson, N. & Cline, T. (2001) *Special Educational Needs, Inclusion and Diversity*. Buckingham: Open University Press.

Gallagher, D. J. (2001) 'Neutrality as a moral standpoint, conceptual confusion and the full inclusion debate', *Disability and Society*, 16 (5), 637–654.

Gersten, R., Baker, S. & Lloyd, J. W. (2000) 'Designing high-quality research in special education: group experimental design', *Journal of Special Education*, 34(1), 2–18.

Gillham, W. (1978) *Reconstructing Educational Psychology*. London: Croom Helm.

Hawkridge, J. (1991) *Uphill All the Way*. London: Michael Joseph.

Hegarty, S. (1993) 'Reviewing the literature on integration', *European Journal of Special Needs Education*, 8 (3), 194–200.

Hegarty, S., Pocklington, K. & Lucas, D. (1981) *Educating Pupils with Special Needs in the Ordinary School*. Windsor: NFER-Nelson.

Law, J., Lindsay, G., Peacey, N., Gascoigne, M., Soloff, N., Radford, J. & Band, S. with Fitzgerald, L. (2000) *Provision for Children with Speech and Language Needs in England and Wales: facilitating communication between education and health services*. London: DfEE.

Law, J., Lindsay, G., Peacey, N., Gascoigne, M., Soloff, N., Radford, J. & Band, S. (2002) 'Consultation as a model for providing speech and language therapy in schools: a panacea or one step too far?' *Child Language Teaching and Therapy*, 18 (2), 145–163.

Lee, B. & Henkhuzens, Z. (1996) *Integration in Progress: pupils with special needs in mainstream schools*. Slough: NFER.

Lindsay, G. (1989) 'Evaluating integration', *Educational Psychology in Practice*, 5 (1), 7–16.

Lindsay, G. (1995a) 'Early identification of special educational needs', in I. Lunt, B. Norwich & V. Varma (eds) *Psychology and Education for Special Needs: recent developments and future directions*. London: Arena, Ashgate Publishing.

Lindsay, G. (1995b) 'Values, ethics and psychology', *The Psychologist: Bulletin of the British Psychological Society*, 8, 448–451.

Lindsay, G. (1997) 'Are we ready for inclusion?' in G. Lindsay & D. Thompson (eds) *Values into Practice in Special Education*. London: David Fulton.

Lindsay, G. (in press) 'Implementing the revised Code of Practice: ethics and values', in D. Galloway (ed.), *Children with Special Education Needs: a response to the new Code of Practice. Occasional Papers of the Association for Child Psychology and Psychiatry*. London: ACPP.

Lindsay, G. & Dockrell, J. (2000) 'The behaviour and self-esteem of children with specific speech and language difficulties', *British Journal of Educational Psychology*, 70 (4), 583–601.

Lindsay, G. & Dockrell, J. (in press) 'Whose job is it? Parents' concerns about the needs of their children with language problems', *Journal of Special Education*.

Lindsay, G., Dockrell, J., Mackie, C. & Letchford, B. (2002) *Educational Provision for Children with Specific Speech and Language Difficulties in England and Wales*. Coventry: University of Warwick, CEDAR.

Lindsay, G. & Maguire, M. (2002) *Modelling the Potential Implications of Graduation on 16 Year Olds in Three Geographical Areas*. Research Report 340. London: DfES.

Lipsky, D. K. & Gartner, A. (1998) 'Factors for successful inclusion: learning from the past, looking forward to the future', in S. V. Vitello & D. E. Mithaug (eds) *Inclusive Schooling: national and international perspectives*. Mahurah, NJ: Lawrence Erlbaum Associates.

Low, C. (2001) 'Have disability rights gone too far?' City Insights Lecture, 3 April 2001. London: City University. (www.city.ac.uk/whatson/city_insights_lecture_3.htm)

Loxley, D. (1978) 'Community psychology,' in W. Gillham (ed.) *Reconstructing Educational Psychology*. London: Croom Helm.

Madden, N. A. & Slavin, R. E. (1983) 'Mainstreaming students with mild handicaps: academic and social outcomes', *Review of Educational Research*, 53, 519–569.

Manset, G. & Semmel, M. I. (1997) 'Are inclusive programmes for students with mild disabilities effective? A comparative review of model programmes', *Journal of Special Education*, 31 (2), 155–180.

Marston, D. (1996) 'A comparison of inclusion only, pull-out only and combined service models for students with mild disabilities', *Journal of Special Education*, 30 (2), 121–132.

Mills, P. E., Cole, K. N., Jenkins, J. R. & Dale, P. S. (1998) 'Effects of differing levels of inclusion on preschoolers with disabilities', *Exceptional Children*, 65, 79–90.

Mithaug, D. E. (1998) 'The alternative to ideological inclusion', in S. J. Vitello & D. E. Mithaug (eds) *Inclusive Schooling: national and international perspectives.* Mahwah, NJ: Lawrence Erlbaum Associates.

Moore, M., Beazley, S. & Maelzer, J. (1998) *Researching Disability Issues.* Buckingham: Open University Press.

Neelands, J., Lindsay, G., Freakley, V. & Band, S. (2002) *Dance and Drama Awards Scheme Evaluation Project: 3rd Interim Report.* Coventry: University of Warwick, CEDAR.

Norwich, B. (1996) 'Special needs education or education for all: connective specialisation and ideological impurity', *British Journal of Special Education*, 23 (3), 100–104.

Oliver, M. (1996) *Understanding Disability: from theory to practice.* London: Macmillan.

Peacey, N., Dockrell, J. & Peart, G. (2002) *'Analysis of the Responses to the Audit Commission's Report: Statutory Assessment and Statements of SEN: In Need of Review?'* London: University of London, Institute of Education.

Plomin, R. & Walker, S. O. (in press) 'Genetics and educational psychology', *British Journal of Educational Psychology.*

Powers, S., Gregory, S. & Thoutenhoofd, E. (1999) 'The educational achievement of deaf children', *Deafness and Education International*, 1 (1), 1–9.

Riggs, C. G. & Mueller, P. H. (2001) 'Employment and utilization of paraeducators in inclusive settings', *Journal of Special Education*, 35 (1), 51–62.

Salend, S. S. & Duhaney, L. M. (1999) 'The impact of inclusion on students with and without disabilities and their education', *Remedial and Special Education*, 20 (2), 114–126.

Sebba, J. & Sachdev, D. (1997) *What Works in Inclusive Education?* Ilford: Barnardo's.

Shield, B., Dockrell, J., Jeffrey, R. & Tatchmatzidis, I. (2002) *The Effects of Noise on the Attainments and Cognitive Performance of Primary Children: Report to DoH and DEFRA.* London: South Bank University.

Skidmore, D. (1999) 'Divergent discourses of learning difficulties', *British Educational Research Journal*, 25 (5), 651–663.

Staub, D. & Peck, C. A. (1994) 'What are the outcomes for non-disabled pupils?' *Educational Leadership*, 52 (4), 36–40.

Tilstone, C., Florian, L. & Rose, R. (eds) (1998) *Promoting Inclusive Practice.* London: Routledge.

Tooley, J. & Darby, D. (1998) *Educational Research: a critique*. London: Office for Standards in Education (OFSTED).

UNESCO (1994) *The UNESCO Salamanca Statement and Framework for Action on Special Needs Education*. Paris: UNESCO.

Vaughan, S. & Klinger, J. K. (1998) 'Students' perceptions of inclusion and resource room settings', *Journal of Special Education*, 32 (2), 79–88.

Wedell, K. (1978) 'Early identification and compensatory interaction'. Paper presented at the NATO International Conference on Learning Disorders, Ottawa.

Wedell, K. & Lindsay, G. (1980) 'Early identification procedures: what have we learned?' *Remedial Education*, 15, 130–135.

Chapter 16

Working with the group dimension

Paul Greenhalgh

Introduction

The import of the group itself has a powerful effect on interactive processes, and since schools are organised around groups, group issues need to be considered in their own right.

Emotional or behavioural difficulties are given expression in relationships, in groups, and so the dynamics of group relations can bring into sharp focus the issues and problems demanding attention. For unintegrated children a key area of difficulty is a lack of the capacity to work and play with others in groups. Mongan and Hart (1989: 26) write, 'If the behaviour of pupils was to be improved, consideration needed to be given first as to how to enable pupils to work effectively in groups.' Yet this can sometimes feel so difficult that such a strategy is often ignored in favour of individualised activities. Croll and Moses (1985) showed that children can expect to spend, at most, only 3.2 per cent of their time receiving individual attention from the teacher. Left to work individually for the greater part of their day, children identified by their teachers as having behavioural difficulties spent twice as much time distracted from what they were supposed to be doing as other children.

Yet the group can be a powerful tool for promoting positive interaction. The first part of this chapter explores the opportunities which groups present for facilitating children's emotional development and learning. However, being in a group presents any of us with a wide range of demanding issues, particularly concerning the relationship between our individual identity and the identity of the group. The struggles which this issue presents in groups can elicit a number of defensive group processes. The second section of the chapter considers group phenomena which inhibit development. It is important to understand such phenomena, since 'unless one understands the character of the helping medium which one is considering using one cannot even begin to make plans and decisions about … how to plan the effort and how to proceed while using it' (Whitaker 1985: 32). The third section of the chapter considers the impact of group size and stage upon dynamics. The final section draws out the themes considered and highlights issues to take account of when leading groups to facilitate development and learning.

These issues in working with group phenomena are pertinent to any group. Those group phenomena which inhibit development are more overt and blatant where group members have limited skills in negotiating and relating with others, or in being aware of and managing themselves. Hence they are particularly pertinent to work with children with emotional and behavioural difficulties.

Opportunities for personal growth and development in groups

In this section I consider the functions of the group in relation to the opportunities for personal development presented by the group itself as a helping medium. Recognition of the positive potential of groups is an aid to promoting the positive aspects of group processes. I present [a number of] images of the group as a helping medium: the group and the churn, the group as a bridge between internal and social reality, the group as matrix, [and] the group as kinship.

The groups which provide the context for the examples cited in this section of the chapter are tutorial class groups, each of which comprises about six children with emotional and behavioural difficulties from different schools, attending for half-days, usually on a twice-weekly basis.

The group and the churn

> Hassan said, 'Wouldn't it be good if Shaheena could have some of my noisiness and I could have some of her quietness!'

The concept of the group as a churn relates to the notion of the emotionally contained environment. A churn is a form of container. The physical act of churning involves agitation and stirring in order to aid transformation into another substance. Two features of physical churning relate to the churning involved in group work.

Firstly, churning requires continuous action for a long enough time to effect changes. In relation to group work, this calls for continuity both practically and psychically. Psychological continuity can be provided partly through the use of structures which provide elements of ritual in the group's life. An example of ritual structures in the tutorial class setting was my division of the half-day sesions into four phases: newstime (when children took turns to share news or concerns of their own choice); work-time (when each child was given work on appropriate aspects of the curriculum); choice-time (when children made use of the varied resources of the room, including the resource of the teacher for help with negotiation, to follow friendships and activities of their choice); and ending, with a coming together for drinks and a story or a game.

Secondly, in the act of churning, the substances in the container move against each other. This is an important precursor to transmutation into a new substance. In a group churn, experiences and ideas are turned over in the mind. A group is an environment in which people can observe what others do and say and then observe what happens next. Even when a person may appear to be doing nothing more than watching or listening, s/he might be noting events which may have a particular personal meaning. For example, someone who has always been afraid to make challenges may be observing others make challenges. A group is also an environment in which people can receive feedback from other members about their own behaviour or participation in the group. Receiving feedback from others in the group is one of its main advantages as a context for helping personal growth. Group members can gain information about the impact of their behaviour on others. Within the containing environment of an established group, a child might productively try out new behaviour patterns which are not part of his/her established repertory.

The group provides opportunities for the child to explore personal meanings and the sense made of life experiences, in relation to a wide range of identifications with others and provocations by others. Freud articulated these processes in terms of 'suggestion' and 'imitation'. Bion (1989: 175) preferred the idea of 'valency', which he defined as 'the capacity of the individual for instantaneous combination with other individuals in the established pattern of behaviour'. Provocations and projections enable others in the group to feel things which they have not felt before, or to rediscover aspects of themselves which have been projected or denied.

These potentially valuable experiences in groups provide, in relation to some types of small-group work, an argument for the value of a limited amount of acting-out. This provides a safe space within which a child's communications through behaviour, which s/he may not yet be able to express in any other way, may be received and thought about. Murray Cox (1990) argues that the group *as a whole* carries the transferences of feeling and that the group together can often bear the intensity of a group member's difficult feeling when the individual cannot.

The group as a bridge between internal and social reality

The group provides a ready-made social context in which the membership provides a forum of social attitudes and expectations. In the group the inner realities of children, as expressed partly in behaviour, are continually exposed to, and sometimes confronted by, what might be called the 'group ego'. This process is continually at work in groups, even though it might not always be expressed in the mature way in which Anna once said, at the beginning of a newstime, 'I'm concerned about Simon's behaviour.' Exposure to the 'group ego' generates the need for each group member to develop responses at an ego level, which are acceptable to the group. Adult interventions can help the child discover the links of meaning between the inner world and social reality. The adult's feedback to the child – of a difficulty or a change – might be given in relation to the child's social reality in the group. The child is thus both required by the group, and helped by the adult, to link inner and outer experiences and the experience of community, and this contributes to the child's ego development. Exposure to the 'group ego' can be particularly valuable for the development of omnipotent children.

Example

When Terry, as a 7 year old, joined the tutorial class group, he was extremely challenging. In the group there were three somewhat macho 10 and 11 year old boys. Terry's desire for a respected and valued place in the group meant that he really took note of the other children's comments about his exaggerated stories and rudeness.

For children who have been emotionally deprived, and whose capacity in life has been damaged, the group setting offers the experience of reliving more positive experiences, over and over again, in concrete forms. The deprived child is thus enabled to internalise gradually a wider range of possibilities in relationships.

The group as matrix

Groups might come to have a symbolic as well as a practical significance for their members. Miller and Rice (1967) termed such groups 'sentient' groups. A significant symbol in facilitating emotional development is that of the matrix, the womb (Cox 1990). Within a known group, the individual potentially has a familiar place, a sanctuary, a sense of safety, of belonging and of trust. Where a group functions as a matrix, the group member can feel free to express and clarify a range of feelings. In defining group developmental goals, Mongan and Hart (1989: 127) place the generation of a sense of belonging – a feeling that 'I am accepted and trusted as a member of this group' – as the first on their list. This is related to what they describe as the development of a sense of achievement ('I have achieved something worthwhile for myself and my contribution to the work of the group is valued') and of shared influence ('I help to decide what goes on in this room, my opinion counts, I take responsibility for my own learning and behaviour').

Cox (1990) maintains, with reference to therapeutic processes in groups, that the therapist is there 'to trust the group. … The root is trust; it grows in trust.' Where there is trust, there can emerge the characteristics defined by Bion (1989) as good group spirit: i.e. a common purpose, a common recognition of boundaries, the capacity to absorb new members and lose old ones, freedom from internal subgroups having rigid boundaries, each individual member being valued for his/her contribution to the group and having freedom to move within it, and the capacity to face discontent within the group.

When children themselves recognise the importance of the maintenance of trust in the group, it can sometimes stimulate a high degree of ethical awareness. I provide a vignette involving two children.

Example

When George returned, somewhat reticently after a missed session, Andrew and Richard asked, 'Why did you tell us George was away because his grandmother had died? You should have just told us he was going to be away. It was for him to tell us the rest if he wanted to.'

In ongoing groups, where individual members leave as they are ready, and new members join established groups, there are opportunities for issues relating to endings, beginnings, loss, separation, greed, envy and feelings about the individual's place in the group to be reworked over and over again. This provides each individual with renewed opportunities to work on his/her subjective constructs about such issues.

The group and kinship

The group provides opportunities for its members to make related, 'living' contributions to each other. In the tutorial class group it was noteworthy how often children brought sweets, crisps, biscuits, fruit and drink to share at drinks-time. In an early work on groups, Ginott (1961: 6) says, 'The therapeutic process is enhanced by the fact that every group member can be a giver and not only a receiver of help.'

A sense of kinship evokes the development of a sense of attachment to the group and those in it. When this happens there is the opportunity for relationship, perhaps unconsciously, with what the group as a whole symbolises, and this has a potentially powerful effect upon individual growth.

In groups, shared themes and kinship build up through associative processes, in which each person makes contributions out of her/his own associations to what has gone before. Issues which are important to a particular person can be explored within the context of a prevailing theme in the group.

> The potential for benefit lies in the opportunity to explore issues of potential importance under conditions in which a number of people are involved and the shared character of the situation leads to courage and support ... an individual finds a theme manageable even though threatening because it *is* shared and because much mutual support for exploring it exists in the group.
>
> (Whitaker 1985: 36–7)

The sense of kinship is supported by the group's evolution of particular attitudes and behaviour patterns, or 'norms' and belief systems. The kinds of belief system on which a group operates are of critical importance and can make the difference between a sterile or even destructive group and a useful one. The evolution of group norms can serve as a means of helping some members to feel safe, for example by allowing group members to express anger in particular ways. Some norms and belief systems have the effect of widening the boundaries of the group, making useful explorations of personal issues possible. For example, the shared belief that 'we all have problems sometimes' supports a group and its members as a positive medium for help, since, if everyone has problems, no one need feel ashamed of talking of problems (Whitaker 1985). Whitaker develops the notion of a 'group solution' as a wider concept than norms and beliefs but encompassing both of these, and she builds the notion into a model of group functioning called 'group focal conflict theory'. In this theory, a facilitating solution is regarded as one which deals with fear, and allows for the safe expression of wishes related to fear. Fears are thus contained and, at the same time, group members can confront and explore the associated impulses and feelings. In a group the motive to precipitate a conflict might relate to a wish which feels risky and which cannot be acknowledged, such as a wish to be close to others, or to be nurtured or loved. Whitaker (1985) argues that during periods when a group is operating on some facilitating solution, processes which she terms comparison, feedback, spectatorship and behavioural try-outs are likely to go on in a co-operative, useful and constructive manner. Bion (1989: 136) examined the relationship between co-operation and on-task behaviour in groups: 'Organisation and structure are the weapons of the work group. They are the product of co-operation between members of the group, and their effect once established in the group is to demand still further co-operation from the individuals in the group.'

From the above discussion it is evident that processes relating to the development of a sense of kinship go beyond individual adjustment and the internalisation of 'acceptable' behaviour. Each group member can being to establish areas of agreement and disagreement with the group, and thus become less dependent and more of an individual. This process is both helped by, and a product of, co-operative learning methods. Such methods help the development of higher-quality cognitive strategies; the improvement of understanding through discussion and controversy; the improvement of long-term retention from the continual restatement and reformulation of new ideas; the enrichment of ideas through exchanges between pupils of different background, achievement levels and experiences; and the increase in motivation for learning (Mongan and Hart 1989: 129).

How does working exclusively with groups of troubled children relate to these issues of kinship, from the adult's point of view? Foukes and Anthony comment:

> maladjusted children can be exceedingly demanding, and drain us of our feeling ... but no unilateral relationship in human society is a good one ... unilateral giving is bad for both sides. It is always therapeutically wise to expect something in return, even from the most psychotic child, for whom the act of giving may become the act of redemption. ... In the group ... it should be shown:
> 1) That unilateral receiving is not therapeutic for the child.
> 2) That unilateral giving is not healthy for the adult.
>
> (Foukes and Anthony 1984: 226–7)

Foukes and Anthony add that the establishment of a reciprocal relationship is as good an indicator of development as any.

The above discussion has elaborated a number of ways in which groups provide opportunities for personal development. Enabling groups to manifest these potentials is a task that calls for skill, since the teacher or other adult is inevitably also struggling with group phenomena that get in the way of development. It is to these phenomena that I now turn.

Group processes that inhibit development

An awareness of group phenomena that inhibit growth enhances the adult's capacity to work effectively with group processes in the service of facilitating individuals' development and learning. Group processes which can inhibit development arise in all manner of groups – groups of adults and of children – and are likely to be most obvious where the individuals within the group have difficulty containing and managing disturbing feelings.

In order to get a feel of the sorts of issue pertinent to this discussion, it is worth nothing Wells' (1981) remarks upon the parallels between the relationship of an individual with a group and the relationship of an infant with his/her mother. Both experiences elicit struggles over the issues of fusing/joining and separating/isolation; both potentially elicit a sense of being nurtured and of frustration; and in both, strong ambivalent feelings are aroused. The last relates to the experience of both love and hate simultaneously, to the generation of the defence mechanism of splitting and projective identification in order to cope with ambivalence, and to the struggle with the tension between engulfment and estrangement.

Group issues are discussed below in terms of defensive norms and beliefs, the toleration of difference, contagion and regression, and task avoidance and regression. The impact of such phenomena depends largely upon the skill of the group leader to work with them preventatively, diagnostically and remedially. To be able to work effectively with processes which inhibit development can have a powerful effect on group experience. Kurt Lewin's research (e.g. 1948) on the forces which drive and/or restrain change in the work situation led him to conclude that working with the factors restraining or inhibiting change is a more effective way of facilitating it than simply reinforcing those forces which drive towards it.

The group phenomena considered here are likely to operate upon individuals in the group in an unconscious manner. This has an impact upon the sorts of fantasy which are harboured by individuals within the group. The dynamics of any group generate fantasies which are commonly held in the group. The fantasies of a group have a part to play in constructing a belief system about what is, and is not, possible in the group.

Defensive norms and beliefs

The positive influences of group norms were considered in the first part of this chapter. Norms and belief systems can also constitute powerful defences in groups. Group norms may serve to suppress feelings which group members find difficult to tolerate, and thereby to keep group members comfortable; but such norms may also reduce or constrict the value of the group by restricting the areas in which individual and group exploration can occur. If such defence mechanisms become a (conscious or unconscious) collusion between group members they have the potential for targeting flak at particular individuals within a group, for example by one person being made the scapegoat. Negative norms and beliefs may be damaging in the direct sense of facing individuals with something which they cannot tolerate, or by placing them in a position where they are blamed or attacked (Whitaker 1985).

Such group dynamics generate norms and beliefs which serve to mask competition and rivalries within the group. Since competition and rivalries are difficult to face up to, groups develop ways of avoiding these issues. Some rivalries which groups commonly avoid are those which relate to the various individual needs and wishes in the group. The question arises of whether the meeting of the wishes or needs of other people threatens the possibility of one's own wishes being met. In unconsciously seeking to mask rivalries, groups may thus generate the belief, for instance, that no one wants to be different in the group, or that no one in the group is interested in certain activities or fostering certain attitudes, whilst everyone in the group is interested in other particular activities or fostering other attitudes.

In circumstances where difficult feelings are present in a group, the group might allow one person to believe that s/he is the only one with a particular feeling, as if s/he becomes a 'carrier' for the group of a particular impulse. This is the mechanism through which group members may (unconsciously) take on particular roles within a group. An individual may thus become isolated within the group, and this mechanism enables other group members to maintain the myth that the particular feeling does not 'belong' to them as individuals. The scapegoat is the particular individual to whom these same feelings or wishes have been ascribed and who is then isolated and scorned for possessing the feelings. So long as scapegoating persists, others are allowed to avoid acknowledging the same feeling or behaviour in themselves. If a group leader keeps the scapegoat in the centre of attention to 'help' that particular individual, this simply continues the pattern of scapegoating in a disguised and devious form. Sometimes, when one person is being criticised or blamed, the underlying dynamic produces displacement activities. Anger which really belongs to one person is displaced onto another, usually because the attackers then feel safe from retaliation, abandonment or other negative consequences.

When group fantasies emerge which relate to the behaviour or motivations of most individuals within the group, these fantasies most often remain unchallenged by the group, *even when* contrary evidence is available to all those engaging in the fantasy. The danger of differentiating feelings in a group is that it might become clear who feels what, and who carries what, and who brings which vulnerabilities to the group. It may often feel easier for individuals in groups to live with a fantasy about a group's behaviour, rather than checking it out. When an individual feels something different from the group's fantasy, this can feel very risky, both for that individual, and for the rest of the group: 'like individuals who reject shadow elements of themselves by projecting them out into the environment, the group will create victims rather than face dealing with diversity and difference' (Colman 1992: 98).

Toleration of difference in groups

In groups we are all faced with the difficulty of tolerating individual differences, differences between ourselves and others. Often unconsciously, we will seek 'sameness' in a group of which we are a member, as a way of avoiding difference, since recognising difference implies recognising different needs, and again, by implication, rivalries within the group. Our strong tendency towards conformity is linked to the experience that 'to be original, or different, is felt to be dangerous' (Rogers 1961: 348). Difference is therefore unconsciously avoided in order to maintain the sense of safety associated with sameness. When faced with the range of such pressures that always exist in groups, it becomes difficult to maintain, struggle with and experience ambivalences, and so in groups we easily slide into omnipotence.

The above discussion suggests that it can feel very risky to acknowledge difference in a group. As soon as the difference of one group member becomes clear and acknowledged, it is possible that the other group members may reject that individual or psychologically eject him/her from the group. Groups most often function to avoid any examination of the differences between members, by taking flight into other 'safer' issues. The struggle between being part of a group and being an individual can be very difficult to deal with.

Where teaching is organised in mixed-attainment (a notion preferred to mixed-'ability') groups, teachers may both recognise the potential of this form of organisation, and yet find some of the issues which get in the way of learning in such groups difficult to cope with. Although teaching mixed-attainment groups demands a high level of organisational skill, the organisational issues in themselves become easier when some of the underlying group dynamics issues are addressed. Of particular importance is the capacity of people to tolerate differences between members of a group. A group may find it very difficult to come to terms with various individual needs within it, since, once different needs are acknowledged, a rivalrous situation exists, which elicits the question for group members, 'Are one person's needs going to be met at the expense of other people's needs?' Hence the significance of the teacher's role in validating and organising for difference. Differences of all sorts can be celebrated: cultural difference, differences in individual interests and areas of attainment, and so on.

Contagion and regression

Feelings of envy or fear of attack which may be aroused in group dynamics provoke anxiety, particularly when they re-evoke previous disturbing experiences. When one is anxious the temptation to act out the difficult feeling and to project it onto others becomes stronger. Panic takes hold of individuals more easily in groups, and groups can sometimes develop particularly intense moods or atmospheres. Quite suddenly, for example, a group can be in a panic, or start behaving hysterically. When groups are 'caught up' in frantic feelings, it can become difficult for group members and the group leader to maintain the capacity to think, and this is particularly so when emotional or physical attacks are likely.

Sometimes groups can be overwhelmed by experience akin to that of the state Melanie Klein described as the 'paranoid-schizoid' position. Reed and Palmer argue that group activity of an omnipotent kind:

> may be precipitated by what are seen as threats to the group from outside, or by anxieties arising within individuals about their relationship to the group. These amount to the same thing, in that the felt threat is to what may be a very primitive fantasy of the group, on which the individual feels he depends for his survival. ... Behaviour is directed towards safeguarding the survival of the group, not by realistic measures, but by designating sources of protection and deliverance on the one hand, and of malign influence and destruction on the other.
>
> (Reed and Palmer 1972, Lecture 2: 10)

People tend to get thrown back to regressive stages under pressure. Another factor which induces regressed states in groups is the entry of a new group member. When a new child joins a group which has become settled and on-task, the group will often regress, with the teacher feeling that s/he is 'back to the starting-point' with the group. This issue is picked up again in the section below on group stages. All groups experience regression at times: the inhibiting factors discussed in this section become reinforced when a group gets stuck in a particular stage as a coping strategy.

Task-avoidance in groups

Bion's innovation in working with groups was to treat the whole group as his patient, and he gave interpretations to the group rather than to individuals. Bion argued that effective work in groups is constantly interrupted by things from other contexts which push them off task. Whenever the group is working, it can behave as if a 'basic assumption' is held in common by all the members, which will affect the activity of the group. By this Bion meant that groups often seem to behave in a particular mode, 'as if' all the members hold a basic assumption in common. The basic assumption relates to unconscious group fantasies about the kind of action which is required to secure the group's survival. these assumptions are seldom voiced. When:

> one kind of basic assumption threatens to overwhelm the group and make work unproductive, the teacher has to try to find ways of mobilizing another, so that new forces can come into play and be used by the group in an increasingly mature and responsible fashion.
>
> (Richardson 1975: 223)

According to Bion, there are three distinct emotional states in groups from which 'basic assumptions' can be deduced. He described these states as 'dependency', 'flight/fight' and 'pairing'. I consider each of these in turn. First of all the dependent group:

> When the shared map of the group is based on the dependence assumption, members behave as though they had access to a person or object which is able to supply all their needs, without their having to do anything except wait and receive. Correspondingly, they feel themselves to be weak, ignorant, inadequate and vulnerable. Capacities which they are able to use elsewhere disappear in the climate of dependence.
>
> (Reed and Palmer 1972, Lecture 2:11)

Of the dependent group Bion says:

> one person is always felt to be in a position to supply the needs of the group, and the rest in a position in which their needs are supplied ... As the culture becomes established, individuals ... begin to show their discomfort. One quite frequent phenomenon is the emergence of feelings of guilt about greed.
>
> (Bion 1989: 74)

When a group becomes taken over by a culture of dependency, what the leader says or does is sooner or later bound to be a disappointment. The group has to work to maintain the fantasy on which, it is felt, their survival depends.

> When the leader's behaviour does not fit the role he has been cast in, it is ignored or explained away. Another member may be unconsciously assigned the role of a disciple or high priest who explains and justifies the words and actions of the leader to the other members. Alternatively the leader may be manipulated to show the love and power he appears to be hiding, by giving him problems to solve.
>
> (Reed and Palmer 1972, Lecture 2: 12)

If the teacher takes the role of leader with a dependent group, the group, although in some ways willing to collude with this, may also become frustrated. In such situations the teacher:

> must contrive to be reliable while continually urging the class to question his omniscience, challenge his opinions and realistically accept his human limitations. And at times he will create situations in which members of his class take his role, and become accepted as alternative leaders in a basically dependent culture, using their own expertise as he uses his when he is the accepted leader.
>
> (Richardson 1975: 223)

In the 'fight/flight' group, task avoidance proceeds through flight away from the task, or 'fight' with peers.

> In the flight-fight culture the danger is that the group will either destroy the teacher or itself by the unleashing of its own hostile impulses or withdraw from the situation altogether. And so the role of the teacher is to channel the aggression into an attack on ignorance and apathy, so that the class rediscovers its powers of co-operation in a learning situation and uses its leaders in a constructive way.
>
> (Richardson 1975: 223)

In the 'pairing group', collusive pairings between group members are entered into as a way of avoiding the task at hand. The pairings may be felt to be collusive by those group members who are excluded from them. Pairing takes place to some extent in all groups, mostly unconsciously. Pairings may take place in many different ways, based for example upon projection, empathy, the desire for sexual liaison, or the ability of some members of the group to relate to others in an honest, direct and personal manner. Reed and Palmer explain the dynamic:

> the hope is built up of creating a group which will be free from all the frustrations and disappointments of most human relationships. This process leads to a shared idea of a group which is highly idealised. All the negative aspects of human relationships are projected outside the group, onto external authorities, careers, marriages and social systems.
>
> (Reed and Palmer 1972, Lecture 2: 13)

Richardson relates this dynamic to the role of the teacher:

> In the pairing culture, the danger is that the group rests in the lazy hope that two members will continue indefinitely to carry responsibility; individuals then become frustrated because their hope of some perfect product from these two is never realized. Here the teacher's role is to break up the task and give each pair or small group a manageable part of it to tackle. In this way achievement becomes possible, because no one any longer supposes that one pair can be left to produce the magic solution.
>
> (Richardson 1975: 223)

I now consider the impact of group size and stage, and then turn to the facilitation and mobilisation of helpful aspects of group life.

Group size and stage

Group size

In the field of education, much is made of the significance of class size, but more from the perspective of the relationship of class size and individual attainment than from a consideration of the group dynamics issues. These are considered below in terms of the impact of group size on individual identity, the arousal of primitive feelings, the development of a shared understanding of the group, the stability of relationships in the group, and the group's relationship with the wider organisation.

Groups of more than sixteen people are regarded in the group relations field as 'large groups'. In large groups it is more difficult for us to hold onto our own sense of individual identity. One way of holding in one's mind an image of a group of which one is a member is to include an image of each individual group member. A large group is a group which is too big for this to happen (Reed and Palmer 1972). Tourquet (1974) argues that a group of twelve is the optimum size for a single group member to encompass so as to take in the rest of the group as individuals, and that sixteen is the very upper limit for this capacity. In large groups a sense of individual identity often develops by individuals identifying in some way with the figure-head. Clearly these issues have implications for the organisation of classes in schools. A group dynamics perspective reinforces the value of dividing class groups into subgroups, particularly when questions of individual identity are pertinent to the task, e.g. for subjects such as personal and social education, for activities such as problem-solving approaches which require mobilisation of social as well as learning skills, and for younger or less autonomous children whose sense of identity is not yet well developed.

In large groups several factors combine to prevent the development of a shared understanding or 'map' of the group. In consequence the capacity of individual members to relate productively to ambivalence in the group is more precarious. Reed and Palmer (1972) suggest that one factor which might inhibit the development of a shared map of the group is a spatial factor. They argue that, given the large size of the group and the space in which it physically operates, the individual cannot always register the effect of her/his contributions on others, and so does not know what feelings are being left with them.

According to Reed and Palmer (1972), another factor which prevents the development of a shared map of the group is that of quantity. In a large group there is too much happening for each individual member to take in. This reinforces the significance of the leader's role in working with group boundaries.

A large group which remains undifferentiated, in terms of emotionally meaningful relationships between members, tends towards instability and is liable to be caught up in impulsive activity or frozen into sterile rigidity. If not provided with structure, the large group frequently breaks down into smaller groupings, either spontaneously or through conscious decisions of the members. Reed and Palmer note three common patterns: firstly, polarisation into two opposing factions – a group and an 'anti-group'. Secondly, there is the formation of an active small group, in the limelight, with others who participate vicariously. The third form of division is into multiple subgroups. This suggests the need to provide structures which link relationships within the group to the whole group identity, and to harness the tendency towards division in larger groups proactively and creatively.

Group stages

Example

In an in-service training session for newly qualified teachers, one of the teachers noted that after he was just getting on top of the demanding process of getting a group settled, on several occasions other pupils were sent in from another group. He observed that on each occasion this seemed to put the whole group process right back to the beginning again. An understanding of group dynamics issues can help avoid this sort of difficulty, and so help functioning groups to pursue their primary tasks.

Groups develop and change their character over a period of time. Their preoccupations are likely to change according to the stage of the group's life. At some time or another, all groups are likely to be faced with issues such as group members questioning their own acceptability within the group, yearnings for closeness and nurturance, anger and its management, issues of power, control and autonomy, personal aspirations and the hopes, fears and despairs associated with them, envy, and personally held fears and guilts. The extent to which an individual's needs are met at the beginning of the group's life disproportionately affects the individual's capacity to participate productively in group tasks. When first joining a group, or at the beginning of a group's life, individuals are likely to have a number of concerns. These concerns are likely to relate to the questions shown in Figure 16.1.

Process

Safety:
>Will I be emotionally and physically safe in the group?

Acceptance:
>Will I be liked or disliked? How will I be treated?

Participation:
>What will my place in the group be?

Task

Definition:
>What will we have to do and what are we meant to achieve?

Competence in relation to task:
>Will I be able to do what is expected of me?

Hierarchy of achievement:
>How will my competencies compare with those of others?

Leadership and group management

Who will be in charge?
How will the rules be made in the group?
What will I feel about the way the group is run, and how will I respond?

Figure 16.1 Concerns at the beginning of a group's life

Group leaders/teachers can be more effective if they are also aware of the processes which a collection of people go through in establishing themselves as a group. Tuckman (1965) identified a number of stages in the life of a group, which are shown in Figure 16.2.

Tuckman also argued that when new members join a group, the group has to rework the previous stages that it has gone through.

When a group has matured and is working effectively, it is able to manage productively the tensions shown in Figure 16.3.

Stage 1 Forming	The group discovers the task in hand and the rules which govern it. They also have to learn about each other.
Stage 2 Storming	During the initial stage a false consensus is often reached. This is challenged in ways which reveal interpersonal conflicts but lead to new rules. The developing trust of group members is tested here.
Stage 3 Norming	Feelings and views are exchanged as norms and practices are established and their limits explored and tested by group members.
Stage 4 Performing	Levels of performance are no longer hindered by the processes of the previous stages. The group is now able to focus on the task in hand.

Figure 16.2 Stages in the life of a group (after Tuckman 1965)

- Links a whole image of the institution and clarity about the group's goals and purposes.

- Shares leadership functions and responsibilities among group members.

- Maintains supportive values and beliefs and facilitates expression and resolution of difficult feelings.

- Facilitates communication, reflection and the development of mutual understanding on the group's tasks and processes, and makes modifications where appropriate.

- Balances group productivity and individual needs, enabling individuals to relate to whole images of the group and of themselves as individuals.

- Balances group identity and cohesion on the one hand, and the capacity to respond flexibly in the environment on the other.

- Selects procedural and decision-making arrangements flexibly and efficiently.

- Works productively with difference, e.g. differences can be expressed and conflict tolerated, minority viewpoints are taken into consideration, the different abilities of group members are valued and made use of.

- Accepts with ambivalence new additions and the losses of group members.

Figure 16.3 Managing the tensions: characteristics of an effectively functioning group

Facilitating and managing group processes

In reviewing the discussion of this chapter so far, I now turn to extrapolate some key functions in facilitating and managing group processes in groups which are concerned with the development of the individuals within them. In general terms, the management of groups designed to facilitate developmental processes requires, according to Menzies Lyth (1988), clear task definition and sustaining the values, roles and boundaries to achieve the task; the capacity to keep in mind the whole group and each whole child; the capacity to mitigate defences (in oneself and others) and anti-task behaviour; and the modelling of good 'management-cum-ego' functioning. Bearing in mind the teacher at work with emotional/behavioural factors in learning, in the discussion which follows I highlight a number of significant leadership and management functions: the capacity to reflect upon process, self-observation, establishing the group as a symbol, boundary control, issues of emotional containment and dependency, supportive group norms, and working with difference and facilitating multiplicity of experience in groups.

Reflection upon process

'Process thinking' is particularly important in relation to group phenomena, as these are so complex. Douglas (1978) emphasises that the effectiveness of group leaders in facilitating emotional development is determined by their capacity to examine and work with 'process' as well as 'content', i.e. with the dynamics, the interactions and the affective realm as well as with the subject-matter of the activities. Working with process as well as content suggests that the group leader needs to be able to work with the many-layered inter-relationships of group members' contributions – group and individual dynamics, conscious and unconscious intentions – as well as the overt subject-matter of the contributions: 'an adult's capacity for listening and seeing beyond the face value of opinions contributes to the functioning of the group' (Barrett and Trevitt 1991: 203). Douglas argues that the key skills in working with group processes are the ability to observe, the ability to assess the group's situation, and the ability to make appropriate interventions. The teacher's effectiveness increases to the extent that s/he can enable group members to make use of the group in what Whitaker (1985) describes as a 'medium for help'.

Whitaker (1985) also suggests that a group leader, as part of the work of reflection, has the following tasks: to develop, refine and expand an understanding of each person in the group; to keep in touch with the dynamics of the group as a whole and as it develops over time; to keep in touch with one's own feelings and to note one's own behaviour and its consequences; and to perceive connections between the group and individual dynamics.

Self-observation

If one is reflecting in a process-oriented way then one is including oneself as part of the equation of evaluation. Given the range of feelings which are part of group life and the projection of painful feelings, a group leader has to act as a projection receptacle and has to be able to bear being used for this purpose (Tourquet 1974). So for the leader of a group to become aware of his or her own feelings can significantly help him/her not only to control his/her expressions and behaviour appropriately, but also to be able to contain feelings which are aroused in reaction to the losses, hurts and needs of others. The use of the leader/teacher's observing ego is essential here. A group leader is like an ego, Janus-like, looking inside and outside (the group and him/herself) as participant and observer (Tourquet 1974).

Group processes and interactions are enormously complex, and it is a demanding task to forge and maintain self-awareness in the face of such dynamic complexity. By way of example of some of the issues which group leaders face in this regard, I refer to Whitaker's (1985) series of questions which group leaders might consider in relation to their role and the group dynamic. What are the implications for the group of the group leader becoming fascinated by the circumstances of problems of one member to the detriment of the rest of the group? What are the implications for a group leader's relationship with a group if someone in the group violates a personally held norm or a norm which the leader/teacher considers essential to the continuing usefulness of the group? Is it possible that sometimes the group leader/teacher gets caught up in the same fears as group members and colludes with some 'restrictive solution' (i.e. an adaptation which reinforces defence mechanisms)? Whitaker (1985) acknowledges that since groups move too quickly and the import of events cannot always be registered in time, all group leaders/teachers are bound to miss some of the opportunities for development presented by group events, and to take actions in the group which may be inappropriate to helping the group with its primary task. She maintains that if an issue is important within the context of a particular group's dynamics, it will enter the group in a similar form, thus providing further opportunities for exploration.

Given the possible negative impact upon the leader of group dynamics, leaders also need to be vigilant about the personal effects of working with such potentials. There are many fine lines to be mediated here. The need to demonstrate genuineness, trust and empathy has to be balanced with developing skill in coping with the pressure which large groups generate. 'The danger is that the form of personality organisation which is developed becomes a rigid persona, a platform manner which the individual is unable to relax or modify' (Reed and Palmer 1972, Lecture 3: 14).

Boundary control

The boundary of the group helps to define it, and holds the persons and things of a group together. It may function partially through the timetable on which the group expects to meet, the regular nature of the membership of the group, the expectations regarding the group's activities. The role of the group membership helps to define the boundary of the group, which has implications for the feelings aroused when group membership changes.

The leader's work on boundary control relates to both the physical and psychological boundaries. Physical boundary control involves issues to do with the way in which group members physically enter and leave the group – their manner of coming in and going out, their presence or absence in the group, and so on. Psychological boundary control is much more complex, and relates to the management of issues which psychologically belong inside or outside the group. For example, what 'material' brought to the group is confidential to the group? In what circumstances might confidentiality be broken, and how might this be negotiated with group members? Are there times when the group's actions have implications beyond the group for the rest of the organisation? Are there times when it is appropriate for the group leader/teacher to refer to events which happen outside the group within the boundary of the group, and what are the implications for the group dynamics of so doing? The communications about such boundaries have implications for group identity, the capacity of individuals to engage with the group and the group's relationships with other groups in the environment.

Another aspect of boundary control is the management of the interface of the group and its environment. The group's relationship with its environment presents a further dimension of determining group identity – what the group is and what it is not. An important element of a group's environment is the other groups operating in the environment. Studies have shown (e.g. Higgin and Bridger 1965) that inter-group relations often involve much rivalry and the emergence of myths about each other's experiences. So an aspect of boundary control is the management of the relationship of a group's perceptions about itself with its perception of other, perhaps rival, groups in the environment.

Issues of emotional containment and dependency

It is important not only that individuals within the group feel emotionally contained by the group leader/teacher but that the group *as a whole* feels safe, emotionally contained. The teacher might demonstrate his/her capacity to contain the group, at one level, through a range of practical measures, such as reliability in relation to time-keeping, the organisation of children's work, the management of classroom resources and the upkeep of displays and other aspects of the environment. The sense of group safety will be further established and maintained by the teacher through his/her management of tensions, rivalries, conflicts and fears between group members. In addition to these management functions, the teacher who is also able to demonstrate the capacity to understand, tolerate and reflect upon the difficult feelings which emerge in the group provides a significantly more meaningful 'container' for, or sense of safety in, the group. With such a sense of safety group members are able gradually to give their trust to the group and its processes, and thus open themselves to greater possibilities of change and growth.

If members of the group do not experience the group situation as a safe enough environment they will not stay in it, but will either flee or psychologically insulate themselves from the experience.

Group members may establish routes of safety within a group by operating within what Whitaker (1985) terms 'restrictive solutions', such as interacting only with the leader, withdrawing into solitary activities, disowning their own problems, interacting with subgroups but avoiding the whole group. Whilst such adaptations enable members to feel safe, Whitaker (1985) argues, they also avoid the risks of emotional development. They have value where they can be used incrementally to build up a greater repertoire of ways of feeling safe within the group. The danger is that the boundaries within which the individuals are operating become so narrow that little in the way of useful exploration, social comparison, feedback etc., can take place (Whitaker 1985). It is part of the leader/teacher's task to monitor this aspect of the group's functioning and look to ways of helping members give up 'restrictive solutions' in favour of being open to emotional growth and development within the group.

Another fine line with which the group leader is working is that of dependency. In containing disturbing feelings one is not seeking to take the pain away, to make things feel better, but to demonstrate that there can be thought and understanding of the feelings. Yet for this process to happen there needs to be trust, some way in which the children can feel dependent upon the adult. Since children with emotional/behavioural difficulties often have to struggle both to avoid omnipotence and to achieve the capacity to allow themselves to be dependent, and then to move into a more genuine independence, testing out in relation to dependency is an important part of the developmental process. So in some ways it is a necessary and healthy part of group experience. But the danger is that dependence might be used as a form of defence against the task. Managing the fine lines and subtle meanings in relation to dependency in groups is a complex task.

During the final phase of a group's life, the issue of emotional containment is highlighted: a sense of threat can escalate, particularly, Whitaker (1985) points out, if the prospect of separation resonates sharply with important and unresolved feelings and fears on the part of a number of members.

Establishing and maintaining supportive group norms

In the earlier sections of this chapter both the value and the dangers of group norms were discussed.

> Balint explains that collaborative group norms follow from the leader's behavior in allowing everyone to be themselves, to have their own say and in their own time ... instead of prescribing the right way to deal with the problem under discussion, opening up possibilities for group members to discover the right answer.
>
> (Perlman 1992: 186–7)

Helping a group to establish and maintain supportive group norms (Whitaker 1985) is generated partly through the sense of safety in a group. The group will be more effective in promoting emotional growth and learning if members can establish norms which are helpful and supportive to members in expressing their feelings and trying out new behaviours. The question is how to help group members feel safe *and yet also* be prepared to take risks without resorting to threatening others. An important way of establishing and maintaining supportive group norms is by making use of events in the group for the benefit of group members (a notion introduced by Whitaker 1985). One can make use of group events for members' benefit on either a collective, i.e. whole-group, or an individual basis.

In terms of interventions which make use of the group for the benefit of individual members, it is possible for teachers and other group leaders to intervene to enable group members to reflect upon their experiences of the group, and to make use of this shared experience in relation to the particular needs of individuals within the group. Group leaders have a role in establishing both a general ethos and particular structures or activities, which invite group members to bring their individual experiences of the group into the arena of group discussion. There are a number of ways of doing this, including sharing a personal view or opinion, supporting individuals in acknowledging feelings, giving and reinforcing feedback to others in the group, acknowledging the new accomplishments and understandings of other group members, and emphasising an important breakthrough (Whitaker 1985). Once the group leader/teacher is successful in facilitating these sorts of process within the group, s/he potentially has a further role in making explicit the links between different group members' experiences. For instance, 'So does that help you to see that if you do … that makes so and so feel …'. Children may also be helped to achieve insight into their problems of social adjustment by the leader/teacher non-judgementally reflecting back to them the manner in which they interact when working and playing with the others.

Working with difference and facilitating multiplicity

Working to promote positive attitudes towards difference and pluralism in the group is one of the most essential yet perhaps one of the most difficult tasks in facilitating group processes for the benefit of members. The defence mechanisms which work against the acknowledgement and valuing of difference are strong: those managing groups walk a fine line between maintaining a positive *group* identity and enabling children with emotional difficulties to develop more of their own *individual* identity. Being both an individual within the group and yet a fully participating member of the group, without identifying with one extreme or the other, demands significant internal resources. For it demands the capacity to be able to struggle with these competing demands, weigh them up, acknowledge them, without falling victim to impulsive desires.

The facilitator's task is to allow difference to be possible in the group, in relation to feelings and the inner world, and the more obvious overt behaviours, interests, cultures, attitudes which manifest in the external world. This might involve acknowledging to group members the value of, and the struggle we have with, difference and the multiplicity of experience. In relation to this issue the function of the group leader also lies in enabling group members to experience the many-sidedness and ambiguities of life in the group, in contrast to relating largely out of fantasies, assumptions and omnipotence.

One way of demonstrating and modelling the struggle with many-sidedness is for the teacher to voice a range of feelings about various events in group life – to acknowledge pleasure at success, and disappointment when things go wrong, for example. One way of doing this relates to the way one acknowledges and deals with the mistakes that one has made oneself. Where the teacher/group leader makes mistakes in relation to particular individuals in the group – perhaps, for example, through a lack of patience or some other insensitivity – then some form of reconciliation or apology initiated by the group leader can be very helpful not only for the individual concerned, but for the group as a whole. The leader thereby demonstrates that that particular group can be one in which the inner omnipotent voices (for example saying 'I'm right') can be struggled with, and aid reconciliation and the development of relationships of a more balanced kind.

The skills discussed in this fourth section of the chapter are relevant to managing and facilitating not only groups, but also the wider organisation.

Summary

- Group processes exert a powerful impact upon development and need to be considered in their own right.
- The group offers much potential as a medium for helping with emotional growth and learning. Groups offer each individual the possibility of assessing his/her own experience against that of a range of other people, and thus of coming into contact with hitherto unrealised aspects of him/herself. The group offers significant opportunities to bridge the experiences and feelings of inner realities with a range of social realities. It is as if there is a 'group ego' against which one can test and assess oneself, which forms both an expectation and a measure of development. Groups potentially offer the experience of a matrix, a womb, which nurtures the capacity for trust. Groups provide powerful opportunities for meaningful relationships with others through the experience of kinship. Groups [also] provide diverse environments.
- However, groups can also be anxiety-provoking and even frightening. Group phenomena can also serve to inhibit development. There is always a

struggle for individuals to experience reflectively both the need and desire for individual identity and the need and desire for group identity, without furthering one of these at the expense of the other. Groups develop defensive norms and beliefs against anxieties. It is particularly difficult for group members to come to tolerate and be able to work with difference within the group. Tasks may be avoided through the mechanisms of dependency, flight/fight or pairing. Defensive and regressive processes in groups can become 'contagious'.

- The impact of group size and stage also have significant effects upon the dynamic of groups.
- Managing and facilitating group processes in a way which supports emotional growth and learning requires clear task definition and sustaining the values, roles and boundaries to achieve the task; the capacity to keep in mind the whole group and each whole child; the capacity to mitigate defences and anti-task behaviour (in oneself and others).
- Managing and facilitating group processes requires the capacity to reflect upon process, and considerable self-awareness. Groups are helped where symbolic structures of their wholeness are provided; where boundary control issues are well managed; where there is emotional containment and the opportunities for some dependency without this reinforcing defence mechanisms; where supportive group norms are established and maintained; where events in the group can be related to the needs of individual members; and where it is possible to acknowledge and explore differences in experience in the group.
- These group phenomena are relevant to any group. They are particularly obvious and pertinent where the individuals' capacities for awareness and management of feelings are at an early stage of development – hence their particular importance in work with children with emotional/behavioural difficulties.

References

Barrett, M. and Trevitt, J. (1991) *Attachment Behaviour and the Schoolchild: An Introduction to Educational Therapy*, London: Routledge.

Bion, W.R. (1989) *Experiences in Groups and Other Papers*, London: Routledge.

Colman, A.D. (1992) 'Depth Consultation', in Stein, M. and Hollwitz, J. (eds), *Psyche at Work: Applications of Jungian Analytical Psychology*, Wilmette, Illinois: Chiron.

Cox, M. (1990) 'The Group as Poetic Playground: From Metaphor to Metamorphosis', Foulkes Lecture to the Group Analytic Society, London.

Croll, P. and Moses, D. (1985) *One in Five: The Assessment and Incidence of Special Educational Needs*, London: Routledge and Kegan Paul.

Douglas, T. (1978) *Basic Groupwork*, London: Routledge.

Foukes, S.H. and Anthony, E.J. (1984) *Group Psychotherapy, the Psychoanalytical Approach*, London: Karnac.

Freud, S. (1933) *New Introductory Lectures on Psychoanalysis*, Standard Edition, Vol. 22. London: Hogarth Press and Institute of Psychoanalysis.

Ginott, H. (1961) *Group Psychotherapy with Children: The Theory and Practice of Play Therapy*, New York: McGraw-Hill.

Higgin, H. and Bridger, H. (1965) *The Psychodynamics of an Inter-Group Experience*, Tavistock Pamphlet No. 10, London: Tavistock.

Lewin, K. (1948) 'Experiments in Social Space', in Lewin, G.W. (ed.), *Resolving Social Conflict*, New York: Harper and Bros.

Menzies Lyth, I.E.P. (1988) *Containing Anxiety in Institutions*, London: Free Association.

Miller, E.J. and Rice, A.K. (1967) *Systems of Organisation*, London: Tavistock.

Mongan, D. and Hart, S. (1989) *Improving Classroom Behaviour: New Directions for Teachers and Pupils*, London: Cassell.

Perlman, M.S. (1992) 'Toward a Theory of Self in the Group', in Stein, M. and Hollwitz, J. (eds), *Psyche at Work: Workplace Applications of Jungian Analytical Psychology*, Wilmette, Illinois: Chiron.

Reed, B. and Palmer, B. (1972) *An Introduction to Organisational Behaviour*, Lectures 1, 2 and 3, London: Grubb Institute.

Richardson, E. (1975) 'Selections from "The Environment of Learning" ', in Colman, A.D. and Bexton, W.H. (eds), *Group Relations Reader*, Sausalito, California: A.K. Rice Institute.

Rogers, C.R. (1961) *On Becoming a Person*, London: Constable.

Tourquet, P.M. (1974) 'Leadership: The Individual and the Group', in Gibbard, G.S., Mann, R.D. and Hartman, J.J. (eds), *Analysis of Groups*, London: Jossey-Bass.

Tuckman, B.W. (1965) 'Developmental Sequence in Small Groups', *Psychological Bulletin*, 63: 384–99.

Wells, L. (1981) 'The Group-as-a-whole Perspective and its Theoretical Roots', in Colman, A.D. and Bexton, W.H. (eds), *Group Relations Reader, Vol. 2*, Sausalito, California: A.K. Rice Institute.

Whitaker, D.S. (1985) *Using Groups to Help People*, London and New York: Tavistock/Routledge.

Chapter 17

Some do and some don't: teacher effectiveness in managing behaviour

Bob Sproson

Introduction

In my teaching career in England I have moved from mainstream education into special provision for difficult to manage students and, latterly, into EOTAS (education other than at school). Throughout that time I have been fascinated by the styles of behaviour management undertaken by teachers and the quality of relationships developed between students and their teachers. I write as someone committed to the right of all students to be treated with respect and to the need for all students to be able to access a safe environment in which to learn. I argue below that teaching is about relationships, and that, while some teachers just seem to be able to form good quality relationships, the rest of us can learn some simple skills that will improve our practice.

Current concerns about student behaviour

I remember listening to an extremely eloquent speaker one early morning on BBC Radio Four following the launch of one of the government's frequent initiatives to reduce truancy. Whilst acknowledging that the 'new' (or at least differently packaged) approach was well intentioned, he was able to use statistics to rather startling effect to show that, since compulsory education had become embedded within the social structure of the country, levels of truancy or unauthorised absence, or whatever terminology was currently in vogue, had remained very much constant regardless of school or local authority or central government efforts to do anything about it. While I would not want to fall into the trap of saying that there is no point in attempting to change 'societal norms', it has always seemed to me that, much like non-attendance, student misbehaviour is a permanent fixture of school life which we fool ourselves that we can eradicate. This article is a very personal trawl through my views on how we (teachers) work with young people in an attempt to enable them to make appropriate life choices – that, after all, is our purpose.

Over the last decade I have delivered a significant amount of 'behaviour management training' in schools and also taken the time to go to listen to other 'experts' (I am always careful to say that I am a practitioner, not an expert!). The question as to whether behaviour in schools, or indeed throughout society, has deteriorated in the last 30 or 40 years, or 'since I was at school', regularly arises in training sessions – sometimes brought up as an 'ice-breaker' by the 'trainer', at other times raised by members of the group. Almost inevitably trainers utilise quotes from Peter the Hermit or an ancient tablet in the British Museum. Sometimes they quote a little Shakespeare, or describe insurrection at Marlborough School in the eighteenth century leading to the murder of a teacher. These examples indicate that, for more than seven centuries, adults have recorded their concern about the willingness of young people to display violence and 'thuggery' at alarming levels and their failure to show due deference and respect to their elders. From the floor there are the inevitable, 'I wouldn't have dared to speak like they do' or 'I'd have got it in the neck at school and worse at home if I'd done a tenth of what they get up to now', but older sages invariably recall difficult students or classes and most adult groups will eventually come round to the view that problems may present in different guises, that the nature of the problems themselves may have changed but that the 'nature of the beast', that is, the willingness and 'need' of some young people to challenge adult values, often in a very frightening manner, has changed little at all.

Teacher characteristics pertinent to behaviour mangement

At a Birmingham (England) seminar held to address the issue of student behaviour, the wonderful title of, 'If there was an answer, somebody would have found it by now' was used. I often use this and think it to be the best start point for anyone wanting to work to improve student behaviour. The notions either that there is an answer or that we can have schools in which misbehaviour does not occur are fatuous.

I consider myself to be a reflective and pragmatic practitioner, thus my concept of 'good practice' constantly evolves. When I entered the world of training (alongside my teaching 'day' job), I believed that there was a package of skills which could be taught to teachers and that, if those skills were implemented, they would greatly reduce the levels of 'unwanted' behaviour in schools. I still subscribe to the efficacy of most of those skills, but I have come to hold the view that not all teachers who have a fairly 'hassle free' life in school, i.e. those teachers with whom students behave pretty well, utilise these skills.

My current position is that the key to students behaving tolerably or better is for them to perceive that the adult who is attempting to 'assert control' cares about them. I also subscribe to a solipsistic view of the world in which perception is all. Thus the teacher may 'care' desperately, but unless the student perceives that, it is worthless for that student. This does not mean that I have forsaken the skills package. It is categorically the case that the vast majority of teachers who are perceived by their students to 'care' also utilise, consciously or unconsciously, a range of skills which is assertive rather than punitive or aggressive and which is not reliant upon a slavish following of specified responses to student behaviour or hierarchical responses.

Just as 'if there was an answer someone would have found it by now' is a core concept, so the understanding that in the whole of behaviour management, be it behaviour modification, 'Assertive Discipline' (Canter and Canter, 1995), or any other approach, there is nothing completely new, is essential. Almost without exception teachers whom I see utilising a positive, assertive, non-aggressive style of classroom management and responses to misbehaviour (Rogers, 1992; Watkins and Wagner, 2000), achieve a high degree of success management if success is defined as having a classroom, indeed a whole school, in which students can learn and feel safe. Painful as it is for the very small number of teachers I see who do employ the skills but still fail to create the desired learning environment, they are not 'cut out' for this particular job. There is something about their interaction with students which leads to 'relationship breakdown'.

This is not an area I have chosen to pursue in length here; suffice to say that I meet a very small number of teachers who are simply in the wrong job. I heard Simon Hoggart (on Radio Four) describe George Bush (senior) as an amsirahc, someone with reverse charisma! I would never wish to describe anyone in this manner, but just as there are hugely charismatic teachers, there are those at the other end of the spectrum.

There is a whole range of jobs which I cannot do, at least with any degree of success, because I lack the wherewithal to do them. The problem in teaching is that it is very hard to categorise just what skills are required to do the job and therefore the profession pretty much has no selection criteria of any rigour. I am fairly certain that, out of any group of people, I could quickly predict which of them would be outstanding pedants, which would be, like myself, journeymen practitioners able to improve their practice by reflection and diligence, and those whom simply I would not want to teach my children. There is no implication here that 'not being cut out to be a teacher' implies any other 'failing'. I have already acknowledged my own inability to perform many jobs. The serious point to be made here is that, because it is so difficult to lay down clear criteria for accessing and remaining in the teaching profession, a very small number of practitioners enter and stay in at huge personal cost to themselves. I can think of few more painful ways of earning a pretty basic salary than working in classrooms where there is no mutual respect, and, far worse, that suffering is at great cost to their students.

To return to my line of argument that just about all teachers who are positive, assertive and non-aggressive in managing student behaviour are successful, my change in view over the last decade is that some teachers do not utilise these skills but remain successful. One aspect of my current job is to manage the out-of-school provision (EOTAS – education other than at school) made within a local education authority (LEA) in England. One of the pupil referral units (PRUs) in the LEA recently moved into refurbished premises. At the 'opening' of the 'new' premises, two of the students spoke publicly about their experiences of learning within the PRU. One talked in some detail about his perceptions of the female headteacher. He described her as appearing on occasions like the 'Wicked Witch of the West' and how she would always be 'on your case' if you stepped out of line. However, what shone through as the student spoke, and what I already knew, is the extraordinary level of commitment and care which this headteacher gives to all of her students. Sometimes she 'does mum'. This is her terminology for when she goes into parent mode and cajoles and harasses her students in much the same way as she does her own sons. She is a very forceful personality and, on occasion, crosses the line, or at least straddles that line, between assertion and aggression. The students, however, will accept 'things' from her that they would not accept from other staff. The key is that they know she cares. Another senior female teacher in a secondary school in the LEA is a regular shouter, something which I continually suggest to teachers is disrespectful behaviour, unless required by some emergency, but, again, she achieves success. The students do not perceive her shouting in the way they do that of other staff and they do experience her level of care.

So, a small number of teachers, do not need to behave non-aggressively. What might the explanation be for this?

The importance of choice

I have already argued that 'care', or perception of its existence, is the key. Another way of explaining this is offered by 'choice theory' (Wobbulding,

2001), developed from Glasser's (1965) 'reality therapy'. This paradigm posits that each of us has a 'quality world' (Wobbulding, 2001): we place within it those 'things' which are important to us. Our quality world may change; that is, people, places and interests may be moved in and out of it. For a young person, in my experience much of what they choose to place within their quality world will be decided by the value systems handed down to them by their parents or carers. Most young people will, therefore, have education fairly and squarely within their quality world. It will be something they want to succeed at and something which they believe can act as a gateway to life success. It may even be deemed to have some intrinsic interest! There will inevitably, however, be those young people who do not place education within their quality world at all. This may be because they choose to reject parental values, because they believe there to be a job available to them which they can access regardless of any achievement in school, because their parents or carers lay no value upon education themselves or, for the most vulnerable of young people, because their quality world is filled with issues of survival which leave little room for anything else.

Wobbulding (2001) argues that when two people share a common aspect of their quality world their relationship will be facilitated by this. Thus, presuming that all teachers have education within their chosen quality world, when teachers meet students who value education, then the subsequent relationship is likely to be positive. Even though it may be desirable to find other shared aspects, the joint commitment to education should ensure that the student is willing to accept basic constraints upon their behaviour in order that they might access something which they value. In my experience students who really value education will even accept significantly poor practice from the providers of the educational package.

Problems occur, however, if either party does not hold education within their quality world. Wobbulding (2001) argues that in those cases wherein students do not place education inside their quality world, then the teacher who wants to work successfully with that student has to enter that student's quality world. In order to do this the teacher needs to value whatever it is that sits within the student's quality world and, through showing that interest, begin to place themselves within it. If the teacher is able to do this, then the student may be willing to take on some of the elements which the teacher values.

I have never found any paradigm which fits all human behaviours, but I come across many which help me to understand what is happening when I am struggling to connect with a student or students. This particular one may be little more than saying that some young people simply do not want what is on offer at school and the only way to work with those students is to work hard to show them respect and to build a relationship with them but that in itself is helpful to me. I am sure that this is where the notion of perceived care comes in. If a young person who will almost undoubtedly have experienced uncaring adults frequently throughout their life and has now become an expert at frightening off anyone who might display care, experiences someone in authority who really cares about them and what happens to them, then they are likely to take that person into their quality world. Once that has happened, then learning (appropriate, desired learning) may occur.

Recognising students' basic needs

What choice theory also offers is a view as to what the basic needs of all people are. It posits the view that, unless each of these is available to young people within their educational setting, then they are unlikely to flourish, even if they value education, and that some will fight very hard, often very painfully for the adults working with them, to get what they intuitively need. I am not suggesting that the following is the consummate or definitive list but I find it helpful to refer back to when things are going awry. I need to consider whether each of the following is available to my students:

- achievement
- belonging
- power
- fun
- freedom.

So, I have argued that all teaching and learning arenas need to provide teachers and students with access to their basic needs. Furthermore, there will be students in virtually all arenas who have little or no interest in what is on offer. The most likely route to enable the teacher to connect positively with the learner in this situation is for the teacher to enter that student's quality world. Most teachers working in the arena require a range of skills to achieve success. Some, by dint of their level of care, some, by their pure charisma and some by their place in the hierarchy can succeed without recourse to such skills, but most practitioners need to practise in a particular fashion. The sorts of adjectives which writers such as Rogers (1992, 1997) and Watkins and Wagner (2000) would choose to use to describe this style of practice would be assertive, appropriately watchful, supportive, and conflict avoiding.

What follows is a very brief summary of my own view of 'good practice' which, I acknowledge, leans heavily upon the assertions of Rogers (1992) in particular.

Good practice in schools

I have noted how all students need to achieve, belong, have a sense of personal autonomy and have some fun in school. My experience concurs with Rogers (1992, 1997) that, in order to address these needs, each student has rights within the school environment. No matter what they do, no matter how awful the behaviour, they should not lose their basic rights. Within a learning establishment these rights should be reciprocal between student and teacher. They are the rights to:

- learn
- feel safe emotionally and physically
- be treated with respect.

It is the responsibility of each member of the community, students and adults, to ensure that rights of other members of the community are not infringed. The position of adult and student differs in that the teacher is charged with the rightful authority to direct and lead learning situations and therefore to ensure that appropriate consequences are the outcome of chosen behaviours on the part of others, while students should seek to further their own learning and to ensure that in doing that they support others wherever possible.

Students and teachers need to have the debate as to what it is that constitutes respect and what respectful behaviour looks like. In doing that they should acknowledge, and will learn, the notion of appropriateness or 'time and place', so shouting is not disrespectful per se. It is sometimes essential, for example, in an emergency such as a fire, and often useful, for example, when instructions need to be heard by people some distance away, but if utilised when two people are in close proximity, and particularly if accompanied by threatening body language, then it is disrespectful and wrong. Some would argue that swearing is always disrespectful, others would employ the appropriateness argument and say that in some places it is acceptable and that in some circumstances, for example, to acknowledge physical pain or shock, it is helpful. Such debates are healthy, and there must be a clarity as to what is and is not acceptable within the learning environment, which comes from the teacher. Teachers who understand the bedrock of respect as a two-way street and reflect upon what it is that constitutes respect are a large part of the way to being effective practitioners.

Rogers (1992) writes very helpfully about the establishment phase in teaching any group. That is the phase in which the teacher establishes what is required within the learning area and makes clear certain chosen behaviours which are unacceptable. Classroom routines are a key element here. They are required at different levels in different environments. Why are they so important? They ensure that key tasks are performed, that students are ready to listen, if that is required, or to start an activity and they offer the teacher a chance to give positive feedback. The routine is taught, then practised, and when a student gets even some part of it right, here is the opportunity to acknowledge that and tell the student that they are 'getting it right'.

Whenever I do any training, most teachers want to know what to do when the student misbehaves and most are disappointed at my response which is that I cannot tell them that. I can suggest some things they might try, but without knowing the student or the situation I would not proffer a solution. Equally many dislike my follow-up which is that actually it is what happens before misbehaviour takes place which is the key to successful teaching. Recent conversations with police officers indicate that they are looking more and more at crime prevention rather than solving crime once it has occurred. The medical and dentistry professions have long understood the notion of prevention rather than cure. I usually refer to my own struggle with mouth ulcers, often known as the 'adventures of the Bonjela Kid'. In summary I spent years purchasing all sorts of jellies and creams which inevitably inflicted great pain when applied to the ulcer and which offered very short term pain relief only. Eventually I realised that it is how I 'manage my mouth', for example, what I eat, my oral hygiene and my general stress levels, which offers any chance of reducing the number of ulcers. Whilst I can reduce them, however, I accept that they will still occur and I will still need to buy some Bonjela. The establishment phase of setting up any learning environment is a key part of the 'hygiene element'.

The most frustrating or, to re-frame positively, challenging aspect of managing behaviour reverts back to the notion of if there was an answer, someone would have found it by now. There is nothing that works all the time with all the students. What works hugely well on a Monday morning with one class or student may not work with the same class or student on a Thursday afternoon, may not work with a different group on a Monday morning, and may not even work with the same group the following Monday. Thus the effective practitioner has to have a range of options available. I find the notion of each of us having a behaviour suitcase a helpful one.

As an experienced practitioner, when I open my metaphorical suitcase I should have a range of clothing items to suit the occasion, whether it be the beach, a cocktail party, relaxing in my room or maybe the gym. When my most difficult to manage student opens his case, s/he probably only has a smelly sock and an item of dirty underwear, neither particularly appropriate. With nothing else in the case, however, s/he has no choice but to use them. Many students, given their life experiences, have no concept as to how to resolve conflict other than through fight or flight. The job of the teacher is twofold: to select from his/her range of clothing effectively and to enable the student to fill his/her case with more clothing. The latter is done most effectively by simply modelling the 'new' behaviours. Thus I, the teacher, need to model ways of resolving conflict which respect the rights of students to learn and feel safe, and

- meet the needs of both parties, that is, provide win–win outcomes wherever possible
- bring an end to the conflict or, at least reduce it
- do not leave either party 'wounded'.

I also need to embed into my daily practice some fairly simple skills that, both from experience and from other researchers and writers (Rogers, 1992, 1997; Watkins and Wagner, 2000), I have learned are respectful of students' rights to learn and feel safe, and enable them to maintain self respect. The key is to make choices as to when and with whom to use each.

'Take-up time' (Rogers, 1992)

Young people rarely do what they are asked immediately, certainly when there is an audience present. Thus the skilful teacher builds in appropriate take-up time. Request made, compliance implied, walk away, acknowledge compliance when it occurs. I watched a head teacher insist that a Year 10 student hand over her mobile phone to him in front of numerous students in the dinner hall. He insisted that the handing over was immediate. She refused, the inevitable argument ensued and eventual exclusion followed. Had that head teacher asked her to bring the phone to his office before the end of the school day, she would have done so and the issue would have been skilfully resolved.

'Partial agreement' (ibid)

A skilful acknowledgement of what a student says, even if what has been said is mildly offensive, may offer much greater prospect of a settled lesson than a rebuttal. Thus when the student responds to a request to 'get on with his work' with an 'it's boring', or 'it's crap', a response of, 'I understand that you're bored (or not enjoying the lesson) and the rule here is that you get on with the work set' together with judicious take-up time is far more likely to elicit the required outcome (student gets down to work) than the confrontational, 'don't speak to me like that' or similar.

'Closed choices' (ibid)

These are my absolute favourite. The key is that they imply compliance without overt direction. So a six year old might be asked, 'Do you want to have your bath at six o'clock or seven?' rather than being directed to 'have a bath'. I managed to enable a very angry (and very large) fifteen year old to leave a site by asking him whether he wanted me to give him a lift, or whether he would prefer me to order him a taxi. Any direction on my part to leave would have had been futile. Bill Rogers (1992) describes how a student with something inappropriate on their desk might be asked whether they want to put it in their bag or the teacher to look after it, and notes that whenever he has done that, the object has disappeared into the bag.

'Broken record' (ibid)

There is some contradiction between this approach and partial agreement. What that indicates is that the skilful practitioner is able to match their response to the student and the situation, rather than having it dictated by the former which is often advocated within discipline 'systems'. The broken record approach simply requires the practitioner to repeat a request/order assertively and calmly without getting distracted by student attempts to 'suck' them into an argument. Thus an exchange might go as follows:

> Teacher: John, start your work, thanks.
> John: It's boring.
> Teacher: John, start your work, thanks.
> John: Didn't you hear what I said?
> Teacher: Start your work, thanks.
> John: This lesson's just so boring … (picking pen up – if you're lucky!)
> Teacher: Pleased to see you getting down to work – well done.

Distinguishing between primary and secondary behaviour

This is illustrated by the previous exchange. A significant number of young people love either to distract teachers from the learning arena or to engage gullible teachers in power battles. If a primary request is complied with (hang your coat up, thanks) even though it is accompanied by secondary behaviours (sighing, moaning, feet dragging), then the response most likely to elicit further future compliance and minimal conflict is, 'Thanks for hanging your coat up'.

Avoiding power struggles

Finally teachers (all those who interact successfully with others) must understand that some people (young and old) simply want a power battle. The outcome is meaningless, they simply love the confrontation. Thus the successful practitioner avoids that confrontation.

Conclusion

Above all I believe that we (teachers) are paid to respond professionally in all cases. I only know my own 'human' responses, but presume that other practitioners experience similar emotions. I frequently yearn to be sarcastic, to use a put down, to make a miscreant feel 'small', to have my revenge upon students who have 'wronged' me. That is fine so long as I manage those legitimate emotions/responses and then behave as a trained professional and respond accordingly. A doctor may be appalled at the actions of someone who has murdered or raped: when that person arrives on their operating table, even if the injuries were sustained in committing a heinous act, their professional response, as dictated by the Hippocratic Oath, is to work to heal wounds and, conceivably, save a life. A teacher should respond in similarly professional fashion at all times, and it is fine for that teacher to go into the staffroom (out of the earshot of students) and be extremely vitriolic about a student's behaviour.

References

Canter, L. and Canter, M. (1995) *Assertive Discipline*. Training materials from course at Loughborough.

Glasser, W. (1965) *Reality Therapy: a new approach to psychiatry*. New York: Harper Row.

Rogers, B. (1992) *You Know the Fair Rule*. Harlow: Longman.

Rogers, B. (1997) *Cracking the Hard Class*. London: Paul Chapman.

Watkins, C. and Wagner, P. (2000) *Improving School Behaviour*. London: Paul Chapman.

Wobbulding (2001) *Choice Theory*. Training notes from seminar at Cambridge School of Education.

Chapter 18

Barriers to belonging: students' perceptions of factors which affect participation in schools

Sandra Davies

Introduction

The issues in this chapter emerge from the data taken from a study which followed six students who experienced problems with literacy over a two year period at Key Stage 3. The investigation took place while the students were in Years 8 and 9 and considered their experiences in the history classroom during these two years. In Year 8 the students were taught in mixed ability tutor groups and were then taught in homogeneous ability groupings in Year 9 for humanities subjects. The school in which the study took place has two populations within each year group and the students were in two different foundation groups within Year 9.

The collection of data in Year 8 had investigated not only their perception of history as a subject, their understanding of it and their reactions to it, but also their views of their participation in the subject and the factors that they considered affected this. The preliminary analysis of this data revealed that the underlying issues were much more complex than I had originally anticipated. The study had always been set within a sociocultural framework with its emphasis on the indivisibility of context and human actions (Rogoff 1990) and the relationships between human action (external and internal) on the one hand, and the cultural, institutional and historical situation in which this occurs, on the other. A sociocultural perspective understands learning as occurring through participation and leading to a transformation of identity (Lave and Wenger 1991). Preliminary analysis of the data indicated that the issues involved in contributing to a sense of belonging to a community of practice (Wenger 1998) were far more salient to this work than I had originally considered.

I found this discovery exciting and it led me in the second year of the study to extend the range of questions I had used in interviews in the first year. While I wanted to revisit the issues I had covered in Year 8 and contrast the students' responses to those given in Year 9, I also wanted to investigate their perceptions of their sense of belonging, not only in the history classroom, but also in other situations. To this end I chose two subjects which were organised differently in the school. These subjects were mathematics, a strictly ability-setted subject, and English, which was taught in mixed ability groups. The analysis of the data collected in Year 9 indicates that the presence or absence of a sense of belonging to a community impacts upon every area of participation within that community, and affects not only the students' subsequent behaviour, but also their perceptions of themselves.

This chapter considers one of these students, William, who had been identified as experiencing problems with literacy and was on the school's register of special educational needs. William has been chosen as an example because, although the behaviour of the other students was also affected to varying degrees, that of William illustrates most graphically the effects of his increasing sense of detachment and marginalisation. In this paper I seek to provide an insight into the experience of one student, among many, with difficulties with literacy. The classroom settings, whether mixed ability or homogeneous ability grouping, and influences that determine his experience of these, are considered through the notion of participation.

Method

The research, set in a sociocultural framework, adopted a case study approach to foreground the learners' experiences and to provide a rich description of these. A range of methods including questionnaires and audiotaped interviews with both students and teachers using a projective technique, 'Talking Stones' (Davies 2000; Wearmouth 2000) and videoed observation were used. Transcripts were made of the audiotapes and analysis of these was undertaken focusing on the mind-in-action and the mediation upon this of sociocultural processes at the level of intrapersonal, interpersonal and community (Rogoff 1995). This paper foregrounds the intrapersonal, that is, the perceptions of William, while briefly acknowledging the interpersonal with reference to my perceptions and those of one of the teachers.

Background

Belonging to communities of practice

Goodenow (1992) reminds us that a sense of belonging and acceptance was recognised by Maslow (1962) as being one of the most basic human needs. Evidence from research with street children has indicated that although their material needs are often unsatisfied they have articulated their desire to be cared for and respected as being their first priority (Griffiths 1995). This need is seen by Noddings (1992) as being so salient that she believes that the most important aim of education should be 'to encourage the growth of competent, caring, loving and lovable people' (p.xiv). Each individual needs to experience the rewards of belonging to a social group which supports, cares for and values its members (Goodenow 1992). These groups or communities and the interactions which take place within them, by engaging and acknowledging the participants, contribute to the formation of the identities of the members (Wenger 1998).

Griffiths (1995) sees the relationships between an individual and others such as parents, colleagues, peers as being a vital part of an ongoing autobiography which works towards the production of the identity of that individual. The narrative of this autobiography is determined by the individual's connections with the other characters, the most significant of these connections being that of belonging. These connections 'are either of love and acceptance, or of resistance and rejection' (p.307). Griffiths (1995) also considers that in no area of the individual's life will there be a situation where the issue of belonging does not arise and as contacts with others increase through school, work and social life, situations of acceptance or rejection increase accordingly.

We are all members of communities of practice. Communities of practice may be seen as groups of people who have a common interest and who meet and share knowledge and expertise. Communities of practice are to be found within the family, the workplace, friendship group, sports team and so on. We are therefore members of multiple communities of practice, although our role within some may be more pronounced than in others (Wenger et al. 2002).

The formation of these groups may have taken place formally or informally (Wenger et al. 2002). Within any community of practice there will be those members who are experienced in the practices of the community who will be assigned or will assume responsibility for instructing and supporting those who are newcomers. A newly qualified teacher, for example, who is appointed to a secondary school in England, will find that not only is there a head of department, whose role includes the induction of new staff and explanation of duties, but there are also teachers within that department who will give support and often tips as to the best ways of undertaking the work.

Some of the instruction in a community of practice is given on a formal basis, but this may not always be the case. Lave and Wenger (1991) cite the work of Jordan (1989) who studied Yucatac midwives and their families in Mexico and discovered that learning the skills of midwifery occurred as part of daily living.

> Girls in such families, without being identified as apprentice midwives, absorb the essence of midwifery practice as well as specific knowledge about many procedures, simply in the process of growing up … As young children they might be sitting quietly in a corner as their mother administers a prenatal massage. … As they grow older, they may be passing messages, running errands, getting needed supplies (p.68).

The effects of the learning that we experience in each of these communities will be taken with us when we enter another. This learning cannot be separated from the context in which it takes place (Rogoff 1990) and indeed is so powerful that it constructs our identities and views of the world. Clearly all the members of one community of practice, scientists, for example, will not hold uniform views on any one issue.

> Nonetheless, an identity in this sense manifests as a tendency to come up with certain interpretations, to engage in certain actions, to make certain choices, to value certain experiences – all by virtue of participating in certain enterprises.
>
> (Wenger 1998, p.153)

Additionally we may be participating in multiple communities of practice (Wenger 1998) concurrently. A student is not only a member of a school population, but is also a member of a family, a tutor group, a subject community, a peer group within the school population, possibly a member of an orchestra or sports team and probably a member of a group of friends who meet outside school. Each of these communities will have its own codes of practice which have been negotiated by its participants and thus behaviour or language, for example, which is considered satisfactory in one context may not be acceptable in another (Gee 1996). Membership of these multiple communities may not necessarily prove to be a comfortable experience. Throughout adult life the web of relationships we form and therefore the range of communities to which we become aligned becomes more extended (Griffiths 1995), resulting in a greater variety of codes of practice to which we choose or are expected to conform. The codes of one community may conflict with those of another, and the realisation that there may never be long-term consonance between them may prove to be a painful process for an individual whose allegiances are put to the test.

Wenger (1998) suggests that these communities have boundaries which are sometimes made explicit by overt symbols such as uniforms. However, even if the boundary symbols are not always as conspicuous as a uniform, they are, nevertheless, powerful and may exclude would-be participants in subtle yet effective ways.

Participation in communities of learners

Throughout the course of a school day the student will find him/herself a member of the different groups of the wider school community with all that it implies in terms of allegiances, expectations and traditions, and a participant, willing or reluctant, of a schooled subject community (Lave and Wenger 1991). These different settings are themselves 'products of human language and social practice, not fixed but dynamic and changing over time' (Packer and Goicoechea 2000, p.232). Participation within these communities signifies an acceptance of their conventions and a willingness to communicate and contribute to their practices (Rogoff 1995). As we become more adept at the practices and our participation becomes more central within these communities (Lave and Wenger 1991) our membership is strengthened and the communities' practices become part of our competences and perspectives and add to our sense of self and identity (Greeno et al. 1999).

The students who are the subject of this research are viewed therefore not only as participants in a school community, but also as 'persons-in-the-world' (Lave and Wenger 1991) and members of sociocultural communities, which are themselves 'positioned in broader social structures' (Wenger 1998) locally and nationally. These communities, some common to all, others particular to individuals, and the learning involved in them are experienced differently by each student. These differences arise through the mediation of students' prior learning and their awareness of the various influences, not isolated and fixed in each separate setting, but carried by the individual to different experiences (Hatch and Gardner 1993). Thus, students enter classrooms as those who have indeed affected and are affected by and defined by the multiple relationships which they have encountered in other communities (Lave and Wenger 1991) and with identities appropriated from the distributed experiences of these associations. They have constructed their own realities therefore which may be seen to be composed of different layers (Woods 1986).

Learning is mediated by the culture in which it takes place (Bruner 1996), with participation being central to learning (Lave and Wenger 1991). In order to belong to or be part of a community it is essential to participate in its activities and participation relies on partnerships between the members of that community. It is 'both action and connection' (Wenger 1998, p.55). It is also the relationships within those communities in which we participate or do not participate that define how we see ourselves (Griffiths 1995; Wenger 1998). Our participation within a community, the understandings developed between participants and the lessons learned prepare us for future activities in which we can utilise the experiences gained (Rogoff 1995). Participants may act in different roles, some serving pro tem as 'memories' for the others, or as record keepers of 'where things have got up to now', or as encouragers or cautioners. The point is for those in the group to help each other get the lay of the land and the hang of the job.

(Bruner 1996, p.21)

Participation, as viewed by Wenger (1998), may not always be the harmonious activity as suggested by the above description. It can, he suggests, also involve conflict and competition. Whatever form it takes, it is, however, transformative not only to those who participate, but also to the groups in which the participation takes place and indeed the practices of those groups. The very act of being able to affect practice is a key element of our experience of participation. Participation and its effects may therefore be seen as something which becomes central to experience and learning generally and which is carried with a person throughout life.

> It is part of who they are that they always carry with them. … In this sense, participation goes beyond direct engagement in specific activities with specific people. It places the negotiation of meaning in the context of our forms of membership in various communities. As such participation is not something we turn on and off.
>
> (Wenger 1998, p.57)

Our sense of belonging to a community is also constructed by the extent to which we are able to both give and receive help (Wenger 1998). When the students in this research were questioned individually about what they considered participation involved, all agreed with the opinion voiced by one that it meant 'joining in with other people and doing stuff with the rest of the class'. However, for William there was an additional clearly defined role of a participant to fulfil a perceived need and thus experience a sense of legitimation. The number of people in a group was, however, crucial to this.

> If they need a group of three and only have two and by going there you make the three I feel I am taking part … but if there's a group of four and then I make it up to five then I don't really feel I am taking part … I don't really feel that I am needed.
>
> (William)

Barriers to belonging to and participating in communities of learners in school

For William the greatest barrier to his belonging to some of the various communities of practice within school was that of his difficulties with literacy. However, some situations, more than others, made these more problematic. We now consider these situations and the effects that these had on William's participation.

Problems with literacy

Schooled literacy

The majority of the secondary school timetable hinges on the assumption that its participants are proficient at reading and writing to a satisfactory level and will become progressively more fluent in the language and the educational discourse of teaching and learning of the school (Mercer 1995). The discourse of literacy here is therefore linked directly or indirectly to the school curriculum and takes place within a forum where its practices, such as talk, may become atomised and abstracted from the discourses which are experienced by a student outside school.

The world of written text with which they are familiar outside school may bear little relationship to language encountered in school subjects such as science, geography, history. Participation at the very margins of each subject community will mean that, unless these students are able to move forward, their self-esteem follows a downward spiral as they see their peers progress towards a more active participatory role where their contributions are acknowledged, while highlighting and reinforcing their own inability. William was not only aware that his participation was minimal, but was clearly affected by this knowledge. As he explained,

> At school I feel quite small because I'm like the little boy in the corner. ... Other people keep putting their hands up and can answer questions and I'm sitting down not saying anything and I feel small.

The Government, through schools, demands that students demonstrate competence through tests. The practices of the specified curriculum have become normalised to the extent that an ideal child is perceived at ages 6–7 and 13–14 to be able to participate in certain ways in literacy.

The report for the tests for Standards at Key Stage 3 in English in 2002 (Qualifications and Curriculum Authority 2002) stated that analysis had been undertaken on a sample of 359 scripts for evidence of skills such as the ability to:

- describe, select or retrieve information, events or ideas from the passage;
- interpret, deduce or infer ideas, eg character, motive, mood, atmosphere;
- comment on the structure or the organisation of the text;
- comment on the writer's use of language, eg choice of words, syntax, imagery, tone;
- comment on the writer's purposes and attitudes, and the reader–writer relationship implied in the text;
- use quotation and reference to the text to support ideas.

(QCA 2002, p.5)

Clearly, for students to attain any marks it is necessary for them not only to be readers, but also to have the requisite level of writing or the 'composing process' (Wray 1994). Additionally the requirements of tests or examinations demand that the students must enact their literacy practices in isolation from ongoing purposes and needs, by addressing externally set tasks in timed conditions. This is a formidable task for those students who may have difficulties with literacy and

a) take some time to articulate the words before making sense of them,
b) not absorb all the necessary information (Male and Thompson 1985) and
c) take longer to write answers and find difficulty in monitoring or revising their own texts (Wray 1994), resulting in a situation familiar to many of them – that of not finishing a task (Male and Thompson 1985).

Ideas which may well be relevant to the questions and contain original and worthwhile thoughts may not be revealed because of the difficulties experienced. As William explained,

> I do understand things … but it's just writing it down … I've got it in my head, but it's writing it down that's the difficult bit. … I get really good answers … It's just I can't spell most of the words … when I write it down it's completely different from what's in my head.

William's level of literacy was not considered by the school to be of a sufficient standard to gain a level 4 and therefore he was not entered for the Standard Assessment Test in Year 9, but undertook a test designed by the school.

For those who have problems with literacy, hearing words articulated may be some indication of the meaning of the subject matter. However, once away from the source of the language, and faced with words which they do not understand, many find it an uphill struggle with which they cannot cope.

Wray (1994) cites findings (Baker and Anderson 1984; Garner and Reis 1981) which indicate that poorer readers concentrate on 'reading as a decoding process rather than as a meaning-getting process' (p.69).

It was clear in the interviews which I conducted in Year 8 on understanding a history lesson, and in which the students were required to read from the set textbook, the efforts of the majority of the students with difficulties were concerned with articulating the text, sometimes deconstructing the words into single syllables. This resulted in a disjointed flow of reading where the meaning of the whole was lost.

I repeated the exercise in Year 9. William was slightly more confident about this task, and he attributed this increased confidence to the amount of time that his father had spent listening to him read. He told me that his father had also experienced problems with reading when younger, had been fortunate enough to have extra help after school and, as a result, now had no problems with literacy. William also felt that his father's experience had enabled him to really understand the problems that William faced and he 'knew how to make it easier'. However, despite this continuing support from his family, William still had difficulties with some three or four syllable words, such as 'provided' and 'materials' which I asked him to read in Year 9, and his reading remained slow and hesitant.

Competent readers are not only able to identify the point at which the subject matter of a sentence becomes unclear and return to it (Greeno et al. 1999, p.137), but also use earlier information to assess the meaning (Wray 1994). For students with problems with literacy, however, there may be few points at which there was understanding to which they might return, thus leading to confusion and possible disengagement. In Year 8 William commented that when he could not understand parts of a lesson, he would

> sort of go off … not go off as like go away, just like go off my work, like speak to people and stuff.

It appeared that a process of disengagement had started to take place in Year 8 and this continued and increased in Year 9.

Reading clearly takes place not just within school and for the reader the opportunities to enjoy this are extended, for example, by the local library. For the non-reader, while the facilities are available the means with which to enjoy them are denied. William admitted that he made very limited use of either the school or public library and did not do any reading which was not specifically necessary for school work. He explained that he found 'it really hard to read' but added that he enjoyed books about the army and weapons which had

> sort of … not loads of writing … with pictures so you know what's going on.

Situations in which problems were more evident

It would seem obvious that the settings in which William had most problems would be those in which he attended lessons which were heavily written-language based. He acknowledged that he enjoyed lessons such as design technology, science and art more than any others because these were all practical subjects and he felt that doing practical work

> does really make me learn … it's much more interesting and you know how to do it.

It emerged, however, from the interviews with William that, in lessons in which he had most difficulty, his experiences were affected by the ability grouping of the lessons and the attitude of peers within them. Secondly the availability of help either from teachers, teaching assistants or friends, and the attitude of teachers whether in mixed ability or setted groups contributed significantly to William's perceptions of whether or not he could cope with the work. These different factors, inextricably linked, wove a complex web which succeeded in so demotivating William that a process of disengagement, which had started for him in Year 8, accelerated in Year 9, leading to long periods of absence from school and displays of poor behaviour in some lessons when he attended.

Ability grouping within lessons

Recent research on student and teacher perceptions fails to reach a clear consensus on the effects of homogeneous versus heterogeneous ability groupings (Hallam and Toutounji 1996; Harlen and Malcolm 1997; Sukhnandan and Lee 1998). What studies have revealed, however, are the features of settings that students consider contribute to their learning. Students who prefer mixed ability teaching suggest that classmates help them and they learn more (Klingner et al. 1998), while sharing ideas can change attitudes (Lyle 1999). While some of the respondents in this research echoed these views, William, however, did not subscribe to them for those lessons in which there might be the possibility of a more overt demonstration of his difficulties. He was taught in a mixed ability situation in English and he considered, rightly or wrongly, that he was

> probably the only one, or maybe another one like ... who finds it hard to work.

He thought that this exacerbated the perception of his difficulties by other people and increased his own sense of inadequacy.

> We're all mixed up ... that means that there's some clever people in there as well and that really makes you like ... if you put, like the clever ones in there ... it makes me look worse than I actually am at work, like if you compare books.

McDermott (1999) suggests that for students with learning difficulties this is not an uncommon experience as the classroom becomes a forum in which the difficulties are rehearsed before an audience which may exploit the opportunity to react to each visible mistake. These lessons in which large amounts of reading and writing were required were clearly a difficult experience for William. I suggested that perhaps he was able to learn from the other students who were more proficient, but he denied this and reiterated the fact that when he was unable to keep up with the work or did not understand he 'switched off', and would 'just sit there and do something else like drawing and stuff'. He was, however, very enthusiastic about English lessons where practical work was involved and where he was able to project his ideas without the fear of being unable to communicate them. He explained,

> We were doing this stuff where you have to write a play, but I had all these ideas, but I couldn't spell them ... write it all up, but then when we came to make one up in a

group to film it … like on a video camera … I really done what was in my head because it's easier doing it in front of a camera than down on paper.

Availability of help and attitude of teaching staff

The factor which William considered improved the situation in mixed ability groupings was the presence of help, whether from friends who understood his problems, from teaching assistants or from teachers who were able to make time to address individual problems. He commented that in a large group there were fewer opportunities for individual help from a teacher and the presence of a teaching assistant ameliorated this. This help was a key element in his sense of belonging and perception of history lessons, both in Year 8 where it was taught in a mixed ability situation and in Year 9 where the students were setted by prior attainment. Mr Tudor, the history teacher, was seen as approachable and available to help,

> I just put my hand up and he comes out and explains it … he just sort of like walks around the class and gives people help.

The teacher was also sympathetic towards the difficulties experienced by some of the students.

> He doesn't put people in an awkward spot. If I say something that's a bit wrong, he makes it funny and makes a sort of joke out of it … and that makes you feel a bit like … even if it's wrong it's like fun … It's fun if you get it wrong and it's fun if you get it right.

This was very important for William who, despite all the problems with coping in a subject in which linguistic demands are high (Haydn et al. 1997), clearly had a sense of belonging in this particular class. He indicated that the teacher and his pedagogy were popular with all the students and that the teacher himself appeared to enjoy teaching his subject and motivated the students.

> I feel like I'm sort of supposed to be in there because the work … it's not easy, but it gives me a little bit of a challenge but not too hard.

In year 9, humanities subjects were taught in homogeneous ability groups, and William was in a 'foundation group'. This had been organised by the faculty in order to have smaller groups for those who had special educational needs and thereby give additional help to those students. Aylett (2000) suggests that students who prefer being taught in a setted situation see the advantages as being that students are all working at the same level and there is lack of embarrassment over incorrect responses. There is also the availability of extra support (Klingner and Kettman-Vaughn 1998). William explained that he felt more relaxed in that situation and 'felt quite normal, like everyone else.' However, if he were unable to cope with something in class he then perceived this problem as being accentuated by the fact that he was in a 'foundation group'.

> It makes me feel like I'm on the bottom of the bottom sort of thing … I'm like bottom of that class. If I can't read or understand then I think this is the bottom of the bottom group as well.

In addition to being taught in setted groups the three humanities subjects were taught in modules. This meant that the students were taught separate modules of history, geography and religious education, by different teachers. While William did not object to this routine per se, he was taught not only by Mr Tudor but also by Mr Stuart, and he found history lessons taught by the latter very difficult. While he perceived Mr Tudor as being sympathetic to his problems and to those of other students like William and 'setting work at a steady pace … so that we can all do it', he commented that the pedagogic style of Mr Stuart was very different.

He considered that the pace of the lessons was too fast, and that Mr. Stuart did not understand the difficulties that William and others like him encountered. He believed that Mr Stuart expected him to be able to keep up with the rest of the class who were able to write more quickly. This was particularly difficult when copying from the board. He explained,

> Mr Stuart takes it that more or less people have done it and rubs it off. Last year Mr Tudor would wait for everybody to finish. That made it a lot better … cos I could actually get work down, not just bits here and bits there.

He voiced disappointment, when comparing his work in his history book in Year 8 to that in Year 9 where there was a considerable amount of unfinished work and much of what was present was 'all jumbled up'.

William also felt that in these lessons he understood far less than in Year 8 although the subject matter, that of the First and Second World Wars, was of greater interest. His perception was that he had participated more in Year 8, although this was not apparent in the lesson which I observed. Neither was it confirmed in the interview which I undertook with Mr Tudor in Year 8. He considered that, in a mixed ability situation, William appeared to be quite insecure and 'painfully aware of his own learning difficulties'. He was reticent about participating and would offer a contribution only if he were asked a question directly.

Mr Tudor did suggest, however, that William's understanding was considerably higher than was evidenced by either his participation in class or his written work. This belief was endorsed in the interview which I undertook with William on his understanding of the lesson which I had observed. It was clear that he had understood the subject matter of the lesson and, with a little prompting from me, was able to analyse possible causes of events and attempt a hypothesis of probable outcomes.

In Year 9 in his lessons with Mr Stuart, because of William's difficulties, and what he considered to be the unsympathetic attitude of the teacher, and lack of help, he felt unable to participate, and was keenly aware of the contrast between his own minimal participation and that of other students in the class who were 'always rushing to put their hands up'. For William, whose attendance in Year 9 was already becoming more infrequent, his sense of marginalisation was increased when he encountered situations in which 'he didn't have a clue.' His sense of belonging to the group decreased and he explained

> I don't feel like I'm supposed to sort of be there.

He admitted that he had hoped that he would be taught by Mr Tudor for all his history lessons in Year 9, not only because Mr Tudor understood William's difficulties, but that he also appreciated the work that William achieved. This had motivated William to greater efforts. As he explained,

> that makes me do more for him, 'cos I feel like if he's proud of it already I'll do more of this.

William considered that Mr Stuart had higher expectations of him that he could actually attain, and that his work never achieved what was expected, with the result that William became progressively less enthusiastic about attempting written work. William believed that Mr Stuart was of the opinion that he actually understood all the work and his unsatisfactory work rate was due to laziness or 'mucking around'. William explained that

> even when I try my best I still don't understand.

He voiced the wish that not only Mr Stuart but also some of the teachers in other subjects could

> sort of like understand more … just explain the work more.

He attributed what he saw as the lack of understanding to teachers' inability to fully appreciate the experience of having problems with literacy, or not having any real solutions. He commented,

> they don't know what to do to make it easier.

This problem was alleviated for William in some other subject lessons by the presence of teaching assistants who were able to give considerable individual help. This was the situation in mathematics, in which students were strictly setted by attainment. William felt more at ease in this grouping as the students were what he considered to be at the same level of achievement or 'only just above'. There were always two teaching assistants, and these and the teachers were understanding, explained the work thoroughly, and were willing to take time to repeat any work not fully understood by the students. William felt confident that the teachers and teaching assistants were not only aware of the difficulties the students experienced, but also anticipated possible problems that they might encounter in the work. This supportive environment, together with the bond which had been built up between the students, encouraged William to participate more.

Attitude of peers

William revealed that his closest friends at school were those who also had similar problems with literacy. He appreciated the support of another boy whom he had known since the primary school and who also had difficulties with reading and writing. Where possible William and he helped each other in lessons and William valued this relationship highly. He preferred to work with one other person rather than working in groups, unless it was in maths where he 'got on really well' with the other students. He enjoyed discussing the work with the other students in maths and felt that, because they were 'all quite close in the work', they were more able to help each other. This co-operation, he considered, fostered a sense of belonging and aided his learning considerably. He was more confident about offering answers, unworried about the responses of the other students to any possible mistakes that he might make as 'they all know what it's like'.

This was not the case in all lessons, and in the interviews William articulated his concern about the reaction of students who had no problems with literacy to any contributions he might make. He felt confident to offer opinions only when working with his closest friend. It was clear in the history lesson which I observed and videoed in Year 8 that, although William was seated at a table with a group of five other students, his participation was limited to discussion with a friend seated next to him. William was clearly uncomfortable when the task required a larger group activity, and continued to concentrate only on talking to his neighbour. His responses to my subsequent questions about this revealed that he was very concerned about the relationships within a larger group situation, and was eager to maintain a pleasant atmosphere:

> Working with one other person there's only two ideas ... and if you are both happy then you can put it down ... and you don't want to fall out with anyone ... and you'll stick together ... but with a bigger group ... there's always someone to take charge ... and if you get picked to say something ... everyone says it's not fair.

William's concern over possible negative reactions from his peers in mixed ability settings was further compounded by the fact that the National Curriculum at that stage demanded that all students study a foreign language. The students were taught in broad bands which meant that there were some in the lessons whom William considered were much more able at this subject than he was. He stated that learning a foreign language made him 'confused' and he was clearly very concerned about what he saw as the unpredictability of the lessons.

> All sorts of things happen. Like sometimes I know the answer, but most times I don't.

His difficulties with literacy meant that opportunities for failure were numerous and very public, and these occasions did little for his self-esteem:

> I feel really small, because most of the people know the answers and I'm just sort of ... like when I get something wrong the other people laugh ... or like speaking to friends and sort of point at me.

In situations such as this, even if William were reasonably confident that he knew the answer, the maintenance of a low profile may have appeared to have been the safest strategy (McDermott 1999).

William was aware that his problems severely limited his participation in lessons where literacy played a major role. He felt, however, that in some lessons, in addition to those of the foreign language, he was further disabled by the dismissive attitude of some of the students who appeared to minimise or ignore the value of any contributions that he or Mortimer – his friend who also had problems with literacy – managed to make:

> Everyone else seems to come out with these really good answers and if we say something not many people agree on it ... most of the people think that what I say is not very important ... and when someone else says something everyone else talks about it.

Lack of recognition or acceptance of one's contributions serves to minimise any possible feeling of belonging.

> Members whose contributions are never adopted develop an identity of non-participation that progressively marginalises them. Their experience becomes irrelevant because it cannot be asserted and recognised as a form of competence.
>
> (Wenger 1998, p. 203)

Goodenow (1992) suggests that, for those students who are encountering difficulties at school, a sense of belonging may be the key factor in reducing absenteeism and encouraging them to remain at school, and that a well defined sense of belonging might counteract other more negative influences. For William, a diminishing sense of belonging and inability to participate set in motion a downward spiral from which he was unable to escape. By the Spring

Term of Year 9 when I interviewed William for a third time it was clear that he was feeling much more detached from the school situation. His attendance had deteriorated dramatically, as he found academic work progressively more difficult and his absences and missed work contributed significantly to his inability to cope. The effects of all the factors were clearly cumulative and each negative experience in school provided the basis for his future expectations. His past was present (Rogoff 1995). William explained that, although he wanted to come into school, he was apprehensive about the possibility of not being able to answer questions in class and the negative reactions of classmates. These reactions caused frustration and suppressed anger in William. He commented,

> I've got like anger building up. I want to let it out, but I can't in school. It's all sort of like locked up inside. Then if I go to another lesson it builds up all the time … If I can't do the work I just sort of lose concentration … I get in trouble and it all starts again.

A learning centre had been established at the school for those students who were not coping in lessons and they were allowed to spend time there working alone under supervision. An individual timetable had been designed for William and he spent several periods a week in the learning centre, going only to those class lessons, such as science or design technology, in which he felt he could cope. Despite this, his attendance remained sporadic throughout Year 9, and he became progressively more detached from school. He felt comfortable only in the company of those friends both inside and outside school, and his family, who understood his problems and didn't make him 'feel sort of small', but as he said, 'just treat me as I am'.

Discussion

The sociocultural framework of this research invited certain methodological approaches (Scribner 1997) which sought to consider the different factors which impact on a sense of belonging and participation for students who experience difficulties with literacy. It has necessarily concentrated on some factors while ignoring others. There may be still others which have not been revealed and it is important to be aware of the possibility of their presence (Becker 1998). Some of the factors that mediated William's difficulties with literacy may also affect other students. They may not, however, have equal importance for every student, the same depth of impact, or indeed, the same long-term consequences. Availability or lack of help, will, for example, be a major influence for all students in a community such as is formed in subject lessons, in which practice and knowing are constantly changing (Lave and Wenger

1991), and in which those who are more experienced in the practices of the community are able to help those who are not.

All respondents in this research considered that the role of the teacher was of major significance to their learning. Clearly, for William, sympathetic and appropriate pedagogy fostered a sense of belonging and a desire to try to participate more, if not always verbally. It is difficult to conclude, however, that this factor would have counterbalanced the effect on William of the negative reactions of some of his peers, which seriously inhibited his participation. It is evident that different settings, and the participants within them, in the school arena, give rise to multiple factors which are responsible for increasing or limiting a sense of belonging and participation. The insights provided by this research indicate how overarching practices such as setting or mixed ability groupings can undermine teachers' aims to enable inclusion and may have unintended consequences, often very damaging ones, for individuals whom the practices seek to support. Further research is needed in this area with a view to investigating the challenges to inclusion in understanding learning as participation, and enabling teachers to arrive at real knowledge of students generally, but with particular emphasis on providing help for those with difficulties such as those experienced by William.

The author would like to thank Patricia Murphy and Carrie Paechter for their help and advice in preparing this text.

References

Aylett, A. (2000) 'Setting: does it have to be a negative experience?', *Support for Learning* 15(1): 41–45.

Baker, L. and Anderson, R. (1984) 'Metacognitive skills and reading', in D. Pearson (ed) *Handbook of Reading Research*, New York: Longman.

Becker, H. S. (1998) *Tricks of the Trade*, Chicago; London: The University of Chicago Press.

Bruner, J. (1996) *The Culture of Education*, Cambridge, Massachusetts; London, England: Harvard University Press.

Davies, S. (2000) 'I've seen Romeo and Juliet. Is that to do with History? Perceptions of students with learning difficulties as to what is history'. British Educational Research Conference, Cardiff.

Garner, R. and Reis, R. (1981) 'Monitoring and resolving comprehension obstacles: an investigation of spontaneous text lookbacks among upper grade good and poor comprehenders', *Reading Research Quarterly* 16: 569–582.

Gee, J. P. (1996) *Social Linguistics and Literacies*, London; New York: Routledge Falmer.

Goodenow, C. (1992) 'Strengthening the links between educational psychology and the study of social contexts', *Education Psychologist* 27 (2): 177–196.

Greeno, J., Pearson, P. and Schoenfeld, A. (1999) 'Achievement and theories of knowing and learning', in R. McCormick and C. Paechter (eds) *Learning and Knowledge*, London: Paul Chapman Publishing Ltd.

Griffiths, M. (1995) *Feminisms and the Self*, London; New York: Routledge.

Hallam, S. and Toutounji, I. (1996) 'What can research tell us about the effects of different kinds of student grouping?', *Research Review*, Institute of Education, London.

Harlen, W. and Malcolm, H. (1997) 'What the research says on ability groups and setting', University of Strathclyde.

Hatch, T. and Gardner, H. (1993) 'Finding cognition in the classroom', in G. Salomon (ed) *Distributed Cognitions*, Cambridge, England: Cambridge University Press.

Haydn, T., Arthur, J. and Hunt, M. (1997) *Learning to Teach History in the Secondary School*, London: Routledge.

Jordan, B. (1989) 'Cosmopolitan obstetrics: some insights from the training of traditional midwives', *Social Science and Medicine* 28(9): 925–944.

Klingner, J. K., Vaughn, S., Schumm, J. S., Cohen, P. and Forgan, J. W. (1998) 'Inclusion or pull-out: which do students prefer?', *Journal of Learning Disabilities* 31(Mar): 148–159.

Lave, J. and Wenger, E. (1991) *Situated Learning – Legitimate Peripheral Participation*, Cambridge, England: Cambridge University Press.

Lyle, S. (1999) 'An investigation of student perceptions of mixed-ability grouping to enhance literacy in children aged 9–10', *Educational Studies* 25(3): 283–296.

Male, J. and Thompson, C. (1985) *The Educational Implications of Disability*, London: The Royal Association for Disability and Rehabilitation.

Maslow, A. (1962) *Toward a Psychology of Being*, Princeton, New Jersey: Van Nostrand.

McDermott, R. P. (1999) 'On becoming labelled – the story of Adam', in P. Murphy (ed) *Learners, Learning and Assessment*, London: Paul Chapman Publishing.

Mercer, N. (1995) *The Guided Construction of Knowledge* Clevedon: Multilingual Matters Ltd.

Noddings, N. (1992) *The Challenge to Care in Schools – An Alternative Approach to Education*, New York: Teachers College, Columbia University.

Packer, M. J. and Goicoechea, J. (2000) 'Sociocultural and constructivist theories of learning: ontology, not just epistemology', *Educational Psychologist* 35(4): 227–241.

Qualifications and Curriculum Authority (2002) *Standards at Key Stage 3 – English: a report for headteachers, heads of department, English teachers and assessment co-ordinators on the 2002 national curriculum assessments for 14-year-olds*, London: Department for Education and Skills.

Rogoff, B. (1990) *Apprenticeship in Thinking*, New York; Oxford: Oxford University Press.

Rogoff, B. (1995) 'Observing sociocultural activity on three planes: participatory appropriation, guided participation, and apprenticeship', in J. Wertsch, P. del Rio and A. Alvarez (eds) *Sociocultural Studies of Mind*, Cambridge; New York: Cambridge University Press.

Scribner, S. (1997) 'A Sociocultural approach to the study of mind', in E. Tobach, R. Joffe Falmagne, M. Brown Parlee, L. M. W. Martin and A. Scribner Kapelman (eds) *Mind and Social Practice – Selected Writings of Sylvia Scribner*, Cambridge: Cambridge University Press.

Sukhnandan, L. and Lee, B. (1998) *Streaming, Setting and Grouping by Ability: a review of the literature*, Slough: NFER.

Wearmouth, J. (2000) ' "Talking Stones": a technique for interviewing disaffected young people', *Reach, Journal of the Irish Association of Teachers of Special Education*, pp. 42–52.

Wenger, E. (1998) *Communities of Practice – Learning, Meaning and Identity*, Cambridge, England: Cambridge University Press.

Wenger, E., McDermot, R. and Snyder, W. (2002) *Cultivating Communities of Practice*, Boston, Massachusetts: Harvard Business School Press.

Woods, P. (1986) *Inside Schools – Ethnography in Educational Research*, London; New York: Routledge Falmer.

Wray, D. (1994) *Literacy and Awareness*, London: Hodder and Stoughton.

Chapter 19

Reforming special education: beyond 'inclusion'

Michael M. Gerber

Often outside the awareness of its practitioners, special education contains elements that make it subversive to universal public education systems. Special education's focus and priorities challenge schools to produce a radical form of social justice: equality of educational opportunity for students who are sometimes characterized by extreme individual differences. Attempting to accommodate these differences raises questions as well about the meaning of equality, the meaning of opportunity, and indeed the relationship between schooling and education. Much of the American understanding of equality of educational opportunity begins with assumptions of normal – i.e. typical or modal – ability and learning potential. School policies and structures have evolved following more or less implicit expectations that children develop and learn 'normally' (i.e. in a tolerably similar manner).

However, it is a simple fact that some children, for a variety of reasons, are handicapped as learners by a complex interaction of individual characteristics and circumstances, on the one hand, and constraints imposed by social structures or material scarcities, on the other. Their observed trajectory of development and learning is atypical, sometimes profoundly so. Mass public schooling was not designed and has not evolved with these children in mind. Therefore, the very concept of a 'special' education can be and has been subversive to the extent that accommodation of extreme individual differences tends to undermine those structures within schools that have evolved to satisfy both expectations of tolerable similarity among children as well as the several social and political purposes of schools.

As I will attempt to show in this chapter, the current reform movement in special education – 'inclusion' – is merely a variation on a theme. I will argue that the stridency of reformers bent on inclusion inadvertently nurtures and legitimizes attempts by school administrators and policy-makers to regain control over an enterprise that for a hundred years has threatened the traditional structure, economy and culture of American public schooling.

Contradiction and conflict

It is not well understood that the conflict between mass public education and 'special' education is fundamental. It has always existed and, during eras of school reform, it frequently has made special education a source of deep discontent, a focus of controversy and a target of criticism. The public tends to view special education as a loose collection of unusual practices used by specially prepared teachers to instruct and manage an exotic, homogeneous population. In fact, special education in the twentieth century is better understood as a school enterprise, as an organizational strategy schools have adopted to accommodate sometimes extreme differences in children. That is, schools create, organize and allocate resources to satisfy instructional demands presented by the challenging behaviours of students with disabilities. Historically, special educational programming emerges as the unavoidable consequence of the immutable fact of human differences in conflict with the ambition to build systems of universal mass education. As a result, special education has proved to be a troubling and troublesome offspring to public school officials, chronically demanding extraordinary effort, contingent resources, and most of all, constant institutional transformation to achieve a radical form of social justice.

In many ways, special education's explicit concern for individual differences has been the source of its moral strength, but also its fatal political weakness. Even in societies professing democratic ideals, individuals are valued more at the high rather than low end of ability, achievement and performance distributions. The history of civil liberties flows from contemplation of social justice for competent more than for incompetent individuals. Historically, the latter individuals have been extended protection more often than opportunity following a common-sense expectation that equal social privileges and opportunities will fail to yield equal successes. Even when, in the first years of this century, special day classes seemed progressive and innovative, the subtle, unrelenting pressure exerted by special education advocacy for individual children was in contradiction to the mass educational system that school managers were attempting to build.

The heart of this contradiction lies in the distinction between access and opportunity. Mere access to the physical environment of schools or classrooms within schools confers no specific or necessarily appropriate opportunity to learn. Children who are very difficult to teach may provoke contingent and individual responses from teachers, but these responses do not necessarily constitute an 'opportunity'. Allowing such children into the schools in the early part of this century was an early form of inclusion that was popularly conceived as new educational opportunity for children with disabilities. But it wasn't until very difficult students received a planful response that was reasonably calculated to promote satisfactory progress in the curriculum that a real educational opportunity existed. It is, therefore, unfortunate that contemporary reformers who urge 'inclusion' have emphasized place over instructional substance and confused 'participation' with real opportunity (Kauffman 1993; Gerber 1995).

Criticism and reform

Despite its origins as a form of inclusion, special education is described today by reformers as a segregating, insulated, self-protecting, racially biased philosophy and array of practices, a product of an outdated modernism and misguided scientific positivism, or merely as an ineffective, overblown solution to easily solvable school problems (Dunn 1968; Heller *et al.* 1982; Tomlinson 1982; Madden and Slavin 1983; Will 1986; Cole 1990; Skrtic 1991). Hardly ten years after the passage of a national special education mandate, its most uncompromising critics had weighed its worth and found it absolutely wanting, absolutely beyond redemption in its current forms (Stainback and Stainback 1984; Gartner and Lipsky 1987; Wang *et al.* 1988). The remarkable policies of inclusion that led in this century from special day classes to mandated public school education for *all* disabled children in the 'least restrictive environment', policies that once were lauded as dramatic signs of a profound social 'revolution', now seem to have lost both the public's confidence and support amid a sea of change in political attitudes about abnormal development, achievement and behaviour.

The current reform movement is complex, containing strands of various interests that converge only on the perceived need to change special education. Administrators and policy-makers, for example, using the rhetoric of inclusion have advocated for integration of funding, more than for integration of students, and deregulation more than improvement of programs (National Association of State Boards of Education 1992; 'Governors seek authority to merge IDEA, other money' 1995). Policy rhetoric and philosophical debate aside, administrators and other public officials recognize a 'bottom line' – attempting to organize instructional resources to suit the learning differences among children is very costly (Chaikind *et al.* 1993; Bacdayan 1994). These critics are focused on managing schools more efficiently and effectively, so their expressed concern for improving special education must be evaluated in that light.

A quite different set of critics who strongly identify themselves with needs and rights of disabled people, advocate a new more radical policy of 'inclusion' in place of existing forms of special education (Catlett and Osher 1994; Fuchs and Fuchs 1994). They aggressively demand and define educational opportunity for all disabled students in terms of its location in regular, age-appropriate classrooms. These critics believe and intend that, under great moral and political pressure, schools, curriculum and instruction will remould themselves to accommodate individual learning needs of students with disabilities and, therefore, produce a fuller and more genuine equality of educational opportunity.

Advocates for special education resist these radical proposals as misguided zealotry and believe that the philosophical and legal framework created by legislation ultimately is a more powerful and reliable vehicle of change (Gerber 1989). Advocates for gradual, research-based improvement in implementing present policies believe that the political stress created by more radical reformers will be expropriated easily by school administrators and policy-makers who seek mainly to gain greater local control and discretion over educational programs for students with disabilities. These 'gradualists' believe that school administrators are supportive of changes in special education only because, as currently constituted, it evades local control and limits degrees of managerial freedom to such an extent that traditional forms of schooling are threatened (Kauffman *et al.* 1988; Gerber 1989, 1994; Kauffman and Hallahan 1995).

If the 'gradualists' are correct, it will be ironic if it is those who have most thwarted current policy by their bureaucratic resistance who ultimately benefit from the intense criticisms and political agitation of radical inclusionists. In fact, radical inclusionists and policy gradualists *both* seek improvement for students with disabilities although they have engaged in fractious, often harsh debate over who best speaks for the interests of children with disabilities (Fuchs and Fuchs 1994; Kauffman and Hallahan 1995). An objective analysis reveals that *both* positions and the courses of action they might recommend have an important underlying commonality. Followed to their logical conclusion, both represent the continuation of the same implicit threat to public schooling that was posed by the establishment of special day classes almost a hundred years ago.

Special education became a formal part of public schooling in the United States during the closing years of the nineteenth century while a system of mass public education was still emerging. The story of its origins reveals why over the ensuing years and especially today it so seriously threatens the *status quo* of public schooling. Beneath the progressivist – some might say, modernist – language of the story, however, is the hard material fact that extant knowledge and technology of instruction, organized for 'schooling' as it has been over most of this century, is incapable of providing either meaningfully equal or equally meaningful educational opportunity for all students. It is in reaction to this fact and its long-term implications that special education is singled out and vilified by current reformers.

Past is prologue

In response to rapid industrialization, urban growth and massive immigration, the institution of public schooling at the beginning of the twentieth century served several different public purposes. One set of purposes wished to secure and improve a democratic society by improving its citizenry and controlling those disintegrative and anarchistic forces thought to be latent in unsocialized – uneducated – people. Another set of purposes sought a general grading and upgrading of the labour force as one component in the production equation to support better expanding capitalist industry and interests.

At an accelerating rate, a subtle political consensus developed following the American Civil War. Different purposes and interests coalesced in support of universal, publically financed compulsory schooling. By 1900, fewer than half of the states had compulsory attendance laws, and those that did varied in the vigour of their enforcement. But public education was far more easily legislated than accomplished. Organizing and operating schools for so many children at the scale contemplated faced substantial practical barriers, especially in fast-growing urban centres. Children appeared in classrooms who, for reasons of ability, background or motivation, caused teachers significant difficulties. Any first-order approximation to the kind of school system intended required management and control, not only of numerous but also highly diverse children. As early as 1894, for example, a researcher, Will S. Monroe, revealed that teachers perceived 2 per cent of their students as 'imbeciles' or 'idiots', and almost 9 per cent as 'mentally dull'. Monroe and others knew that children who were extremely low functioning would eventually find their way into state institutions. But he crystallized the core problem of universal compulsory education by pondering if schools were or could be the proper place for so many 'mentally dull' students who were so 'below the general average' (cited in Trent 1994: 147).

At the turn of the century, teaching consisted of oral presentation and recitation of subject-matter and an array of drill and practice for acquiring basic academic skills. Teachers expected and sought to command student behaviours conducive to large-group instruction in classrooms. Professional teaching, still in its infancy, was wholly unprepared for students who differed in so many obstructive ways. Teachers were not trained or encouraged to develop repertoires of adaptive methods or techniques suitable, let alone optimal, for addressing significant individual differences in learners.

In conventional wisdom, learning was a product of crudely understood interaction of opportunity, provided by schooling, and ability and character, sufficient amounts of which were assumed to exist in a 'typical' student. There was as yet no psychology of child development or useful educational psychology. Neither the intelligence-testing nor 'child study' movements had begun. In practice, school personnel made little formal distinction between students who were unwilling or unable to learn the curriculum teachers presented to them. Rather, they and the public at large believed that merely being at school provided students with an opportunity to learn. If they succeeded, then they had obviously used this opportunity to good advantage. If they did not succeed, then just as obviously they had squandered their opportunity and must accept responsibility for doing so.

The first reform

In the first years of the century, however, a new progressivist philosophy gained a foothold in urban affairs and spread easily to urban schools in particular. According to Ravitch (1974), new ideas contributed to a vision of a 'new education' that undermined traditional thinking 'that school was a place to learn reading, writing, and arithmetic, and that students who failed had only themselves to blame' (p. 167). Progressivists urged schools as agents of the community to assume and accept more responsibility for the success of students' learning. Ultimately, the public's perception of the source of educational success or failure shifted away from students to what schools were thought to provide – how instruction was organized, the curriculum offered, the quality of teachers, and the nature of teaching itself. In this view, schools did not merely manufacture education by a set of technical production processes. Rather, schools, through the kind of educational opportunities offered, were vanguards of societal redemption and renewal.

It was natural, therefore, that someone would view educating children with learning and behavioural problems as similar to public health nursing or social work. One of the most prominent leaders of a new movement to establish special day classes for these children in schools was Elizabeth Farrell, a teacher in New York City. Farrell gained the active support of social activists associated with Lillian Wald's nearby settlement house and from other progressive figures, including New York City's Superintendent of Schools, William Maxwell (Sarason and Doris 1979; Hendrick and MacMillan 1989). As Farrell herself describes it, the idea for special day classes

> was not the result of any theory. It grew out of conditions in a neighborhood which furnished many and serious problems in truancy and discipline. The first class was made up of the odds and ends of a large school. There were over-age children,

so-called naughty children, and the dull and stupid children … They had varied
interests but the school, as they found it, had little or nothing for them.

(cited in Sarason and Doris 1979: 297)

Thus, while the still-emerging concept of 'public school' emphasized universal
exposure to a common curriculum in age-graded classes, early special
education advocacy by teachers like Farrell promoted *differentiated* treatment
and curriculum in *ungraded* classes for students considered wayward, mentally
deficient or simply difficult to teach (Hoffman 1975). Despite what appear to be
obvious contradictions in trying to incorporate special classes, teachers and
curriculum within the otherwise rigid framework of public schooling, the idea
caught fire. By 1913, there were special day classes and special schools in 108
cities. Ten years later, this number had increased by 55 per cent with over
33,000 students in special education programs (Trent 1994: 147). Clearly, not
every teacher or administrator shared Farrell's and Maxwell's enthusiasm for
special class programs for retarded students within the context of graded
public schools. Indeed, it isn't clear that Farrell and Maxwell had precisely the
same motives or vision. It seems, rather, that the concept of special day classes
was embraced widely because it satisfied different needs for different
constituencies.

When Farrell, encouraged by local support, finally presented her ideas to
members of the Board of Education, she was praised as a 'genius whose vision
was essentially practical' (Lillian Wald, cited in Sarason and Doris 1979: 299).
That phrase – a vision that is essentially practical – is a succinct expression of
the unusual consensus achieved by the new 'special' education. To
administrators, special day classes appeared to meet two important goals,
attendance *and* containment, while also providing an orderly professional
context for addressing significant management difficulties. However, although
administrators won control and containment of a segment of the school
population who were difficult to teach and manage, they failed to see how
porous and troubling the boundaries between general practices and the new
special education actually would prove to be. On the other hand, advocates for
special day classes won a kind of autonomy within the school from which they
hoped to organize more appropriate, more meaningful curriculum and
instruction for students with disabilities, but failed to see how potentially
threatening they would become to the deepest interests of those who built and
supported public schooling.

Almost immediately, these different purposes began to conflict, surfacing as
debate over how special day classes were to be administered, to what extent
their curriculum would vary from normal curriculum, methods of
identification and classification, and the nature of professional preparation and
certification. Most school districts established separate supervisorial authorities

and administrative channels to manage those specially designated teachers assigned to special day classes. It was separation, to be sure, but separation by mutual consent (Sarason and Doris 1979: 360). If special educators pushed the boundaries of their autonomy, general educators worked as aggressively to circumscribe, contain and limit the overall impact of special education on the general structure and operation of schools. Thus, the bifurcation of the public school system into two mutually contradicting, asymmetrically empowered strands – one for 'special' and one for 'normal' students – arose not from the insistent advocacy of any particular group, so much as from a tacit agreement about the practical conditions and possibilities of public schools. It was – it is – an unworkable arrangement as long as schools maintain their traditional structure, economy and culture.

In remembering Farrell's vision as it was shared with members of the Henry Street Settlement House, Lillian Wald in 1935 understood more accurately than most the implications of what was being proposed by the young teacher. It was *not* simply about optimal development of every individual's potential. Rather,

> Miss Farrell's originality lay in applying the idea to the education of the atypical in the public schools. She was optimistic enough to believe that the largest and most complex school system in the country – perhaps in the world – with its hundreds of thousands of children, its rigid curriculum, its mass methods, could be modified to meet the needs of the atypical – often the least lovely and potentially the most troublesome of its pupils.
>
> (Wald, cited in Sarason and Doris 1979: 298)

Education, income and social justice

Without some reference to material well-being, the concept of social justice is ultimately a philosophical abstraction. Differences and variations in status or power or specific rights are important because they ultimately contribute to greater equality or inequality of material well-being. After 1900, greater social equality and material well-being, as indexed by distribution of income, was presumptively related to access to and equality of educational opportunity. In these terms, social justice does not require strict equality of income, but it does demand that some basic level of material and psychological well-being (i.e. income) should not be withheld from individuals by society for arbitrary or capricious reasons. There is historical confusion and room for debate, however, over what constitutes 'arbitrary' or 'capricious' justifications for social inequality.

In capitalist societies, apologists explain observed inequalities of income distribution as a product of supply and demand for qualities of labour as they are differentiated and allocated blindly by competitive market mechanisms.

Beneath this explanation is a broad-based and tenacious conventional wisdom that lifespan social achievements of individuals reflect unfettered expressions of innate differences in ability in competition with one another. For some, this belief provides a satisfying explanation for income and social class disparities because natural abilities do not seem arbitrary or capricious. The concept that education obtained in schools frees natural ability for fair competition also establishes an explicit strategy for social advancement and, therefore, the value of an *equal* educational opportunity.

Much of the social value of publicly supported education in this century begins with an abiding faith in the transformative or modifying effects of learning as a process leading to expression of natural abilities. In American society, at least, there was no expectation that schools would produce absolute equality. Despite educational opportunity, income disparities certainly would still exist because individuals differ in natural ability. Following from this logic, public schools were embraced as an instrument of social justice for individuals in the marketplace and in society at large. For example, in a recent call for educational opportunity for African-Americans, John Hope Franklin has written: 'Economic and social progress in the United States has long been rooted in access to quality education. What worked so well for millions of immigrants must at last be made to work for black Americans' (Committee on Policy for Racial Justice 1989: ix). His statement succinctly captures how strong still is the popular expectation that American public education has the ability as well as the purpose to transform American social and economic life and promote social justice.

In the 1960s, when this belief was applied to the problem of substantial domestic poverty through a series of unprecedented education policies, it seemed logical that public schools could be recruited to redress income disparities simply by offering compensatory educational opportunities for those who were unfairly disadvantaged. The expected result was not the elimination of poverty so much as a correction of *disproportional* poverty among some social groups. Thus, the equality of opportunity sought was equality of opportunity to *compete* without restrictions other than those imposed by differences in ability. The core belief was unchanged that ability differences, once freed from unacceptable social suppression and enhanced by educational opportunity, were still the legitimate determinants of income disparities.

Limitations and disability

Individuals with disabilities occupy an ambiguous and sometimes paradoxical space in this scheme of things. In particular, there is only a tenuous relationship between access to schooling and economic well-being. As a group of learners, individuals with disabilities are heterogeneous. Despite confusion in individual identification, as a group they are neither like immigrants nor racial minorities. Also unlike these latter groups, we make no assumption that their social identification distorts or disguises an underlying average ability. Instead, we presume that they will face serious and chronic barriers to achievement over their lifespan and generally will not compete successfully with non-disabled individuals for employment.

To be sure, there is considerable debate over whether these perceived limitations are a product of innate characteristics or the result of arbitrary social assignment or some interaction of both. Teachers recognize children with disabilities less by diagnostic signs and more because they are relatively difficult to teach and less likely to benefit from typical instructional arrangements. On the other hand, inclusionists stridently argue that teachers underestimate their achievement potential if professional training is improved, instructional environments modified and adequate support provided. Whichever view one holds, it is difficult to dispute the fact of 'disabled' students' lower achievement compared to that of non-disabled peers. There is also little dispute that available remedies will cost more on a *per capita* basis than the public typically expends for students not considered disabled. And therein lies the source of the durable concern special education of any kind raises for school managers.

When the public perceives disabilities as unalterable barriers to achievement and, thus, future employment, it is unwilling to invest scarce resources in what seems to be futile educational opportunities. On the other hand, especially during times of economic prosperity, the public also rejects the social devaluation and economic disadvantage that follows from little or no educational opportunity for individuals with disabilities. These two views ultimately are not reconcilable within the current economic and organizational framework of public schooling. The special day class curriculum was designed with alternative, not simply lower, achievement and employment expectations. Contemporary special education is more complex, allowing for remedial and compensatory academic programs for some, alternative curricula for others. Nevertheless, whatever special education the public has supported inevitably reveals a critical paradox in nominally 'universal' schooling. It really cannot accommodate the full range of human differences without substantial cost and structural change.

Paradox revealed

To achieve its ambitious scale of universality, public schooling largely ignores individual differences that contribute to variable instructional outcomes.

Special education throughout its almost one-hundred-year history has been concerned *mostly* with individual differences and how they might be accommodated by institutional transformations. The intrinsic nature of this paradox is revealed best by asking whether the claim that public schools work for *all* children, without exception, is supported by any extant evidence? More specifically, is equality of educational opportunity really offered to each and every American child, again without exception? What, indeed, does it mean to provide equality of educational opportunity for children with disabilities if these children will always be at a competitive disadvantage compared to their more normally achieving peers?

Under most existing instructional arrangements, exposure to precisely the same instruction designed for more normally achieving peers condemns children with disabilities to achievement below their potential and at great disadvantage for developing socially valued levels of independence and productivity. This, in essence, defines disability and is axiomatic in any construction of a 'special' education. Equal physical access to school and strict equality of instructional resources therein are precisely the conditions that created special education in the first place. The subversive quality of special education arises from the organizational disruption and fiscal burden imposed on schools when they legitimize attempts to provide individually variable levels of access and instructional resources.

Early special day class programs revealed this paradox because, in an attempt to gain control over the consequences of enrolling diverse, often difficult students, school officials legitimized the internal organization of special effort that was fundamentally antagonistic to the organization of the school as a whole. Special class teachers required *additional* resources but also used these resources *differently* to create instructional arrangements meant to obtain *different*, not just lower, achievement outcomes from those expected for students in the general program. Although now criticized by inclusionists and others, is it instructive to consider how special education seeks to establish equality of opportunity? That is, in what sense can a *different* instructional program aimed at *different* goals with *different* resources be considered equal? Clearly, any such description of equality must accept not only that children may consume different resources to reach similar goals, but also that they may consume different resources to reach *different*, equally valid goals.

In past decades, policy-makers have overemphasized the amount of school resources, or inputs, for calculating equality while ignoring whether similar resources provide an equally substantive educational opportunity for students who differ. For students with disabilities, substantive opportunity is not necessarily provided either by access or by social participation in universally accessible programs, but is provided when and if an individually tailored educational program exists that is reasonably calculated to promote at least satisfactory levels of development and achievement. If such opportunity is provided to each child, then educational opportunity is equally meaningful. The public school establishment, focused on equal access to equal resources, constrained by fiscal limitations and conflicting political demands, has recognized from the beginning both the resource and organizational implications of special education's more radical formulation of equality and, therefore, has resisted it at every turn.

Public schools may have *attempted*, at varying times and to varying degrees, to give access to *all* children, but truly universal public education remains really more of an ideal than a reality. Despite early advocacy for special day class programs, public schools in the United States have always acted to deny or restrict access – sometimes absolutely, sometimes contingently – for some students. As a matter of law, *all* American children were not guaranteed equal access to public education until 1975 and the passage of the Education of All Handicapped Children's Act (popularly known as Public Law 94–142, or simply PL 94–142 and revised and reauthorized in 1990 as Individuals with Disabilities Education Act, or IDEA). Even so, schools still require students to demonstrate desirable general standards of conduct to *remain* in normal public school programs. Students with severe behaviour problems, particularly those whose behaviour is considered dangerous or otherwise criminal, tend to be segregated and eventually expelled from public schools.

The hot dispute currently raging over suspension and expulsion policies in the United States illustrates how special education disturbs school administrators and their sense of control over schools. Court decisions like *Honig v. Doe* underscore how strongly anti-exclusionist contemporary special education policy is in its philosophy and current regulatory scheme (Bartlett 1989; 'House IDEA draft would lift discipline barrier' 1995). Once identified, students are explicitly entitled to appropriate educational interventions that cannot be limited or interrupted by unilateral decisions by school administrators. School authorities perceive this policy as serious interference with their ability to suspend or expel unilaterally any student who is disruptive, aggressive or violent regardless of whether such behaviour is related to disability. Special education policy, on the other hand, permits no exclusion and, in any case, intends an active search for educational rather than administrative solutions to undesirable behaviour.

More important than loss of discretion over misbehaviour, schools balk at the open-ended and contingent commitment of resources that special education demands. In other recent litigation, *Timothy W. v. Rochester*, school officials sought relief from what they perceived to be a burdensome and inappropriate expenditure of scarce resources for a completely unresponsive profoundly retarded child. An appeals court, overturning a lower court's ruling in favour of the schools, indicated that federal law mandating special education required no test of educability as a precondition for the provision of special education and related services (Whitted 1991). Simply stated, children do not have to prove they can learn before schools must commit themselves to an exploratory effort to teach them.

This principle, central in special education history and policy, contradicts the traditional assumption around which traditional school organization has evolved, namely, that learning opportunities are provided and children may or may not take advantage of these opportunities. Either way, whether students are successful or not, the school's obligation ends with provision of whatever instructional arrangements it chooses to designate as an opportunity. Special education policy, on the other hand, imposes on schools an obligation to seek actively and continually means to instruct all students without exclusion. Society cannot presuppose or legislate individual outcomes, so what is required by such a mandate is effort itself. That is, special education law in the United States commits schools to invest effort in educating children who may not, when all is said and done, promise much return for that effort. Although from the perspective of educational resource managers, such a policy may seem folly, the *Timothy W.* case emphasizes how radically American special education policy endorses true universality and redefines equality of opportunity.

American special education policy also includes at least two other principles that have proved a chronic irritant to school officials. One is the requirement that parents formally participate in formulating and consent to an individualized educational plan (IEP) for their children. While not a legal contract, the IEP shares important characteristics with contracts. Most fundamentally, IEPs represent a negotiated agreement between parents who wish to lay claim to school resources for their child, and school administrators who manage and who are accountable to the public for the use of these resources. The IEP requirement, therefore, confers on parents an unusual degree of power over how schools respond to children. No tradition of schooling or other law so explicitly and so effectively extends to parents the right to modulate the school experiences of their children. Even though it is doubtful that all parents of disabled children take equal advantage of their legal rights, including judicial relief if necessary, enough do so that public school administrators feel challenged and burdened. Beneath their apparent support for the values espoused by inclusionists, administrators also clearly seek greater discretion and control when IEPs are contested by parents.

Another principle enshrined in contemporary American special education policy that can be antagonistic to traditional schooling is the requirement that special education, when provided, should occur in the 'least restrictive environment' (LRE). As a matter of law, the LRE requirement intends to separate questions of educational program and physical setting. That is, once parents and schools agree on an appropriate program, it is incumbent upon the school to provide that program in an environment that is different from regular classrooms and schedules only to the degree necessary. Gradualists have argued that the LRE provision provides and protects precisely what inclusionists propose – opportunity to learn in the same education environments as non-disabled children.

There is no disagreement that schools often circumvent the intent of this requirement by failing to acknowledge the possibility of providing some special education in regular classrooms, particularly for students with severe disabilities. But the failure in this regard has been a failure of schools, not special education policy, a failure consistent with schools' historical reaction to the intrusiveness of special education. Acknowledgement of possibility requires an attempt; and the attempt to provide special education in regular classrooms, as inclusionists are beginning to learn, immediately creates demand for supplementation and contingent reconfiguration of resources available to any given class, including the kind of training and consultative support required by teachers. Schools attempting to exchange special education's current regulatory strictures for a vague inclusion policy will find themselves recreating the very thing they are trying to escape. Ironically, by adopting inclusionist philosophy to counter the perceived burden of special education policy without fundamental restructuring, administrators risk conflicts with general classroom teachers who, without adequate support, will resist the increased instructional burden of 'included' students. One hundred years after the first special day classes were instituted, then, schools will have come full circle.

Can schools change?

It really was not until the *Equality of Educational Opportunity (EEO)* report that the belief that public schooling promoted social mobility and was a force for social equality was ever seriously questioned (Coleman *et al.* 1966; *Harvard Educational Review* 1969; Mosteller and Moynihan 1972; Jencks and Brown 1975; Levine and Bane 1975). The massive study commissioned by the Office of Civil Rights and produced by Coleman and his colleagues sought only to demonstrate the magnitude of the injustice that almost everyone agreed must exist. Much to everyone's surprise, Coleman's data showed rather small differences in the resource infrastructure that characterized segregated white and black schools.

It is difficult to recapture in 1995 what profound implications seemed to attach to these findings in 1966. Coleman's findings were surprising because they could not demonstrate the expected inequality of resources that hypothetically accounted for achievement inequality. But they were shocking because they offered little evidence that schools, even with massive federal investment, could correct achievement differences in any case. This contradicted precisely the policy course the federal government had already chosen by the time Coleman's data became known. And more darkly, it appeared to support the view that the real cause of unequal achievement was familial and not social (Jencks *et al.* 1972; Jencks and Brown 1975; Levine and Bane 1975).

Coleman's study instigated two decades of vigorous research to refute the politically unacceptable inference that schools sorted but did not really educate children (*Harvard Educational Review* 1969; Mosteller and Moynihan 1972; Hodgson 1975; Rutter 1983). Ever more sophisticated analytical methods were brought to bear on the general search for an educational production function – that combination of resource inputs that reliably and strongly would predict achievement outputs (Averch *et al.* 1972; Bridge *et al.* 1979). But after two decades, the evidence is still ambiguous and forcefully debated (Hanushek 1989, 1994; Wainer 1993; Hedges *et al.* 1994a,b).

Despite differences in analytical strategy, though, most research habitually focuses on average achievement in the school as the proper indicator of school effectiveness or success. Although policy-makers acknowledge that schools might produce more than one outcome, there has been an unwavering conviction that these multiple 'products' of schooling are simply different domains of achievement or growth, estimated as the *average* performance or status within a school.

Such blind faith in the arithmetic average has led us far astray and helped schools avoid recognizing that they 'produce' a distribution of human beings, not average levels of performance. Ignoring the fact that different outcomes are distributed by schools' instructional arrangements for different students causes periodic paroxysms of reform without ever changing traditional approaches to curriculum and instruction. Enshrining average rather than distributed outcomes permits schools to continue their historical treatment of diverse students as tolerably alike in learning characteristics and, therefore, tolerably alike in their responsiveness to a given curriculum or particular instructional method. Student diversity is reduced to a slogan and the organizational and resource implications of disability continue to be avoided or ignored (Gerber 1989; Gamoran 1992; Biemiller 1993a,b; Slavin 1993).

Questioning the importance of average performance in terms of its underlying distribution also threatens traditional notions of school effectiveness. Do we expect that as a manifestation of some natural law that high achieving students will always make the greatest gains? If so, we are actually expressing a preference for a particular achievement outcome, a distribution that is skewed towards already high achieving students. Because low achieving students, including most considered disabled, achieve at a lower rate, more instructional effort is required to obtain more similar (equal) levels of achievement. If we are committed to universal education for *all* students in a world of scarce and limited resources, then we must contend with the fact that effort invested in many disabled students may alter the distribution (narrowing it) while having little or no impact on the mean outcomes of schools (Gerber and Semmel 1985; Gerber 1988). This formulation has serious implications for the concept of school effectiveness.

When is a school effective?

The challenge that special education posed to public schooling in the first decade of the last century – and still poses – was the insistence that design and deployment of instructional effort within schools could and should be modified to accommodate individual differences rather than expectations for modal students. This insistence implies a value that suggests a non-intuitive definition of school effectiveness. Schools are effective when and if their poorest-performing students demonstrate significant achievement gains.

Very little serious attention has been paid to such an alternative view. Yet, organizational prescriptions drawn from case studies of schools that appear to be effective at the mean (Purkey and Smith 1983, 1985) are not useful for predicting school effectiveness with their disabled students. Schools that rank high on performance of their modal students do not necessarily rank similarly on performance of their disabled students (Semmel and Gerber 1995).

Unlike Coleman and related studies, these findings do not mean that instructional efforts by schools are fruitless, only that they are distributed in such a way so as to make the *average* a poor measure of a school's effectiveness (Brown and Saks 1981). That is, effects of intentionally organizing instructional effort within schools to meet needs of slower-learning, lower-achieving students are not likely to be detected by changes in mean tested achievement. Special education constitutes an institutionalized, explicit pressure for schools to distribute instructional effort in this way.

The next reform

Special education poses difficult technical problems for universal education, but also reveals a challenging view of our real, as opposed to professed, values and commitment to social justice. School effectiveness cannot be meaningfully inferred from an achievement distribution until these values are made explicit. If equality of educational opportunity means equalizing *substantive* opportunity, then school effectiveness can be demonstrated only in one of two ways. Either achievement variance will decrease by increases in achievement in the lower half of the distribution or mean achievement will rise without increases in variance in the higher half of the distribution (i.e. the entire distribution will shift upwards) (Brown and Saks 1981; Gerber and Semmel 1985; Gerber 1988; Bacdayan 1994). To obtain either of these outcomes in the next reform movement will require not only new resources and new technologies of instruction, but also a fundamentally different structure, economy and culture of schooling to permit and support individually variable programs of instruction.

Despite prolific reform rhetoric, the achievement of disabled students as an indicator of school effectiveness has been specifically ignored by blue ribbon panels and commissions (Gerber and Semmel 1995), as well as in state and national assessments of educational progress ('Students excluded from education data' 1991; National Center for Education Statistics 1995). Such a profound silence regarding an aspect of public policy that schools view as intrusive and expensive seems odd and worrisome.

Moreover, the apparent and formal lack of interest in assessing the progress of disabled and other low-achieving students on a national scale prevents the possibility of understanding school effectiveness as explicit, intentional instructional effort. Instead we can only perpetuate discredited concepts of effectiveness, equality and opportunity that represent a tangled, ambiguous mix of socio-economic and instructional effects. More disturbing, though, if such lack of interest is actually a tacit, consensual policy, one that the public silently embraces, then it is reasonable to infer that school authorities, policy-makers and many reformers consciously or unconsciously reject either the value or cost of a truly universal education as well as the kind of social justice that follows from it. The reform of special education currently advocated or supported thus must be viewed with profound scepticism.

References

Averch, H., Carroll, S., Donaldson, T., Kiesling, H. and Pincus, J. (1972) *How Effective is Schooling? a Critical Review and Synthesis of Research Findings*. Santa Monica, CA: Rand Corporation.

Bacdayan, A. W. (1994) Time-denominated achievement cost curves, learning differences and individualized instruction, *Economics of Education Review*, 13: 43–53.

Bartlett, L. (1989) Disciplining handicapped students: legal issues in light of *Honig v. Doe, Exceptional Children*, 55: 357–66.

Biemiller, A. (1993a) Lake Wobegon revisited: on diversity and education, *Educational Researcher*, 22: 7–12.

Biemiller, A. (1993b) Students differ: so address differences effectively, *Educational Researcher*, 22: 14–15.

Bridge, R. G., Judd, C. M. and Moock, P. R. (1979) *The Determinants of Educational Outcomes*. Cambridge, MA: Ballinger.

Brown, B. W. and Saks, D. H. (1981) The microeconomics of schooling, in D. C. Berliner (ed.) *Review of Research in Education*, vol. 9. Washington, DC: American Educational Research Association.

Catlett, S. M. and Osher, T. W. (1994) *What is Inclusion, Anyway? An Analysis of Organizational Position Statements*. Alexandria, VA: National Association of State Directors of Special Education.

Chaikind, S., Danielson, L. C. and Brauen, M. L. (1993) What do we know about the costs of special education? A selected review, *The Journal of Special Education*, 26: 344–70.

Cole, T. (1990) The history of special education: social control or humanitarian progress? *British Journal of Special Education*, 17: 101–7.

Coleman, J. S., Campbell, E. Q., Hobson, C. J., McPartland, J., Mood, A. M., Weinfield, F. D. and York, R. L. (1966) *Equality of Educational Opportunity*. Washington, DC: US Department of Health, Education and Welfare.

Committee on Policy for Racial Justice (1989) *Visions of a Better Way. A Black Appraisal of Public Schooling*. Washington, DC: Joint Center for Political Studies Press.

Dunn, L. M. (1968) Special education for the mildly retarded: is much of it justifiable? *Exceptional Children*, 35: 5–22.

Fuchs, D. and Fuchs, L. S. (1994) Inclusive schools movement and the radicalization of special education reform, *Exceptional Children*, 60: 294–309.

Gamoran, A. (1992) Is ability grouping equitable? *Educational Leadership*, 50: 11–17.

Gartner, A. and Lipsky, D. K. (1987) Beyond special education: toward a quality system for all students, *Harvard Educational Review*, 57: 367–95.

Gerber, M. M. (1988) Tolerance and technology of instruction: implications for special education reform, *Exceptional Children*, 54: 309–14.

Gerber, M. M. (1989) The new 'diversity' and special education: are we going forward or starting again? *Public Schools Forum*, 3: 19–32.

Gerber, M. M. (1994) Postmodernism in special education, *The Journal of Special Education*, 28: 368–78.

Gerber, M. M. (1995) Inclusion at the high-water mark? Some thoughts on Zigmond and Baker's case studies of inclusive educational programs, *The Journal of Special Education*, 29: 181–91.

Gerber, M. M. and Semmel, M. I. (1985) The microeconomics of referral and reintegration: towards a new paradigm of special education evaluation, *Studies in Educational Evaluation*, 11: 13–29.

Gerber, M. M. and Semmel, M. I. (1995) Why do educational reform commissions fail to address special education? in R. Ginsburg and D. N. Plank (eds) *Commissions, Reports, Reforms, and Educational Policy*. Westport, CN: Praeger.

'Governors seek authority to merge IDEA, other money' (1995) *Special Education Report*, 21: 1–2, 9 August.

Hanushek, E. A. (1989) The impact of differential expenditure on school performance, *Educational Researcher*, 18: 45–51, 62.

Hanushek, E. A. (1994) Money might matter somewhere: a Response to Hedges, Laine and Greenwald, *Educational Researcher*, 23(4): 5–8.

Harvard Educational Review (1969) *Equal Educational Opportunity*. Cambridge, MA: Harvard University Press.

Hedges, L. V., Laine, R. D. and Greenwald, R. (1994a) Does money matter? a meta-analysis of studies of the effects of differential school inputs on student outcomes (an Exchange: Part 1), *Educational Researcher*, 23(3): 5–14.

Hedges, L. V., Laine, R. D. and Greenwald, R. (1994b) Money does matter somewhere: a Reply to Hanushek, *Educational Researcher*, 23(4): 9–10.

Heller, K.A., Holtzman, W. H. and Messick, S. (eds) (1982) *Placing Children in Special Education: a Strategy for Equity*. Washington, DC: National Academy Press.

Hendrick, I. G. and MacMillan, D. L. (1989) Selecting children for special education in New York City: William Maxwell, Elizabeth Farrell, and the development of ungraded classes, 1900–1920, *The Journal of Special Education*, 22: 395–417.

Hodgson, G. (1975) Do schools make a difference? in D. M. Levine and M. J. Bane (eds) *The 'Inequality' Controversy: Schooling and Distributive Justice*. New York: Basic Books.

Hoffman, E. (1975) The American public school and the deviant child: the origins of their involvement, *The Journal of Special Education*, 9: 415–23.

'House IDEA draft would lift discipline barrier' (1995) *Special Education Report*, 21: 1–2, 9 August.

Jencks, C. and Brown, M. (1975) The effects of desegregation on student achievement. Some new evidence from the Equality of Educational Opportunity Survey, *Sociology of Education*, 48: 126–40.

Jencks, C., Smith, M., Acland, H., Bane, M. J., Cohen, D. K., Gintis, H., Heyns, B. and Michelson, S. (1972) *Inequality: a Reassessment of the Effect of Family and Schooling in America*. New York: Basic Books.

Kauffman, J. M. (1993) How we might achieve radical reform of special education, *Exceptional Children*, 60: 6–16.

Kauffman, J. M., Gerber, M. M. and Semmel, M. I. (1988) Arguable assumptions underlying the Regular Education Initiative, *Journal of Learning Disabilities*, 21: 6–11.

Kauffman, J. M. and Hallahan, D. P. (eds) (1995) *The Illusion of Full Inclusion*. Austin, TX: Pro-Ed.

Levine, D. M. and Bane, M. J. (eds) (1975) *The 'Inequality' Controversy: Schooling and Distributive Justice*. New York: Basic Books.

Madden, N. A. and Slavin, R. E. (1983) Mainstreaming students with mild handicaps: academic and social outcomes, *Review of Educational Research*, 53: 519–69.

Mosteller, F. and Moynihan, D. P. (eds) (1972) *On Equality of Educational Opportunity*. New York: Vintage Books.

National Association of State Boards of Education (1992) *The Report of the NASBE Study Group on Special Education*. Alexandria, VA: NASBE.

National Center for Education Statistics (1995) *The Condition of Education*. Washington, DC: US Department of Education.

Purkey, S. C. and Smith, M. S. (1983) Effective schools: a review, *Elementary School Journal*, 83: 427–52.

Purkey, S. C. and Smith, M. S. (1985) School reform: the district policy implications of the effective schools literature, *Elementary School Journal*, 85: 353–89.

Ravitch, E. (1974) *The Great School Wars: New York City, 1805–1973*. New York: Basic Books.

Rutter, M. (1983) School effects on pupil progress: research findings and policy implications, *Child Development*, 54: 1–29.

Sarason, S. B. and Doris, J. (1979) *Educational Handicap, Public Policy, and Social History*. New York: The Free Press.

Semmel, M. I. and Gerber, M. M. (1995) *The School Environments Project*, final report. Santa Barbara, CA: Special Education Research Laboratory, University of California.

Skrtic, T. M. (1991) The special education paradox: equity as the way to excellence, *Harvard Educational Review*, 61: 148–205.

Slavin, R. E. (1993) Students differ: so what? *Educational Researcher*, 22: 13–14.

Stainback, W. and Stainback, S. (1984) A rationale for the merger of special and regular education, *Exceptional Children*, 51: 102–11.

'Students excluded from education data' (1991) *Outcomes*, National Center on Educational Outcomes, University of Minnesota, no. 1.

Tomlinson, S. (1982) *A Sociology of Special Education*. London: Routledge and Kegan Paul.

Trent, Jr., J. W. (1994) *Inventing the Feeble Mind*. Berkeley, CA: University of California Press.

Wainer, H. (1993) Does spending money on education help? A reaction to the Heritage Foundation and the *Wall Street Journal, Educational Researcher*, 22:22–4.

Wang, M. C., Reynolds, M. C. and Walberg, H. J. (1988) Integrating the children of the second system, *Phi Delta Kappan*, 70: 248–51.

Whitted, B. R. (1991) Educational benefits after Timothy W.: where do we go from here? *West's Education Law Reporter*, 68: 549–55.

Will, M. (1986) Educating children with learning problems: a shared responsibility, *Exceptional Children*, 52: 411–15.

Index